The Acts of the Holy Spirit

Our Personal Journey

Dear,
Keep the faithful
Chris

Chris Morris

ISBN 978-1-64349-066-3 (paperback)
ISBN 978-1-64349-067-0 (digital)

Christian Faith Publishing, Inc.
832 Park Avenue
Meadville, PA 16335
www.christianfaithpublishing.com

Printed in the United States of America

I can do all things through Christ who strengthens me.

—Philippians 4:13

All things are possible to those who believe.

—Mark 9:23

To one who has faith, no explanation is necessary. To one without faith, no explanation is possible.

—Saint Thomas Aquinas

Introduction

I write this book with a certain degree of trepidation. As you read this book, you will discover that someone in our government tried to murder me at least three times. How many attempts were really made, I will never know.

Twenty years after I went to college, a friend of mine who had been in the Navy, after hearing about the mysterious death of my parents, and after learning my dad was a general in the Army, decided to determine what happened to him. Cliff, my friend, reached out to a captain in the Navy, and they started a full-fledged investigation in hopes to get to the bottom of the mystery surrounding my parents' disappearance at sea.

A few weeks later, I was late to my office. It was after 9:00 AM. Cliff had been waiting in front of my office. He was wiping tears from his eyes and cheeks as I approached him.

He said, "Thank God, Chris, I thought they killed you."

As he regained his composure and stepped into my office, Cliff said, "Chris, we have to cancel trying to determine what happened to your parents. They will kill us if we investigate this any further. An ambassador is going to call you to send his sympathies. Talk to him, and let this investigation go. Do you understand me, Chris? Let this go!"

I have waited another twenty years since then to complete this book as it was originally drafted over thirty years ago. By now almost all the players I knew in our government are dead. The one or two who are still alive are so old I can't imagine this hurting anyone. The things that could be very negative, I have taken out of the story, leaving only the things I feel are necessary to adequately tell my story and the story of how God has intervened in my life.

When I wrote the book originally, I believe I did it under the power of the Holy Spirit. I would come home from long hours at work exhausted and would sit in our den and type out these stories at breakneck speed. I wrote over two hundred pages in two months. My original intention was simply to tell the story of my mom and dad for my children, who never met their grandparents. I also wanted them to learn how God had saved me and to keep a written record of the miracles that we encountered in our lives. My memory of the details of the incidents was far more accurate then than now. So it is fortunate that I am more of an editor today than a storyteller.

The most important point I want to emphasize is this: I truly do not know what happened to my parents. All the conclusions about what happened to them are speculations on my part. Some may be accurate. Others are at best hearsay and would never stand under a rigorous trial in court. So why retain these stories in this book? I suppose these stories have given me a sense of closure. And I suppose these stories are needed to tie the loose ends of the story into a book, instead of just a series of disconnected short stories.

But there is still one theme that is left that is the real reason for writing the book. I have spent my life learning about God and Who He is and how He communicates with me, my family, and mankind. And that story is real and absolutely based on facts, not fiction, and is told with absolute clarity, absolute veracity, and to the best of my abilities. I know that different people may come to different conclusions about each reported miracle. But as the story unfolds, it should become apparent that there isn't one or two or three miracles; there are many miracles that have been needed to keep me alive and for my children and my wife to have survived.

Say what you may, but if you believe there may be an explanation for these miracles and the chances are 1 in 10 that any one of these supposed miracles occurred by accident, then let's look at the odds that all these miracles could have occurred by accident. Starting with the assumption that there is a 1-in-10 chance that any one miracle was a freak accident, then the odds of a dozen such events having occurred are 1/10 to the 12th power, which is 1/10,000,000,000,000. And there are many more than a dozen such miracles in this book.

6

If you carefully consider the events that had to occur for one of these miracles to have happened, then the odds could be a lot less than 1 in 10. Perhaps the odds should be 1 in 100 to 1 in 1,000,000 or less depending on the specific event. Other miracles simply can't be explained by any scientific reason.

As far as I am concerned, one can only reach one conclusion after reading this book. There is a God. God is active in our lives. And the evidence of God's existence in my life and my family's lives is simply irrefutable.

The next question you may ask is, Why is God not this active in your life? One possibility is that you haven't needed His help to the degree I have needed it. That's almost a certainty. A second possibility is this: Jesus said you need faith the size of a mustard seed. But the most likely possibility is that miracles are occurring in your life just as they are in my life and you attribute them to karma, good luck, or accidental benefit.

The fourth possibility is that you are reluctant to tell others about the miracles that have occurred in your life as you are afraid of criticism or rejection by friends and family. I have often asked seniors to tell me about their lives. I have found this exercise fascinating. Then I would ask them if they ever had a miracle occur in their lives. Every person I have asked this question has told me of one or two miracles that occurred. Typically, they told me this with tears in their eyes as they recalled one or more events they believed were guided by God.

I like to think of my son's faith, and my lack of faith, when he prayed that a volcano would erupt. He prayed, and God moved a mountain, just as promised. I must say, I failed that test that day, as you will see later in this book. But while I failed the test, I didn't doubt that God could do anything!

Secondly, the Bible teaches us that we must be righteous before God. What does it mean to be righteous? I don't know, as I am far from perfect, and if you ask some people, I am an outright sinner. I guess that is the mystery. However, in my old age, I can say I have tried to keep the law to the best of my abilities, by doing what is right by others throughout my life. The emphasis is on trying. If you dig into my thoughts, as you will soon find out, I have a convoluted, self-centered, egotistical way of viewing reality. As some would say, my view of reality is not much different than yours. You see, "it is all about me," and my sense of my self-importance is unrealistically great and often needs to be kicked down a notch or two daily. To the Messiah Yeshua (in Hebrew), or Jesus, that means I have sinned in my heart, mind, and soul! Yet He still loves me, despite my flaws . . . which is simply amazing!

So I guess the answer to this must fall back on your willingness to have faith the size of a mustard seed and to try your best to do what God asks of you and realize that when you fall down, He will pick you up and redirect you on the path He wants you to take. I am reminded of St. Peter. You see, he decided to get the heck out of Rome while the getting was good. As he was leaving, a stranger appeared and began walking with him. It turns out this stranger was, indeed, Jesus Whom Peter did not recognize at first, Who came down to tell Peter to turn around and return to Rome. What price did Peter pay for that decision? He was crucified upside down.

One must assume that if you are willing to follow Jesus, the result may be persecution and even death. So the question on the table is this, "Are you willing to follow Him and share in His fate?"

And to that I will say, "But as for me and my household, we will serve the Lord" (Joshua 24:15).

> Phillip said to him, 'Lord, show us the Father and we ask no more.' Jesus answered, 'Have I been all this time with you Phillip, and you still do not know me? Anyone who has seen me has seen the Father. Then how can you say, "Show us the Father"? Do you not believe that I am in the Father, and the Father in me? I am not myself the source of the words I speak to you: it is the Father who dwells in me doing his own work. Believe me when I say that I am in the Father and the Father in me; or else accept the evidence of the deeds themselves. In truth, in very truth I

tell you, he who has faith in me will do what I am doing; and he will do greater things still because I am going to the Father. Indeed anything you ask in my name I will do, so that the Father may be glorified in the Son. If you ask anything in my name I will do it.

'If you love me you will obey my commands; and I will ask the Father, and he will give you another to be your Advocate, who will be with you forever—the Spirit of Truth. The world cannot receive him, because the world neither sees nor knows him; but you know him, because he dwells with you and is in you. I will not leave you bereft; I am coming back to you. In a little while the world will see me no longer, but you will see me; because I live, you too will live; then you will know that I am in my Father, and you in me and I in you. The man who has received my commands and obeys them—he it is who loves me; and he who loves me will be loved by my Father; and I will love him and disclose myself to him.' (Jesus speaking in the gospel of John 14:8–21)

Dear Jessica and Joshua

This story is about your daddy and his family. It is also about how God revealed Himself to me and how He has revealed Himself to us. It is a story about faith; it is a story about love; and it is a story about the struggle we all face in keeping God's law, learning to trust God and ultimately learning to trust others. I hope it helps you understand a little more about me, your mother and our Lord the Messiah Yeshua called Jesus Christ by gentiles.

A Little Boy on the Grass

I remember sitting on the grass on a nice summer day. My best guess is I was two or three years old. My hands were in the grass. It was a warm summer day. My parents were in the backyard with me. The sun warmed my body. And I couldn't help but realize that God had given us a beautiful day.

I do not remember being in a church in my life up to that point. I don't remember talking to anyone about God. But I knew He existed and that He knew who I was. And I knew He took care of me. Have you had feelings like this before?

Grandfather Henry
(Your Great-Grandfather)

I only met my grandfather once in my life. I was about three at the time, and we met at his home in San Antonio, Texas. My grandfather was a minister but at the time was a chaplain at a local hospital.

I remember playing in front of their home by myself, in a dried-up creek bed. I picked up a rock, and underneath the rock was a beautiful small snake, with diamonds on his back. I felt a hand on my shoulder, as if my daddy was saying "Don't touch the snake." So I ran in to tell my family. They all went out front and searched for the snake. He had slithered away.

Then I found a lizard on one of the trees. I called them "horny" toads, and for some reason my Aunt Hank kept correcting me. She would say they are horned toads, not "horny" toads. She was rather picky about words. I loved running my hands through the soft grass behind the house.

One day we went to church with my family, and my grandfather, who walked in with us, disappeared. I wondered where he had gone. Then I saw him in front of all those people, speaking. I kept saying to my mother and father "Why is Grandfather talking to all of us about God?"

My father had been raised in a Baptist church with his parents. He often went to church three and four times a week when he was growing up. He went so much that he never wanted to go to church again when he grew up. Thus, I was not raised in a church. In fact, I don't believe I had ever entered a church before that day.

My grandfather took me into the carport by himself and let me blow bubbles. He held me in his lap and seemed to enjoy holding me so much. I really knew he loved me, and I was so happy to be with him.

Grandmother Alma

When I was about five or six, Grandmother invited my sister Karen and me over to her apartment to spend the weekend occasionally. Since our grandfather had died, shortly after our trip to Texas, Grandmother moved to Washington, DC, to live nearby us and next to her daughter Aunt Hank. On Sunday she would take us to church. It was fun but a little boring. We usually colored on paper. When we got a little too loud, Grandmother would grab our hands and squeeze hard. It hurt!

Grandmother could paint beautiful paintings. She tried to teach Karen and me to paint oil paintings. We would put on smocks. She would open paints, put up a canvas on an easel, and show us how. She had taught painting at a finishing school in Atlanta when she was a young girl! I loved Grandmother, but I always felt she worried a great deal and cried about little things that upset her. Every time we ate with her, she left the dining room and went to her bed room to cry. I thought she was silly.

One day, after church, we got home on a sunny chilly day. My sister and I enjoyed running to the top of the apartment building that overlooked Washington, DC. There was a gazebo on top of the roof, with some flowers. It was so beautiful to be in a garden in the middle of a bustling city. We also enjoyed running up and down the steps in the apartment building. It was exciting and fun to run fast and race. After sitting up on the roof, Grandmother said that we were to have some company for dinner and that she would like to have some flowers for the dining room table.

At the time I didn't know how terribly poor Grandmother was. My daddy paid for the apartment she lived in. And my grandfather, the minister, who had died a few years earlier, never had two

15

pennies to rub together. So when he died, Grandmother had nothing. It turns out Grandmother and Grandfather often skipped meals and went hungry trying to feed their children. So Grandmother had to learn to rely on God for everything. Being poor and dependent on God was quite foreign to me. I didn't know Grandmother really couldn't afford to buy flowers.

Well, Grandmother perked up and said, "Children, let's ask God for some flowers so that we can put them on the dinner table."

I said, "Grandmother, you don't believe God would answer a prayer like that, do you?"

Never had my Grandmother been so sharp with me. Lifting her walking cane, she shook it in my face, and with the meanest look my grandmother could conjure—I really thought she was going to hit me—she said, "Come with me." She grabbed me, called my sister, and dragged me down the staircase, along the hallway and into her apartment. "Young man, we will have to pray that God will forgive you for your sin."

I did not know what sin was, but I figured it must have been bad. Frightened and holding back tears, I went into her bedroom, knelt by her bed, and listened to a lengthy prayer where Grandmother asked God to forgive me. Grandmother asked God that He would show me that He could answer prayers, and she asked God to show me a miracle so I would believe in Him.

Grandmother didn't have a TV set, so we helped her cook. And just as we were finishing cooking, the doorbell rang. Grandmother stopped cooking, and she sent me to the front door to open it. I did as she instructed, opened the door, and a woman about my mother's age—blond, I guess pretty—walked in carrying flowers.

She said, "Alma, I was thinking of you upstairs, and we had some beautiful flowers that I wanted you to have. These are for you!" handing them to Grandmother.

"Thank you so much and God bless you," Grandmother said.

She looked back at me as she held the flowers. Grandmother gave me a dirty look as she walked by carrying her flowers. We helped her put them in a vase on the dining room table. I was confused and amazed at my grandmother.

"Maybe she really talked to God," I thought.

Our Neighborhood

When I was two years old, I walked through our backyard, past a house that backed up to our home, and found a boy who was a couple of houses down on the cul-de-sac where he lived. He became my best friend. Carlton and I were a lot alike. He became a civil engineer. I was a physics major in college. We were both athletic. But Carlton was a gifted athlete who took up canoeing in C-2s, which is a type of covered canoe designed to run the rapids. It has two holes in it for two canoeists. Ultimately Carlton became the best C-2 canoeist in America and was selected to represent America in the Olympics in Munich. Unfortunately, the Germans decided to skip the white-water part of the competition, and Carlton never got to race in the Olympics.

I went to Carlton's house frequently. But as I passed the house behind us, a nice man discovered me and would invite me into his home, and we would sit on the porch and he would tell me stories about mountain climbing. His name was Barry Bishop, and he worked for *National Geographic* as a photographer. One day Mr. Bishop caught me walking by his porch. He was talking to an older man who had a British accent.

He introduced me to the man and said, "Chris, this is my boss. He is the head of *National Geographic.*"

I had a top with me, and I showed them how to spin it. They seemed to like watching the top spin.

The nice man said, "Working for *National Geographic* is the best job a man can have."

One fall day the wind was blowing and the leaves were falling off the trees. I cut through past Mr. Bishop's home, and Mr. Bishop asked me into his house. I sat down, and he showed me some pictures of men climbing a mountain. Some were of him climbing Mt. McKinley. He loved climbing Mt. Denali, as it is now called, in Alaska. It sounded like so much fun.

Then he showed me pictures of Mt. Everest and said, "We just climbed Mt. Everest last summer. I made it to the top." Then he said, "But Mt. Everest is not like Mt. Kinley. Mt. Everest is hell," which I thought was strange, since he loved to climb so much.

"Chris, I was the photographer for the American team. We were climbing Mt. Everest, and I had to haul this camera across the crevasses and up the ice field, with the film and the lenses here," which he showed me. "It was a lot of work but fun as we started out."

"When did you do this, Mr. Bishop?"

"Last June [in 1963]," Mr. Bishop said. "We reached the summit of Mt. Everest, but we were a couple of hours late, and it was getting dark. We were the first team to summit the West Ridge of Mt. Everest, and my partner and I were really excited.

"Well, we started to descend the mountain. But because we were late arriving to the top of Mt. Everest, it started to get dark, and we couldn't continue our descent, so we had to pitch a tent right on the side of the mountain. A little while later, two others from our team arrived and joined us.

"Typically, the wind blows every night on Mt. Everest and the temperature drops. It is not uncommon for the temperatures to drop to thirty below zero. When the winds are strong, the temperatures feel far below that, and you can freeze to death.

"Well, there we were, stranded on the side of Everest in a tent with no oxygen. I remember praying all night that night. And God did something miraculous for us. The wind, which had been blowing hard all day, just stopped blowing. It became completely calm." Mr. Bishop was crying and wiping his eyes with a handkerchief.

"Had the winds continued to blow, we would have died that night." Mr. Bishop wiped the tears from his eyes again. "While I prayed, I told God I wanted to see my wife and boys again."

"You wanted to see Paul?" I asked. I played with his son Paul.

"Yes, Brent and Paul," he replied.

"Well, when the sun came up, I knew we had experienced a miracle that night, and I thanked God. We climbed down the mountain to base camp, but when I got there, I knew I had lost some toes to frostbite," he said.

"What's frostbite?" I asked.

"It's when your toes freeze and they have to be cut off," he said. "But, Chris, I survived. And you know why I survived? Because I asked God to save me and the others by calming the wind, and God answered my prayer," Mr. Bishop said quietly. "And now I can see my family and friends like you."

This story had an impact on me.

Mr. Bishop would come to our home every Christmas dressed as Santa Claus. He would give me a big hug. My mother knew to expect him and would put out cookies and milk for him. I don't think Mr. Bishop liked the milk much, but he would eat the cookies and ask for a glass of whiskey!

A few years later, my mother called me into the living room and had me sit down. This was not like her. She had a very serious look on her face and said, "Chris, you know your friend Paul Bishop?"

"Yes, Mom?"

"Well, his dad died yesterday in a car accident."

"Mr. Bishop died?" I asked, as tears rolled down my face.

"Yes, the man who dressed up as Santa Claus, remember him?"

I asked a lot of questions about how it happened and cried. My mother was surprised. She thought I would be more worried about my friend Paul than about his dad. She did not know how Mr. Bishop would invite me onto his porch and tell me stories about mountain climbing and play with me. He was like a part-time dad who helped raise me. And I wondered why God had taken this wonderful man from my life.

I Begin to Grow Up

My dad was a psychiatrist. He helped people with "emotional problems." I was six or seven, and I remember my dad hoping into a 1956 Chevy to go to work. He had come home and eaten lunch with us that day.

I asked him where he was going and added, "Why can't you stay home?"

He said, "I have to go to work, Christopher."

"Where do you work, Daddy?"

"I'm going to work at Chestnut Lodge," he said.

I thought he worked at some kind of clubhouse. I learned years later that Chestnut Lodge was a mental hospital, and he worked for a woman named Frieda Fromm-Reichmann. Frieda Fromm-Reichmann had been married to Erich Fromm, who wrote many popular books about the human psyche, some of which my dad had given me to read when I was in high school. Mr. Fromm was famous to laymen and was a celebrity. But his ex-wife was a far better psychiatrist according to my dad. You see, Mrs. Fromm-Reichmann was probably the greatest psychiatrist of our time.

She had a patient who wrote the book *I Never Promised You a Rose Garden*. In this book the patient described how Ms. Reichmann helped cure her. You see, Ms. Reichmann and Harry Stack Sullivan are the only psychiatrists known to cure schizophrenics. And I am not aware of anyone else that could replicate this . . . other than God.

As I got older, I began to realize how successful my dad was. He went to John's Hopkins Medical School and did his residency at Yale University Hospital where I was born. He worked for Frieda Fromm-Reichmann and later worked for the National Institute of Mental Health and was head of psychiatry at Walter Reed Army

Hospital. Many years later, my daughter came home with a psychology textbook and asked if the full-page picture of the "Father of Sleep Deprivation," a specialized field in psychology, was her grandfather.

I told her, "Yes, Jessica, that is your grandfather. I wonder where they got the picture from?"

It turns out Aunt Henrietta sent the publisher the picture.

But I want to digress briefly and talk about my Aunt Henrietta, whom we kids called Aunt Hank. Aunt Hank was single her entire life. She was a devoutly religious woman, raised a Baptist but, after spending ten years working in the embassy in England, joined the Anglican church. She was a contradiction in terms. While devoutly religious, she understood people and could talk to someone like Mao Tse-Tung and treat him with great respect, even though he had killed more people than anyone else in history.

Aunt Hank started her career working with the embassy in Mexico. She later moved to Washington, DC, where she worked for President Kennedy as one of his secretaries.

After President Kennedy was assassinated, she worked for Lyndon Johnson for a while and then was moved to England in the US embassy and worked for Ambassador Bruce. She spent almost ten years in England and was moved with Ambassador Bruce to China in 1972. This was after President Nixon opened diplomatic relations there and sent Ambassador Bruce as the first ambassador to China. When Ambassador Bruce died in 1973, a new ambassador was appointed, George Herbert-Walker Bush, who would later become the forty-first president of the United States. Ambassador Bush's son, George W. Bush (president number 43) and Aunt Hank used to ride bicycles together during the Cultural Revolution through Tiananmen Square.

John F. Kennedy Years

It was 1961, and we were in the middle of the Bay of Pigs invasion in Cuba. My dad was extremely worried about "the Cuban missile crisis." Apparently, the secretary of state had asked my dad and his other psychiatrist partners a simple question:

"Would Khrushchev 'push' the nuclear button and bring on World War III?"

My dad told me years later that the psychiatrists told President Kennedy, "Yes, Khrushchev would definitely push the button if he was backed into a corner."

I remember being awakened early on a Sunday morning. We drove out I-270 to a Ramada Inn. We didn't go into the hotel but sat in the car in the parking lot for about fifteen minutes and waited. Then Aunt Hank drove up in her little yellow VW Beetle with its open sunroof. Aunt Hank got out of her car, and Dad hopped out of our car, and he told Mom and us kids to stay in the car. Aunt Hank was dressed up as she just left the White House. She waved to us kids and walked down a hill with Dad to the side of the interstate and stood on the shoulder of the road and they talked. After about ten minutes, Aunt Hank and Dad walked back up the hill. Just as mysteriously as she arrived, Hank waved goodbye to us as she got in her little yellow VW and drove away.

We did not stay at the hotel; we didn't eat lunch; we simply sat in the car. Dad then turned the wrong way on I-270 and said to Mom, "President Kennedy has decided to give one relative to each adviser in the White House a thirty-minute head start to get out of the city before he pushes the button should we have a nuclear war with Russia."

Since Aunt Hank was not married, she picked our dad as her contact.

"Gary," our mother said, "do you think this Cuban mess could result in war with Russia?"

"President Kennedy asked us if Khrushchev would push the button if we invaded Cuba. We told him he would."

There was dead silence as dad pulled out onto the expressway.

"Jane, I want you to teach Chris how to run home from school. If I call you, get the kids in the car, and start heading for the school to get Chris."

"Chris?"

"Yes, Dad?"

"If you hear the siren in front of the school, do you know what siren I am talking about, Chris?"

"I think so."

"It's that big yellow speaker thing on a pole in the front of your elementary school."

"The really, really big telephone pole and a yellow metal speaker thing on top?"

"That's it. If it goes off, I want you to run home as fast as you can. Your mother will show you the route. You aren't to go the back roads, you need to run on the main road, do you understand?"

"Yes, Dad."

"Jane, show Chris the way you drive to the school, and make sure he knows where the siren is so he knows when he is to head home, okay?"

"Okay," Mom said.

"Chris, if they try to stop you at the school or make you duck under the desk, you are to run as fast as you can out of the school and run home. Dodge anyone who tries to stop you, and head home as fast as you can, can you do that?"

Dad was really serious now, and I said, "Sure, Dad."

"Jane, once you have Chris with you, you are to head for West Virginia. Go as fast as you can. I am now taking you to where we must meet in West Virginia. They are rapidly building an underground facility there, and it is President Kennedy's wish that we be there to advise him in underground bunkers. I will show you where the bunkers are, okay? Pay attention to where I am going. The government will be there if war breaks out."

When we arrived at the location, Dad pointed out two rivers that met and said, "There is plenty of water here. There are mountains all around this area, so radiation should not be able to reach us. Radiation travels in straight lines, and these mountains will block it out. Food is already stocked in the shelters. We can survive here for ten years. They are now putting in the communication systems so the president can communicate with the military from here."

After seeing the place, Dad headed home. When we arrived, Dad, not Mom, took me to the school and showed me the route to run home. He reiterated again and again that I was to run as fast as I could and that I was to dodge anyone that tried to stop me from getting out of the school. He told me to fake people out like a running back in football and head home as fast as possible.

The Bay of Pigs Invasion

I t was April 17, 1961, and 1,700 Cubans launched what turned into a failed invasion of Cuba. These young Cubans disembarked from boats and ran up the beach toward the capital where Castro resided. Fidel Castro had only one World War II vintage airplane with a machine gun mounted on the nose of the airplane. As our CIA-trained Cubans ran onto the beach to attack Castro, the plane gunned them down. They were helpless. Those not killed were captured and put in prison for life. It was a tragedy. Trained by our CIA in St. Lucia, expecting support from the US Marines and jets, they were abandoned last minute by presidential order. You can imagine how many people in the military were furious with President Kennedy.

I'm sure, in hindsight, had President Kennedy acted as the military wanted him to act, nuclear missiles would have been launched by Russia and World War III would have ensued. The real question was, If we weren't going to give the Cubans air support, why did we let their young men invade in the first place? I suppose that was the tragic mistake we made. I believe President Kennedy did not know that this old, vintage airplane even existed, much less flew and had a machine gun that worked. And that is probably the real reason we sent good men to their tragic ending.

Years later I became good friends with a man who was one of President Kennedy's best. In fact, he is the man who trained Jessica to scuba dive. What are the odds that our paths would cross? As I am sure, Aunt Hank knew Tom as did President Kennedy. Tom would have been a Navy Seal had he lived in recent times. He was one of our Navy's best scuba divers in the 1960s. He was often called upon by generals to do the impossible during the Vietnam War. Tom was not only a great diver, but he could fly airplanes and helicopters, and few people can transition back and forth between the two. The best description I can use to describe Tom is "Rambo." Tom was so important that President Kennedy sent him to Cuba during the Bay of Pigs invasion to spend the night in a closet in Castro's bedroom the night before the Cuban invasion occurred.

Tom had a wire on him and was able to talk to President Kennedy while Castro slept. Tom awaited the order to kill Castro in his sleep. But President Kennedy, for whatever reason, decided not to assassinate Castro. By morning it was obvious the kill order was off, so Tom snuck out of the house. He went down the streets and slipped into the ocean and was never detected by the Cubans.

One more story about Tom you may find interesting. Many years after the Bay of Pigs invasion, Tom was walking down a street in Miami. A crazed drug dealer had grabbed a woman and was holding her hostage. Police officers were doing their best to save her. The crazy man screamed at the police as he held a gun at the woman's head. Tom, feeling sorry for the woman, with only a knife, slipped up behind him, slit his throat, took the gun from him, and freed the woman. How did Tom do this? I don't know, but he is that good.

On numerous occasions, Tom and I spoke about God. You can imagine, being our best killer, he had mixed views about God's existence. He even feared God's wrath because of some of the things he had done in his past. I patiently explained to Tom that he was acting in behalf of his government and anyone who did what his government asked him to do was not responsible for the death of men he killed. That Jesus's blood could cover all sins and that he could go to heaven if he just turned his life over to Christ.

Tom was skeptical!

President Kennedy Is Assassinated!

Aunt Hank worked in the White House as a secretary for President Kennedy. Don't bother checking; they never used her real name in the press. She told me Harvey Mudd, a famous TV broadcaster at the time, would call her and beg her to give him information on what was really going on in the White House. Of course, she never told him anything unless authorized by the president.

Hank spoke fondly of President Kennedy, and I was proud she knew him. I also felt we were safe because he was president. I expected to see a nuclear bomb explode and to die shortly after I saw it. I expected to have to run home and not make it to the designated hiding place. I had nightmares about dying from a nuclear bomb. Yet President Kennedy somehow made the right decision and did not get us into a nuclear war. He was accused of being weak, but I never thought he was weak. I personally thought he was somehow in touch with God, Who spoke to me too.

In hindsight, President Kennedy only had a few short years to be president of our country, yet he probably was one of the most effective presidents we ever had. As president the economy did very well, we landed men on the moon, we helped out the poor and the blacks, and we avoided World War III. President Kennedy's dad was a stock market genius who set up the Federal Reserve. It is not a surprise that President Kennedy did such a good job with our economy. But the most important thing is this: I believe God put President Kennedy in the White House to save us from certain destruction, and I am forever thankful for what that man did for my dad, Aunt Hank, and our family.

It was November 22, 1963. I was in elementary school. I was pulling leaves off a mulberry tree to feed the silkworms I had in a box at home so my mother could have a silk dress . . . at least that was what I thought at the time.

Suddenly there was a great commotion as screaming people ran out of the school, saying, "The president is dead, the president is dead!"

I sat silently on a tree branch. Were they talking about President Kennedy? Then I heard other kids saying President Kennedy was just killed. I remember feeling numb. I couldn't believe it. I wondered if Aunt Hank was okay. This was her boss. When we went home, our mother turned on the TV but would not talk.

It did not take the authorities long to catch Lee Harvey Oswald and to accuse him of killing the president. I remember our dad coming home and sitting in front of the TV set. He was in shock. Hank called him on the phone and talked to him. I knew that our world just changed, and the man who looked after our family was no longer alive, and I was frightened.

Our dad said, "President Kennedy was warned not to go in that convertible. They told him there would be an assassination attempt in Texas."

My mother said, "Don't they get those warnings all the time?"

"Yes, Jane, but this one was unusual in that we got a number of different warnings. The warnings were of an assassination attempt in Dallas. Kennedy must have chosen to ignore the warnings."

A few days later, our dad said, "Jane, someone changed the route President Kennedy was supposed to take through Dallas. He was supposed to take a different route and someone, someone very high up in our government, changed the route last minute. Whoever the assassin was must have been high up in our government. If I had to make a guess, I would say Lyndon Johnson did it. He so wants to be president. And he had the authority to change the route of the parade."

"Gary, you said Lyndon Johnson was organized crime. You said everyone in Texas knew this about him. Did organized crime kill Kennedy?"

"Believe me, I have thought about that, but we have no proof. Lee Harvey Oswald was a sharp shooter in the Army. Someone high up in our military put him up to this. They set him up and planned on his getting caught. And they didn't even provide him with an escape route. It could have been Johnson, but I don't know for sure."

A Big Boy

About the age of ten, my mother knew I believed in God. She felt it was important to take me to church, even though my father wouldn't go with us. Mother and I went together on Sundays to a Lutheran church. During that time, I learned to really believe Jesus was God. I seemed to know it all my life. But I didn't know why.

My mother had given me a *yamaka*, a Star of David, and a Jewish harp. At the time, I did not understand the significance of these gifts. Then one day she gave me a Bible. I took it up to my room to read. It fell open, and I flipped through some pages and arrived at the beginning of a chapter. And I read:

> In the beginning was the word, and the word was
> with God and the word was God. (John 1:1)

After reading those words, I was shaken. You see, I only read this far. I paused. I closed my eyes. Then I repeated the rest of the paragraph silently to myself. I had memorized these words before I read them and didn't recall reading them before that day.

> He was in the beginning with God. All things
> were made through Him, and without Him was
> not anything made that was made. In him was
> the life, and the life was the light of the world.
> The light shines in the darkness and the darkness
> shall not overcome it. (John 1:2–5)

How did I know these words? Did I learn them before I was born? Did I learn them in a past life? Was there such a thing as past lives? I was confused. But I knew I absolutely knew I had memorized these words. I knew every word. But how was this possible? This was the first Bible I had ever owned and the first time I had opened that Bible and read those verses.

I then thought about church service. Had I ever heard these words in church? No! At this point in my life, we had only gone to this Lutheran church for a few months. I never studied these words as far as I could remember. It was as if they were indelibly written in my memory . . . from before my birth.

The Bright Light

I was afraid to tell my dad and mom that I somehow knew this section of the Bible and had memorized it before I was born. But I wanted to know how this was possible. So I decided to ask God to explain it to me. I lay facedown on my bed, covered my eyes with my hands, and prayed.

"Dear Lord," I thought, "I don't know how I know those words, but I am certain Jesus is God. I know I have read these words before, but I don't know when. If it is possible, please reveal Yourself to me so I can better understand You."

Just after praying those words, lying on my bed with the Bible above my head, I heard this fire in the room crackling and popping behind me . . . It made my back tingle, as if electric fingers were running up my back. It tickled. I rolled over to see this white ball of lightning with a black spot in the middle of it . . . It was floating there in the room with me. It made my hair on my arms stand up like static electricity. I was terrified.

"God has entered my room," I thought.

I felt a tingling over my whole body, a tingling that indicated that God was touching me, answering my prayer, or so I thought. As I watched the glowing ball of lightning in front of me, a thought entered my mind: "I will reveal Myself to you."

With that I rolled over and covered my face. I was terrified. The static noise only lasted a moment or two, and then it went silent. I turned over to see the fireball had disappeared.

Only one other time did I have an experience with a fireball in the room—once again, my bedroom—when I was in college, after an intense day of prayer and worship. But that is another story for another time.

I Read the Gospels

I studied the Bible over the next few months. I struggled with trying to understand more about this book as, apparently, I learned part of it before I was born, before I even came into existence. I started by reading the Gospels first. Then I found this in Matthew 15:21–28:

> Then Jesus went thence, and departed into the coasts of Tyre and Sidon. And, behold, a woman of Canaan came out of the same coasts, and cried unto him, saying, Have mercy on me, O Lord, thou son of David; my daughter is grievously vexed with a devil. But he answered her not a word. And his disciples came and besought him, saying, Send her away; for she crieth after us. But he answered and said, I am not sent but unto the lost sheep of the house of Israel. Then came she and worshipped him, saying, Lord, help me. But he answered and said, It is not meet to take the children's bread, and to cast it to dogs. And she said, Truth, Lord: yet the dogs eat of the crumbs which fall from their masters' table. Then Jesus answered and said unto her, O woman, great is thy faith: be it unto thee even as thou wilt. And her daughter was made whole from that very hour.

I remember being greatly distressed after I read this. I was not a Jew. Was I just a dog in God's eyes? I was so upset when I discovered this that my mother detected that something was wrong. As she so often did, when I was upset, she sat down next to me on the couch in the den.

"Chris, something is bothering you. Is it a girl?"

"No, Mom. It's what Jesus said."

"Oh, and what would that be?" she asked, looking a bit relieved.

"Well, I was reading in the Bible, and Jesus said He came only for the Jews and not for the Gentiles, and I'm just a Gentile. He said the Gentiles are like dogs. So how can He love me? I wish I was a Jew."

"Well, Chris, I understand your concern, but I have a little secret I will tell you, if you promise not to tell anyone else. Will you promise?"

"A secret?"

"Yes, a secret. But you must promise not to tell anyone."

"Okay, sure, I promise."

"Well, Chris, I am a Jew. And I believe the rabbis say that the Jewish lineage passes through the mother to their children, not from the dad through his children. If I am correct, that makes you a Jew. So I don't think you have anything to worry about, okay?"

"Mom?" I asked. "So, Mom, why did you say I can't tell anyone this secret?"

"Chris, our country club does not allow any of their members to be Jews or blacks, and I'm a Jew and so are you. If they find out, they may throw us out of the country club," Mom said, getting quiet.

"But you're a Lutheran, Mom."

"I may have converted, but they don't need to know anything about my ancestry. Can I count on you to keep this a secret?"

"Sure, Mom. So if Jesus was sent for the Jews, why do they hate Jews?"

"The Jews, my dear, have been persecuted and hated for centuries. If you think you have it tough, you should have grown up with me. I was raised in Germantown in Baltimore during World War II, and we were Jews," she said.

I didn't understand the hatred of Nazis and the persecution of the Jews in Germany at the time, nor did I understand how the

Germans in America were treated during this time. It must have been traumatic for Mom and her brother. Her brother chose to remain a Jew and never converted to Christianity.

"Hey, Mom?" I asked.

"Yes, Chris?"

"Does this mean I am supposed to hate part of myself? And if so, what part of myself am I to hate?"

Mom looked confused. Then she said, "No, you're not to hate yourself. But this is why this little secret must remain between you and me. Karen and Eric can't know that we are Jews, and they can't tell anyone this, or we might be thrown out of the country club. They're too young and can't be trusted to keep a secret. Do you understand?"

"Mom, I don't understand why they would discriminate against us because we are Jews when Jesus said He was sent for the Jews first?"

"Chris, life is complicated. I don't expect you to understand, but Jews have been persecuted throughout history. And that's why you can't tell anyone."

"Does Dad know we're Jews?"

"Yes, of course, he does, Chris. And he loves you and me and Karen and Eric, and we are all Jews except for Gary," my mom said, almost whispering.

"Mom, did you know my favorite math teacher is Mr. Dempsey? And did you know he's black?"

Mom nodded in the affirmative.

"And did you know my best friend in school is a Jew?"

"Of course, I do, sweetheart. And I'm not surprised that your best friend is a Jew. But now you know Jesus loves you as a Jew and as a Gentile, as you are both. Just remember, you can't say a word of this to anyone, promise?"

"Yes, Mom, I promise."

My Future Wife

Every boy and girl wants to know whom they will marry. I was in love with a girl up the street named Peggy when I was thirteen. She wasn't interested in me and said she had a boyfriend. One day I hugged her at the bus stop. She giggled and told all the other girls, and I felt so sad because while I loved her, she certainly didn't love me.

I loved Sundays then because I got to go to church to worship God. After the ball of lightning appeared to me, my mother decided I needed to go through catechism. I was also made an altar boy in the Lutheran church and had to go to church every Sunday, which made me happy.

There was something special about those days. After church I watched football with my dad and mom. He loved the Baltimore Colts. Johnny Unitas and Raymond Berry were my heroes. But Sundays meant something more, because I knew God took care of each of us and blessed our whole family. No one had to tell me this. I just knew it.

After being very sad about this girl Peggy, I knew I would never get married. No one could love me. And then, after lying in bed, I felt my spiritual friend come into my mind. I knew it was Jesus, but He seemed to be more like a woman who loved me . . . like my mother loved me and took care of me. This Spirit of God asked me to get out of bed and look out of my window, which I did. Then the strangest thing happened.

I didn't hear a voice, but I knew I was hearing someone else's thoughts, as if they were placed inside my mind. The thoughts went like this:

"Chris, don't be sad, you're a young man, and it is important that you live at home with your parents for a while longer. You're not ready to get married yet. But you will marry one day. I have already selected a wife for you. Her name is Beth, and she lives in Georgia. She's a pretty girl with blond hair. You're looking toward her home in Georgia. And she will love you, and you will love her."

Years later I decided to go to Emory University in Georgia because I liked Southerners. They were just nicer, I thought. I did not meet Beth in college. It wasn't until I was twenty-seven years old and working for a Big 8 accounting firm when I met her. And I never could have picked a better wife had I spent eternity looking. God made Beth for your Daddy Chris! And He made Chris for your Mommy Beth!

Life Is a Circus

I had always wanted to swing on the flying trapeze. I was fascinated by the flying trapeze when the Ringling Bros. & Barnum and Bailey Circus came to town, and so I wanted to do this one day. At this point in my life, I believed if I told God I wanted to do the flying trapeze, he would change my life so I could fly!

When I was in seventh grade, a friend of mine would juggle in class. I asked him to show me how to juggle. He could juggle four or five balls at the same time with no problem. Determined to learn to do this, I practiced at home over and over again and finally was able to juggle three, then four, and finally five balls. I had trouble with six balls but could keep them going for a few seconds.

My friend talked about working in the circus that came to Washington, DC, every year. He said it was a lot of fun and they were always looking for good athletes. I asked my friend Mark what he did.

He said, "They dress me up as a clown, and I run around on the stage. That's when I can juggle and do flips and cartwheels and things."

This was interesting to me, so I asked if I could help in the circus. He said he would check with his friend whose parents owned the circus and he would let me know.

To my good fortune, I was asked to come by and meet the circus owners. Mark introduced me to this older couple, and after I answered a few questions, they asked me to show up at rehearsals in a couple of weeks.

At the circus, a woman showed us a little house under the big tent, and she told us exactly what the clowns did. Then they took us out to climb on a fire truck and into the house and hang out the windows. They then set fire to the house. They didn't actually burn the house, but fire poured out from the ground around the house, making it look like the house was burning. We screamed, slid down a slide, and climbed out a window and rolled between the flames on the ground. Having escaped the fire, we went around the circus floor, on the edges, and juggled and did flips and cartwheels as we made our way off stage.

One day in practice, my friend asked me to climb up on the flying trapeze with him. I did. Holding on to the bar, he jumped up in the air and swung out over the ground, back and forth, until the swinging stopped. He then did a backflip off the bar and landed on the net below. He then let me do the same thing. It was a lot of fun. To get down, we released from the swing and landed in the net, but we practiced different gymnastic dismounts where we flipped to the net. We had fun climbing up the telephone pole, climbing on the little stand, grabbing the bar, jumping in the air, and swinging back and forth. We then practiced swinging from one side to the other telephone pole. So we would hold the bar jump straight up and swing out under the tent. Then another person would push an empty swing toward us just as we jumped in the air. As our swing approached the top of the swing, we would release from one bar and try to grab the new bar in the air. If we missed, we fell to the net. If we caught the other bar, we could swing to the other pole and dismount there. After several times doing this, I was asked by the owner's wife if I would like to learn a routine for the flying trapeze. Of course, I said yes.

An older gentleman hung upside down with bent knees over the bar. I was to hold a swing and at the right time I would jump in the air and swing out holding the other bar. At the right spot I would do a backflip and reach out toward the other swing, where the man who hung upside down would grab both my wrists with his hands. We would swing back to the other pole, and I would dismount. I got good at this. We then added two flips and even twists as I released from the one bar and grabbed the man's arms. I missed his arms several times and landed on the net below. But after practice, I got good at it and never missed again. We did this over and over to ensure we did this right when we performed.

A couple of days later, we spent every day performing several shows each day. I invited my parents to come down for the last weekend. They were given seats about four rows back in the center. I did my part as a clown. And then I got up on the flying trapeze and did all the tricks I had learned. Our show was perfect. I was so proud of myself.

I was surprised when my dad looked extremely agitated and said, "Chris, you are not allowed to do this again, because you could get seriously injured or worse if you missed the net."

My dad was so careful and conservative, I thought. Then I told him, "I don't understand you. Don't you know God answered my prayer and allowed me to do the flying trapeze? If He allowed me to do this, don't you think He will protect me? He will not let any harm come to me, Dad."

My dad shook his head and walked away speechless.

A Family Trip to South Carolina

Our dad's family was from South Carolina. My grandmother had family members who had fought in the Civil War. Her sister and she took care of their grandfather who had fought for the South. She remembered many atrocities that were committed against Southerners after that terrible war, but her response to such things was to simply pray.

That summer, when I was eleven, we went to Myrtle Beach in South Carolina. Our dad had rented a beach house, and our entire family showed up. There was Aunt Hank; Aunt Clarice, Uncle LB, and their two children; my dad's mother was there; and my parents and sister and brother stayed there. I was put in a room in the basement of the house on the ground floor. I had a door out of the side of the basement that I could exit and if I turned left, I could walk straight onto the beach. I thought this was the most beautiful beach I had ever seen in my life.

I would wake with the sun every morning. I would get up, go upstairs, and make an egg for myself and look at the ocean. Grandmother also woke up early and would sit with me and talk. To keep from bothering our sleeping relatives, she asked me to walk on the boardwalk with her, which I gladly did. After the first morning, I would wake up early and she would join me, and the two of us would walk on the beach and watch the sun rise across the ocean every morning. While we walked, Grandmother would tell me stories about Jesus and His life. Many of the stories were new to me, and I had never heard them before. Others I had read, but never fully understood what they meant, and Grandmother had a wonderful way of simplifying these stories so I could understand their implications.

That summer I really began to understand and trust Jesus. Grandmother taught me to trust Him for everything. Anything she needed, she asked God for, and then she expected Him to give her what she needed. She was a Southern belle and yet faultless in the way she treated others. She always stopped and listened. She judged no one. She treated everyone with great respect, even black people—which at the time few white people did.

When I asked her why she was so nice to everyone, she said, "We are to love others as God loves us."

"What about bad people?" I asked.

"People aren't bad out of choice. They usually had bad experiences and haven't learned to trust God. God can take care of any need they have if they trust Him and ask Him for help. But they don't know this, Chris. So I try to reflect the love of Jesus to them and teach them that He can give them anything they need if they ask and have faith."

"What is faith?" I asked.

"It is confidence in someone else. It is a way of being where we know God can and will do anything we ask of Him," she said.

For the first time in my life, I began to understand that Jesus really loved me and wanted to help me be happy and that He was there for me, if I simply put my faith in Him and trusted Him to take care of me and my family. Knowing this instilled a sense of confidence in me. And I started asking God for things, and little by little, I learned that Grandmother was correct. God did answer my prayers. There were occasions where He didn't answer my prayers, but I realized that when He didn't answer my prayers, there was a good reason for it: either my prayer was misdirected, because I asked for something that was bad for me, or my prayer interfered with a path God wanted me to take. But apart from that, I learned that if I had enough faith, God could do anything.

Aunt Hank Takes Our Family to Visit Her Best Friend

Aunt Hank had lots of friends. One of them, Rose, lived on the beach at Virginia Beach. One year Aunt Hank took us to the beach with her to stay at Rose's house. I was about twelve when we went on this trip. The house was right on the beach, and it had a beautiful view of the ocean. But it was cold when we went there. Unlike Myrtle Beach, where we burned in the sun quickly, you had to wear a jacket, long pants, and a hat to walk on this beach. Of course, the fact that it was October might have had something to do with the cold weather.

Even though it was cold outside, that wasn't enough to keep me from wanting to walk on the beach. No one wanted to go with me, even though I asked everyone. Rose, seeing my plight, offered to take me for a walk up the beach. I bundled up. I put a coat on, gloves in my pockets, and my mom added a hat to my head. Then she kissed me and sent me on my way with Rose. It was windy, and the waves were large. I would walk out toward the water. The waves would break, thundering and crashing, and I had to run back as fast as I could to keep from getting soaked by the waves. These large waves rumbled like thunder as they broke, and the water flowed with a sloshing sound as it ran over the sand. White foam glistened on the surface of the water, reflecting the sun as the sun set over the building tops.

Rose seemed to enjoy walking fast. I had trouble keeping up with her pace. But then I would run ahead and wait for her. Salt foam blew in the air, and I tasted salt in my mouth as the wind blew over the frothing water from the ocean. Occasionally cold water sprayed my face. It was cold. I asked God, in my mind, if He would let me see something special that day. I often talked to God as a young man.

After my brief prayer, I ran ahead and saw something moving on the beach just ahead.

"Maybe this was what God wanted me to see," I thought.

I sprinted to see what it was. And there, lo and behold, I saw a big black seahorse, flopping around in a puddle left by a giant wave that was retreating across the sand. I called Rose over to see it. I asked her if I could keep it.

She said, "Sure. Let's take it back to the house, and we can pin it up for you, and you can keep it."

I thought that was a grand idea.

Just then a man wearing an overcoat and a hat approached us from the left. He had been sitting on some steps and watched me when I ran to pick up the seahorse. He was a neighbor, and Rose apparently knew him. They spoke for a few minutes. It looked like a serious conversation. And then just as quickly as he appeared, he walked away, and we turned and headed back to Rose's home.

When we got home, I took off my cap, dropped my coat on the floor, and ran over to show my mom the seahorse I had found. Rose had retrieved a piece of foam, an old small cigar box, and some pins. By this time the seahorse was no longer moving. I cringed as she stuck the needles into the seahorse's head and then its tail, as if I felt the needle penetrating my brain. She pressed a couple more pins into the seahorse, holding it fast to the foam board. Then she cut the particle board piece and put it into the cigar box. It fit perfectly.

When done, she handed me the box and walked over and began talking privately to Aunt Hank. Aunt Hank then called my mom over. The three women were discussing something important and arguing a bit.

Aunt Hank said loudly, "Should we tell Chris what this man said about him?"

Mom said, "Why not? It can't hurt him."

"It's probably not true, Jane," Aunt Hank retorted.

"Maybe it is! Maybe not! But if it is true, he should know, don't you think?" Mom replied.

"Okay, I'll tell him. Chris, come here and have a seat."

I promptly walked over to the kitchen table where the ladies were sitting and sat next to them.

"Chris, Rose says a man saw the seahorse wash up on the sand, and then he saw you run and pick it up."

"I know!" I said. "I saw him when I picked it up. Do I need to give him back the seahorse?" I asked, feeling guilty.

"This man is related to Edgar Cayce."

"Who's he?" I asked.

Rose stepped in at this point and said, "Chris, Edgar Cayce was a famous prophet who lived here on Virginia Beach. He passed away a long time ago."

I wasn't sure what she was talking about.

She continued, "A prophet is someone who can predict the future. Mr. Cayce would go into a trance and talk to God and then tell people what to do to be healed. Over the years many people with diseases like cancer would seek him out, and he would tell them what was wrong with them and what to do to be healed. And they would do what he said and would be healed. He also would go into trances and predict future events in America and around the world. It is said he predicted the Crash of 1929, and he predicted World War II. He also predicted future climate and seismic events that would change the shape of the world as we know it. The last ones haven't happened yet."

"He could have been talking to God, or he could have had other spirits influencing him," Aunt Hank interjected.

"Hank, really!" Rose said firmly. "Edgar Cayce was a very good man who helped out hundreds who had illnesses. He would pray for them and lay his hands on them and tell them what was wrong with them and what to do to be healed. He really had an unusual gift, and it must have been given to him by God," she said, chastening Aunt Hank.

Aunt Hank took over the conversation. "Apparently, this man was waiting to see you, Chris. He said Edgar Cayce predicted you would be there that day at that time and that you were a prophet. He was expecting a young man, and he wanted to see you . . . this boy prophet."

"What's a prophet?"

"A prophet," Rose said with sincerity, "is someone who can predict the future with God's help."

I never felt special, and I thought this guy must have been mistaken because there was nothing about me that made me believe I had any special gifts. But I did love God, I feared God, and I trusted God to provide for all of my needs and desires, and He seemed to be doing that at this point in my life. And that was all I cared about!

Israel Is Reformed as a Nation

I was fourteen years old. Aunt Hank had come to visit and stay with us. I always loved it when Aunt Hank visited. She would take us down to the capital, or to the Jefferson Memorial, or to see the Cherry Blossoms, or into the White House and the Smithsonian. She was so prim and proper, and when she wanted to, she spoke with a British accent. I thought she was funny.

But that paled in comparison to her greatest talent. She could speak to you and you would feel good about what she said. Then a day or two later, it would hit you . . . what she said wasn't a compliment at all; it was outright mean. But instead of being mad at her, you would laugh, because she made a good point. I guess that is what happens when you work around politicians all the time.

Aunt Hank so wanted to talk to Dad about Israel. It was the summer of 1967, just after Israel had won a war in six days, something both my dad and Aunt Hank viewed as impossible. But Aunt Hank was less interested in the politics of the war than she was in comparing notes with my dad about what Grandfather Henry, the Baptist minister, had told them.

"Don't you remember, Gary," Hank said to my dad, "father told us that Israel would be reformed as a nation."

My Yale-educated dad appeared to have an attitude about religion that was one of indifference. He had taught me that God was a projection of our mother and father, who took care of us when we were very little. So I found it interesting when he spoke with Aunt Hank about biblical details. This was a side of my dad I had never really experienced before.

"Yes, that is what our father said, Henrietta." That was dad's name for Aunt Hank.

"Gary, remember?" Hank continued. "Father said that wasn't enough. He knew Israel was reformed as a nation in 1948 . . . he was still alive then." Aunt Hank paused, as if she was about to cry thinking about her daddy. She regained her composure and said, "Wasn't that the day before the expiration of the British Mandate when David Ben-Gurion declared Israel to be a nation?"

"I think you're right," my dad continued. "In 1948, when Father was alive, I believe he said their conquest had not yet fulfilled prophecy. He believed Israel had to take back Jerusalem and then it would begin."

"What would begin?" I asked.

"Something like the period of the Gentiles would come to an end and God's favor would turn from the Gentiles back to the Jews," Hank continued. "Israel controlled a limited stretch of land in 1948. I just wanted to confirm that my memory is correct and that Father said when Israel controlled Jerusalem, the countdown would begin."

"Jerusalem?" Dad asked, as if his memory was shaken. "Yes, Father said they had to take back the temple mount so they could rebuild the Temple of God."

"That's what I thought he said," Aunt Hank recounted triumphantly.

Aunt Hank pulled out a Bible and flipped through pages, looking for something. "Here it is," she said. "Remember Father reading this to us?" She continued reading from the Bible. "Jesus said this just after the Olivet Discourse."

> Now learn a parable of the fig tree; When his branch is yet tender, and putteth forth leaves, ye know that summer *is* nigh: So likewise ye, when ye shall see all these things, know that it is near, *even* at the doors. Verily I say unto you, This generation shall not pass, till all these things be fulfilled. Heaven and earth shall pass away, but my words shall not pass away. (Matthew 24:32–35)

I asked incredulously, "Aunt Hank, what does the fig tree have to do with anything?"

"Chris, the fig tree symbolizes Israel," Aunt Hank said.

Israel, I thought. "How do you know it symbolizes Israel?"

"That's complicated," she said. "Before this Olivet Discourse, Jesus was walking along and saw a fig tree that did not bear fruit. Since there was no fruit on the tree, He believed the fig tree was worthless, so He cursed it and it withered and died. Father thought that was a prediction that Israel would be destroyed because the nation was no longer bearing God's fruit of the Spirit.

"Later, Jesus was walking along, and He saw another fig tree. Perhaps it is the same fig tree that has come back to life. Jesus said, 'When ye see these things know that summer is near even at the door.'"

"What does He mean 'summer is near'?" I asked.

Aunt Hank paused and said, "Chris, it means the return of Christ is near."

"Gary," Aunt Hank continued, "so it is your memory that Father said Israel had to recapture Jerusalem and that would end the period of the Gentiles and usher in the end of times?"

Dad had picked up a newspaper and was reading it. He seemed to give a mindless answer as he said, "Yes. That is what Father told us."

Aunt Hank flipped to a page in the Bible and began reading. "Listen to this, Chris. I'm reading from Matthew 24:26–31."

> Wherefore if they shall say unto you, Behold, he is in the desert; go not forth: behold, *he is* in the secret chambers; believe *it* not. For as the lightning cometh out of the east, and shineth even unto the west; so shall also the coming of the Son of man be. For wheresoever the carcase is, there will the eagles be gathered together.

"Jesus is the Son of man," she said. She continued reading:

> Immediately after the tribulation of those days shall the sun be darkened, and the moon shall

not give her light, and the stars shall fall from heaven, and the powers of the heavens shall be shaken: And then shall appear the sign of the Son of man in heaven: and then shall all the tribes of the earth mourn, and they shall see the Son of man coming in the clouds of heaven with power and great glory. And he shall send his angels with a great sound of a trumpet, and they shall gather together his elect from the four winds, from one end of heaven to the other.

"I don't understand, Aunt Hank," I said.

"God's blessings are leaving the Gentile nations like America and are moving back to Israel since they recaptured the Holy Mount last week. And we may be the last generation that lives before He returns."

"The last generation?" I asked.

"Yes, notice, He said, 'This generation shall not pass, till all these things be fulfilled. Heaven and earth shall pass away, but my words shall not pass away.'"

Aunt Hank added, "Father believed 'this generation' did not apply to the generation that was alive while Jesus spoke. It applied to the generation that saw Israel retake the Holy Land."

Apparently, I looked concerned, and my dad peering over his newspaper wanted to calm me down.

"Chris, don't worry, people have been expecting these events to come for thousands of years, and they haven't happened yet."

I said, "Aunt Hank, you're saying Jesus predicted that Israel would be destroyed, and it would be reformed as a nation at a later date?"

"Yes, and that's exactly what happened. In AD 70, Israel was destroyed, and they regained the Holy Land this month," Hank said triumphantly.

"So how long has Israel not been a nation?" I pressed, wanting to understand.

My dad had a serious look on his face. "In AD 70, about forty years after Jesus died on the cross, Titus of Rome invaded Israel. His men routed and destroyed Jerusalem. They tore down the Temple, a beautiful building, and destroyed the other buildings and killed almost all people in Jerusalem. It was a tragedy, Chris."

"How do you know this happened in AD 70? That was a long time ago," I asked.

"A historian named Josephus documented these events in a history book he wrote back then," Dad said, turning a page in his newspaper.

Aunt Hank jumped in and said as she was flipping through the Bible . . . "I can't find it here, but Jesus said just before He was crucified, 'Don't weep for me, but weep for yourselves and your children.' This would have been about forty years before the invasion, so His warning came true pretty quickly." Oh, in Matthew 24:

> Then Jesus went out and departed from the temple, and His disciples came up to show Him the buildings of the temple. And Jesus said to them, "Do you not see all these things? Assuredly, I say to you, not *one* stone shall be left here upon another, that shall not be thrown down."

"This is exactly what happened to Israel in AD 70," Aunt Hank continued. "So Jesus predicted the destruction of Jerusalem by General Titus, and this resulted in the Jews being spread throughout the world. You see, Jesus prophesized this destruction of Israel. Now if you subtract 70 CE from today, which is 1967, then we are three years short of 1900 years since King Titus invaded Israel and destroyed the Temple. They call this a prophecy that Jesus made where He predicted the future before it happened.

"Gary, help me," Hank said as Dad looked over the top of the newspaper. "There were two thousand years from Adam and Eve to Abraham in the Bible, right?" Dad nodded. "Then two thousand years from Abraham to Christ. That would make it four thousand years. It's currently 1967, which is since Christ was born. So in thirty-three years, we will have completed six thousand years since the creation of Adam."

"Correct," Dad said, looking immersed in his newspaper.

"That totals 6,000 years if you count all of the people who lived in the Bible. God said He gave mankind 7,000 years. That means we have 1,033 years to go and the last 1,000 years is called the millennium."

"I'm confused," I said.

"Chris," Dad said, "Aunt Hank believes Israel's quick victory this past month was a miracle. Put another way, God helped the Jews take back key strategic areas and Jerusalem because God had to fulfill this prophecy."

"And without God's help, the Jews would never have beaten the Arabs," Aunt Hank said.

"Are there other prophecies about our time?" I asked sheepishly.

My dad said, "You will have to talk to Aunt Hank about those, she knows far more about the Bible and prophecy than I ever did." And with that, my dad said, "Would anyone else like to stretch their legs and get a nice cool glass of iced tea?"

He stood up, and he began to stretch his legs and walk gingerly out of the den toward the kitchen.

Back to the Country Club

There was a nice general practitioner physician who had invited my dad to move into the country club. My parents applied to the country club with his recommendation, and we were approved to buy a lot near the eighth fairway. So we occasionally spent time with this family and played with their children.

A few years later, my mother said, "Chris, do you remember Dr. Swindell's wife?"

"Yes, I do, why?"

"Last Saturday morning, she told her husband that she couldn't keep her balance and sat back down in the bed, saying she felt light-headed. Dr. Swindell, being a GP, took her pulse felt her forehead, essentially did everything he could to identify what was wrong. And then she died in his arms."

My mother couldn't continue as tears rolled down her cheek. "She just died."

"How is that possible?" I asked.

"Turns out her spleen ruptured and she bled to death in her husband's arms. There was nothing Dr. Swindell could do. She was fine one minute and dead the next."

Then our mother said something strange. She said, "Chris, I don't know how I know this, but I have always known I would die and never see my children grow up."

I replied, "Don't say that, Mom, I'm sure you're mistaken."

"Chris, you need to know this. I'm going to die suddenly before you children are grown." Putting her hands over her eyes, she ran out of the room as she began to sob.

About six months later, my mother asked to see me.

"Chris, Dr. Swindell had just married the nurse that worked in his office. He had four children from his first wife, so I am sure he needed all the help he could get to help raise these kids.

"Dr. Swindell was in his garage picking up some things off the floor. His new wife was coming home from the grocery store when her accelerator in her car stuck. She hit the brakes, but it was too late. The car plowed into the garage door and rode up the door into the garage. The door collapsed on Dr. Swindell. By the time she climbed out of the car, he was dead."

"Dr. Swindell is dead?" I asked in disbelief.

We went to pay respects for the survivors. Dr. Swindell's new wife looked like she had been in a war. She looked terrified, confused, and like she hadn't slept in weeks.

Our sitter, Mrs. Seaton, the elderly lady who took care of us when our parents traveled, went to the funeral with us and said, "I know whose foot was on that accelerator."

"Whose foot?" I asked naively.

"His dead wife's foot!" she whispered to me.

"Mrs. Seaton, did you learn that type of thinking in the hills of West Virginia?" I asked.

She didn't answer me.

My mother had a different take on what happened. When we were alone, my mother confided in me this little secret.

She said, "This country club is cursed because they don't let Jews live here. God loves the Jews, and He blesses those who bless the Jews and curses those who don't."

I'm not sure she knew where this came from in the Bible. But it came from Genesis 12:1–3:

> Now the LORD had said unto Abram, Get thee out of thy country, and from thy kindred, and from thy father's house, unto a land that I will shew thee: And I will make of thee a great nation, and I will bless thee, and make thy name great; and thou shalt be a blessing: And I will bless them that bless thee, and curse him that curseth

thee: and in thee shall all families of the earth be blessed.

*****

I was walking to the bus stop a few weeks later. A miniature poodle that frequently barked at me saw me coming from my driveway that morning. As I walked his way, he would circle and back up and circle and back up, barking the whole time. A bus was coming down the hill toward the bus stop. As the bus got closer, I saw the dog was right where the bus was heading. I swung my arms in the air and yelled at the dog, trying to scare him. He jumped back and then ran forward under the bus's tire. He was dead instantly. The owner of the dog ran out of the house.

I apologized to him, saying, "I tried to stop Max."

In tears he said, "It's not your fault, Chris, I saw the whole thing from my living room window. That driver should have slowed down, he was going too fast . . . too fast." With that, Mr. Snow took a shovel and scraped what was left of his dog off the road while he wept.

I don't know why, but these things seemed to be warning beacons to me. The only thing I knew was something was wrong, very wrong. And my parents were in trouble. God kept telling me I needed to pray for my parents.

At times it is not so much the events but what sticks in our mind later that tells the story. This time in my life, I was focusing on the negative things instead of the positive things. I want you children to focus on positive things. All great men have negative things happen to them but tend to always see the silver lining. They have a dream, a vision. They have well-defined goals. And they do not let a tragedy or obstacle get in the way of achieving their goals. But at this point in my life, the negative was winning.

I remember my father sitting at the dining room table, doing accounting, one Saturday. I played the piano in the background. Over and over I worked on the *Appassionato* by Beethoven. My father would get up and pace. Finally, he started talking to himself.

"I do not have enough money to do what I need to do."

After hearing this a second time, I felt a tingling all over my body. I thought, "God has entered me." I walked into the dining room and stood next to my dad.

Finally, he looked up. "What can I do for you, Chris?"

"Dad, you must trust Jesus. He is the only one Who can save you now."

I wasn't sure what I meant by that . . . There was no reason to suspect that my dad was in any kind of trouble at that point. That comment didn't seem like it came from inside me . . . It was totally out of character for me. Even worse, I never dared talk to my father with that authoritative tone of voice, as if I was the parent and he was the child.

He looked dumbfounded. "What did you just say?"

"Listen, it is impossible for you to save yourself. The only way you can be saved is to trust Jesus."

I was shocked, and I believe my dad was so shocked he didn't know what to say. I expected to be punished or at least questioned about my clearly out-of-order, truthfully crazy comments. But the punishment never came. Neither did the questioning. Somehow what I said seemed to resonate with my dad.

A few weeks later, my mother blew up and yelled at me for not cleaning up my room. I went upstairs to clean it up, and she called me a rotten brat. I didn't know what to do or say. I cleaned up my room as requested but was so upset. I left the house so I wouldn't say or do anything that I would regret later. I was trying to get control of my emotions and foster a more positive relationship with my mother and father, especially since I knew my parents were under a lot of pressure.

*****

I walked out the front door and just started walking. Faster and faster! I had to get away from the evil. The evil, as if demons encircled me! I walked toward my childhood home—the home in the normal neighborhood I grew up in until I was ten years old. It was roughly five miles from our country club home. I was searching for the life I had when I was younger. We had a happy family that was warm and loving, a family that God protected. I searched for that family that was cohesive and unified . . . the family that God loved.

Somehow I walked all the way to that old home that was five miles from our new home. When I arrived, it was late afternoon! It took me an hour and a half to make the one-way trip. I walked into our backyard. I examined the tree I climbed to pretend I was on a rocket heading for space. I thought of Paul's dad, the mountain climber, now dead. I thought of my grandmother who taught me about Jesus. Now she was dead. I was seventeen years old. I thought of my best friend, Carlton, who lived a block away. I even thought about walking to his home and getting a ride back to my house. But I wasn't done with my internal battle that was eating me alive. Finally, I left our old home and headed back to the country club.

About halfway home, I arrived at the top of a hill that looked down upon Rockville. I walked up the hill in front of a house to the highest point in the area. I could see five miles. A storm cloud in the distance was brewing with lightning firing out in all directions. But it wasn't raining where I was. I sat down, feeling helpless, and wept.

Abruptly I stood up and said out loud, "God, why are You going to take my parents from me? God, why are You going to abandon us? Why must they die?" I had no idea why I said that. I thought I must be going crazy.

Getting control of my tears, I continued the walk to our country club home and asked God to keep the rain from falling on me as I walked. I did not feel a drop of rain as I completed my unexpected journey. Just after I arrived home, the storm broke loose. It poured; the wind howled, and lightning flashed.

*****

Things got worse at home. One day after playing the piano, my mother sat next to me and began weeping. Once she gained her composure, she said my dad needed hemorrhoid surgery and that he might die. She asked me to pray for him and said that he was worth more to us alive than dead.

"Dying from hemorrhoid surgery, really, Mom?" I asked. "The only way he will die from hemorrhoid surgery is if the doctor kills him."

I realized my mother was worried. "Does someone want to kill Dad?" I asked.

"If a president wants you dead, Chris, no one can save you."

"Richard Nixon wants our father dead?" I asked. "How can a president have someone killed?"

"The president says something like, 'Joe is in my way, take care of him,' and the CIA does exactly what he asks. If the president gives an order, it must be carried out. That is the only way to protect our nation and our government." At that point, my mother got up and left the room.

Around this time, I was instructed by my dad to put a knife over the front and back doors so if the door opened, it would make a noise as the knife hit the floor. I was also instructed to check all the locks in the house, especially the ones over the windows, every night before going to bed. You could not purchase security systems at that time, so I became the home security system.

About a month later, I was awakened in the wee hours of the morning. Someone was pounding on the front door. I got up and stood at the top of the stairs, wondering what I should do. My dad and mom came out of their bedroom and walked over to me.

My dad stood behind my mother and said, "Chris, open the front door. You're not in danger."

I walked down the steps, pulled the knife out from above the door, and held the knife behind my back. I then opened the door, and a man dressed as a police officer pushed the door open and entered the foyer, screaming at the top of his lungs. He wanted to talk to my dad.

Dad stood at the top of the steps behind my mother and looked at the police officer.

The police officer said, "Mr. Morris, get down here now, we need to talk."

My dad said, "We can talk from a distance. What is your problem?"

"My partner was murdered. You found his body. I need to know who murdered him."

A week earlier, we had been walking to our clubhouse to eat lunch on a beautiful Sunday, and I discovered a man facedown in a blob of his blood on the side of the road. He had been shot in the head. My dad tried to resuscitate him. He sent us on. We called the police, and they picked him up. It was a depressing Sunday, and it began to rain as we arrived at the clubhouse to eat dinner.

It was apparent my dad would not come down the steps, and I stood between this man and the steps. My dad was probably armed with a gun. So this man, after five minutes of screaming, left our home. As he left, I locked the door and returned the knife over the door. I was visibly shaking when he left. Mom came down to comfort me while Dad went back to his bedroom. It was after 3:00 AM.

"What kind of police officer drops by your home at 3:00 AM?" I asked Mom.

She said nothing.

We looked around the house the next morning. Whoever this person was, he tried to enter our home through several windows and doors. Apparently, my home security system—made up of nails, knives, and furniture—had worked for one night.

My mother kissed me on the head and went off to bed. I followed her upstairs to my room and did not sleep that night.

The Teenage Years

When I was a teenager, I became difficult for my parents, or so they say. I thought I was easy to get along, but they thought I was terrible. Sound familiar, Jessica and Joshua? I did go to football parties and parties with friends in the country club where they served beer, but I never could drink a whole beer. I suppose it didn't help when I snuck out of the bedroom and went to a striptease joint with a bunch of friends. I also drove too fast. I rode our thoroughbred horse too fast and got thrown frequently. I played football and loved to hit other people as hard as I could. I guess that's why I became a linebacker. I had the lead role in a high school play. Kids all around knew me. And I could play the piano as well as anyone—well, except for the boy in high school who went to Julliard and became a music professor at a college. I loved Beethoven and Brahms. I could play piano concertos. I think Chopin was my favorite composer. And I thought one day I would be discovered and become a famous pianist. But amidst all our blessings, I knew something was not right.

My dad worked all hours of the day and night. I hardly ever saw him. That hurt my self-esteem. I now believe a boy's self-esteem largely comes from his father. And while I loved my dad, I wished he had spent more time with me.

I had a good friend who lived at the end of our street whose dad was a US senator. This senator liked me and liked my friendship with his son. But his son suffered because this senator was too busy to spend time with his son. I hope that I am always there for you, Jessica and Joshua. I believe that is why God gave me a business to run, a business you have grown up helping me run, so you have ready access to me. And trust me, I am your greatest fan and will stand behind you forever.

Teenage years are tough. I even partially abandoned my love for God. And I wanted to grow up fast so I would play golf a lot. Then I would practice the piano. I was told I was brilliant by various people. I thought school was boring. I didn't think I was popular. You see, I had the same problems all teenagers have. Somehow I was adjusting to pressures that were mounting. Not family problems, but problems and pressures mounting on my parents.

Then it was no longer an uneasy feeling about things; it became obvious things were going wrong at home. I felt a different spirit in the house. Something was very wrong, but I was unable to identify what it was. Like a dark cloud covering our home, I couldn't get away from the pressure.

A bird flew into our house. We tried to nurse it back to health, and it died. I had never experienced asking God for something and not getting a positive answer to my prayer. Our sitter Mrs. Seaton had a lot of superstitions. When she heard about the bird, she became distressed and said someone was going to die. I felt evil walking up the sidewalk to our home. This dark force became darker and darker, and the darker it became, the more frightened I was.

Around my sophomore year, my dad suddenly said out of the blue, "Chris, I want you to become a psychiatrist and work with me and my partners. But until then, I want you to help me with some of my research I am doing at the Army Hospital."

Shortly after he told me this, he asked me to go to work with him in the summer when school was out. He gave me assignments. Some involved reading his papers and helping him edit them. I helped him with a number of menial tasks. Some of these tasks helped him prepare exercises for his psychoanalytic students that he was training. Other things were connected to his work with the military. At the time I suppose some of these things were classified, so I was told I couldn't tell anyone what he was doing.

I remember the first time he took me into the Army base. When my dad drove up to the guarded gate, the guards stood up and saluted my dad. A little while later, while we walked through the hallways, everyone saluted him. Get this, when they talked to him, they didn't call him by his name; they simply said, "General . . ." and stood at attention until he saluted them back in his black suit.

I remember, as a young boy, I loved to watch TV shows about World War II heroes. I even remember asking my dad if he served in the military. His answer was simple: "I was a private first class." And with that he never discussed his military career. So you can imagine how surprised I was when we went to a Naval base or Army Base and everyone saluted him and called him General. Clearly, he omitted some of his background and was unwilling to discuss his credentials.

One of the things I helped my dad do was write papers on his research on sleep deprivation. Why did my dad do this research? During the Vietnam war, a platoon of men had been in the jungle and hadn't really slept in several days, other than a catnap here and there. They arrived back at a little clearing to bunk down for the night. The captain of the company grabbed a man and posted him as guard while the rest of the men slept. During the night, the guard fell asleep in the bushes. Viet Cong found the camp and killed every man who was asleep in tents. The guard who had fallen asleep in the bushes, upon hearing the commotion, froze for fear he would be killed too. The Viet Cong cleared out. The guard checked and found all his comrades were dead. Extremely distressed, he made his way back to main camp and told the chief what had happened. He was summarily arrested and charged with abandoning his post. He was discharged immediately and sent stateside. During the court-martial hearing, the question came up: "Could a man who had not slept for a couple of days stay awake and guard the camp all night long, or was it impossible?"

To answer the question, my dad would keep men in the Army awake to see what happened to them. There were various phases of problems people went through after staying awake for a day or two that surprised my dad. Periods of emotional breakdowns where people cried uncontrollably, screamed out of character, and extreme cases of depression occurred. Then after time, hallucinations occurred, a hallmark of schizophrenia. They kept increasing the time they kept the people awake, and finally kept one man awake for something like five days with no sleep. He became ill. He was so ill that my dad put a halt to any further testing. The minimal illnesses that this soldier had didn't go away. They got worse and worse, and every medical treatment they tried—from antibiotics to complete rest and sleep in a darkened room—none of them worked. Suddenly the man died. My dad was horrified, as were all the other physicians who worked in desperation to save this soldier's life.

For a year after the death of this soldier, my dad felt responsible for the death of this innocent man. Another change our dad went through as a result of this testing was to tell us to get sleep, as much as we needed. He no longer got up after sleeping four hours a night. Our entire family was cautioned to sleep as much as we needed and not to cut short our sleep. Somehow he concluded that our immune system, our brain functioning, and our mental health were heavily linked to the amount of sleep we got.

These psychiatrists were looking for ways to gain classified information from the enemy. The traditional ways of torturing captives went against these men's consciences, as they had limited success, you could only hit a man in the head so many times before you did permanent brain damage or worse. And those who survived these brutal hits often had so much brain damage that they never returned to normal. Their personalities changed because of the brain damage, and often they were unable to take care of themselves.

My dad tried hypnosis to see if he could get classified information from the enemy. After several years of research, he concluded that people under hypnosis will not do anything that they wouldn't do when completely awake. So that was a dead end.

One of my dad's partners tried testing soldiers with all types of drugs, including LSD and other mind-altering drugs, to see if these drugs would work like some sort of truth serum. These didn't work well either. Dad was very upset when he found out one of the doctors took the LSD to test the effects it would have on him.

I remember telling my dad about a friend of mine who smoked pot regularly, and I told him that my friend's personality had changed substantially since he used pot. I asked my dad what had happened to him. Based on research his partners had done, he told me my friend had brain damage. You can imagine I never smoked marijuana after hearing this, whether my dad had all the facts. I wouldn't put it past him to lie to me to keep me from smoking pot.

These psychiatrists were not typical psychiatrists. They were not only involved in the military, but they had been in combat. One of the men who worked with dad had walked the Bataan Death March carrying a friend the whole way on his shoulder. I don't know of a greater war hero than this man, with the exception of those who gave their lives to save others during the war.

The question became, How do you get the enemy to provide our government with information we need that might be classified? It turns out one of the best solutions involved sleep deprivation. And why was sleep deprivation so effective? Because people lost touch with reality and often didn't know where they were or who they were talking to and as a result would do anything to get some sleep. The other beauty of sleep deprivation was that once these men got adequate sleep, they returned to normal, as if nothing had happened to them. It was the best of both worlds. You could interrogate people and not permanently hurt them. It seemed to be a lot more effective than hitting people in the head repeatedly.

Years later, Jessica, my daughter, who had never actually met her grandfather, came home with a high school textbook on psychology. At the front of the chapter was a full-page picture of a man Jessica showed me, and she asked, "Is that my grandfather?"

I answered, "Yes, it is, Jessica." As I recall, the caption under the picture said, "Father of sleep deprivation research." That chapter was about sleep and sleep deprivation and all the research that was going on in this field at that time.

And now you know more about your grandfather and your father.

To Dulles Airport

My stable father, who was always happy and in control of himself, had changed recently. He had made several trips to the Caribbean with my mother in the last few months. He went to the Caribbean sometimes two times a year as far back as I could remember. By this time, I learned that trips to the Caribbean were often not to the Caribbean, but I also learned not to ask questions.

This should have been an uneventful trip. When they traveled, our sitter, Mrs. Seaton, would take care of us while they were gone. She was a wizened seventy-year-old woman who believed in ghosts, superstitions, and premonitions—you see, she was raised a hillbilly girl in the Appellation mountains.

When we said goodbye to our parents at the airport, we got in the car to drive away; and there were our parents, waving to us from the entrance to the airport. As I drove away, I had this terrible feeling of impending doom. I drove down the highway from Dulles Airport, and no one said a word.

I broke the silence and said to Mrs. Seaton, my sister, and brother, "I don't know why, but I know we will never see Mom and Dad again."

Mrs. Seaton said, "Chris, don't say that. You take that back."

"What do you mean by that?" I asked.

"You take that back. Don't curse your parents like that."

"Curse them?"

"What you say may come true, Chris," Mrs. Seaton elaborated. "I knew when my mother was going to die. The phone rang, and I didn't want to pick it up because I knew if I picked up the phone, a person on the other end of the line would tell me my mother was dead. I picked up the phone and a man I didn't know said, 'I'm sorry to tell you, Mrs. Seaton, but your mother passed away tonight in the hospital.' I believe in these things," she continued.

I said to Mrs. Seaton, "It doesn't matter what we do, they are going to die, and we can't change that now. Should we go back and say goodbye again?" I pulled off the interstate. The car remained eerily silent as I drove back to the airport.

When we arrived at Dulles, we found our parents sitting in the same place we left them. I looked at my dad. Then I said, "I came back to tell you we will never see you again. I love you both."

My dad looked horrified. My mother cried. She believed me. Just like the last time I spoke with authority to my dad, I wondered who had taken possession of my body and said things through me.

At this point, my dad stood up and took me to show me an airport lockbox. He opened it with a key. There wasn't anything in the lockbox. He then said, "Someone was supposed to put a case of money in the box for me, but the box is empty."

I didn't know what he was talking about at the time. Years later, I learned that the CIA used these airport boxes to pass things from one agent to another. Clearly my dad was expecting some kind of help from a CIA agent.

We hugged and kissed them goodbye, and they walked us to our car and sent us on our way. Was I going crazy?

I wondered!

As we got in the car, they said, "Don't come back again, we will be on the plane in less than half an hour. It's time to go home, Chris."

As I thought about this experience later, I was puzzled. The first time I confronted my dad, I said to him that he would be fine if he put his faith in Jesus. This time there was no opportunity to save him or Mom. He had his chance and did not take it. I felt ill. There was a pit in my stomach. I knew Who spoke through me. I recognized Him, and His name was Holy Spirit.

Tragedy Strikes Home

That was the last time we saw our parents. Many people came by to visit us. A reporter named Bob Woodward from the *Washington Post* called me at home every day for almost a month, asking for information about our dad's disappearance. Our dad was written up as a VIP on the front page of the *Washington Post* and the *Washington Star*. I had been through enough training with my dad to know the stories in the *newspapers* were planted by our government in hopes to get a response as to who did this.

A newspaper article, printed about a year later, connected our dad's disappearance with a woman who died in a plane crash. The article said Mrs. E. Howard Hunt had died because the pilot had been poisoned. Mr. and Mrs. E. Howard Hunt were friends of the family and Mr. Hunt had trained the Cuban's for the Bay of Pigs invasion. It also said she had a satchel full of money and in the satchel was our parents' names and address and a lock box number.

I knew many things about my dad because he had been training me to work for him in the government. A psychiatrist named Dr. Pierce that worked with my dad contacted me. He invited us, the three kids, over to his house where he asked prying questions. Every time I went to answer, I felt someone that was not there put pressure on my shoulder as if to say "Don't answer that question." Suddenly the play Hamlet entered my memory.

"To be or not to be, that is the question."

If I told this man what I knew, I was surely going to suffer my dad's and mom's fate, I thought. I wondered where the thought came from. It was as if an alien put it there. I decided to remain stupid and say nothing. In hindsight, I believe God was leading me, and the best thing I could do was to be silent and say nothing . . . like Hamlet.

Over the next few months, I blamed myself for my parents' death. I knew I was to blame. I had failed to reach my dad and convince him that Jesus was real. I remember pleading with my dad one night. For some reason, the Holy Spirit had entered me and pleaded with my dad through me.

I said, "Trust Jesus, Dad. Trust God. It doesn't matter how bad things seem, God is great enough to do anything. No matter what problems we face as a family, God can overcome anything."

I did not know why I said this. At the time there was no reason to believe our dad was in danger. Remarkably, after I said this, my dad, who had not been in a church in decades, returned to church and went with us every Sunday until their disappearance in the Caribbean.

I felt I was responsible for their death, because I failed to bring my faith into our parents' lives. My mother believed, but I felt I hadn't done enough to really teach my dad about our Lord. This was a difficult subject for my mother, a Jewish woman, and my dad, a Baptist minister's son. Nevertheless, this guilt I felt expressed itself in a feeling of loss and a deep and dark depression.

A few days later, a policeman came to our home. He knocked on the door. I opened the door. He asked to see me and my sister and brother. We all three sat on the floor of our den with Mrs. Seaton sitting on the couch in her usual position, smoking her Salem menthol cigarettes.

He said simply, "Your parents are missing at sea. They went out on a boat, and they never returned. The hotel in St. Lucia contacted our police station and asked me to tell you what happened."

The nightmare had begun. I went into my dad's office and picked up the phone. I called Aunt Hank, who was now in London working for Ambassador Bruce. She was having a party in her flat. She said, "Let me shut the door."

"Christopher," she said, "I will go to the British government and get help immediately. I will also contact the White House and have the secretary of state search for Gary and Jane."

Someone entered her bedroom. I could hear them say, "Henrietta, is everything okay?"

"No, my brother and sister-in-law are missing at sea. I have to handle this call with my nephew."

Aunt Hank flew in from London two days later. She stayed with us and called Ambassador Bruce, who assured her the British government had dispatched three ships to search for Gary and Jane. She had also heard from Secretary Kissinger, who said the White House and the US Coast Guard had dispatched several airplanes and a couple more ships. They were searching night and day over the Caribbean Sea for their little boat that disembarked from the hotel with our parents and a captain.

Every morning I would get up and make coffee for Aunt Hank and me. She would read the *Washington Post, Washington Star* and other papers and magazines . . . searching for stories about our parents. I pointed out articles that I felt were planted by our government. She agreed and wanted to know how I knew. I told her dad had been training me to work for him one day.

Our parents were lost at sea. The US Coast Guard and the Royal Navy from England—thanks in large part to Aunt Hank, Henry Kissinger, and Ambassador Bruce—searched for our parents for eleven days. There were five ships and three airplanes all searching for them. They found three boats that had lost power, and they rescued those people; but the search did not turn up a floatation device, an oar, or any other part of the boat that our parents were on when they went missing. The odds of the Coast Guard and Royal Navy not turning up some part of the boat were less than 1.5 of 1 percent when they halted the search.

Another man from Washington showed up at my uncle's home and said he had been asked by the US government to determine what happened to our parents. Uncle Stuart, who had no idea what my dad really did for a living, went to St. Lucia to investigate what happened. When this man flashed his card, he got whatever he wanted— and I mean, immediately. He turned the island upside down in a week. He interviewed over a hundred witnesses. Over time the story came together . . . Several people saw our parents getting off the little boat. It had pulled up to a larger boat, and they saw three people who fit the description of our parents and the captain boarding the larger vessel. That was the last anyone heard or saw the three.

The Mysterious Woman

After my parents disappeared, a woman called me at home. She would not tell me her name. She said her husband was a lawyer and worked with my dad in the White House and that I would know who he was if she told me anything else. She confessed having been a patient of my dad and was going to save him. I asked her how she could do that. She said her husband was a very important and powerful man in the White House.

Her first call occurred a few days after our parents were declared missing.

About this time, the impeachment hearings against President Nixon had started to be aired in the press and became the hottest story. I didn't know that Bob Woodward, my morning caller, was breaking the story on our president. One story that hit home that surfaced involved a person that had broken into a psychiatrist's office in DC and had stolen many records of his patients. The psychiatrist had a name that was different than my dad. But after doing some checking, I realized the name was a false name used to protect my dad's actual identity. They used another name in the story because so many things in Washington are classified and altered for the general public. How did I find out there was a break-in? I went to his office. The windows were broken through, as mentioned by the press. The file cabinets had been jimmied open. This was a professional job.

I confronted a partner of my dad who worked in his office. When I threatened to go to the police and worse, he suddenly asked me into his office and closed the door. At that point he admitted he had staged the break-in so he could get access to the files on important people who worked in the White House. These records could not come into the hands of anyone else as they were classified. So they used a key that I gave them to get into his office, took the records, thanked me, kicked out a window, and knocked over some furniture and goods to make it look like a break-in and reported this to the police and the press. They then reported that a burglar had stolen the records to keep this quiet.

After about ten days, my aunt and uncle from Texas joined Hank in our home, and we all knelt down together and prayed for their safe return. I made a desperate prayer, a sincere plea with God that he would not let our parents die. But I knew, I knew all too well, for I had told my parents at the airport, we would never see them again.

A few days later, I felt ill and lay down in my bed. Aunt Hank noticed I was missing and came upstairs searching for me. When she found me, I was holding my stomach with my knees up toward my chest.

"Chris, are you okay?" she asked.

"No, Aunt Hank. No, I'm not. I just felt Dad die. Someone shot him in the chest. He fell on the floor in a lump and died a senseless death."

What happened to Mom, I don't know. Perhaps our Lord kept her alive after all. But I am certain our dad died that night. Death certificates searched for years later indicated Dad died at the time of the disappearance but that my mother never had a death certificate filed. Perhaps that is why my dad was so concerned about having enough money. He was trying to change their identity and get away. Perhaps he succeeded in saving our mother!

Are Others Being Murdered?

I t was decided that I would stay in high school for a few more months, stay in the home, and graduate from high school. A couple of weeks later, a friend of mine who played football was walking down the hallway and started accusing me of flirting with his girlfriend. He then swung a punch at my head. I ducked. He hit me again and again, and I refused to hit back. Tears streamed down his face. I was bruised but not badly hurt. That evening I explained to Aunt Hank what happened when I got home. The next day she showed up at school and demanded to talk to our principal and this boy.

After I got home from school, Aunt Hank asked to speak with me.

"Chris," she said, "I went to school to talk to the principal about that boy that hit you. The principal called him into his office and interrogated him. I'm sorry to say, his dad died last week. He was shot in the head. Chris, I recognized his dad's name and did some checking. His dad worked for our CIA."

"He did?"

"Yes. Don't be mad at your friend. He wept when I confronted him. I was upset because he beat up on you just after you lost your parents. But he also lost his dad. He was clearly very upset with what had happened." Hank paused for a moment. "Chris, Jeff believes someone in our government murdered his dad."

"Aunt Hank, I wasn't after Marcie . . . his girlfriend, at all. I liked her, and we were friends and worked in chemistry class together, but I never flirted with her."

"Well, he didn't take it that way, and his girlfriend Marcie, was it? Well, she came in to the principal's office and told him there was nothing between you and her, and she insisted with tears streaming down her face that he had to believe her."

"I understand, Aunt Hank. That's why I didn't fight back."

"Chris, there is something else I need to tell you. Jeff's dad wasn't the only operative killed recently. Agents are being killed across America by someone, we don't know who. I believe this is somehow connected to your dad's death. But I need more information to get to the bottom of this."

"I love you, Aunt Hank," I said with my voice breaking. "I just don't know what we would do without you. Thank you for everything."

The Mysterious Woman Calls Again

A few days later the mysterious woman called. I answered the phone. "Chris, good news. There may be an opportunity to save your parents. They were picked up and transported back to Washington, DC, and are currently held in a military facility."

"Walter Reed?" I asked.

"I don't know," she answered. "But with the help of my husband, I believe we can save your mom and dad."

Then I heard clicking on the phone line.

She said, "Chris, do you hear that clicking?"

I said, "Yes, I do."

"They are bugging our phone calls. We will have to keep the calls brief. I will call you back later," and she hung up the phone.

I remember saying to Aunt Hank, "Isn't it illegal for our government to bug our phones?"

"Yes." Aunt Hank laughed out loud. "Chris, no one in our government pays any attention to those silly laws."

I was shocked that she took it so nonchalantly. This proved to confirm what my dad had previously said about bugs on our phones.

One day when this woman caller was on the phone, a man in the background called her.

"Martha," he said. "Martha, are we out of coffee?"

I now knew the first name of my mysterious caller. Her name was Martha. Martha Mitchell, I thought, the wife of the Attorney General. And at least once a week every week for the next two years, she picked up the phone and called me.

Friends of Our Dad Emerge

Aunt Hank took us on a tour traveling from Washington, DC, to South Carolina. We stopped frequently on the way to stay with friends who knew Aunt Hank and our dad. These people took us into their homes and treated us with true Southern hospitality. At a home in Charleston, South Carolina, a Navy captain asked to speak with me privately outside of his home. He was afraid people might have wired his home.

We stepped out into the breezy evening air, which was still blowing warm on our faces.

"Chris, your dad reported to the secretary of state," Roger said. "You see, he was the top psychiatrist in the Army, and all of the psychiatrists in the Army reported to him. I liked your dad a lot. He was honest. He always did the right thing by everyone. He loved your mother, he loved you kids, and he loved America."

Another friend of Hank's was a psychiatrist. He said, "Chris, you have an amazingly strong ego. I am proud to know you, and I'm sure your dad would be proud of you as well. I know you have been through a lot. Be strong. This too will pass, and you will be fine. If you ever need anything, let me know."

I happened to overhear Aunt Hank talk to a friend of hers at another home. They had stepped outside, and I was throwing a football back and forth with this man's boys at the time. Hank and this man stood by his car on the side of the road. I couldn't hear what he said very well as he spoke quietly. But I could overhear Aunt Hank saying, "They have names locked in a safe at the Democratic National Headquarters?" Then silence. I walked closer to the car and told the boys to go long as I threw the ball high into the air.

Then I heard him say, "Hank, these are the names of all of those in the CIA who assisted in the assassination of President Kennedy. Teddy Kennedy is killing them all one by one. He has already killed dozens of men."

"But Gary would never have been involved in such an operation. I know that, Bill."

"I don't think he was either. But a number of men who reported to Gary, good men, have been dying recently. Teddy Kennedy is killing them in revenge for Jack's death."

"Can someone get to the list they have?"

"I don't know. Only the president could authorize such an operation. I believe Gary was asking President Nixon to get the list at all cost and stop the senseless killings. Hank, there were over one hundred names on that list."

I had my answer. There had been several men who had been coming to our home, strangers I didn't know, looking extremely agitated and asking to meet with our dad. I was afraid of these people as Dad talked to them privately. He typically kept me informed on work he was doing, but I was not allowed to hear anything that was going on when these strangers showed up. I guessed they were CIA operatives. They went to great lengths to keep everything hush-hush. If this was true, this would explain a lot about what was going on in Washington.

When we returned to our home in DC, I spoke to Aunt Hank about what she had learned. She wouldn't tell me, so I finally said that I had overheard the conversation. Hank looked horrified as I explained what I knew.

"Chris, I am certain your dad had nothing to do with President Kennedy's death."

"What really happened, Aunt Hank?" I asked.

"Nixon won the election against President Kennedy. Joseph Kennedy, President Kennedy's dad, stuffed the ballot box and threw the election. Johnson was able to help stuff the ballot boxes in the South and had used these tactics before when he ran for the US Senate."

"He had that much power?" I asked.

"Joseph Kennedy was organized crime, Chris, and ruthless. They would go to great lengths to get in the White House as it would mean huge financial rewards for their family if his son became president."

"So what happened?"

"Richard Nixon made two important decisions. He decided to bide his time and not contest the election. Then he decided to ally himself with the Texas Mafia."

"The Texas Mafia?"

"Actually, yes, with Lyndon Johnson's boss. They call them Mafia, but they are nothing like the Italian organized crime, Chris."

"Lyndon Johnson? I thought you liked Lyndon Johnson."

"I do, Chris, he is a good friend. You know he is a Texan? Well, he and his wife, Lady Bird, are wonderful to me."

"Did the CIA really kill Kennedy?"

"I don't know. Apparently, they were involved somehow."

"Why did Lyndon Johnson help kill Kennedy?"

"That's easy. So he could be president. And as president, he was able to funnel a lot of money to his family."

"Did you ever read the book *A Texan Looks at Lyndon*? This book makes Lyndon Johnson look like a monster."

"I gave that book to Gary, Chris. Yes, I read it. Did Gary give it to you to read?"

"As a matter of fact, he did last winter."

"His way of teaching you how the government really works," Aunt Hank commented. "Chris, you have to understand. All men who have great power do things that might be considered unethical. That's how they get ahead. Don't judge President Kennedy because he is connected to Mafia. As you now know, President Johnson was connected to the Mob, and so is President Nixon. You don't get that much power by being a nice guy!"

My mind had switched back to the book about Lyndon Johnson.

"I remember when Johnson wanted to take over a radio station that was worth over $1 million. The man who owned the station had a cash flow problem and had found a buyer for the station. The buyer made a concrete million dollar offer, but the FCC had to approve the deal. After several months, the FCC disapproved the sale. The seller found two other people who wanted to purchase his radio station. In each case, the FCC disapproved the sale. The owner of the radio station, after a year, filed for bankruptcy. While the business was in receivership, Lady Bird Johnson went to the judge and made an offer to purchase the radio station for a trifling amount. The FCC immediately approved the sale. And Lady Bird wound up with a million-dollar business for peanuts.

"When Johnson ran against Stevenson, wasn't that his name? At any rate, I think it was Stevenson . . . he won by fewer than one hundred votes. Stevenson accused him of stuffing the ballot box with names of dead people. A Texas judge, I believe, ordered a recount of the votes. The story goes that Lyndon Johnson surrounded a bank with his boss' men, who wore holsters, guns, western hats, and boots. They guarded the bank vault that night so the votes would be there for the recount in the morning. When they opened the safe in the bank, lo and behold, all the ballots were missing. Lyndon Johnson told the press, 'The maid must have gone into the vault and thrown out all the votes that night.'

"Stevenson was about to drag Lyndon Johnson into court for trial over these missing votes, and the dead person ballots, but before he was prosecuted, Supreme Court Chief Justice Black gave Johnson a full pardon. Lyndon Johnson was put on a plane to Washington to serve as the senator from Texas the next day."

"Chris, you are naive, my dear boy. Anyone who becomes president of the United States is ruthless. They have to be! The things you are describing are nothing, believe me. And it is also probable that Vice President Johnson planned to kill President Kennedy. Gary and I both believed Johnson would kill Kennedy if Kennedy made him vice president."

"You knew that would happen . . . really?"

"Yes, I know Lyndon Johnson, and as evidence to this, his timing was perfect! It was certain that after his one-year term, where Johnson was made president by Kennedy's death, he would easily win reelection because of the sympathy vote. You see, he had only been in office for a little over a year when President

Kennedy died, and the next election took place. Johnson couldn't lose."

"Did he use the CIA to redirect the traffic and to pull the trigger when President Kennedy was assassinated?" I asked.

"I don't know the answer to that, Chris, but I am confident Oswald was a CIA operative."

"Dad checked this out. He speculated that Oswald would talk if interrogated. So they had Jack Ruby kill Oswald to shut him up. Apparently, Ruby was dying of cancer and needed money for his wife and children. He agreed to kill Oswald in exchange for a large financial gift that was given to his wife.

"Which brings me to my next question. If Nixon did cut a deal with the Texas Mob after losing the election to Kennedy, could he have been working with Lyndon Johnson's boss and been part of the plot to kill Kennedy?"

"That's certainly possible," Aunt Hank said.

"Kennedy used Johnson's skill in stuffing the ballot box with the names of dead people . . . it only makes sense that Nixon might want revenge," I speculated.

"Chris, all of the presidents in the past have been picked by men in smoke-filled rooms. The American people never really have a say in who becomes president," Hank stated matter-of-factly. "At least that was true through President Kennedy. This may change that fact, and the people may now be able to pick the president."

Years later I heard Tip O'Neill, a previous Speaker of the House, say the same thing in a TV interview. I laughed, because Aunt Hank was always correct when it involved politics.

"Dad stated flatly that John F. Kennedy did not win the election. So it is possible these CIA operatives thought they were acting in our country's best interests by eliminating the man who stuffed the ballot box and who never won the election. By the way, Aunt Hank, I thought the Democratic Party was essentially run by the New York Mafia. Am I right?"

"It's connected to the Kennedy machine, which was more the Irish Mob, which really doesn't exist anymore. But they have many connections with other gangsters, including the New York Mob."

"So it doesn't matter which party we support. We are support-ing one Mafia group or another. Why does the Mafia care about the presidency so much?"

"It means a lot of money to them and incredible power if they get their man elected as president. They might pay millions to help a man become president, and they will receive billions in return through government contracts."

"Aunt Hank, another friend told me what you said. She said anyone connected to Kennedy's death is now being executed by Teddy Kennedy, and he is using the Democratic Party to help him pull this off. So that confirms your speculation earlier."

"Chris, if I am going to help you, you will have to tell me who this friend is."

"Hank, it is a woman that has been calling me every week for the last couple of months. She says her husband is a lawyer, is very powerful, and works for the president. Her name is Martha."

"Martha Mitchell?" Aunt Hank said. "It can't be."

"If there is such a list and dozens of people, like my friend's dad, are being killed by Teddy Kennedy, can Nixon get to the list and stop the killings?"

"I don't know," Hank mused.

I didn't sleep a wink that night. I thought of trying to revenge my dad's and mom's death. But how do you kill a president? Then I thought of Jesus and realized I couldn't get revenge. Jesus would not allow it. Not now, not ever. I lay in bed praying, crying, asking God for forgiveness for my anger. And I was bitter with God for allowing this to happen. And then it hit me . . . God tried to help my dad out, but my dad would not take His help. And then I really cried.

Ambassador Bruce

A few weeks later, I was invited with Aunt Hank over to Ambassador Bruce's home in Georgetown. I remember being greeted by a lovely woman in a traditional maid's dress who escorted us into the living room. After sitting on the couch for a while, I turned around in my seat and got on my knees on the couch to look at the painting on the wall behind us. It looked like an impressionist. I read the signature on the painting. It said "Renoir."

"Aunt Hank, I don't recognize this painting. I have seen all of Renoir's paintings in art books. Is this really a Renoir?"

"Yes, it is, Chris. And the painting over there is really by Claude Monet. The reason you don't see these pictures in books, is they are privately owned by Ambassador Bruce. The pictures you see in the books are of paintings in museums."

We ate lunch with Ambassador Bruce and his wife. He said he had just returned from a meeting with President Nixon. He asked lots of prying questions; he was apparently interrogating me to see what, if anything, I knew. I felt the pressure on my shoulder again, from the unseen angel. I knew I had best act stupid. And I was particularly good at that, so I said absolutely nothing of consequence to him and talked about high school.

I believed I had satisfied Ambassador Bruce by my naïveté. So he stopped interrogated me, and he and his wife talked to Aunt Hank about an affair their butler was having with one of their maids. After lunch I was asked to drive Ambassador Bruce to his club so he could play cards with his friends. Aunt Hank and I gladly drove him to a nondescript building and dropped him off at the corner and waited for him to disappear into a door before we headed for home.

Graduation

I n May I graduated from high school on schedule. My sister, brother, Mrs. Seaton, and Aunt Hank showed up as everyone else had returned home. It was an unusual graduation. Our speaker was Hubert Humphrey, the Democratic presidential nominee. As I listened to him speak, I decided I really liked this man. He must have mentioned God at least one hundred times. He feared and trusted God. No one could fake that genuine appeal for faith and trust in God Almighty. He was a good man trying to do good in difficult times. I wondered how he got tied up in the mess we call Washington, and I concluded a good man like that could never be elected president of our nation.

While he spoke, I wondered what inspired him to come to our high school graduation. Was it me? Was it Jeff? Or were there other children of dead parents in our high school? Did we have the most children of assassinated parents in our high school? Or were we just convenient to Senator Humphrey because we were in the suburbs of DC? I thought about Teddy Kennedy's wrath. I could understand his desire for revenge. But I believed in Jesus so much I knew revenge was a direction I could never take. I felt tears on my face during the graduation, as I thought about all the innocent deaths, and I had become content with my role, which was the same role Hamlet selected.

"To be or not to be, that is the question . . ." We both chose "to be."

The Summer after Our Parents Disappeared

Once I finished my senior year in high school, we immediately moved to Baltimore, where Karen and Eric, my sister and brother, lived with our mother's brother Stuart and his wife, Joanne. They had three children and had taken in a foster child from the state named Timmy. Three's company, seven is a full house. Uncle Stuart handled the estate and was trying to get money for us kids. But the judge wouldn't let us access it.

The judge essentially said, "No bodies to show, then no access to their assets."

I planned on working in the oil fields, at my Texas uncle's suggestion, so I could pay my way through Emory. I wanted to spend the summer with my sister and brother, so we decided to move to Midland, Texas that summer where our dad's sister Clarice and her husband, LB, lived. We also brought our dog, Folly, with us to Texas that May. I drove for three days to get to Midland, Texas and stayed at cheap hotels. I used some cash Stuart gave me and even stopped in Six Flags over Texas in Dallas on the way.

LB was an oil geologist and, with our parents' death, had lost his job as an independent oil geologist. He worked for a partnership our dad had set up . . . The partnership was made up of a bunch of my dad's friends, who were physicians. LB had an above-average success rate in hitting oil wells. LB was just about ready to drill on land in the Permian Basin when our parents went missing. The business my dad and LB had set up had mineral rights, allowing him to drill a well there. But our dad had made one major mistake. He set up a partnership instead of a corporation. And with his disappearance at sea, the partnership was dissolved and had to be reformed. Try though he may, LB could not get the remaining partners to reform a new partnership without Gary to run it. The result was that LB had to sell off all the assets of the partnership and close it down. This also meant LB was now unemployed just at the time we three kids arrived in their tiny three-bedroom home.

To tell you how bad our luck was, Uncle LB had identified where he was going to drill the next well. He subsequently sold the land lease to Shell Oil. Shell drilled where LB told them to drill and hit a fifteen-well field, worth many millions of dollars. My dad and LB owned 20 percent each of this partnership. As it was, we got nothing. Had our parents lived six more months, they would have both been much better off financially. I remember thinking the devil's timing was perfect. We were not to become truly rich, and Satan made sure of that!

As it was, I had to pay my way through college. The only way I could make enough money to do that was to work in the oil fields. Through Uncle LB's connections, I got a job working on a drilling rig as a "dope man." Not the type of dope you smoke, but the type of dope that is grease. My job was to use a big stick with a rubber end and to put the dope on the drilling pipe threads as they added a pipe to the column so the joints would hold firmly together and not unscrew.

I would get up at 4:30 AM, drive to Odessa, Texas from Midland, about a thirty-minute trip, get in a car with a man in Odessa, and drive an hour into the Sonoran Desert where we would work on a drilling rig. We worked from 7:00 AM to 3:30 PM. We had a thirty-minute lunch break. And I typically got home at about 5:00 PM. The job was a lot of hard manual labor. It was also dangerous. Three big diesel engines that were loud ran nonstop. They pulled steel cables, which ran from draw works on the oil platform, up into the top of the rig. They dropped down where there was a device that gripped the pipes and held them. The ninety-foot pipe stands descended into a turntable where they attached to a square pipe. The square pipe fit into two steel bushings that sat in a rotary table called the "turntable." The two steel bushings weighed tons and held the pipe . . . say up to fifteen thousand feet of steel pipe with a drill bit at the bottom. So we were dealing with extreme weights and pressures, and if anything snapped or broke, it would kill a worker or two.

I was working on the job one day. Something unusual had happened. When I had left the day before, the driller was fishing for a drill bit that had broken off in the well. *Fishing* is just what it sounds like. We had pulled all the pipe out of the ground, and the driller was sending down metal grippers in hopes to grab on to the expensive diamond-studded bit and haul it up and continue drilling.

The next day, I arrived at work; he was drilling again, but this time the pipes were at an angle. I asked, "What happened?" They were not able to get the bit out of the ground and had to start over again and drill at an angle. No problem, I thought, except for the expensive loss of a drill bit.

Every thirty minutes or so, we would add a stand of pipe as the drill bit cut ninety feet deeper into the ground. Every day or two, we would pull all the pipes out of the ground and change drill bits. Some bits do a better job in hard rock, others in soft rock, and occasionally you would need to replace a worn bit with a new bit. This involved pulling out as many as a hundred ninety-foot pipe stands and hanging them on the drilling rig.

The next day, when I arrived at work, we were pulling all pipe stands out of the ground. Not a big deal, but as we did this, because the driller had angled the pipe in the well, the wide pipe connectors were catching on the bushing and pushing one of these steel multi-ton weights that sat in the turntable up a foot or two out of place. To reset it, the driller would hit a button and spin the turntable, and the steel bushing would fall back into the turntable as it slipped off the collar of the pipe. I had been watching this for about an hour when suddenly, this thought occurred to me: "Chris, get out of the way . . . NOW."

First, I wondered where that thought came from. It was my thought, no question about that, but I had no reason to think that thought at that moment in time.

I had been concerned that when the driller spun the turntable, instead of the two-ton steel bushing falling back into the hole, it might be slung out and hit one of us. Obviously, if it did, it would kill us. So I climbed up on the draw works, which is a large metal frame that houses the cable that moves the pipe up or down. I would climb up five feet and then hop down to dope the pipes and reset them every minute or two.

The driller yelled at me, "Get down here, worm."

That was the affectionate name they gave me. I shook my head no. He yelled again. I ignored him. Being a nicer, older gentleman, he decided to ignore me and let me climb up on the draw works.

Then he spun the turntable. Only this time, instead of the two-ton steel bushing falling back in the hole, it flew out away from the drill pipe. Traveling at thirty miles an hour or so, it went exactly where I was supposed to be standing, and it broke through a steel wall and chain and flew down into the mud pit about fifty feet below the steel platform where we stood. I shuddered. The steel bushing disappeared into the mud. If I hadn't moved, I would have been killed for sure.

I was saved by that still, quiet thought in my mind. I paused. The driller looked at me, knowing I was alive because I disobeyed his orders.

The chain thrower looked at the driller and said, "Who is going to report this to management?"

I then paused, closed my eyes, and thought, "Dear God, what would I do without Your warnings? Thank You for saving me."

Summer Progresses and Our Dog Folly Gets Ill

Folly was like a fish out of water in Texas. She loved our mother. She knew we three kids were under tremendous stress. She must have gained fifty pounds that summer, and by August she died one night in her bed. I couldn't cry. I loved that dog. I understood why she gave up and died. Uncle LB gave me a shovel, and I dug the hole and buried her in their backyard.

I was emotionless as we prayed over our now-dead dog. I felt like a zombie, as did Karen and Eric. Death seemed to follow us to Texas.

My Driving Companion, Bob

The old man I drove to and from work with every day rarely spoke. His name was Bob. He was a strange bird. I would talk occasionally, and he would grunt. He had to be in his forties. I was eighteen, so he seemed like an old man to me then. One day he asked me into his house after work. He wanted me to meet his wife. I met her and thought she was a really nice lady. She looked so sad. I was curious.

His wife, Cynthia, asked, "Chris, I heard you lost your parents recently. I'm so sorry to hear that. What a tragedy."

"Yes, ma'am, it was a tragedy."

"Do you have any sisters or brothers?"

"One each," I responded.

"Are they okay?"

"I think they're fine."

"How old is your sister and brother?"

"My sister is fifteen, and my brother is thirteen." I paused to think about how Karen and Eric really were doing. Then I added, "I feel so helpless, because I want to help them out, but my sister, Karen, doesn't want any help. She treats me like she hates me."

"I'm sorry to hear that, Chris. She's a young girl, I'm sure she will grow out of that over time. The loss of her parents is difficult on her, and I'm sure she's taking it out on you because she has no one else to be mad at. The good news is that you're okay and working, and you'll be fine. Are you going to college?"

"Yes, I plan on going to Emory University this fall."

We finished our small talk, and I simply thanked Cynthia for the iced tea, got in my car, and drove home.

Bob's wife liked me, and I think she asked him to bring me into the house every now and then.

One day I felt extreme anxiety from Bob. It was like he was going to explode. Something was really wrong. Bob, I guess out of habit, drove me to their home. I went in and started talking to Cynthia. As she did so often, she asked me if I wanted something to drink . . . I said no, and then she asked me to have a seat.

She looked at me with tears in her eyes and said, "Our son James was killed on this date last year. Racing a car, he tried to beat a train across the tracks and lost. Cost him and a friend their lives."

"Oh my god, what a tragedy," I blurted out, not knowing how to respond.

"Yes, sir, it sure was. He was eighteen years old. Just graduated high school and was looking for a job. Bob here says you remind him of our son."

I was so uncomfortable I didn't know what to say. But I tried to comfort Bob and his wife by saying things like, "I'm sure James is in heaven."

After that, I wasn't often invited into their home. We would go by their house, I would hop out of Bob's car if he drove, or he would hop out of my car if I drove, and I would head home.

One day when we reached Bob's house, I got out of the car, and a young woman came out to meet me. She invited me into Bob's house. Her name was Denise.

"Hey, boy, what's your name?"

"Chris."

"You're the guy that works with my dad, right?"

"Yes, I do."

"You're a college boy, too, right? My, you're a mighty handsome man. You have a girlfriend?"

"No," I said.

"Chris, can I have your phone number?" she asked.

I gave it to her. But I noticed her glow was missing, and I became very concerned about her health.

"Are you okay, Denise?" I asked her. You should have seen the looks that drew from her. "I mean, you look a little pale." Realizing I misspoke, I added, "Ah, um, you look really nice, I mean." That drew a smile, and she grabbed my hand, dragging me into their house.

"No, I'm fine, Chris. We need to have some fun, boy."

I did not feel comfortable with her. It was almost as if there was evil surrounding her. But I could not put my finger on it.

"So, Chris, why don't we go out for a date tomorrow night? Will you take me out?"

"Sure, I would be glad to go out with you. I have wanted to see a play and really would love it if you would go with me."

"I'd be glad to do that, Chris," Denise said.

So that night, I called the Shakespeare Theater in Odessa and asked about tickets. This theater was built as an exact replica of the Shakespeare Theater in London and was the only one in the world like that, I was told. At any rate, I was able to order two tickets over the phone, and they were to hold them in will call for Friday night.

On Friday night, I got a call from Denise. "Chris, remember you said you would go out with me?"

"Yes," I responded.

"Well, let's get on out tonight and go dancing down at this bar."

"I don't like bars particularly, Denise. I don't drink. But I have reserved two tickets to Shakespeare's play called *Macbeth*. Let's go there, and I will take you out to dinner afterward, is that okay?"

There was dead silence on the other line. Then she said with extreme Southern sarcasm, "You want me to go to a Shakespeare play?" There was silence followed by, "Really?"

"Sure, I already made reservations."

"No way, honey, you don't know what's fun! If you want to have fun with me, we need to go to this bar, and I promise you, you will have the time of your life."

I don't know why, but once again I had this terrible, dark feeling, and I began to panic. Then I had this thought that didn't seem to belong to me. It was that still, small voice that told me not to go to that bar.

So I began to plead with her, "Denise, please don't go to that bar tonight. It's not safe. I don't know why, but let's go somewhere else, anywhere else, please."

After several minutes of my trying to persuade Denise not to go to the bar, she said simply, "Are you for real? If you will not go with me, that's your loss," and with that she slammed the phone down.

I went to see the play *Macbeth* in Odessa by myself that night. I enjoyed the play but was disappointed no one wanted to go with me. It was a lonely evening. And I drove home quietly and went to bed exhausted.

The next day I was going to work at 5:00 AM. You see, we worked seven days a week when we were drilling a well. Then we waited for weeks typically for another job. The old man seemed grouchier than normal. He didn't say a word to me all the way to work.

About two hours later, the driller called me into his office. He asked me how the old man was doing.

I said, "He seemed really quiet, even upset."

The driller said, "I'm not surprised. Chris, Bob's daughter was murdered in some bar last night. He said you were supposed to escort his daughter to that bar but refused to take her there."

I almost dropped the thermos in my hand and stumbled backward. "What did you just say?" I asked.

"What are you, stupid? Didn't you just hear me tell you his daughter died last night? Someone pulled a knife on another guy, she tried to stop the fight, and she wound up stabbed. She was dead on arrival. Why didn't you go with her and protect her?"

I didn't know what to say. I had remembered the old man's son had died a little over a year ago.

I had gotten out of Maryland and run away to Texas, and there was more death. I saw his wife on the way home. She looked like a woman gone mad. I understood like few people could. I had been too close to death and tragedy, and I hated facing the cold brutality of death. I worried that Cynthia and Bob blamed me for their daughter's death. But there was nothing I could do now. I had tried every way I could to get her to go with me to the theater.

The story ends with a twist. The next summer I returned to work in the oil fields. These guys really liked me and wanted me to work a full year with them.

The driller said, "Chris, if you delay going to college by just one year, you will have saved enough money for four straight years in college. Stay and work with us, Chris, you're a good worker. Plus, you saved the company when you got out of the way of that bushing."

I prayed about it, struggled with the decision, prayed about the decision, and without any clear indication from God . . . I chose to go to college. I wondered all year long if I made the right decision, especially with what transpired while I was in college that year.

The following summer, I went back to the drilling company's headquarters to get my old job on the oil rig back. I asked to work with the same guys.

The manager of the drilling company said, "We are in the process of closing our doors and selling off our equipment, Chris."

I asked, "What has happened to my friends?" thinking if I could track them down, I could work with them.

He put his arm on my shoulder and said, "Chris, we need to talk, son, have a seat right here."

I sat across from his desk where he pointed.

Under what looked like a great deal of pain, this man said pathetically, "All four men you worked with last year, and one other man, the man who replaced you, died on the rig last January. There was a fire on the rig. The only man who was far enough away to survive the fire was the old engine man, Bob. From what we can tell, he saw his friends burning, so he ran to their aid and died with them."

God, I thought, what a cold cruel world it is indeed. I felt tears on my face.

"How's his wife?" I asked.

"Not well, Chris" was the response.

I left the office visibly shaken. My thoughts about Bob's wife returned. I thought I had it bad. I just couldn't understand what she was going through, yet somehow I did feel her pain. The loss was great. The tragedy for one family was beyond belief. Only one woman was left from a marriage with two children.

Why God chose to destroy a family as this one made no sense to me. Granted, they were not saints by any measure, but they were good, hardworking people. Bob didn't steal. He didn't lie. He just worked. He worked hard and did his job. He didn't talk much. Why Bob? Why his family? Why had I been sent into their midst? Was it to test me? Was it just another attempt by the devil to kill me? Or was I sent there to offer a little comfort and to help this family spiritually? But if that was the case, I failed and miserably. Perhaps I was not a total failure! I wish I had tried to tell Bob more about our Lord Jesus and His love for us.

My Favorite Psychology Professor

When I was a student at Emory my freshman year, I took a psychology course. I got a kick out of this teacher. One day we arrived at class, and the door was locked. A roommate of my girlfriend played with a fire extinguisher hose in a very seductive way that morning. The professor, upon seeing this, motioned to the class to look at her, and he held his finger over his lips so we would keep quiet. During class, he talked about how you could identify a hysterical neurotic. He said they often did extremely seductive things when they play with things like a fire hose. I think everyone but the girl got it that day.

During the course, the professor asked me to meet with him in his office. I thought I had done something wrong and was extremely nervous when I entered his office. His office walls were lined with books; he had a dozen books and papers lying open on his desk; and he had magazines stacked up by the side of his desk. His office was such a mess I wondered how he could ever get to his seat past the papers, much less work there.

The interrogation began. "Look, Chris, I don't know who you are, but you know things about psychology I am trying to teach my doctoral candidates." He looked perturbed as he threw a paper in the trash. "And, Chris, I'm having trouble teaching my doctoral candidates these concepts. Yet you, a freshman in college . . . well, you fully understand these things already. So, Chris, how do you know all of this at such a young age?"

"My dad taught me," I said succinctly.

"Your dad taught you. And who is your dad? What's his name?"

"Gary Morris?" I said, as if apologizing.

"I haven't heard of him. He must not be that important."

"He wrote some papers with another psychiatrist named Dr. Schultz, and he worked for Frieda Fromm-Reichmann for a while," I replied, surprised he hadn't heard of my dad. "Plus, he was a part-time professor at Duke Medical School."

"I know the other two psychiatrists. They are famous. Well, at any rate, Chris, I believe you should become a psychiatrist. I predict you will be a great psychiatrist one day. Keep up the good work, and thanks for coming by."

And just as quickly as I had entered his office, I was summarily dismissed.

Problems Build in College

After my first few weeks, the phone rang in our room, and I picked it up.

"Hello?" I asked.

"Hi, Chris, this is Martha."

"Martha? How did you find me?"

"I knew you were going to Emory, so I called the dean's office, and they gave me your number."

We talked for a while. She was just checking up on me. After that I would get a call once or twice a week from my mysterious friend, Martha. The only other piece of useful information I received from her was one day, when she was extremely upset, she blurted out she was trying to get to Nixon to save a bunch of people's lives.

Martha said, "The Democrat National Committee occupies a hotel in Washington called the Watergate. They have a safe in the hotel, and in the safe is a list of names of people who helped in the assassination of Jack Kennedy. If we can get that list out of the safe, we can save many people's lives. I have been trying to persuade President Nixon to get that list out of their hands."

By now it was apparent that I had been talking to Martha Mitchell, the attorney general's wife, but she didn't know that I knew who she was.

My question to Martha was "What makes you think they only have one list?"

She did not respond to that question.

An Older Psychologist Befriends Me

During my freshman year in college, I played the piano on a regular basis. One day after playing the piano, this older man showed up and congratulated me for my talent. He asked my name. I told him. He seemed extremely interested in me after that and followed me back to my dorm room.

I asked him who he was. He said he was going to graduate school to study psychology. He was very pushy. He wanted to get to know me, and I wondered why. It was like he had been waiting for me to show up at the music school where the pianos were kept. But he was friendly, I was young, and I thought I could trust him.

"I mean, what are the odds this guy was sent to check up on me anyway?" I thought.

He started turning up like a bad penny several times a week to talk to me.

One day he asked me about my parents. I had cut an article out of the *Washington Post* connecting my father's death with government leaders and a woman's death. This was E. Howard Hunt's wife who had a satchel of money and my dad's name and address and a lockbox number in the satchel. I put this newspaper article over my desk in my room. He saw the article and asked to read it. This man looked extremely displeased with me when he read the article that connected my dad's disappearance with the woman on the plane whose pilot had been poisoned. He took the article and did not give it back to me even though I asked repeatedly for the article. By now his pushy attitude scared me, and I asked him to beat it. He suddenly befriended my roommate.

A few days later, this psychologist showed up and asked my roommate and me to go to see where he worked part-time, and then he would take us to Krispy Kreme to get a donut. My roommate said he had to run an errand and we would meet him at Grady Hospital in about an hour. I reluctantly agreed to go with Mark, my roommate, and thought I would be safe if Mark was with me. When we arrived at Grady Memorial Hospital, this psychologist met us at the entrance and took us up to an empty floor.

He said to both Mark and me, "This is where I work."

"This is an empty floor," I said.

"No, no, I work downstairs. I took you up here so you could see a beautiful view of the city."

"Mark," he said to my roommate, "would you be a sport and run downstairs and get us all Cokes please?" John reached in his pocket and gave Mark some money.

The minute my roommate was out of sight, this psychology "friend" opened the window to show me the view. After stepping back to admire the view, he slammed into my back to push me out of that open window. There was a wall about waist-high that was between me and a seven-story fall to the concrete below. I grabbed the wall and luckily sank my right-hand middle finger into a quarter inch crack in the wall. I held fast. John pushed as hard as he could, and I hung out of the window, looking at the concrete sidewalk below. He released me and in a moment slammed into my back again harder. I screamed. I didn't know what to do or how much longer I could hold on. I was hanging halfway out of the window and looking at a concrete path that led into the hospital again. I was afraid to turn to fight him because I would lose hold of the concrete protrusion.

As I looked at the concrete below me and imagined my fall to my death, I began to pray frantically.

"God, if You want me to die, fine, but I really don't want to die yet. Please save me."

At that moment, I heard a voice. John, the psychologist, backed off and released his grip on me. I turned around and saw a police officer who was walking toward us from the stairwell. He told the psychologist to beat it or he would haul him off to jail. John, the supposed psychologist, walked away quickly and got on the elevator.

This security guard then told me to stay away from that crazy fellow if I knew what was good for me.

As I left to get on a separate empty elevator, I looked back at the security guard. I could see right through him, and as the door on the elevator began to close, he disappeared completely. He didn't even exist.

I thought, "I must be losing my mind."

I arrived on the ground floor and found my roommate carrying some drinks, waiting for me when I exited the elevator.

"My god, Chris. Are you okay?" he asked.

I must have looked bad! "I think so," I said.

"Where's John?" Mark asked.

"He had to leave. And I think we need to go as well."

Mark agreed, and we got into his car and left. I never told Mark or anyone else at college what had happened.

The next day I went to a private phone at the dorm and called Aunt Hank, who was in England working at the US embassy. I told her what had happened. She seemed to panic over the phone.

She said, "Chris, stay away from that psychologist. I will see what I can do. What was his name again?"

"John Maxwell," I told her.

Then she said, "I want you to check in to a nearby hotel and drop out of school until I get back with you. This psychologist is CIA, and someone has given the order to have you killed. I'll do my best to save you, Chris. Until then, stay low and out of sight." Aunt Hank hung up the phone.

I then decided to call my sister to say goodbye and to ask her if she had anyone following her at college. She said she had someone who was older ask her a lot of nosy questions about her parents. But she said he could ask all the questions in the world; she didn't know anything.

"True enough," I thought.

Dad was training me to work for him, not her; she was too young. I was the one that had been involved in all the odd exchanges among my mother, my dad, and the US government.

I wanted to do what Aunt Hank said, go off campus. But I didn't have any money. I had to work to pay my way through college and could not afford a hotel for a day, much less a week or month. I couldn't even afford a tent. So I thought about it and decided to stay on campus and rely on God to save me. If I stayed in crowds, in class, and locked the door at night, my odds improved.

My Life Is on the Line

The next weekend, I began to drink a small glass of crème de menthe, which I had kept in the room. It probably sat there for over a month . . . You see, I was not much of a drinker. When I began to sip the drink, I felt a distinct pressure on my shoulder, and immediately words came to mind: "Don't drink that." I followed the lead of the strange thought inside of me. It had barely touched my tongue when I pulled the cup from my mouth and set it on the desk in my room.

Within a few minutes, I felt light-headed, I had a headache, and then fell on the floor, trembling and shaking like I was having convulsions. My whole body had spasms. I shook and shook. My heart raced. I thought I was going to die. I could not figure out what was happening. As I got control back over my body, I went into the shower and stood in the hottest shower I could stand, tears running down my face the entire time. After about an hour, still trembling, still a bit out of control, I stumbled back into my room and lay down in my dorm bed.

"What had just happened?" I wondered.

As my body settled down, I began to think of Jesus. He must have saved me. I thanked Him and praised His Holy Name. I had survived this bizarre experience.

Since I had no money and had to pay my way through college and since I had thoughts of becoming a physician, I took a job as a nursing assistant at Emory Hospital. I knew a number of medical students. Everyone thought I would become a doctor. They treated me wonderfully, both nurses and doctors alike. I took the liquor bottle to the hospital and told a medical student friend a short synopsis of what had happened, trying to not sound crazy. He laughed and said he would check it out. A few weeks later, I got a phone call. It was my friend Jim, the medical student.

He said, "Chris, meet me outside of the AMUC building, I want to talk to you now!"

It was February 1973. It was cold, and I had my pajamas on, but I felt this was important, so I put on a jacket, a pair of blue jeans and tennis shoes without socks, and walked up to the AMUC building. Standing outside in the cold night air surrounded by darkness, I waited for him. Then he appeared from nowhere right behind me, and I jumped. He had been hiding behind a tree, waiting for me. After the informal introduction, Jim got very serious and looked at me harshly.

"Chris, I don't know where you got that, but whatever is in that bottle is lethal. Where did you get that from?"

"What are you talking about?" I asked.

He was almost yelling at me when he said, "I killed two dogs with that crème de menthe you gave me." His voice was shaking and loud. "I then ran tests on it and couldn't figure out what was in it. So I asked a chemistry professor to help me. It took us a while to figure out the chemical, but then Professor Miller got it. The drug in that drink is illegal to possess. Tell me, Chris, how did you get that drug?"

"Well, this guy has been following me and my roommate around. He asked me if that was my bottle, and I said yes. Perhaps he put something in that drink."

"If he did, he meant to kill you. As far as I'm concerned, I never met you and never knew you. Stay away from me. And you're lucky I don't turn you over to the authorities."

"Are you serious?" I was extremely concerned.

"Chris, one more thing . . . If you didn't put that drug in your drink, and if someone else did, it has to be the FBI . . ."

"Or CIA?" I said.

"If that is the case, Chris, they meant to kill you." He paused for a moment and then said, "Take extra good care of yourself . . . I wish you luck, you're going to need it," and with that Jim walked off into the cold, dark night, never to be seen again.

What a thing to hear when a freshman in college. Not only were my parents murdered, but now the CIA meant to murder me, and I didn't know why. I think it was at this point that I really began to understand the concept of the devil. I realized the devil's stronghold was in the governments of the world, because that is where power and money reside.

I walked back to my room with the cold night air giving me chills. In my room I lay down on my bed and prayed.

"Dear Jesus, if the CIA wants me dead, I'm going to die. No one can save me except for You." I pushed my head into my pillow, and tears dripped onto my pillow. "What have I done? I don't deserve this."

Then I reflected about my pathetic situation. There was no one I could go to for help; there was no place I could hide; not even my aunt could save me now.

My mother sat by me when I played the piano just before they disappeared in the Caribbean, and she said, "If the president wants you dead, there is nothing you can do . . . you are as good as dead."

She was talking about my dad at the time. I doubt she thought she would die. But now she too was dead. And I never thought this meant that the president of the United States would demand my execution. What had my parents or I done? It was at this point that I really understood the concept of the devil who hated the saints and who wanted to kill us without reason.

While I lay their helplessly, with tears in my eyes, feeling completely at a loss, it was as if a woman who was like my mother stood by me. I wondered if this was the Holy Spirit trying to comfort me by giving me pleasant thoughts.

"There, there, Chris, I know how frightened you are, and I understand how you feel. It's okay. I love you. You're going to be fine. Life is unfair, especially to my children. Everything is going to be fine. But you must listen to me, and you must do exactly what I tell you to do if you want to live."

I retreated far into my mind and reached out for God as if to touch Him. As if facing Him, I asked Him, "I believe You can hear my thoughts, and You know everything about me. I have tried to keep Your commandments. Okay, I haven't always honored my father and mother, when I argued with them, but I always did what they asked me to do. I don't steal. I don't lie or bear false witness against my neighbor. I don't cheat. I have never murdered anyone and would not murder anyone, not even this psychologist John, although I have thought about it. I haven't committed adultery, and I do everything You ask me to do.

"At least I think I do everything You ask me to do. Okay, I will do everything You ask me to do if I know it's You. I fear You and love You. I'm only eighteen years old. I'm a freshman in college. Just tell me before I die, What have I done to deserve death? You are in control of this world. You are in control of everything. If You could have saved my dad, surely You can save me!'

I paused in deep thought. "Will You save me?"

As I lay there and ran through my options, I knew the sad truth. There wasn't anything I could do. Perhaps I should stay in large crowds, go to class, and stay with people I knew I could trust. If caught in my room, should I jump out the window three stories into the courtyard below?

Thoughts kept running through my mind over and over again, and I always came to the same conclusion: "I am going to die no matter what I do."

I then argued with God. "I have always tried to be a good person. I aspired to be like Jesus and be good to others even when they weren't good to me. I love You and have always trusted You to protect me and answer my prayers. I somehow survived the poison in the drink, thanks to You. But sooner or later, our government is going to kill me.

"My dad was not a bad person. You gave him a chance to live, I know. All he had to do was to simply trust You and follow Your lead and do what You asked him to do, which, by the way, is sometimes difficult if not impossible to do . . . and I thought women were difficult to understand, but You are much more complex. I don't always know when my thoughts are from You or when they are from within me.

"Perhaps I am going to die because my dad failed to do what You asked. I know both of my parents are dead. What had happened that the president of the United States ordered their executions? Lord, I know You can save me." I felt more tears well up in my eyes because I knew at this point I wasn't worthy. "Surely, if my parents weren't worthy to be saved, I'm not worthy." This thought was directed back to me, not to God. And then, exhausted, with my mind spinning out of control, I remembered a story about Jesus:

> And Jesus being full of the Holy Spirit returned from the Jordan, and was led by the Spirit into the wilderness, being forty days tempted of the devil. And in those days he did eat nothing: and when they were ended, he afterward hungered. And the devil said unto him, "If you are the Son of God, command this stone that it be made bread." And Jesus answered him, saying, "It is written, Man shall not live by bread alone, but by every word of God." And the devil, taking him up into a high mountain, showed unto him all the kingdoms of the world in a moment of time. And the devil said unto him, "All this power will I give you, and the glory of them: for that is delivered unto me; and to whomsoever I will I give it. If you therefore will worship me, all shall be yours." And Jesus answered and said unto him, "Get you behind me, Satan: for it is written, you shall worship the Lord your God, and him only shall you serve." (Luke 4:1–8)

My thoughts resumed. "Back in Jesus's day, Satan ruled over all the kingdoms of the earth. We were now enlightened, and it is commonly believed the devil or Satan no longer ruled over our kingdoms. My dad and aunt worked for presidents in the White House and advised our government their entire lives. Both felt America was the one good country that stood up for You, Lord. That's why none of this makes any sense to me."

For the first time, I realized that the governments of the world had not changed since the time of Jesus. Satan still ruled over all the kingdoms of the earth.

"My parents, Martha Mitchell, and I had done nothing wrong, except somehow threatened Satan and his powers . . . am I right, Jesus?" I asked. "President Nixon needed to remove my parents because they somehow threatened his power . . . someone Satan wanted to protect, so he—meaning, the devil—could continue to rule over the earth. We were simply collateral damage," I realized. Finally, after arguing with God for an hour or more, trying to make sense of what was happening in the world and in my life, I drifted off to sleep.

When I woke in the morning, I searched for verses in the Bible that had something to do with how to fight the devil or Satan. I asked God to help me, so I blindly opened the Bible, and this is the first thing I read in 1 Peter 5:8–11:

> Be of sober spirit, be on the alert. Your adversary, the devil, prowls about like a roaring lion, seeking someone to devour. But resist him, firm in your faith, knowing that the same experiences of suffering are being accomplished by your brethren who are in the world. And after you have suffered for a little while, the God of all grace, who called you to His eternal glory in Christ, will Himself perfect, confirm, strengthen and establish you. To Him be dominion forever and ever. Amen.

The next day I went to the psychology department to find the psych professor I knew and liked, the professor who told me my first quarter at Emory that he wanted to know who I was and who my father was because I knew so much about psychology.

"Professor, have you got a moment?" I asked.

"Come in, Chris, of course I do," he said.

I sat in the chair in front of him and said, "I met a guy who says he is a doctoral candidate here, but I am not sure whether I can believe him. His name is John Maxwell. Can you tell me if he is a student here?"

"Chris, I know all of the psychology graduate students. There are none with that name. Perhaps he is going to the medical school and is becoming a psychiatrist or is doing some specialty there. It's possible he is a psychiatric student," he said.

I thanked him and decided to hike over to the medical school admissions office and ask if there was such a person in the medical school or enrolled anywhere else with that name. The admissions department pulled their files and said no one went to the college or medical school by that name. They had asked some questions, and I told them he was following me around on campus.

That's when they said, "Please let us know if he shows up again so we can throw him off campus. He's not allowed to be here, Chris."

Finally, I had a little success. Someone was willing to protect me after all. I felt exhilarated.

A few weeks later, I was in my room studying. I had a desk to the left of the bed by the window, and as was my norm, I kept the window wide open so I could look out on the dorm courtyard when I studied. All the windows on the inside of the rectangular dorm faced in to the courtyard, and to let the light in, I would either lean back on my chair on its back two legs or slide back in my chair and hold books I was reading in my lap. One day while leaning back in my chair, this crazy thought occurred to me: "Lean forward now."

I leaned forward, and the chair snapped forward off its back two legs and onto all four legs. Just at that moment, I heard a gunshot ring out. Scared, I dropped off the chair onto my knees and crawled to the middle of the room. After a few minutes, I lowered the blinds so no one could see in the room. I then darted across the room to turn the lights out and leave. Just as I began to close the door, I noticed a hole in the wall, to the left and above the light switch just below the ceiling. I have no other proof that someone shot at me that day, but it sure looked like it. And once again that little voice in my head saved my life. Later that day, when I returned from studying at the library, I filled the hole with toothpaste to cover it up.

I never studied in my room again. I would slip out in the morning when all the students were going to class. When I needed to study, I went to the library and sat at a table with many other students surrounding me. Yes, John or another member of the CIA could kill me, but whoever it was had to do it in front of a bunch of students. And given the recent killing of my parents and investigations into their death and the fact that my aunt in London knew the CIA was after me and had contacted the secretary of state on my behalf, it might bring a lot of attention to my murder and even another investigation of President Nixon, who was now embroiled in a scandal called Watergate.

Every night I slept during those days, I thought could be my last. But somehow God was sufficient. He had saved me from being poisoned by telling me not to drink more than a tiny sip of liquor. He provided a little place for me to grip the wall followed by a ghost that looked like a security guard who emerged just in the nick of time. And my aunt later reported that she called the secretary of state, her boss, and pleaded for my life. Apparently, her plea did not go unheeded. I was still alive.

I Damage My Hopes of Being a Doctor

My psychology professor told me I was a genius, and he said he wanted to help me. He introduced me to a female psychology PhD candidate for testing. So I let her give me an IQ test. I knew my IQ was really high.

During the test, she said, "I have never tested anyone who has tested as high as you have. You're probably smarter than many of the professors in this university."

Sarah was beautiful, and I had a good rapport with her, so I opened up and told her about my parents.

"Sarah," I began, "I am having some problems concerning my parents' death, and I need some advice. Can I trust you to tell you a little more about what happened to them?"

"Sure, Chris, go ahead."

"Look, I told you initially my parents were lost at sea in the Caribbean, right?"

"Yes."

"Well, that's not the whole story. I believe my mom and dad were murdered by our government. You will never find any evidence that this happened because it was a CIA job ordered by the president of the United States."

"Really?" Sarah said.

"What's worse is, I believe my life may be in danger now. My aunt told me to leave campus and go into hiding, to get away from this psychologist guy who is trying to kill me. I paid tuition, and I don't have the money to go into hiding. What would you do?"

Sarah looked shocked. But she was cordial and said she would get back to me.

I noticed when I went to class the next day, my psychology professor asked to talk to me privately. In his office he started to retract what he had told me previously. Instead of my becoming a psychiatrist like my dad, he recommended I not go to medical school, not become a psychologist and not pursue a field where I would work with people. He knew I played the piano well and that I had thought about becoming a concert pianist. Suddenly he jumped all over that as a possible career.

Later my psychology professor went to talk to the Atlanta Symphony conductor, Robert Shaw, about me. He then recommended I work with Robert Shaw and become a conductor. Robert Shaw was interested and asked my professor to test me. These tests were time-related. Apparently, Robert Shaw had the ability to know what time of the day or night it was without a clock, to the minute. He had other time given skills that are rare. If you gave him a tempo, he could hold that tempo in his mind perfectly for an indefinite period. His mind was like a metronome or a clock that worked perfectly. Needless to say, I did not have those skills, so my conducting opportunity evaporated.

Because of my musical talents, I was asked to write an article in the school newspaper to rate a new pianist from Israel. His name was Daniel Barenboim. I went to the concert with a few friends and listened to him as he played Chopin's Polonaise in A major. I believed I played that piece better than he did, at least so I thought. His expression was better than mine. But he kept missing notes. Had he hit those notes, I would have said he was a superior pianist. I was asked by the music department to come and meet Daniel Barenboim at a reception later that evening. He was about ten to fifteen years older than me. When we shook hands—well, pianists don't really shake hands for fear of having their fingers damaged—I turned his hand over in my hand. His hands were much smaller than mine. And suddenly I realized why he missed those notes.

I blurted out, "Daniel, look how small your hands are compared to mine. And I have trouble reaching some of those keys with my big hands. I don't see how you can become a concert pianist. Your expression is beautiful. I think you need to become a conductor and give up the concert pianist goal."

He was a nice quiet, introvert of a man. He didn't know what to say. Then he said, "Thank you for your recommendation."

It was a bit inappropriate for me to say that to him. No one invited me to perform around the world as a pianist. So who was I to talk to him in that manner? Perhaps I should have kept my mouth shut. Truthfully, I wasn't surprised when I found out Daniel Barenboim had become a conductor. Maybe he listened to me after all! Or maybe he figured it out on his own and performing on the piano was a way of showing off his genius when he was a young man. The truth is, I was not surprised to find out he became one of the greatest conductors of our time.

A little while later, a strange thought occurred to me. "How is it I always know things will happen in a certain way before they happen? Do I have the gift of prophecy? Can I tell future events before they happen? And if so, do I have to touch someone or look at someone to know these things will happen? Was that crazy guy at Virginia Beach right about me? Maybe I really have this gift?"

Apparently, the psychologist girl thought I was crazy. In hindsight, what else could she think? Word traveled fast on a small campus like Emory. It wasn't long before it became obvious that people knew I was crazy. The question kept running through my mind, Had I really gone crazy? But my dad told me I was one of the most normal people he had ever met and he was proud of how well I had turned out.

He said, "You are really mature and emotionally mature for your age, Chris."

And then one of his psychiatric partners said, "Chris, you have a really strong ego, and I am really pleased at what a fine young man you have become."

Perhaps I snapped under the pressure of my parents' death. Had I really gone crazy? Many highly intelligent people are nuts. I had always wanted to become a physician; I had never thought about another career. It really worried me when Dr. Moskowitz told me not to become a physician.

The night my professor told me "Don't become a doctor," I lay in bed and talked to Jesus.

"Jesus, You allowed my parents to be murdered. I know there have been attempts on my life to kill me. If I really have gone crazy, I don't want to become a physician. I would be a terrible doctor and hurt people rather than help them.

"What am I going to do with my life? Two years ago, I had a family that loved me, we had plenty of money, and my parents were supportive and wanted to help me. Today all their money is tied up in court. We will have to wait seven years before we can access their money since they were legally lost at sea. We have lost their home, my dad's life savings, and now my uncle in Texas has lost his job. I work my way through college. A man Aunt Hank says who works for the CIA is trying to kill me. My sister doesn't want to talk to me. She almost blames me for our parents' death. I have no family. I have no money. And now I have no career to aspire for. All I ever wanted to do was to help others. And You have taken that away from me. Do You really hate me this much? I don't want to die. But maybe I would have been better off if I had drunk that whole bottle of liquor and died. I can truly say I am beginning to understand Job and what he went through.

"Jesus, am I really crazy? Have You also taken away my ability to be objective in human relations? You might as well have given me leprosy. If I am crazy, I will probably never marry. I don't know what to do with my life. And I may be killed any day now. Why am I fighting so hard to stay alive?

"And, Lord, what about the strange happenings that surrounded those events? I had strange thoughts that warned me of impending disaster, did I not? And I can't explain where they came from, before tragedy struck. How did I know things were going to happen before they happened? I know those thoughts only occurred to me on those extremely rare occasions, just before disaster happened.

"That is not a symptom of schizophrenia. Schizophrenics hear voices all the time. And I didn't hear a voice, I thought a thought. It was just that those thoughts seemed out of character, as if I would typically not think that way, so I concluded they must have come from outside of me. I in turn credited God for those thoughts. But what if they didn't originate outside of me? And what is the definition of being crazy?" I thought.

"Then what about the time that man saved me at Grady Hospital? I saw through him and he disappeared. I began to believe I was going crazy that night.

"On the other hand, let's say I went to see Dr. Moskowitz to prove that I was not crazy. Let's say I proved beyond a shadow of a doubt that the CIA was trying to murder me. What then? Questions may be asked of people in the government, and word may get high enough up to ensure my execution."

I thought and thought about it and came to the only possible conclusion. Did I want to live or die? Hamlet chose life by letting them think he was crazy. Perhaps that's why God told me when I was in high school, my only chance for survival was to become like Hamlet.

"Be like Hamlet if you want to live," I thought and laughed at myself.

More than forty years have transpired since college. No one has tried to murder me since then. Any fears I had at the time of being murdered are long gone. I became controller and CFO of several large publicly held companies and helped take three companies public. Each time, before I took a new job, psychologists gave me personality and intelligence tests. They all told me I was completely normal and had no trace of mental illness—oh, and I got all the questions on the IQ test correct. Years later, after I left industry and started my own business, I hired a psychologist to test me in every way possible to see if I had any mental illness and to determine if my career choice was the right career for me. He gave me four hours of tests. After the tests, he met with me and told me that I was perfectly normal. I missed one question on the entire psychological profile test. He showed me a chart. There was a line down the middle. The last point on the graph, I was one notch up on that topic, but I was still well within the dashed lines on the page, which represented normal.

He said, "Chris, if you are inside those dashed lines, you're emotionally 'normal.' You see, every part of the test, you were on the line in the middle. You answered every question correctly and only missed one question on the last topic. That question for me shows you trust people a little too much."

I told him I debated on one question and wasn't sure of the answer and I guessed wrong. He then said that I needed to be a little more of an extrovert. You see, I was an INTJ under the Myers-Briggs test. Then he said, I was on the border between *I* or introvert and *E* an extrovert and to be a president of a Fortune 500 company, I needed to be an ENTJ. He was willing to help me become a little more *E* than *I* if I wanted his help.

By the end of this testing session, I realized that if I had any mental illness, I no longer had a problem. And maybe, just maybe, I was completely normal when I was a college student. Perhaps the sad truth was this . . . the president of the United States was indeed trying to murder me, through this psychologist named John.

The Summer after Freshman Year

Aunt Hank came to check up on us that summer. She was upset with me when she found out I did not check in to a hotel as she instructed me to do. I told her I didn't have the money.

The realization that I really didn't have any money hit home, and her face changed.

At this point, Watergate was in full swing. Woodward and Bernstein, the guys who had called me frequently when I was in high school, were behind a huge investigation into Nixon, and a special prosecutor would be appointed to investigate Watergate.

Martha Mitchell kept in touch with me my entire freshman year, but the frequency of the calls had diminished to less than weekly. That summer, after leaving college, she did not call once.

That summer was an odd summer. I went back to Texas to work in the oil fields. I now was a derrick man and worked in the derricks which are ninety feet above the floor of the drilling platform. I enjoyed this work more even though it was considered more dangerous. But the men I worked with were unsavory fellows. They bragged about being members of the Hells Angels. They swapped wives. And they were scary guys. I learned to do my job and not interact with them.

*****

Aunt Hank visited Aunt Clarice and us kids that summer. One day she joined me as I sat alone in the living room. The sun was setting outside, and I decided to talk to her about our parents' death.

"Did you hear about the three guys who were caught in the Watergate Hotel trying to break in to the safe? I believe I had met

E. Howard Hunt through Dad. Wasn't he training the Cubans to invade Cuba?"

"You may be correct, Chris."

"The press says they were low-level thugs. I don't think that is accurate."

We paused to admire the sunset and sip our iced tea.

I continued, "Martha told me there is a list locked in a safe in the Watergate Hotel in the Democratic Convention's headquarters. That list has the names of all those in the CIA who participated in the killing of Kennedy. If she is correct, maybe that is the safe the three guys were trying to break in to, to stop the executions."

"Those three thugs, Chris, are all CIA agents. And you are correct, one of them was very high up in the CIA and a good friend of Gary's," Hank stated. "It was unfortunate that they failed."

"Hank, don't you think there are other copies of the list? I believe Martha has been pressuring President Nixon to get to that list to stop the killings. What if Dad and Martha Mitchell had some goods on Richard Nixon and threatened him if he didn't do something about that list? Then it would make sense that President Nixon would have executed Dad. Perhaps he feared killing Martha Mitchell, because of her proximity to the White House through her husband."

"Chris, this may or may not be true. Our problem now is keeping you and me alive. I don't care what happens to those monsters in either party," Hank said with tears welling up in her eyes. "You're too young and too precious to die now, Chris. I've already lost my brother, and I'm not going to lose you too."

"Hank, is it possible that Dad helped kill Kennedy?"

"Anything is possible, but if he did, he made a grave mistake. Gary should have known better than to get involved in this type of military coup." Hank paused for a minute. Then she said, "No, I was President Kennedy's secretary. I don't believe he could have done that, so put that out of your mind. But if that drunk Teddy is getting revenge . . ."

"You don't like Teddy Kennedy, do you?"

"No. I liked John but not Teddy," Aunt Hank said. "If Teddy is killing a bunch of CIA operatives, and if any of them worked for

Gary, he might have decided it was necessary to ask President Nixon for help in hopes of saving some of his men's lives."

"And if Nixon was caught up in this mess, he may have feared that Gary was getting too close to the truth . . . that Richard Nixon helped kill John F. Kennedy," I blurted out. "One thing is for sure. No one in the press would ever believe any of this."

"No one else will believe it either," Hank said. "We have to keep this quiet. If Gary got mixed up in trying to stop this killing of CIA operatives, it is no wonder that he was killed, especially if he threatened President Nixon to obtain his objective. President Nixon might feel he had to shut Gary up to protect his presidency.

"Chris, all of this is speculation. You can't tell anyone what has been spoken here today. I'm sorry you got caught up in this. If Nixon was connected to the Kennedy brothers' assassinations, and if Teddy Kennedy is killing all of those who are connected, neither man will want this to come out."

"I guess Martha Mitchell is these agents' last hope," I responded.

"Come to dinner, everyone," Aunt Clarice said from the kitchen.

Hank and I stood up and obediently left the living room and our conversation behind.

*****

I never heard from Martha Mitchell again. I was afraid they had caught up with her and killed her! Why else had she not called? I hoped she moved to a beach house and lived happily ever after. But that seemed unlikely.

It was reported that Martha Mitchell separated from John Mitchell in 1973, my sophomore year. Nixon was later to tell interviewer David Frost in 1977 that Martha was a distraction to John Mitchell, such that no one was minding the store, and "if it hadn't been for Martha Mitchell, there'd have been no Watergate." I believe Nixon meant to say, if it hadn't been for my dad and Martha Mitchell, there'd have been no Watergate.

Martha Mitchell, my friend who kept in constant contact with me, was reported to have died at Sloan Kettering Hospital in 1976, the year I graduated college. However, a friend of my dad's told me she had been held hostage, as a prisoner, in Walter Reed Army Hospital, where she was executed. The truth is so blurry whenever the CIA is involved.

Years later I heard Nixon interviewed, and he said he felt terrible about three people he had killed before he left office. I believed he meant he felt bad about murdering my parents, Dorothy Hunt and Martha Mitchell, because murdering them did not help him stay in power.

Another Health Issue

During those tough days in college, where family members cared for us and made tremendous sacrifices for us, during those tough days when my life was apparently in jeopardy, during those tough days when I struggled to rediscover my faith in God, for I felt God had abandoned me during those tough days—my health began to suffer seriously.

One day in Baltimore, the day before I went back to Emory to begin my sophomore year, I ate raw oysters at a restaurant with my Aunt JoAnne . . . oysters on the half shell. I loved oysters on the half shell and steamed crabs. Remember, we grew up near the Chesapeake Bay, and I learned to sail at a young age. Having eaten oysters and crabs that day for lunch, I headed in my car back to college.

When I got to Richmond, Virginia, I called our baby sitter, the woman who was with us when the police told us our parents were missing at sea. Mrs. Seaton, whom I loved dearly, and who sacrificed so much for our family after our parents died, was one person who loved me and my sister and brother. I tried to talk to her in Maryland but was told she was staying at Nan's house in Richmond. As I drove to Atlanta, from Washington, I decided to pull off the road and call her on a pay phone. I was really pleased when she answered the phone. I told her I was on my way back to college and just wanted to say hi to her. She begged me to come spend the night in Richmond with her and her family's children for whom she was babysitting while the parents were traveling. She said there was a room for me. I didn't want to impose. I had only driven a couple of hours. But she insisted. I reluctantly agreed. Having gotten directions over the phone, I went to Nan's home in Richmond. Mrs. Seaton met me at the door, and I felt so blessed to be in her company.

As we ate dinner, and I barely could eat, I felt sick to my stomach. Finally, I excused myself and went to bed early. I woke up three times that night, vomiting and with diarrhea. I was so sick. I went into a delirious state. I remember looking at myself in the mirror, and I had turned yellow. My eyes were bright yellow. My skin looked yellow. I didn't recognize myself. As soon as I had used the restroom, I would go back to sleep. After what seemed to be an interminable period, I woke up and knelt at the side of the bed. I knew death drew nigh. Now shaking from chills, knowing it was appropriate to die with Mrs. Seaton caring for me instead of alone at a college campus, I wept and called out to heaven.

"Dear Jesus," I said, "I ask Your forgiveness for my sins. It seems that every time I try to step forward, once again I am attacked for some sin or evil I don't recall doing. I love You and fear You. But I am no longer afraid to die. If it is Your will, please take me tonight and end my suffering. If it is Your will, and I know You can do this, please heal me. I care not which You do, but let me not wake up tomorrow if this disease is going to continue."

With that prayer I crawled into bed and fell asleep. The next morning, I remember hearing the television set downstairs. I climbed out of bed and went into the bathroom. My color in my face was normal. Illness had completely left my body. I was fine. The disease was gone. I sang out to God and gave praises, for I knew, I absolutely knew I had been healed. I bounded down the stairs half dressed, skipping every other step. I ran into the room where Mrs. Seaton and the kids sat, and I told her I was fine and thanked her and thanked God for her. I asked her how long I had been in bed and found out it had been five days. Five days I don't remember.

Later that day I drove to college and got there just in time to register for the fall quarter. I could not shake the thought that had I not had the urge to call Mrs. Seaton, had she not been in Richmond, had I not gone to be with her, what would have happened to me? Would I have lived through the night? I had twenty dollars in my wallet to buy gas. No money for a hotel room. No way to pay for a hospital room. Would I have tried to make it to college and died trying? I was sick within an hour of arriving at the house where Mrs.

Seaton was, and the trip was many more hours. Surely God encouraged me to call Mrs. Seaton and in so doing saved my life once again! Blessed be the name of the Lord!

Healing Our Government

I want to comment on a few of the men who became president after Nixon. Gerald Ford was appointed to replace Richard Nixon. Gerald Ford appointed George H. W. Bush as his director of the CIA. I don't know which of the two came up with the idea, but the decision was made that CIA operations on US soil would never be allowed again. That was another miracle that helped save me. Additionally, George Bush wanted a kinder, gentler nation. I owe my life to Gerald Ford and George Bush, good men who healed America from a terrible past. And of course, I owe everything to Jesus.

Aunt Hank moved to China with Ambassador Bruce. We never talked about the college incidents after that, although we talked at length about the government. I believe Ambassador Bruce became ill and died shortly after that. This left the ambassador post empty in China. George H. W. Bush became ambassador to China and became Aunt Hank's boss.

Aunt Hank was in China during the Cultural Revolution when all the Chinese wore the same uniforms and rode bicycles. She called me in college and told me I was one of thirty Americans in the world that could come to China at that point, as she listed me as her nearest relative. She asked me to come to China. Finances once again got in the way of my taking a China excursion.

Aunt Hank had many wonderful stories about China. She even told us she liked to ride bicycles with George W. Bush in Tiananmen Square. She was close to four presidents of the United States: John F. Kennedy, Lyndon B. Johnson, George H. W. Bush, and George W. Bush. Granted she was a low-level secretary for these men, but if you're a man and you have ever relied on a secretary . . . well, that is one of the closest relationships with a person you will ever have in your career.

The State Department had tried to send Aunt Hank to Russia, and she never trusted the Russians, for good reason. It was later discovered that the Russians continuously x-rayed the American embassy, exposing Americans to dangerous levels of radiation. Aunt Hank liked and admired Mao Tse-tung, and she repeatedly said she trusted the Chinese, as they had respect and honor as a part of their culture. It was who they were. So even though you might be their purported enemy, they would always treat you with respect, and you had to treat them with respect; and if you did, you were, in an important way, a person they could work with.

You Can Sum Up the Bible in a Word: Israel

A good friend of mine in high school was a Jew named Joey. He was a wonderful friend. When I went to college, I was on a dorm floor where I was the only goy, which is a not so complimentary Hebrew word for *Gentile*. The dorm head was a Jew. And many of my classmates were also Jews. We did all the things other college kids did, with a few extras. We periodically had lox and bagels for Sunday brunch. We played ice hockey (we were all from the North). We fasted on Passover and Yom Kippur. I fasted right along with the guys. And we didn't celebrate Christmas formally. I had to fly to Texas to celebrate Christmas, as my aunt and uncle in Maryland were Jews.

These people were good friends. They were excellent students. They were honest. They had high morals, as I did. And they had been carefully taught about the time in Germany where family members or friends had been greatly persecuted and killed by Hitler.

As boys do in a Southern college with little money, we often road buses. One day we were on the bus to town. We were going out for the evening. When we got on the bus, I noticed that there were a bunch of black people sitting at the back of the bus. Having ridden the bus frequently, I felt this was leftover from segregation times. These black people looked down when you looked at them. They were nice people, but they felt inferior for some reason. And I thought of my Jewish friends. What did they go through in Germany? I headed to the back of the bus, my friends following. We were told by the black people we couldn't sit there. It wasn't where white college boys sat.

I said, "It's a free country, move over."

To my surprise, all the Jewish boys sat together in the back. The bus driver stopped the bus and asked the college boys to move forward in the bus where we belonged. We said we were content to sit in the back of the bus and if he didn't like it, to take his complaint up with the dean of the college.

After that day, we championed a cause on campus, for students to ride at the back of the bus. Was this the Holy Spirit? I believe all love, all justice, and all searching for justice is inspired by God. Before we graduated from college, the buses were no longer segregated. Whether our college changed the city, I doubt. I suppose we were just one of many forces at play in the change, something that was facilitated by those Jewish boys at Emory!

Superstitions

S tarting in my sophomore year, I worked at Emory University Hospital as an orderly to help pay my way through a ridiculously expensive school. I enjoyed the hospital staff. The nurses reminded me of my mother, who was a nurse. They were smart, efficient, and I swear, totally detached emotionally from what was going on around them. And they took care of me. The young college boy orderly, who handled the sheet-changing, cleaned out the bed pans and ran errands for the nurses. I worked hard but found the job depressing. Again, I was an observer more than an interactor. Every day they would bring in another heart patient. I was staffed in the cardiology ward. They had just started performing major heart surgeries. They replaced valves. They cut open hearts to save lives. And I watched people die; one after another they died!

It was there that I discovered I had the gift of foreseeing the future. So what parent of mine transferred this gift to me? My mother reported a variety of things to me before they happened. She would take me aside and predict future events, and she wasn't right just once; she was consistently right. And I knew, as a boy, arguing with my mother's feelings was futile. She knew the future before it happened. Just as I knew many things were going to happen before they happened. How did I know so many things in advance, before they happened? I can't explain it. But there is no question I have a gift from God that was the same gift my Jewish mother had.

Well, here I was at this big university hospital. But being in a ward where open heart surgeries were performed, I watched many people die. At first I didn't think it was affecting me. But I remember this young black man who came in to the hospital. He was breathing very hard. He was having trouble catching his breath. I looked at him, and something seemed very wrong with him. I could not put my finger on it, but he was missing something that other people had. One afternoon, they called doctor 99. It was an emergency. I ran to the room referenced on the intercom. I was late. The room was filled with nurses and doctors, hooking up electrical paddles. They shocked him, again and again. But to no avail. This dear black man was dead.

After this I noticed another patient that looked like they were missing something. This patient was cheerful yet sick. He didn't breathe hard. He didn't have any external symptoms. In fact, he was a famous doctor. He was considered one of the best surgeons in America.

One day I asked him what it was like being a well-known doctor. It must be wonderful, I thought. The man was bitter. He said he had no family. All he had done with his life was work. And he regretted his choice to be a physician. I knew something was wrong with him. I could see it in his eyes and around his body. The light around his eyes and around his head was missing. I remembered it when my black friend died. And this man too died within a couple of weeks.

At this point I recognized I could identify death before it happened. Being somewhat naive, I blurted this new gift I had discovered out to a nurse whom I liked named Jean. She was a sweet friend.

She laughed at me. "Chris," Jean said, "you have access to the patient charts, do you not? You hear our reports each morning. Don't you think that you can tell from that?"

I responded, "No way. This isn't from scientific evidence, it is from a glow that all people have around their eyes and face that they lose just before they die."

At this point, several other nurses chimed in with her and told me I was imagining things.

Jean asked me, "So tell me, Chris, who is going to die next?"

"That's easy," I said. "Do you see that woman they just wheeled into room 305?" I asked.

"Yes" was the response!

"Well, she is going to die soon, very soon."

Four nurses laughed out loud.

Jean then said, "Chris, she is on this ward because of an over-flow on third floor east. She just had an appendectomy. That's all. She will go home tomorrow." Jean said, "Chris, go take her blood pressure and temperature, and report back to me."

As expected I walked up to her room and took her temperature and blood pressure. In the room I noticed her nervousness. She was shaking. Somehow even she knew something was wrong. But it was certain; from up close there was no light around her eyes or head. The aura was missing.

I went to find Jean to give her the blood pressure and tempera-ture results and then said, "She is going to die."

When I left the hospital, our friend in room 305 was still alive. I felt terribly embarrassed that I had opened my mouth to a friend I trusted. Word spread throughout the ward, and I was a laughing stock; even the doctors thought I was nuts.

The next morning, I returned to the hospital. Jean had been waiting for me.

"Chris," she called as I walked onto the floor, "I need to talk to you now. Step into this room."

I did as she bid. I stepped into the closet, and she closed the door behind me.

"They are going to ask you a lot of questions. I know you didn't have anything to do with it, but they want to know where you were yesterday."

"What are you talking about?" I asked.

"Your patient, Mrs. Elway, in room 305, died last night unex-pectedly. They are performing an autopsy on her now."

"An autopsy, why?" I asked.

"Because they think you murdered her last night."

"That's crazy. Of course I didn't murder her. I just warned you that her aura was missing. I was only trying to help!" I responded.

"You were right, but people are investigating you now, and you had better be careful in how you answer questions. I can't help you now, Chris," she said ominously.

She was right. You would have thought I pulled a shotgun on this lady to prove some kind of point. But I no more wanted her to die than I wanted my mother to die. By now I hated death. It was depressing and full of tragedy for the survivors. But I could see something, and I simply was reporting on what I could see.

They investigated me all right. The Georgia Bureau of Investigation turned my dorm upside down, talking to my roommate, his girlfriend, who spent the night with him and me (they slept on the top bunk and interfered with my sleep the night of the death), and other students in my dorm. They all reported I was there all night long, and Mark's girlfriend made a desperate plea that there was no way I left the room during the night—that she heard me snoring all night long and she would have known if the snoring stopped.

I was vindicated by the GBI, so I wasn't fired, but I was transferred off the floor at the request of the head nurse of 3 west.

Fortunately, the head nurse of the hospital liked me and transferred me to 5 south, the brain ward.

Illness Strikes Again

During the winter of my sophomore year, I noticed that I had frequent problems with light-headedness, headaches, swelling in my lymph nodes around my legs, and malaise. I also had flulike symptoms. I would get a fever and chills at night. But unlike a flu, they didn't last just a week or ten days; they kept dragging on and on. I didn't know what was wrong. I went to the infirmary on multiple occasions explaining these symptoms. The doctors didn't seem to be able to determine what, if anything, was wrong. He kept squeezing on my gut, saying my spleen was swollen. I thought of the doctor's wife whose spleen ruptured.

I missed my mother. When I got the fever or chills or the flu, she would take care of me. No one was taking care of me now. I had no parents and no wife, so I wondered if I was reaching out for a little comfort. The Holy Spirit filled the void. Who else was listening? So I would talk to Jesus in my mind almost continuously. Of course, it was a bit of a one-sided conversation.

I finally went back to the student clinic for the third time that December to see their top physician. I explained how I was weak all the time, I felt light-headed, and had trouble studying. I had this cold that had stayed with me for months. I couldn't shake it for some reason. Dr. Julian listened to me and took a lot of notes. He checked my lymph nodes and said they were swollen. Then he punched on my spleen, which hurt. He said it was inflamed. Then he ordered a series of blood tests.

A few days later, I was told to come to his office. I went there the next morning before class, and he pulled the chair up close and, leaning very close, said quietly, "Chris, I ran a series of blood tests. I'm sorry to tell you that you have a rare form of lymphoma."

"What is lymphoma?" I asked.

"It is similar to cancer of the blood. It is 100 percent fatal, and there is no cure."

"Will you give me chemo or any treatment?"

"Chris, there is no cure. I can't do anything. You have three to six months to live."

I was dumbfounded. I couldn't believe what I heard.

"After all this struggle to stay alive, I am going to die from lymphoma. Go figure!" I told Jesus. "Everyone I love has died. It makes sense that I'm next. Think of all the miracles You have done to save me so far. I am a walking miracle, and now I am going to die alone at Emory Hospital," I said to Jesus.

I walked back to my dorm room. At first I was concerned because I was about to miss class. But then it dawned on me. "What's the point? Why go to class? I have three to six months to live at most, Jesus."

So I lay on my back, stared at the ceiling, and prayed in an irrational, confused, sad, and angry manner to my Lord. I was numb. After an hour or so, I imagined the ceiling was breaking and was going to fall on me and kill me. I wondered if I was going crazy. When the roof caved in, there was no escape. I imagined my death was preordained before I was born and that my attempts to save my life only changed the manner of my death and only added a few more months to my life. Jesus said our days are numbered like the hairs on our head. Maybe I only had a few days left. I didn't know, and I was confused from circular stupid arguments with a God Whom I still feared and Who repeatedly had saved me.

A few hours later, I got up out of bed, washed my face, and dressed. I decided to go to class after all. What else was I going to do with the time I had left?

Have you ever thought about suicide? I did after this diagnosis. No one would miss me. No one would care. And if I was right, God would forgive me for my sin. He said He can forgive all sins.

After careful consideration, I decided to forget what the doctor told me and pretend his diagnosis was wrong, and I decided I was not going to die after all.

"That's it," I told Jesus. "I'm not going to die, and You're just going to have to heal me."

I was going to absolutely hope—nay, I was going to absolutely *know* that God was going to heal me.

"Lord, You have to heal me. You have saved me in the past, and You will save me again, and I will not think about my death from lymphoma ever again."

By the way, Freud called this denial, and I was pretty good at this defense mechanism.

The Voice in the Car

Having come to these conclusions, I realized I was hungry, and it was way past lunchtime. So I decided to get in my car and drive to the village to get lunch. I remember sitting in the car and putting the keys in the ignition and starting the car. Just after I started the car, I swear I heard a voice.

"Chris." It was a voice directly behind me in the car. "Take vitamin B." It was as simple as that.

I jumped. "Who said that?" I exclaimed, glancing over my shoulder and turning the car off immediately.

The voice repeated what I had heard. "Chris, you must take vitamin B."

I turned again to look in the back of the car. There was no one there.

I hopped out of the car and looked around. There was no one within fifty feet of the car. And the students I saw were all walking away from me at a casual pace up the hill.

I called out, "Did someone say something?" but my voice echoed in empty space.

No one turned, no one heard me, since no one was within earshot of the car. I sat back in the car and thought, "What just happened?" I wondered if that was an angel talking to me.

Either way, I decided I better purchase vitamin B at the store, so I headed to Emory Village. At the Kroger in the village, I bought a multivitamin named Centrum and didn't know what B vitamin to take, so I bought a B-complex vitamin. I started taking the vitamins that day in the car on an empty stomach. Big mistake! I didn't do that again.

Over the next few months, my weakness got worse, and the vitamin doses didn't seem to help. I found each day harder and harder to study. I had flulike or cold like symptoms continuously. I lost weight so you could count my ribs. My gut hurt all the time. I figured that was my spleen. I periodically passed out in the middle of the day, with my head falling into my study material. I would fall asleep at the strangest times. Waking up and getting out of bed in the morning was more and more difficult.

Finally, I decided I needed to pray in preparation for my death. I needed to ask God for forgiveness and get completely right with God so I was ready to face Him. One night after intense prayer, just before I fell asleep and having resigned myself to the fact that I might die any day now, I prayed to the Lord. I asked Him to either kill me or heal me that night, remembering what had happened in Richmond.

"Lord, in Richmond I turned yellow as a Chinaman. I prayed and prayed that night and asked You to take me if it was Your will or heal me. I really didn't care what You did, I simply trusted You would do what was best for me. And the next morning I woke up feeling 100 percent A-OK. Once again, I come to You—weak, alone, and lost. And I don't really care whether I live or die. I am tired, Lord. I have been fighting to stay alive. But I no longer care whether I live or die. I just don't want to suffer anymore. Let this be my last night on earth and take me tonight, or as You did in Richmond, heal me once and for all. Thy will be done, not my will."

Then something strange happened. I woke up the next morning right on time. I went to class and wasn't tired. I continued to improve. Over the coming weeks and months, my illness disappeared. In fact, by May, I forgot I had been sick. During finals week, I decided I needed some help with my allergies, so I went back to the infirmary. Dr. Julian looked shocked to see me.

Then he said, "Chris, it has been five months since I first diagnosed you with lymphoma. How do you feel?"

"I feel good. I even forgot how sick I was a few months ago," I said. "I came here because my allergies are driving me crazy."

He seemed very concerned and said he didn't expect to see me in such good shape. After doing the normal things doctors do, like listening to my heart, taking my blood pressure, feeling my lymph nodes, pressing on my spleen (which no longer hurt), and asking a series of questions about my allergies, he decided to run a full battery of blood tests on me again.

A couple of days later, Dr. Julian called me in my dorm room and asked to see me again. I went back to his office later that day. He sat me down and asked me how I was feeling. I said I had a head cold that had developed, but it was probably allergies.

Then he said, "I thought you were light-headed, fainting, and passing out and had difficulty getting to class?"

"Yes, that was true a month or two ago. But after that I started feeling better and better. I bet it was the vitamin B-complex and the multivitamins I have been taking," I said. "I got over the flu I had, but my allergies started acting up last Wednesday."

Dr. Julian looked at me like he was studying something he had never seen before and said, "Chris, you have no trace of lymphoma in your body."

"Is it possible that you misdiagnosed me initially . . . like the lab had someone else's blood tests by mistake?"

"Chris, I ran the tests twice . . . On two separate occasions, you had the exact same diagnosis, lymphoma! I had two other experts at Emory look at the blood work, and they both confirmed the diagnosis. Plus, you had other symptoms of lymphoma. You were weak, you were having trouble getting to class, your spleen was swollen and it hurt when I touched it, your lymph nodes were swollen, you were constantly ill from flulike symptoms, and you fell asleep in the afternoons . . . Chris, I don't think I missed the diagnosis."

"Could the vitamins and minerals have cured me?" I ask.

"No. No way," Dr. Julian said.

"If it is not that, what is it?"

"We call it spontaneous remission. And it falls in the category of we just don't know how you got better."

I paused and thought about what had happened. I announced out loud, "It was a miracle, and I believe God healed me."

Dr. Julian had a wry smile on his face and didn't speak immediately. "By the way, Chris, can I give you anything for your head cold?"

"Sure."

He prescribed an antibiotic and sent me off to class.

"You know, Doc, I feel better already," I said as I stood up, shook his hand, and headed back to class, pondering what had really happened to me.

Many years have since transpired. I never had a similar diagnosis again. Did I have cancer? Was I on the verge of death? According to Emory Hospital, I was! What really happened? I can't explain my miraculous recovery other than God saved me.

Richard Nixon Is Impeached

During my sophomore year in college, the press roiled with Watergate. Watergate dominated the news, as did the investigation. I never saw the psychologist that tried to kill me after my freshman year. I stayed on the alert, ate in crowds, changed dorm rooms, and moved in with a good Jewish roommate I really cared about named Ted. I studied in the crowded halls and was never alone after that. During that year, I met a pretty blond girl from Jackson, Mississippi. We fell in love. She had been a professional model. And everyone that saw her asked me why a girl who looked like that would be my girlfriend. I couldn't answer them. Nancy and I stayed together until I went off to graduate school.

My Friend Mary!

I hated the brain ward. So I went back to the head nurse and asked for a transfer. That was a mistake I realized after the transfer. You see, she put me on the cancer ward. That was the most depressing job I ever had. In those days they didn't have hospice. So critically ill patients were left in the hospital until they died!

I remember one old man who was dying of cancer. He screamed night and day; you could hear him anywhere on the floor crying, then saying, "Momma, help me, I hurt. Momma, please help me. I hurt so bad!" There was nothing they could do until he died several weeks later.

A pretty nurse named Mary became my friend. Mary was a good nurse, and she had real compassion for our patients. She loved other people, and she told me secrets; and I respected her secrets, and she respected my secrets. And she never told the head nurse I could tell who was going to die by looking at the light in their eyes and around their face. She must have been ten years older than me, but we were good friends. She was someone I could say anything to no matter what. And I could say whatever was on my mind, and she still cared for me. That's a very special friend. I suppose it's love. As I get older, I understand what love is, and I have to admit, I loved Mary.

I came into the hospital running one morning. I was late to work. Huffing and puffing, I went into the nurse's station for the report but found the morning meeting breaking up.

"Chris," said nurse Chapman, "glad you could make it today."

I was dense, but I knew she was being sarcastic. I grabbed Mary and found a place where she could brief me on what I had missed. Mary was not herself. She seemed agitated. She wasn't cool, calm, and collected as usual. It was as if part of her mind had left the room.

Then I noticed the light around her eyes was missing. I guessed she was not feeling well, as fatigue or illness can affect one's aura.

"What's wrong, Mary?" I asked.

Mary began to cry. She put her face in her hands and tried to stop the tears.

I hugged her and said, "What's wrong, Mary?"

Mary was single and didn't have a family, so I guess I was one of her best friends, but I was very young and a bit clumsy in relationships. I really didn't know what to say or do.

"Chris, something terrible has happened."

"Did someone die?" I asked.

"No. But let me ask you a question. What do you think about suicide?"

"Suicide?" I asked. "Why would anyone consider that?"

"Well, let's just say that one of our patients is dying of cancer. Would you think God would approve of suicide?"

"Mary, I don't know."

I thought of my best friend Carlton Gutschick's mother. After my parents died, she took me aside and told me suicide was a terrible sin because it demonstrated a lack of faith in God. I think Mrs. Gutschick was afraid I would commit suicide.

But cancer, I couldn't think of a worse way to die. I hated to watch people die of heart attacks, but they typically went relatively quickly. Cancer was a different beast. These people often suffered traumatic ends.

I said, "I know God is a God of love and all things are possible through Him. But cancer has to be the worst way to die. I'm sure He can forgive us for any sin, don't you?"

Mary then dropped the bombshell. "Chris, I just found out I have a melanoma behind my right eye. It is inoperable. I'm going to die. Worse, I have less than six months to live."

"Oh my god, what had I said? What had I done?" I thought.

"Mary," I said, "isn't there anything they can do?"

"No, I am going to die soon, Chris. And I think I've made up my mind. I am not going through the slow, painful death most suffer. Not with what our patients go through."

"Mary, God loves you. Did I tell you I had lymphoma and that God healed me? It had to be God. I am sure he can heal you too if you ask Him to and if you believe He will do it."

That night I prayed in my awkward way for Mary, and I begged God to save her.

The next day I arrived at work early. It was Saturday morning. I was eager to talk to Mary and see if there was any improvement. She wasn't there. She was late. Mary was never late. But I guess under the circumstances, I might be a few minutes late myself.

"Chris," Head Nurse Chapman called to me from the other end of the floor. I ran up to her, and she asked, "You're running around like a chicken with your head cut off?"

"Ms. Chapman, where's Mary?" I asked.

There was a long pause. Nurse Chapman was looking at me, trying to assess something. "Let's have a seat here at the nurses' station."

I complied with her request.

"Chris," she said, "Mary died last night in a train wreck."

"Oh my god, was she driving across train tracks?"

"No, she was sitting on the train tracks."

I began to cry. "Oh no, it's my fault," I blurted out.

"Your fault?" she asked.

"Yes, she came to me yesterday talking about suicide. She said she had a melanoma behind her right eye and asked me what I thought of suicide. I said I believed God would understand."

Nurse Chapman looked very stern. "Chris, you told her to commit suicide?"

"No . . . well, not exactly. But I did say God would forgive someone who committed suicide."

Word travels fast in a hospital. I was told to go to the head nurse's office within the hour. This was the nurse who was head of the entire hospital. This nurse was beautiful and as cold as ice. She showed no emotion.

"Chris, I heard you spoke to Mary Reynolds and you told her that suicide was okay, is that correct?"

"Why, yes, it is, but . . ."

With real anger, she said, "Chris, that is not something we condone in this hospital."

I was speechless.

Her tone of voice changed, and rage entered her cool face. "Well, Chris, we have appreciated your help, but we have to let you go. We will mail your last check to the address we have on file. Have a good day."

I couldn't speak. I was frozen. I simply got up and left the hospital. I wondered how I was going to make ends meet and pay my bills. But there was nothing I could do. Sometimes I froze and did a poor job asserting myself when I was verbally attacked. As I got older and had more responsibility, I became more assertive and had no problem defending myself. But in this case, I simply left the hospital and never worked in a hospital again.

I didn't want to lose my job. But the greater loss was Mary.

What Should I Do Now That I Am About to Graduate?

As my senior year was winding down, I had to make a career choice. I was accepted into graduate school in physics. I decided to go ahead and get a PhD at Emory as I was given a full scholarship, called a grant.

April came, and my physics professor asked me in to talk. I showed up on time.

He said, "Chris, congratulations on your acceptance into the graduate program. I would like to know what area of physics you would like to specialize in so I can craft the correct course program for you in the future."

"Dr. Jackson, I would like to study general relativity."

There was a pause as Dr. Jackson simply stared at me in disbelief. "Chris, Einstein is famous, granted. But special relativity is a simplified physics theory. I showed you how to derive special relativity with algebra. I think that is a poor choice for a physics career. Why do you want to study general relativity?"

"I believe the Bible is correct on its description of the creation. General relativity predicts a singular event, a point where the creation of the universe began. Since it is consistent with the Bible, I think it must be true."

Dr. Jackson was taken aback. He got up and paced the room. He then said, "Einstein was a terrible mathematician and a lousy physicist. It is a waste of time to study his theories. I will not let you study that here. If you want to study general relativity, you will have to go to another university."

With that he dismissed me from his presence. About a week later, he called me up and told me my grant had been canceled and that I had to pay my way through the doctoral program if I wanted to study physics there. I was devastated. I had counted on working part-time and going to get a PhD at Emory in physics. I didn't know what to do.

*****

There is a hostility in academics to the Bible that I was ill-prepared to deal with at the time. It turns out I was right to want to study general relativity. Today physicists recognize Einstein was two or three generations ahead of all other physicists in his theories. General relativity predicted the existence of black holes that have been essentially proven to exist. More recently, gravitational waves have been observed, another prediction of general relativity. While I have been vindicated, it did not help me and my physics career to express my faith in God.

*****

I then sent an application to Georgia Tech and was accepted. But then one of the professors said that jobs in physics were hard to come by and that university professorships were very hard to get. I needed to support a family, not hang unusable degrees on my wall. I wondered if I should go back and talk to the president of the American Medical Association who said, "Name the medical school and I will get you in there." But where would the money come from to pay for medical school? I couldn't work my way through medical school. Then there was my girlfriend who wanted me to get an MBA.

I remember praying for several nights. One afternoon, I dropped to my knees and felt the Lord come over me in a way I had not experienced since I was a young boy. And my prayer turned into something that was not expected. In fact, the words seemed somehow alien to me. But I knew this was from God and I wanted to please Him and be obedient.

"Dear Lord," I began, "I know that this world is very wicked. I know that mankind is disobedient and evil. I know that man has become totally depraved and is only worthy of destruction. Somehow I know that You are going to destroy us all. We deserve destruction. Please tell me what You are going to do so that I can prepare myself for what is coming. And, Lord, I need help with my career. I want to choose a career that is pleasing to You. I ask for Your help, Lord."

The prayer was not that long. It was concise and short. I was tired and went to bed early that night. I was expecting help and a miracle, but I was not expecting what was to happen.

I fell asleep as usual. But during the night, someone came to me and said, "Chris," there was a moment of silence. Then again, "Chris, I want you to leave your body."

"Leave my body," I thought. "Have you lost your mind? I can't leave my body."

I then realized he heard my thoughts.

"Look up to me, Chris, and I will help you leave."

"Look up to you? Okay, I'll try."

And I tried. Not knowing what I was doing. But I seemed to see some light above me in my dream. I strained to see what I was looking at, and then I could see a glowing figure. An outline of a body that was not concrete and not clear. Let us say opaque. Yes, that's it, but he was brighter than my surroundings. He motioned down below me, and I looked in the direction of his motion, and there, lo and behold, I slept in bed on my side. I could see the whole room. But I was not in my body. I did not know what was happening, but I began to bow and worship this light being. He immediately pulled me up and scolded me for bowing down to him.

"Worship only the Lord," he replied. "I am an angel, and we are equals. Now follow me."

"Where are we going?" I asked.

But there was no answer. The path was long, but the time seemed to pass quickly, like a walk in the park. After a brief walk, we had arrived somewhere in outer space with stars surrounding the darkness.

I entered a large room. Light illuminated everything. It was beautiful. The walls were clear with hues of colors—red and green,

I believe. They were translucent. Clear. You could see through the walls, and you could see the black sky of space with stars in the distance right through the walls and the floor—although I seemed to be floating, not walking. The color was more of a hint of color. The floors were also transparent but had hints of gold. You could even see multiple walls through the wall next to you and then still see the stars. It was breathtaking. As I walked, following my angel, he disappeared in an instant. Perplexed, I began looking for him, but he was not there; yet in front of me, as I looked up, I saw the source of all light in the building. The light was in the form or shape of a man. He glowed like bright white light. It would have hurt my eyes had I seen Him with human eyes. But just as this thought ran through my mind, I realized I was looking at Jesus. How I knew this, I cannot say. But I knew this was *Yeshua*, which is Hebrew for Jesus.

A moment passed of admiration, wonderment, bewilderment, and simple rapture. But then I retrenched into myself. I stopped observing and became aware of myself before God. Yes, the realization was true. Jesus is God, Lord and King of the universe. And here I was before Him. Then I realized He saw through me, and I was horrified at what He saw, for I was a terrible sinner.

I panicked. I wanted to hide behind a rock, anything to escape the gaze of His eyes. I was not worthy to be here. I was a terrible, disobedient sinner. A feeling of incredible shame overwhelmed me. Not unlike a person who found themselves naked in front of an audience. He saw and knew everything about me. I wept at my evil self and begged God to forgive me for the bad things I had done.

This perfect building had no rocks. There were walls. So I hastily darted behind a nearby wall, and as if in tears, I hung my head low to the floor. I looked within myself and was ashamed. Then a thought occurred to me.

"The walls are clear, Chris." Clear they were. Clear indeed. "Chris, there is no place in heaven on earth or in hell where you can hide from My eyes."

I walked out into the room before my Lord, holding my head low. I stood in front of Him and waited for what was to come.

Then all thoughts of me and my sins melted, and a sense of love and peace encompassed me.

Suddenly movies appeared before my eyes. I recognized nuclear weapons. Bombs. Fire and destruction. It was a terrible and wondrous vision. I knew it was of future events. I knew the prayer the night before was being answered. I was witnessing the very destruction of the earth. He showed me many future events. Terrible and frightening events. And I was shown the destruction of the planet earth as we know it.

Some of what I was shown, I was cautioned not to reveal. The fact that the end was coming was certain to me in that place. And the vision of the end I saw was horrifying yet incredible. But the reason for my prayer was still a mystery to me. I never had studied that the world would be destroyed. I never had heard of a war called Armageddon. I was not aware of this, except through Aunt Hank who said that the return of the Jews to Israel was probably the hallmark that "the end" was coming soon. I didn't know what she meant, and she never elaborated. I considered my aunt's stories a little fantastic, anyway, and didn't give her a lot of credibility.

I was then shown a brief vision or movie where I was still a young man and where an event occurred that was brief.

My Lord then said, "Go back to your body." And the dream was over.

The next morning, I woke up with the dream hanging in my memory in perfect detail. The question arose, Was this a dream or something more? I was not certain. But I was perplexed. The dream was chronological. It revealed all new information to me, information I had never experienced before. It provided no clue to unconscious revelation or internal struggle. None of these experiences were like a dream. They were like a waking experience, an experience with something I had never encountered before. But being a science student, the thought occurred to me that this was not provable without additional information.

That day I had a traffic ticket to pay. I drove to the local police station where I was to meet with a judge. I explained the ticket was not my fault. I did not know I had to have local tags when I was an out-of-state student at Emory.

The judge's verdict was immediate and concise. "Ignorance of the law is not an excuse or a defense." He slammed the gavel down and said, "You are guilty."

I went to pay the fine. And in the room, when I began to write a check, events played out before my eyes that were incredible. I had seen this scene the night before in my sleep. Someone standing in the background was speaking. And as she spoke, I said every word she said with her. The person who responded, I mimicked as well. The person I was writing a check to looked at me in shock. I felt weak all over.

I spoke, "I know you are not going to believe this, but I saw this in a dream last night, given to me by God. Everything that has been spoken, every action, every motion, I saw last night before it happened." I paid the bill and left the station confused.

Back in my room I prayed again. "Lord, I know I don't understand what I just saw. It must be confirmation that the dream wasn't a normal dream. It couldn't have been just a dream. What I just witnessed must have been some type of confirmation so that I would believe what You revealed to me about the end. I know it is not time yet, but in my life these events will occur, and the end will come to pass. I only ask for help from someone who understands what this means. I pray that You will introduce me to someone who can help me, Lord. Please, for I am so limited in my intellectual ability, I can't possibly understand what You showed me without help."

Terry to the Rescue

Within a week, my life was turned upside down. I was asked to move out of my apartment by my roommates, including Nancy, the girl I was in love with at the time. I knew that this was from God. I also knew where I was to go. I was to go to graduate school in business. I learned this in my dream the night before. I applied to and was accepted to get an MBA at Georgia State University.

I began looking for an apartment and selected a room in a home to rent in Midtown Atlanta. I moved in and had just unpacked and was walking up the steps of this gargantuan house. On the way up the steps, I encountered a young woman, about my age, who immediately began speaking to me.

"Hi, my name is Terry, what's your name?"

"Chris," I responded.

"Chris, I am pleased to meet you. Are you a Christian?"

I had to hesitate. I never thought of myself as a "Christian" before that; in fact I thought of the word *Christian* as being a bit derogatory. I was a Jew. I was confirmed in a Lutheran church. Because of my recent experience, I now believed Jesus was God, so I guess I was, in fact, a Christian.

"Yes," I said, "I am a Christian."

"Oh, it is so wonderful to meet a Christian in this evil place," Terry responded.

I immediately became concerned, for I did not recognize the evil to which Terry referred.

Terry invited me upstairs. And we began to talk about the Lord. She told me about her concerns about where we were living. She knew that we were sent there to do good, but she felt she needed help because the evil was great in that house.

I tried to explain my dream and asked her if she was the person I prayed to meet who could help me understand the dream's meaning. I relayed the contents of the dream to her, as quickly as possible, and she beamed.

"Chris, I studied this under a minister when I grew up in my home in Ohio. Our minister said there was a special blessing to ministers who taught Revelation to their congregation."

"What is Revelation?" I asked naively.

"It's a book in the Bible. It looks like you need a lot of help."

She then described a war that would destroy the planet by fire. She described an Antichrist, as she called him, a world of terrible evil, the church amid a worldwide Sodom and Gomorrah, the return of Christ, and a millennium of years where there would be peace on earth, with Christ as King and Lord.

Her explanations were more detailed, but it did not take five minutes before I was reduced to tears as she spoke. Everything she said, I had seen in my vision, I had seen with my own eyes. And there was no way I had ever read Daniel, Ezekiel, or Revelation in my life. The only thing I might have read was Thessalonians, but I didn't remember reading it. I only remembered reading the four gospels several times, the book of Jonah, the Acts, and parts of Genesis.

This was a second confirmation that the "dream" I had was not just a "dream" but something much more. It was real, I thought, it had to be real. I saw Jesus in heaven, and He revealed the end of the world before my eyes. Why? I had no idea. But nevertheless, I had been shown these things, and perhaps, as I experienced events the day after the dream, the end-times would unfold as a bad dream I had already witnessed. The parallels between my dream and the events Terry described to me were eerily similar.

At this point in my life, I was very much alone. My girlfriend had dumped me. Visiting my relatives was okay but not encouraged. How does one say I was always accepted, but never hoped for? My sister and brother had basically disowned me as a pushy older brother who was trying to manipulate them. And I was terribly lonely and frightened, though I denied my fear and my loss of my family.

All I can say is, God bless Terry and her family. Her grandmother moved into our house and was a spiritual warrior. She prayed and quoted the Bible to me continually. And she was a friend. She cared for me. I think she wanted me to marry Terry. But the Lord did not want us to get married, from what I could tell. Then there was Terry's mother, Marvine. I really loved Marvine. We were best friends. She had great faith. Abandoned by her husband, she raised Nan, her youngest, and lived with Terry, who helped her. These people were now my best friends. They were not angels, but if my Lord were to send angels, none could have been as good to me as these.

Marvine later became secretary to the president of the Presbyterian Church USA. When Marvine went to this president's house for parties, I was often her guest. And I felt honored to talk to this important man and humbled to be there with him and with Marvine.

Terry's grandmother and mother, Marvine, have gone to be with our Lord. Terry has married and had a son. And no demon will be safe near Terry. I thank God for Christian friends like this. Friends that God provided for me exactly at the time I needed them!

Spiritual Help

The home we lived in was run by an ex-minister who had turned against God and walked from his faith. I never found him to be as evil as Terry and her family said he was. But I found his life sinful, as he had three beautiful women living in his room with him. And he treated all three as his wives. I had an opportunity while living there to talk to two of these women, and two finally left him to strike out on their own. They didn't have confidence in their ability to survive without him. And our Lord sent me to them to explain that God was sufficient to meet their needs and that they would not need to be dependent on this man in the future. One married a successful man. The other left, and I never heard from her again.

God sends us into the world to do small tasks. Sometimes it is to provide someone with a word of comfort. Sometimes it is a word of faith. Sometimes it is to heal the sick. And sometimes it is to drive out demons. But it always involves loving others as our Lord loves us and to carry out His works on earth on His behalf.

Investigation into the Spiritual

After I had experienced this incredible dream, and before meeting Terry and her family, I thought back to my girlfriend Nancy. She read a lot of books about the transfer of the soul and out-of-body experiences. Personally, I thought she was nuts. She also said there was a book called *Life after Life* by a physician named Dr. Raymond Moody that I should read. She gave me a copy of the book. I had not read it until after I had the unbelievable dream where I went to heaven.

Dr. Moody had studied people who had near-death experiences. He described many situations about people who, upon near-death experiences, saw a light and traveled through a tunnel toward the light. When they got to the light, they could look down on their bodies and see their bodies on operating tables, in car accidents, and they could hear events around them, often as others tried to save them. At some point, they might see their deceased family and friends and have an incredible sense of peace and joy. Then they were sometimes given a choice, to live or to die. And if they chose to live, they would hear a command to go back to their body, and they would live.

I felt this was like my out-of-body experience, with one minor exception . . . I was not on the verge of death when this happened. I could only leave my body by looking at an angel-like person, a light, and I traveled to him to leave my body. I then saw my body asleep in bed. After my dream, I was commanded to go back to my body.

But one of his stories that intrigued me the most was of a patient, blind from birth, whose heart failed on the operating table. As they tried to save him, he remembered looking down from the ceiling of the operating room. He watched them as they made several attempts to save him. He described everything that was done with great precision by the medical team; he described what the participants in the operating room looked like; and he saw a clamp drop below a table in the corner of the room. Dr. Moody went to the operating room and looked under the table in the corner, and lo and behold, he saw the clamp lying exactly where the patient said it fell. The patient was excited because he had finally been able to understand what sight was and what things looked like.

My First Experience with Demons

I began to have unusual experiences after this vision. While in Texas, after the vision, the Holy Spirit descended on me and had me write a prophecy to the Jews. It was not read by anyone of any significance, except to offer prophetic advice for the last days. After writing the prophecy, a minister came to me and said I was Moses as predicted in the Bible, who had returned for the last days. I don't believe I am Moses. But one thing was true . . . I realized people sensed I was not the same person I had been. I was then taken to retirement homes and played the piano for services with encouragement from the assistant pastor of the First Baptist Church of Midland, Texas.

Back in Atlanta that fall, I had numerous experiences with people who said I was an angel or an apparition from God. Others said I was a saint, which I believe is the title every Christian has. There was no doubt; people sensed something different about me.

One day I was driving down Virginia Avenue through Atlanta. I stopped at a light at an intersection. It was cool outside. The window on the driver's side was down, and I was leaning my elbow out of the car. It was a beautiful day. I was not in a hurry that afternoon. I was lost in thought.

A noise in the distance and a screaming from the street caught my attention. I looked to my left, wondering where the noise came from. A man was running toward me. A big man! He was screaming something at me. I realized he was saying, "Child of God, I will kill you."

I was not prepared for this. I thought being a Christian was love, joy, and happiness—not fear, anxiety, and running from demons. I had heard of demons in the Bible but never encountered anything of that nature before. The man was crossing the other side of the street; in moments he would be upon me. The light was still red.

I did all I knew to do. I called out at him, "In the name of Jesus, get thee behind me, Satan."

He stopped in his tracks in the middle of the road.

"If you come closer, I will be glad to cast the demons out of you," I said with all the authority I could muster.

The man looked horrified and took off running as fast as he could in the opposite direction. I noticed people on the side of the road staring at us. I am not sure they heard or understood the words that were exchanged. The light was green by now, so I rolled up my window and drove off.

Paying Rent in School

After several months, I was approached by the ex-minister who managed this giant house I lived in because I had been late in paying rent that month. What was my problem? Rent was due by the first of the month. He said, if I did not pay by Monday, he was going to evict me. But he didn't really want to evict me because he thought I added something to the milieu. I played the piano and was always cheerful. Everyone liked me.

I didn't dare tell him I didn't have the money to pay rent. My uncle shipped me funds from time to time but was often very late in paying me. I had asked my uncle over four weeks ago to send me a thousand dollars, and he had not sent me anything.

I realized there was no money coming and I had to get a job. I wanted a job immediately. But I knew, even if I had a job that day, my first check was going to be late. I prayed that night desperately.

"Lord, where will I go if I am evicted? Where can I go? Will I live outside in the cold? What am I to do?"

Monday morning came, the rent was due, but the funds had not arrived. Frightened, I went to the post office to see if my uncle had sent me any money. But to my surprise, I had a notice from the IRS. I opened the notice, and inside was a check. And the check amount was for fifteen dollars more than I needed for rent. After preparing returns for over twenty years, I have never made a mistake on a tax return. This was the first and only time I made a mistake. Even better, I had a refund coming, and the refund was for the exact amount I needed.

By Monday afternoon, I had a job with the State of Georgia and could pay my rent from that point forward.

Who Was This Beggar?

I began to read the Bible on a regular basis after these strange spiritual experiences. And I became very interested in Paul. He was a soldier for God. He had a purpose. He knew where he was headed. I loved Paul. He was committed to Jesus; he was on a mission; and he fought for Christ until he died. When a poisonous snake bit him on the hand, he simply shook it off. Such was his faith, and this faith was something I wanted. Jesus was God. I loved Him and feared Him. But I could never be like him. Paul, on the other hand, was a man—an educated brilliant man, a man who attacked the church and murdered one of the saints, a man who was so committed to God that God decided to save him when he was on the road to Damascus. This was a man who sinned like me and a man I could identify with and a man who had unshakable faith. I was not worthy to be like Jesus or to even be the lowest servant to Jesus, but I could aspire to be more like Paul.

I also identified with Paul because I felt I was lost and the Lord intervened into my life and saved me. Paul was lost, and then he saw a light on the road to Damascus that changed his life. Paul was someone I wanted to meet. I prayed that. I remember telling the Lord, "I would like to meet Paul if that were possible."

The next day after class, I went to catch a bus back to the house. I waited with a lawyer who was getting an MBA with me. While we waited for the bus, a beggar approached both of us and asked us for money. I was opposed to giving beggars money, not because I didn't want to help, but because I didn't want to help a beggar buy more liquor as hobos often do.

The lawyer I was with handed this man a quarter. Feeling convicted by the Lord, I did the same. The minute he took the quarter from me, this beggar began to speak directly to me in a bold way.

"Chris," he said, "I have been sent by the Lord to encourage you. Yes, I am Paul. Yes, the end of the world is at hand. The Lord will be returning soon. You must keep the faith. Do His work and finish the tasks He gives you to completion. God loves you. Stay strong in your faith to the end, and follow the Lord. Finish the race and glorify God." And just as quickly as he arrived, he simply turned and walked away.

After the encounter, I asked the lawyer friend how this man knew my name. He didn't know. "Perhaps you look like a Chris," he said.

To this day I can't let go of the coincidence where I prayed to meet Paul of Tarsus and the next day I met a man who claimed to be Paul. Could this have been Paul? He said nothing that would make me think he was other than Paul except for the fact that Paul was dead.

This Paul guy talked to me about the end-times, the very thing I saw in the recent vision, and he knew my name. But he looked so aged, so worn from stress. He looked so much like a poor pauper with no money. Just like a beggar. He looked nothing like I imagined. But his words sounded like an intelligent and spiritual man. Coincidences are amazing. We sometimes see what we want to see. I am sure this man was just a man who happened to say the right words and stirred my curiosity.

Falling Down the Steps

During my first semester at Georgia State in graduate school, I took an accounting course. There was a guy from India who sat next to me in class named Shashi. We competed to be the best student in that class. At the end of the semester, Shashi and I had the two highest grades in this class, but Shashi beat me by two points. Apparently, I impressed him. He would often strike up a conversation with me after class. Then, one day, out of the blue, he said he needed a roommate. He wanted to save money on his place in Midtown, so he asked me to move in with him that semester.

Terry, her mother, and her grandmother had moved out of our house. Her grandmother had moved back to Ohio to be with her sister who was dying of cancer. She wanted to witness to her, to save her soul. Terry had moved into a friend's house and had become interested in astrology. Marvine moved into a house with her younger daughter, Nan, who was attending high school. Left alone, it made sense for me to move in with Shashi and share rent.

Shashi Kapoor had been an actor in Bollywood. It turns out he was one of the greatest actors in all of India. His family consisted of some of the most powerful people in India. His cousin ran the entire Army. And Shashi Kapoor was one of the smartest men I have ever met. I really liked him. He was a genuinely kind and good man. He felt Americans looked down on him because of his dark skin. He thought we believed he was a "nigger" and that all white people would persecute or hate him. I found such defensiveness inappropriate, for I felt nothing but great admiration for Shashi. And I certainly didn't approve of discrimination against blacks or anyone with different skin color.

Shashi became an invaluable friend to me. He was sixteen years older than me. He was like an older brother and a father to me. I really grew to love Shashi. When I had trouble studying, Shashi would give me advice. He helped me improve my study habits. My grades jumped to mostly As, and I was taking twice as many courses a quarter as was normal while I worked forty hours a week. Shashi and I often talked about the Lord. He was a Hindu, but he believed in God and feared God.

One day I was in a hurry to get to the bus. Shashi had already left, and I was afraid I would miss the bus that morning. I went bounding down the stairs, skipping every other step, and suddenly I slipped. Having played football, I had a great sense of balance. I grabbed the railing on the side of the steps, and with a gentle push, I flipped over and flew in the air to the bottom of the steps and landed on my back. Thankfully I had landed with my back on the last few steps, and my bottom slipped down to the first floor of the condo. I tried to sit up, but I couldn't move. I lay there unable to move. I was frozen in place on my back. Minutes seemed like days. After about a half hour, I began to pray.

"I can't move Lord, help me," I thought.

I assessed my chances of having someone find me that morning. Shashi was on his way to class and would not come back home until late that night. I couldn't reach a telephone. I couldn't call for help where anyone could hear me. The front door was locked, and the room was largely soundproof. With time on my hands, I began to praise the Lord and sing praises to Him. I began to thank Him for my life and the blessings I had received, and finally I asked Him for help . . . provided it was His will to help me.

After another half hour of praises a thought entered my mind. "Chris, I'm here to heal you."

No one was there. But over the next few moments, my back heated up, especially the backbone below my shoulder blades where I had hit the step. I tingled all over.

Another stupid thought entered my mind. "You're fine, Chris, you can get up now."

I laughed at myself and wondered how on earth I could describe myself as being fine. I was paralyzed, lying on the floor, and I had to go to the bathroom. What was I supposed to do, pee on the floor in my clothes? I wasn't fine.

Anyway, I decided to see if I could sit up. I tried to sit up. It must have been a miracle. Or did I stun my back somehow and the stun wore off? I didn't know. I then gingerly stood up, and I realized, by gosh, I was fine. Without a moment's hesitation, I went into the living room, picked up my bags, and headed to work. I was a little late to work that day but none the worse for the wear.

Later that evening I conveyed this story to Shashi. He said that I probably had stunned my spinal cord and that no miracle had happened that day. I do not know whether my spine was stunned or broken, but I was thankful, very thankful, that I was able to get up and go to work and to school with no permanent damage.

Sensing Others

In college and graduate school, I met some truly interesting people. One young lady was a medical student at Georgia College. Her name was Kathy. We had a wonderful friendship. I told her of spiritual experiences I had, including parts of the recent vision. As a medical student, Kathy said that some of the experiences I had could be explained in medicine as a part of the brain that had generated something akin to supernatural experiences. She spoke of LSD and similar hallucinogens that created spiritual-type experiences.

I was disappointed, because I had concluded that there was much more happening than brain anomalies. But my experiences came from faith and could not be proven in a laboratory.

My friendship with Kathy was just that, as a sister in Christ. Whenever she came back to Atlanta from medical school in Augusta, she would call me up and ask me to take her out, which I happily agreed to do.

I had a date with her one evening. I came by her house to pick her up, and her dad answered the door. When I saw him, I was perplexed! Something was wrong with his aura. It was a mix between death and evil. I had this sick sense of sin resonating from this Christian man. I didn't know how to interpret what I saw. But that evening I felt it was important to tell Kathy as we drove to dinner.

I said, "Something is wrong with your father, Kathy. I don't know what it is, but you and your mother must pray for him."

That was what God said through me. I wasn't quite sure what that meant at the time.

That evening Kathy confided in me. She said her dad had asked her to have sex with him earlier that day, not something I would expect from a Christian. She asked how I knew that they had to pray for her dad. I couldn't answer that question.

*****

About a week later, my friend Chuck was visiting Shashi and me at our apartment. It was a rainy evening, so we decided to stay in and discuss politics, girls, and homework. Chuck had a master's in history and was an amazing source of information.

While we were talking, I had a very strange feeling. I knew someone was very distressed. It was someone I knew . . . and it was a young woman.

"Chuck and Shashi," I said, "I have just had the strangest feeling that a young woman is thinking about me and that someone else, an old man, just died."

Chuck was a polite Southern gentleman, so he was careful with words. He asked, "Is everything all right, Chris?"

Shashi looked very concerned but remained silent.

I responded, "I know this is hard to believe, but I am concerned. Dee, my grandfather is in his late nineties and has had two serious heart attacks. I hope he is fine. But it could be my cousin Jana who is thinking of me. Oh God, I hope my last living grandparent is fine."

About that time the phone rang. I went and picked up the phone.

"Chris." It was Kathy. "Chris, I just found out my father died in a car accident. He hit the car in front of him. There was a heavy object in the back of the car, and it flew forward and hit him in the head and killed him."

"Kathy, when did you hear about your father's death?"

"About half an hour ago," she said.

"Were you thinking of me Kathy when you heard this news?"

"Yes, I was, Chris, because you told me something was wrong with my father and that my mother and I were to pray for him."

I relayed the facts to my friends Chuck and Shashi. Shashi was stunned. Chuck laughed.

Bolder in Faith

I was seeing color and beginning to enjoy life again. I loved children and was thankful for the beauty God made in the world. I had trouble handling anything that reminded me of my mother after her death. But as I was emerging from my depression, I was beginning to think of my mother and was dealing with her death in positive ways. One thing that reminded me of my mother was opera. My mother loved *La Boehm*, a beautiful yet tragic opera where a young woman dies of tuberculosis. I could not listen to that opera for years after she died. I would leave the room if I heard it as it reminded me of my mother and her death. So it was a good thing I wanted to listen to this opera. It meant I was getting over her death and was ready to move on.

My mother struggled with her mother's death, as her mother died of rheumatic fever when she was in high school. My mother also worked at a tuberculosis, or TB, hospital in Denver when she was young. In the opera *La Boehm*, a young woman dies of TB, and that was an important connection to my mother as she saw many people die from TB. Perhaps this had something to do with her love of this opera. But I agreed with her, as it was my favorite opera.

One Saturday I decided to cook a ham for Shashi and me. I pulled out my mother's gourmet cookbook and decided to listen to music while I cut up and prepared the ham for the oven. What opera to listen to, though? One opera I had not listened to was *Mephistopheles* by Berlioz. I pulled the shrink wrap off the album, pulled it out of its cover, and put it on the turntable in my apartment. I had just bought the opera the previous weekend, probably because I loved *Symphony Fantastic* by Berlioz.

I had a gourmet recipe for ham that called for honey and cherries. Shashi was in the living room reading and didn't seem to mind the opera. With greasy, messy hands, I cut off the fat and began putting honey and cherries and other seasoning on the ham.

Then the music turned dark and sinister. I did not understand the chant in the background, but I felt weird. It was beginning to scare me. I asked the Lord if I was listening to something that was evil that should be turned off. My thoughts were simply, "Then turn it off."

"Lord," I said out loud, "my hands are a mess and are covered with honey and fat, and by the time I am able to turn that opera off, another five minutes will have gone by. If You want the opera to stop, please help me out and turn it off Yourself."

The moment I finished speaking out loud, the music stopped. I wondered if we had a power surge even though the lights did not flicker. If we had a power surge, it probably ruined my stereo, I thought. But I didn't see any change in the lights. It was odd. Then I said, "I spent a lot of money on that stereo, and I can't afford to buy another one Lord."

I finished preparing the ham, put it in the oven, washed my hands, and as quickly as possible went into the living room to the stereo and carefully lifted the album off the turntable and put it up.

I turned the turntable back on and gritted my teeth, knowing it wasn't going to work. To my surprise, it worked perfectly. I pulled out a different album and put it on the turntable to see if the speakers or amplifier had failed. To my surprise, everything worked perfectly. That stereo system worked until I replaced it with a DVD player many years later.

Shashi was in the room studying. He just looked at me with a confused gaze. I guess he overheard me ask God to turn off the stereo, and of course, he heard it stop.

*****

Shashi, Chuck, and I later went to a dance club to dance and to have a drink with friends. It was an odd evening, and I sensed evil emanating from the bar—something I had learned to ignore, as evil was everywhere. I enjoyed the swing dance that was popular at the time, where guys would spin girls around, sling them in the air, and hold them in their arms.

My mother had danced with Fred Astaire on television and felt it was important that I learn to dance. After all those lessons she put me through, in everything from ballet to ballroom dancing, I finally found a type of dance, which was an impromptu type of swing that I really enjoyed. And I could dance this with anyone and just have fun feeling free to express myself on the dance floor.

But that night there was to be no dancing. A bouncer singled me out and started calling me names.

He said, "I don't like the way you look." I wondered if he was demon-possessed. "You can't enter with those shoes."

Shashi, being a man of reason, said simply, "Let's go, Chris, they don't want our business."

As we began to leave, the man ran after me, screaming, "Get out of here, and don't come back!"

This really freaked Shashi out. I turned, and feeling the Holy Spirit descend upon me, I stopped him cold in his tracks by simply saying "Stop." He froze like he couldn't move. "I curse this place," I said. "Tonight this place will burn to the ground."

Everyone in line was staring at the two of us. With that I turned and walked away, leaving the man frozen. At this point I was sure he was demonic.

We decided to eat pizza that night at our favorite pizza joint.

When we sat down to eat, I said, "I'm sorry, guys, that you had to get out of line because of me."

"Chris," Shashi said, "that's not your fault. He threw us out of line because my skin is dark."

"Shashi, he singled me out, and my shoes, not you or Chuck."

Chuck politely changed the subject. "Well, it will be a cold day in hell before we go back there."

"Hear, hear," we said, holding our iced teas in the air and clinking the glasses together.

*****

The next morning Shashi and I were riding together in his car to go to class. The dance club we went to the night before was just off I-75. As we turned onto the interstate, I looked to see the dance club. There was nothing left but a few blackened logs and ashes. Smoke still drifted from the middle of the slab where the building had stood.

Shashi had been with me the entire evening, and I slept in our apartment that night. But he asked, "Chris, you didn't burn the building down last night, did you?"

"Of course not, Shashi, I was with you all night. Plus, you know God would never allow me to do something like that to anyone."

"You cursed that business before we left."

"Well, if anyone did anything, it wasn't me."

Shashi was driving; he looked agitated but nodded politely.

I continued. "The problem is this, Shashi. I feel terrible about what happened. I have been before the Lord. I know what a terrible person I am. I am no better than the owner of this business and that man who threatened me."

"But, Chris," Shashi said, "that man wanted to harm you."

"Was it the man or the demon inside him?" I said. "Besides, Shashi, God would not let him harm me."

"He seemed pretty intent on chasing you last night. Maybe that is how God protected you, by burning the business down."

"Either way I feel terrible about what happened, and I hope I never have to curse another business or person again."

Silence prevailed in the car the rest of the way to Georgia State that day.

I Pray to Hold Our Leaders Accountable

Realizing the Lord was listening to my prayers, one night before bed I prayed:

Dear Lord, you have blessed me repeatedly by answering my prayers. I struggle with the loss of my parents. Martha Mitchell my friend is dead. And what of all the other men and women who lost their lives tragically in the Nixon administration? I've been thinking about how out of control the leaders of our Country have become, and I have wondered…what if we could create a news channel that delved into the real political issues in Washington and around the world, perhaps we could reduce or eliminate the corruption that has destroyed the lives of so many. Lord if it is possible, will you please provide me with a way to help keep eyes on these corrupt leaders in Washington?

I uttered this prayer on a Saturday night after I watched a thirty-minute news broadcast that was practically a waste of time. The thirty minutes news was divided into 10 minutes of commercials, 15 minutes pertained to local Atlanta news and 4 minutes concerned Georgia politics. They spent less than 30 seconds on US news and no time at all on world news.

A few days later I had a strange dream. I was once again standing in Heaven before Jesus. I had no recollection of how I got there although I believed I had just ended a lengthy conversation with Him. Jesus then said, "Get up Chris, or you will miss the bus." I opened my eyes and looked at the alarm clock. It was 6:50 AM, ten minutes before I normally got up. I thought about closing my eyes for ten minutes but decided I had better get out of bed. I stumbled in to the shower, brushed my teeth, washed as quickly as possible, dried, combed my hair, jumped into my blue jeans, pulled a shirt over my head, put on my socks and shoes, grabbed my bag and headed for the bus stop. I walked to the bus stop as quickly as possible, and just as I was arriving there I noticed the bus was pulling away. I ran and was able to knock on the door to the right of the bus driver. He recognized me, stopped and let me on the bus.

Our bus went through Buckhead, where the wealthy lived. I was reading a finance book and doing homework when a gentleman in a suit, carrying a briefcase sat down next to me and started talking.

After brief introductions, he asked about the book I was reading.

"I'm reading an international finance book. I'm a graduate student at Georgia State in business."

"Chris is it?"

"Yes sir."

"It's nice to meet you Chris." He paused as if he wanted to ask me a question, and then said, "Hey Chris, I work for Ted Turner." Everyone had heard of the mouth of the south. He was quite the ladies man. Then he said, "My boss wants to get on board with this cable television thing. He believes this is the future of TV. But he doesn't know what type of shows to air. You seem like a bright guy. What would you recommend?"

This was exactly what I prayed for, and I had already stated my position to my Lord, so it was easy for me to explain. "I leave my home by 7:30 AM each day and often don't get home until 11:00 PM. I haven't seen the news in two years. They have the 8 AM news, the 5 PM news and the 10 PM news. That's it. If you miss these times you don't get the news.

And then when I do hear the news, say on the weekend, out of a thirty-minute broadcast less than a minute is spent on National news and I almost never hear any mention of world news. When I was in Washington, DC, they had two thirty-minute shows that only spoke about national and international news. I don't know how the people in Georgia know who to vote for much less what is going on in the world. I swear, the world could blow up and we wouldn't hear about it down here in the south."

"So, you want national and international news? Remember the cable news channels will run 24 hours. Is there enough news for that?"

"I believe so. I would create two different news channels. One channel could run for thirty minutes and could be repeated, over-and-over again. Then as new stories come in they could simply replace the oldest or least important story with the new story or stories."

"What about during the night?"

"Just rerun the same news over-and-over again until your journalists get back into the offices and update stories."

"So, you would just rerun the same news repeatedly all day and all night."

"Yes, I would run the news 24 hours a day. But let's say a newsworthy event occurs that they wanted to run, they could tape that, fit it in to the thirty-minute show that is running, delete the part they want out and start playing the new tape. That way they could run the news continuously. They would just update the thirty-minute segments as news came in and pick which stories to pull out and replace those segments with a new segment or segments."

"By gosh, Chris, I like that idea. I think that is a good idea."

"Then anyone can watch the news anytime."

"I see. So, you recommend Ted get into the news business. You know Ted doesn't know anything about news."

"He has to know more than the local channels in the south know. He can only improve the content for most of America."

"I like that idea. But you mentioned a second channel."

"Yes, that's true. I think we need a second channel that really delves into national and international news. My Dad worked in Washington and I knew things no one knew and was shocked at how little people understand about our Government. I also found much of the news to be totally wrong or misleading even in Washington. I believe the leaders in Washington have become too powerful and too corrupt. That's why we had Watergate. I believe we need a news channel that really holds these people accountable in Washington, so they don't run willy-nilly all over the rest of us."

By now the bus was pulling up to the newly built Omni hotel. My newly found friend shook my hand and thanked me. "Chris, I think I'm going to recommend Ted get into the news business. Thank you for your recommendation. I think it was a great idea!" And with that he disembarked from the bus and headed for the hotel. I didn't think anything more about that day until a year later when a channel was introduced on the air called CNN.

I wondered, even mused that I might have had a positive influence in the creation of this television channel. About a year after that Mr. Turner introduced another channel, the real reason I recommended the news. We now had the headline news channel and an in-depth news channel called CNN. It did not matter to me whether I recommended CNN, what mattered to me was I believed if in fact I was behind this, it was truly Jesus who did this, and it was Jesus who answered my prayer, and I was awe inspired at the majesty and wonder of my Lord and savior Jesus. I also realized, if this was a creation of my Lord, then I had no right to be paid for helping fulfill His will on earth. All I could do in my heart was continuously praise and thank Him for his wonder and majesty. The verse, "Who is like thee, Oh Lord," kept running through my mind....for there is none like Him.

Graduate School Helps Spiritual Growth

To get exercise, I either rode my bike or ran every night, provided I got home early enough from school. I found an area I loved to bike or run through. It was a water purification plant with a beautiful creek that ran through downtown Atlanta. I prayed as I ran, asking God for help, asking God for companionship, and asking God for direction. Never in my life have I felt so close to my Lord. Never have I felt such an intimacy. I studied a lot of hours. I worked at a Steak and Ale, which was a restaurant, and I ran at night.

One evening I was performing my exercise routine, running four or five miles. I ran through the water purification area. I felt pressure on my shoulder, telling me to walk. I became curious.

"Why was I to slow down?" I thought.

Then I noticed a quaking aspen, a type of tree that was not quaking or shaking, that usually danced in the mildest of breezes.

"Very unusual," I thought.

I stopped to investigate. Then I realized the insects had suddenly become silent. I looked up into the sky and noticed a pressure difference and a yellow-and-red bright sky and immediately realized a tornado was in the area. I ran as fast as I could toward the creek. Hopping down the hill, I crawled up under the bridge that cars drove over, wedged right up in the corner. I heard a roar, a high-pitched whine, trees snapped, winds blew, and then silence. After a few minutes, the insects began making noise again. I crawled out from under the bridge and ran back to my room. Within a few blocks, a tornado had touched down and taken the roof off the governor's home. They said Governor Carter was not home that evening. But I felt a sense that God had warned me, spoken to me, not in words, but politely nudged me to get out of the way.

A month later I was running through the same water purification plant. It was dark. There was no light, except from the stacks that burned the gases, that lit up the night sky. They reminded me of hell. I had just run around the bend, and I felt a hand on my shoulder as if to say "Slow down." Again I felt pressure on my right shoulder, so I stopped running. I began walking quietly, trying to see what was in front of me. I was scared for some reason. Then I heard an incredible growl. It sounded like a tiger or lion. I stood there and could barely see the outline of a large cat moving back and forth on the path in front of me. I had trouble seeing it, but it was moving back and forth. I wondered if demons took animal form. I decided it was really a wild cat. But how did it get here?

I decided to back up on the path and walk away from it while facing it until I got back to the road. It stayed and did not follow me. Back at the road, I felt it was safe to continue running and headed back to the apartment.

When I got to the house, I wondered what I had encountered. I had no idea. Then on the news they reported a panther had escaped from the zoo and they were looking for it, and it had last been spotted a few miles from where I was that night. Had I continued running, I would have come right up on that darn cat! Thank God, I stopped. Then I remembered the pressure on my shoulder to slow down.

I called the zoo and reported the sighting. They thanked me and said they were sending a team over to investigate. The news reported they found the missing panther at the water purification plant the next day.

The Elevator in Graduate School

I was studying in the graduate school library on a regular basis. I enjoyed studying there on beautiful days. I saw all types of students: students I competed with, students who were my friends, and others who became my friends. We had a camaraderie that made this place a special place to really get a lot done in a short time.

One day, getting off the elevator, I saw a young woman who was in undergraduate school. Her aura was completely missing. I stared at her and wanted to speak to her but didn't know what to say. I tried not to stare. Then she looked hard at me as if to say "Stop staring." So I turned away. As with most of these experiences, I chose to disregard what I saw.

I put a lot of books in a cart and was wheeling the cart behind me to the elevator. While I was standing at the elevator door, it opened. I turned to line the cart up with the elevator, something I didn't always do, and I noticed there was no elevator inside the doors. Panic flooded through me. I stepped forward away from the doors.

"One step and that would have been the end of me," I thought.

The doors closed. After a moment or two, the elevator doors opened, and the elevator was there. I prayed and felt it was okay to ride the elevator. I went to the lobby to the front desk and urgently reported that they had to close the elevator and get a repairman there immediately. The student behind the desk looked unconcerned, but after some pleading, he agreed to call for help.

The next day I heard the bad news. A coed had fallen to her death down the elevator shaft. A picture confirmed it was the girl I had seen.

What Career Should I Choose?

One day I was driving with my friend Chuck, and I took off without a specific direction for a long ride. We were both single men on a Saturday, with no one to date, so we wanted to kill the evening. As I drove I seemed to follow a direction that was into an undeveloped neighborhood. I had an eerie feeling and stopped the car. I got out of the car and walked on this empty lot. Chuck followed me. He asked why I stopped there.

"Chuck," I said. "I believe I will be a financial officer of a big company right here . . . right on this land, one day in the future."

"Well, I guess anything is possible," Chuck responded with a chuckle.

I, too, could not believe those words left my mouth, and I disregarded what I had spoken, except for this uneasy feeling that perhaps those words came from God and not from me.

*****

Little did I know at the time, an office complex would be built at that location and that a multibillion-dollar company would hire me as their top financial officer to work right there.

My title would be vice president and corporate controller, yet I had many responsibilities that were far more complex than a typical controller. Additionally, I regularly reported to the chairman of the board. It was everything I had hoped and prayed for many years before, and it was in the exact location of that Saturday-night drive! Don't ask me how I knew, because most of what this book is about are things that make no sense to me as a scientist but that happened nonetheless.

Karen, My Sister

Karen is a Christian. She left our aunt and uncle's home in Texas and set out across America to win the lost to Christ with a boy she met when she was in college. No money. No assets. She just packed a backpack and took off. They were gone for a couple of months before they returned home.

Knowing that Karen was a Christian, I chose to tell her about some of my unusual experiences. One question she had for me was why I had not become a doctor. The answer was obvious. I didn't have the money.

I chose to tell her about some of my spiritual experiences, my visions, prophecies of doom and destruction, miracles, and the like. But the one that hit her was when I told her that I could see death in people's eyes.

"Oh, you can see that too?" she quipped. "Remember, I worked in veterinary hospitals for many years, thinking I would become a vet. Well, I could always look at the animals and see which were going to live and which were going to die by this strange light around their eyes. I didn't need to know what illness they had."

"Wait a minute," I responded. "You can see that in dogs and cats?"

"Sure, can't you?"

"I never thought about it and haven't had enough experiences with dying animals to know," I replied.

"But you predicted Folly would die, didn't you?" Folly was our dog that died in Midland, Texas.

"Yes, I did, but that was out of pessimism."

"But she did die, Chris. I had another interesting experience you may like to know about," Karen continued. "Remember the guy who went bumming with me across the country to witness to the world that Jesus was God?"

"How can I forget, although I never actually met him," I responded.

"Well, about two years ago, I had a dream. Richard, my friend, you know, the one who traveled across America with me, was in a dream. He was in a hospital and dying. He needed help. I was allowed to leave my body in the dream and visit him."

"You can leave your body too?" I asked.

"Yes. Can you?"

"Why, yes, I did in a dream . . . but I've never met anyone else who had that experience."

Karen looked at me as if to say "I feel your pain!"

She regained her composure and continued, "He was in a comma. I knew the room and the nurse who cared for him because I had this dream on multiple nights. I decided I needed to track him down. It took several weeks. Some nights I would leave my body and visit him, and I begged God to help him. Other nights I wouldn't. But I somehow knew Richard had no one to pray for him. He was all alone.

"Well, to make a long story short, I finally got him on the phone. I asked him how he was doing. He said he had a near brush with death and had just gotten out of the hospital. I asked about the hospital room he stayed in. He described it, and it matched my dream to perfection. I described his nurse to him . . . you know, her hair and eye color, the glasses she wore, her height and body type, and the type of hat she wore in the hospital. He couldn't believe it. I told him I was at his side many nights when he was in the hospital from the night I found out he was in trouble until the night he was healed. And I prayed for him continually, and the Lord saved him. I remember Jesus telling me that he would die without intercession, and that is why I was asked to intercede in prayer."

"What a dream," I said. "I have had similar bizarre experiences where I have left my body, and I find it difficult to confide in others and to tell others about these experiences. Thanks for sharing that with me.

"Come to think of it, there was a patient who had an appendectomy who I predicted would die in the hospital, and she indeed did die that night. The doctor did an autopsy and found nothing wrong with her. So you could be correct," I concluded.

"We agree?" Karen said.

"Then there was the girl whom I saw before she fell to her death down an elevator shaft. That had nothing to do with health. So I guess you are correct."

"Sounds like it. Wait, you saw a woman and decided she was going to die soon, and she fell down an elevator shaft? When did that happen?"

"When I was in graduate school, I saw this student who didn't have an aura at all. A few minutes later, I went to the elevator, and the doors opened but there was no elevator. The next day I saw a picture of the person who fell to their death in our elevator shaft at GSU, and it was her, the same girl I saw who was missing her aura. So there was no physical illness that could have cued me in to her impending death."

Karen just looked at me and shook her head. "By the way, I have been meaning to ask you, when you go to see eye doctors, do they freak out on you?"

"Actually, yes. This nurse was checking my eyes and dropped her instrument on the floor and ran out of the room. But when the doctor came in and checked my eyes, he said I had a flap that protected my eyes that looked like cancer, and the nurse thought I had cancer, but it actually protected my eyes to a degree."

"That happened to me last month. Only the student doctor at college dropped the instrument and got the head doctor to examine me. Same thing. I wondered if I was the only person. Perhaps that has something to do with our ability to see death in people, we may have extra sensory capabilities."

"Maybe so," I said. "Karen, this is morbid, but I had a friend who worked with me at Emory Hospital. She was a wonderful and kind nurse whom I really liked. Her name was Mary. Well, her doctor told her she had a melanoma behind her right eye. I wonder if they misdiagnosed her."

"They could have . . . so why is that morbid?"

"Because she committed suicide by sitting on a train track the day she found out."

"Ouch," Karen said. "That is tragic."

"If nothing else, that has convinced me to never commit suicide."

"Plus, suicide shows you don't have faith in God, Chris. And I don't know about you, but I want to show God I have faith no matter what."

"Agreed! But sometimes having faith is difficult, especially when bad things happen to you . . . like you are told you are about to die of cancer!"

"Chris, do you think God forgives people who commit suicide?"

"I don't know. Jesus said all sins can be forgiven. The only sin that can't be forgiven is denying or rejecting the gift of the Holy Spirit. At least that is what I believe."

Karen nodded her head in agreement.

On Suicide

Raymond Moody, in his book, *Life after Life* was asked "Have you ever interviewed anyone who has had a near death experience in association with a suicide attempt? If so, was the experience any different?

A man who was despondent about the death of his wife shot himself, "died" as a result, and was resuscitated. He states:

"I didn't go where [my wife] was. I went to an awful place....I immediately saw the mistake I had made...." I thought, "I wish I hadn't done it."

One man who had a near-death experience after an accidence said:

"[While I was over there] I got the feeling that two things it was completely forbidden for me to do would be to kill myself or to kill another person....If I were to commit suicide, I would be throwing God's gift back in his face....Killing somebody else would be interfering with God's purpose for that individual."

Sentiments like these, which by now have been expressed to me in many separate accounts, are identical to those embodied in the most ancient theological and moral argument against suicide—one which occurs in various forms in the writings of thinkers as diverse as St. Thomas Aquinas, Locke, and Kant.

God can forgive all sins. As evidence of this fact, I met a young woman at a Waffle House who tried to commit suicide and was miraculously saved. She had three young children at the time. Now she is a single Mom raising those three children and is thankful she was given another chance.

That does not mean one should put the Lord to the test.

Canoes at the Lake

My friend Chuck and I were going with a young woman named Judy to Stone Mountain to rent canoes. I used to canoe with my friend Carlton Gutschick who was on the US white-water Olympic team. Carlton taught me a great deal about white water, but we were merely going to be paddling on the lake that day. On the way to the lake, I was reminded of the book *Life After Life* and was telling Chuck and Judy about this book, and I was trying to use this as a witness to both; neither of whom really believed in God.

We rented two canoes. Judy paddled her canoe, and Chuck and I paddled the other, with me at the back of the second canoe. While we were paddling, two young boys passed by us. They were really moving, and their canoe rocked back and forth. It was apparent they didn't know what they were doing. I noticed they didn't have life preservers on, and I called out recommending they put on life preservers. I didn't want to get too far from these boys for some reason. Judy was ahead of us in a separate canoe, and the boys were between Judy and us.

Then it happened. Their boat capsized, and both boys hit the lake. It was a cold November Sunday. The wind was blowing. And swimming in the lake was life-threatening in this cold. To make matters worse, based on my lifeguard training, I realized almost immediately that neither boy knew how to swim. They were drowning! Why is it boys who can't swim will not wear life preservers while great swimmers will wear extra protection?

We pointed both boats in their direction. As we got close, I noticed Judy standing on the bow and clasping her two hands together, as if readying to dive in.

"No!" I screamed, "Don't jump in, Judy, you can save them from inside the boat better than in that cold water."

Judy sat down, and I silently thanked God. The two boys had totally disappeared below the water by now. I thought I remembered where they were but was not sure. It is difficult to pick out references in an open lake. Both boys were about fifty feet apart when they finally sunk.

Judy said, "Chris, I don't know where they went. How can I save them from the boat?"

"Put the paddle and your hand in the water where you last saw him. I'll head for this boy and help you out with the other boy in a minute."

Chuck and I paddled to where we last saw the first boy. We put our hands in the water. I felt the head of one of the boys. He grabbed my hand. And with surprising strength, I pulled him out of the water and into the middle of the boat with one yank. I thought it was a miracle that our canoe had not capsized, and I wondered where my newfound strength had come from. He turned quickly and sat down in the boat, shivering.

With one boy securely in the boat, we turned for the other. Over two minutes had passed when we pulled the first boy out. The other boy had been in the water for what seemed like ten minutes by the time we turned toward where he fell into the lake. I asked everyone to put paddles and hands in the water. The first brother suddenly grabbed his brother's hands, and in one pull, he was lying across the top of the boat, over both sides. It was a miracle that the canoe had not capsized the second time.

This boy did not move for the longest time. Then he began speaking with a shaking voice.

"Get in the boat, and sit down please," I said.

"Let me collect my thoughts first," he responded as his arms stretched in the water and legs in the water on both sides of the canoe. "The most amazing thing just happened to me. While I was under the water, I saw a light, and I began traveling through a tunnel. The next thing I knew, I was floating above you, watching you try to save me. That woman in the other boat stood up on the end of the

183

boat and was going to jump in, and you," he pointed to me, "stopped her by telling her she would drown. You then went over and pulled my brother out of the lake. You pulled him out with one pull. When you came over to me, I heard a voice say, 'It is not your time yet, go back to your body,' and about that moment, I felt someone touch my head, I grabbed his arm, and here I am."

"Maybe you heard our Lord," I said.

"I don't know what I heard, but it was amazing, whatever it was," he said.

Both boys were fine. Several people saw everything from the shore and waited for us with warm towels, and both boys were none the worse for their experience. But they did reassure me they would use life preservers in the future!

To me, this was further evidence that the book *Life after Life* was true.

Travel Abroad

As I finished graduate school, the dean of our university became my greatest advocate. Dean Black recommended me to several companies. After I graduated I learned Dean Black was my Dad's cousin. He convinced AT&T management to have a Georgia State graduate student do an internship with them. So AT&T said yes, and Dean Black recommended me for the internship. I spent several months doing a study for AT&T about the long-term viability of traditional phone lines and the impending threat of wireless phones. My recommendation was this: AT&T should spin off all their Bell carriers and only keep the long-lines and cell phone operations. As a result of my paper, I was offered a job in New York where I was to enter the executive training program. I was the first student to be offered this prestigious position that had not graduated with an MBA from Wharton or Harvard.

Oddly enough, I turned AT&T down, which was truthfully a stupid business decision, and accepted a job with Arthur Andersen consulting, which was a two-block walk from my university. Funny how things work out! After the partner offered me a job, I asked to take several months off so I could travel in Europe. I was surprised by his reaction.

He initially said, "Chris, I need you now, or I would not have hired you." But after some thought, he reconsidered and said, "Let me discuss your proposal with another partner."

He left the room, and about twenty minutes later, he returned.

"Chris, we want you on our team. You have an excellent background. But more importantly, we believe it would be a good educational opportunity if you were to go to Europe. In fact, our headquarters is in Switzerland. So after further consideration, we have decided to let you go to Europe for six months. Your starting date has been moved to June when you get back from Europe."

With that I set out on a new experience that would prove to be exciting and, indeed, educational.

All I had in the world was about three thousand dollars. I purchased round-trip airline tickets for $299 on Icelandic Airlines. I scheduled a trip to New York and called my ex-roommate Ted in hopes to see him. I arrived in New York. Ted met me, and we walked all over Manhattan. We had a delightful time. About three hours before I was supposed to fly, I went down to catch the subway to La Guardia. I stood there for forty-five minutes, and the scheduled train never arrived. Finally, the train showed up. They had taken the train offline due to some mechanical problem. I arrived forty-five minutes before the plane left. I was told they had given my ticket away fifteen minutes earlier.

"Oh my god, I'm not going to Europe, what should I do, Lord?" I thought of Paul who spoke with boldness when in trouble.

The employee who worked for Icelandic asked me, "Chris, why were you late?"

I said, "There was some mechanical problem on the subway, and the train was forty-five minutes late."

"I'm sorry to tell you, the next trip you can take is about thirty-five days from now."

I couldn't afford such a delay as I had already spent money on Euro rail passes. I began to realize the magnitude of this subway delay. I stepped away and prayed silently to myself.

The Lord said, "When in trouble, I will speak through you and for you."

I didn't think this was exactly what He meant, but after a brief prayer, I stepped forward.

"I am going to work for Arthur Andersen Consulting, one of the largest consulting firms in America. They have numerous offices in Europe, and they are a Swiss company. I will do what I can to encourage the partners there to fly Icelandic if you will help me out."

The man stepped away from the desk to speak with a supervisor. When he returned he inquired, "Chris, why were you late?"

God did not want me to lie. "I waited for the train in Manhattan to La Guardia. I arrived at the train station around 1:00 PM. The train was supposed to arrive at 1:15 PM, but it did not show up until around two o'clock. I suppose I could have tried to hail a cab, but I would have had to leave the subway station and walk above with no guarantee that I could catch a cab easily at that location and no guarantee that the cab could get here more quickly than the train."

This nice gentleman seemed to be concerned. He disappeared behind the counter for a while.

When he returned, he simply said, "Tell me where you want to fly in Europe. I will get you to Paris. You will be flying Air India. Since they do not fly directly to Paris, you may stop at any other location before you arrive in Paris."

I had prayed to go to England, where my aunt had served in the embassy for ten years. But I could not afford to fly to England and then take a separate plane to the Continent.

So I said, "How long can I stay in England if I go to London first?"

"As long as you want," he responded.

"Can I stay there two weeks?"

"Sure," he said.

I knew my prayer had been answered. But my heart couldn't take too many more of these last-second answered prayers!

He wrote up the ticket, and I disembarked on a 747 to London within two hours on Air India. Through adversity, a prayer had been answered. I couldn't believe what had just transpired.

I loved London, but it rained a lot. Out of two weeks, I only had six sunny days even though I prayed continually for sunshine. Years later my aunt said three sunny days in a week is unusual for London, so perhaps I had God's help after all.

I visited Buckingham Palace and met these extraordinarily rude men with funny hats. I asked this guy for directions three times. Not only did he not answer me but he didn't move. Apparently, they don't like Americans. I made a mental note to speak to my aunt, who personally knew the queen, about these rude servants who hated Americans. But after some thought, I decided there must have been some silly reason they didn't talk to me, because they didn't move either. Years later I learned about the Beefeaters, who are not to talk to anyone. Once again, I displayed my naïveté as I traveled through Europe!

I had heard they had a wonderful circus in London called the Piccadilly Circus, and I planned to visit this circus. I had been in a circus, and I wanted to compare the American-style circus to the British circus. I hopped on a double-decker bus and, for the first time, made my way to the top of the bus. Out of the blue, an elderly man sat right down next to me on these tight seats and began talking to me.

"I say, you must be an American."

"I am," I responded.

"Where are you headed?"

"I want to see the circus at Piccadilly."

After he chuckled, he said, "It's not a circus, Chris. But I'm sure you will enjoy the visit just the same."

We spoke for a while about England and what sights I should see. After a pleasant conversation, he said he had to get off the bus at the next stop.

Then he said, "By the way, Chris, hide your wallet, there are a lot of good pickpockets in Piccadilly Circus."

I did as the gentleman instructed.

When I got off the bus, I walked around, finding the people more interesting than the lights on the buildings. Then I noticed a place where one could play video games. I was quite good at video games. So I walked on up and began to play on one of the machines. You get lost playing these games and become unaware of what is happening around you.

About fifteen minutes later, a young guy and a pretty girl walked up to me. While the boy talked to me, his girlfriend put her hand in my back pocket. I grabbed her hand. Fortunately, my wallet was safely locked in my briefcase that was between my legs. Had I left my wallet in that pocket, I could have lost all my traveler checks, and once again the trip would have ended abruptly.

Being spiritual, I believe God often speaks to us through others. Why this man sat on an empty bus next to a young American and offered help just in the nick of time, I do not know, but I am grateful. God is in me and my family, and He calls upon me from time to time to do little things for others. I guess God worked through this nice gentleman to save me from disaster.

After a wonderful time in England, I flew to Paris and began my tour of that beautiful city. The people were difficult if you did not speak French. I knew some Spanish, but not enough to be fluent. I understood about 50 percent of what people said, but when I paused to try to interpret the other half, they just kept talking and lost me. So I found it very frustrating. I stayed in France for about a month and understood more and more of what they were saying.

Within a few days of arriving in Paris, being alone, and not being liked by the French, I became mildly depressed. I prayed to the Lord for help, for someone who could keep me company. I was riding on the Metro the next day, and a young Brit girl sat next to me. We had a delightful conversation. She was teaching English to the French children in school. She said if I needed a guide, she would be glad to take me on a tour of the city, and she left me her number.

Yes! I thought. So I called her. After waiting for about half an hour on the phone for the school to get her out of class, she came to the phone. Right away she agreed to take that Friday off and take me on a tour provided I bought her lunch and dinner. First, she took me to the Eiffel Tower, the Louvre, and the Cathedral of Notre Dame. All three were on my prayer bucket list. Jamie also spoke to the waiters, ordered for me, and suddenly the French became nice. My resolve was never to return to France again unless I spoke the language fluently.

After a few weeks travelling in Paris I realized my rental was up and it was time to move on to a new location. It was an early Sunday morning when I awoke. I had this thought, another strange thought that seemed to be from outside of me. "Get up Chris, I want you to meet an Antichrist."

"This was a strange thought," I concluded. "What are the odds I would run into the Antichrist today?" But just in case this was a thought put in my mind by the Holy Spirit, I decided to hop out of bed, comb my hair, brush my teeth, pull on a shirt and blue jeans and set out walking. The streets in Paris where I was staying were winding and cobblestone. I understood they were wound around to help police capture criminals who were trying to escape. I left the steps in front of the room I rented. I turned left and headed off walking with no specific direction. I simply wandered off.

No one. There wasn't one person anywhere. It was 7 AM on a Sunday in downtown Paris. I didn't even know if the streets I followed were safe. Then I heard a raucous cacophony of people talking as they approached from behind. I turned to see I was being followed by gypsies that must have come down that branch road on the right. Gypsies were an unsavory sort that could rob or even worse so I picked up my pace. Someone called out from behind me in French. I assumed he was speaking to me but didn't know what he was saying. Then the same person called out to me in Spanish. I walked faster. Finally, this person called out to me in English, "Hey American. Hold up a minute. I would like to talk to you." I stopped and turned.

This young man emerged from the crowd of gypsies and ran up beside me. I felt I was safe with this one person and the others simply stopped and waited. "Hey…what's your name?"

"Chris," I replied.

"Hold on Chris, let me get my friends to join us. It's OK, they work for me and you will be safe I promise."

We stood as this entourage of about twelve people joined us and surrounded us in a circle. He then began to ask me questions.

"So, where are you from and why are you visiting Europe?"

"I'm from Atlanta, Georgia and came here to see the sights and learn about Europe."

"I live in Europe. Like you I am here to be educated about the world. My friends are here for my protection. What do you think of your Government?"

"I think America is the greatest country on Earth."

"I see. I think American's are out of touch with the real world. To Europeans you are still a bit like the wild west. You don't take care of those in need. You abandon the poor. And yet you have some of the richest people on earth."

"Yes, that is true," I agreed. "But I think there is a disparity between the rich and poor everywhere."

"I believe Europeans have superior morality and can build a truly great civilization that is far better than your United States of America."

It became more and more apparent, the more I defended America the less he liked what I said. Quite frankly he had an open and hostile disdain for America and Americans. He did not want to converse, he wanted to tell me how to think. Not liking my defense of America, he said, "It's been nice meeting you Chris, but I must move on." He jogged away leaving me in the dust. As I walked in his direction, two 350-pound men emerged from the group and stepped between me and the rest of the crew and held their hands up indicating that I was to halt and stand still. I was a bit concerned but obeyed their command and stood still.

"Who is that man who I just spoke with," I asked the man on the left.

"He is a prince in his Country. He will one day be the leader of his Nation. He is in Paris to further his education, so he will one day be a better king." As this big man with a beard finished speaking, the entourage disappeared around a bend ahead. They both dropped their arms and ran ahead to catch up with their fellows leaving me standing alone wondering what just happened.

Having fulfilled the command of God, I simply turned around and headed back to my room. I packed up my things and checked out of the room. I decided to catch a train to the south. I was heading for the Riviera.

****

Did I meet the Anti-Christ, or did I meet an anti-Christ? I don't know. It was not clear to me at the time. I did not mention the name of the prince who is now a king to protect him and his country.

There is a hidden message here. After this encounter, Europe has been united, it has created a single currency, and it has created a Constitution. This Constitution has been created by men who believe they can make a more just civilization than one founded on the principles and teachings of God. Attempts throughout history by men to create great nations apart from God have always failed.

On the other hand, America, with all its flaws, was founded by men who were devoutly religious, who believed and feared God and who tried their best to create a new nation based on the laws of God. That is the reason I defended America to this Prince.

Europe will probably be the final beast spoken of in the Revelation. If it is, the leader of that reunited Nation made up of clay and iron toes may indeed be the true Anti-Christ. Could it be this man? Possibly. But my takeaway from this chance encounter is not to indict him, but to be wise as a serpent and gentle as a dove, and to keep a watchful eye on the developments in Europe.

*****

I specifically wanted to go to Nice, France, a little town on the Riviera, and I especially wanted to visit the Monte Carlo Casino, but I had no idea where it was. I hopped on a train, which was free as I had a Euro rail pass. The countryside in France reminded me of America. The farmland was beautiful. After a pleasant ride, I arrived in Monaco. Having heard of Monaco, I decided to disembark and check out the scenery. Monaco is tiny. But then I stumbled on this strange building that backed up on the Riviera. I wanted to see the scenery, so I entered the building, and to my surprise, I was in Monte Carlo. How's that for God answering prayers, I thought. The casino was really small. But the view from the balcony in the back was breathtaking. While standing there, an Aussie started talking to me.

"Hey, mate, what are you doing?"

"Well, I'm on vacation, and I'm traveling through Europe to see the sights."

"Me too," he said succinctly.

"Are you staying nearby?"

"Well, I was planning on going to Nice and staying in a youth hostel there."

"Well, mate, I just came from there, and I'll be happy to show you the way. Plus, it's nice to talk to someone who speaks English. Are you up for dinner?"

"Sure, why not," I said.

So the two of us went to the station, we hopped on a rail, and we headed for Nice. It was even more beautiful than I imagined. I wanted to walk on the beach. The two of us headed down to this rocky beach and walked on the water's edge.

We had a delightful chat as we walked on the rocks. We took off our shoes, and the water lapped over our feet as we walked in the Mediterranean. At one point I heard some talk, and not knowing that people were sitting in chairs to our left, I looked up and saw a row of twenty naked people. Then this nearly perfectly shaped woman leaned forward as she looked at me. Naturally, I stumbled, flipped over on my back in the water, and received a nice applause. I think they were saying something like, "Stupid American."

I ultimately rented a room in an apartment. A French grandmother let me stay in a bedroom, and I paid her by the week. She liked me. Every night when I came home, I prayed to God for help and guidance the next day and thanked Him for the day that just passed. When I left her apartment, she cried, hugged me, and thanked me for the blessing I brought to her home. She then confided that she listened to my prayers every night.

*****

It is fun to travel when you travel with someone you love or care about. Traveling alone is difficult. There is no one to share your discoveries with, no one to talk to, and no one to spoil, whether it is a wife or children. I felt so alone I prayed to travel with a beautiful woman, someone I could possibly get close to, even kiss. I decided to visit Luxembourg the next day so I could sleep on the train. This is a tiny nation that is the size of a small city. I had heard they had a wonderful youth hostel, and they liked Americans.

When I arrived, I checked into the youth hostel! I signed the paperwork and paid for the night just as a group of Americans headed out. Apparently, they were gathering to go get dinner in town. So I asked a friendly guy if I could join them, and he said, "Sure, why not, we're going to get some beer and sing a few songs."

It sounded like fun, so I followed the crowd. We entered a bar, ordered beer, and sang German songs. This beautiful and friendly blond named Jennifer sat a couple of seats down from me. She was a flirt. She flirted with all the men, and they all died inside. She was unquestionably the center of attention, and everyone loved her.

After singing German songs and drinking beer, the crowd broke up. I simply followed the crowd back to the youth hostel but wound up outside a residential flat. When we arrived, I made a point of talking to Jennifer. She asked me questions about where I was from and what I did.

I told her I had just graduated with an MBA from Georgia State and had accepted a job at Arthur Andersen consulting in Atlanta. This girl was so beautiful she was a distraction as I would forget what I was saying when I looked into her eyes.

After a while, Jennifer sat down and I sat down on the steps next to her. I really liked her, and she seemed to like me. So we continued to talk well into the night. Slowly everyone disappeared, leaving Jennifer alone with me.

After this trip to Luxemburg, I planned on traveling to Pompeii to see the streets and possibly some of the ash remains that were in the shape of people and dogs.

I said, "Hey, Jennifer, I am traveling to Italy tomorrow, and I plan on going to Pompeii to see the ruins. Would you like to join me?"

It seemed like a ridiculous request, but English-speaking people that stay in youth hostels often partner up and travel together for company.

Jennifer smiled politely and said, "Chris, I can't go with you, I'm sorry."

I said, "Don't you want to run away with me?"

She smiled, pushed me away gently, and said, "No . . . I can't, silly."

She then stood up, took out a key, and opened the door to the flat we sat in front of that evening. So that was her place that everyone had gathered around, and we were sitting on "her steps." I had no idea. I thought she was staying at the youth hostel with everyone else.

"Come in, Chris," she said.

I stepped into this little flat, and oh my god, it was huge.

As we stepped into the house, she said, "Chris, I can't go with you because I'm the reigning Ms. America."

I laughed. "And I'm the reigning Mr. America," I said sarcastically.

"Silly boy . . . I really am, and this is where I stay when I am in Europe."

I didn't believe her. Jennifer said, "Kay, are you here?"

A woman appeared around the corner and walked up to us. I guessed it was her mother.

"Kay, tell Chris who I am please."

"Odd she called her mother Kay," I thought.

Kay looked at me to size me up. "What do you do, Chris?"

"I just graduated from graduate school in business."

"What does your father do?"

"He was a psychiatrist."

She then took a very formal pose and said, "Jennifer is the reigning Ms. America, Chris. This is her European home. And I am her assistant."

"Oh," I said with a mixture of embarrassment and confusion. Who was I to ask Ms. America to travel to Pompeii? I felt ashamed. I bit my lower lip and said, "I'm sorry, Jennifer. I didn't know."

She looked like she was evaluating me and said, "Kay, Chris asked me to go to Pompeii with him in Italy. I told him I can't go. I'm sorry, Chris."

Kay said, "Perhaps you can."

"No, I can't," she replied, and I was politely shoved out the front door with the door closing behind me.

I deserved worse, I thought. But I wasn't mortally wounded, so I returned to the youth hostel, climbed up on the top bunk, and went to sleep.

Around 7:00 AM the next morning, I heard some woman talking loudly as she entered the youth hostel.

"Hello, I'm looking for Chris Morris." That woke me up. "Hello, Chris, are you in there?"

Another voice of a woman, "He's in the men's dormitory. This is the women's dormitory."

"I see. Where is the men's dormitory please?"

"Across the hall."

Next thing you know, a woman walks right into our room of bunk beds. One poor guy was naked and was trying to put on his underwear when this beautiful woman strolled in unabashed. She was wearing an overcoat with the collar pulled up, a hat on her head, and she was wearing big sunglasses. Who wears sunglasses inside a dormitory with the lights turned off? Who else but . . .

"Jennifer?" I said as I sat up.

"There you are, Chris! Get up and get dressed. Let's go, we're going to Italy together."

"Of course," I said. "Could you wait outside please while I get ready?"

Getting the message, she said, "I'll just step outside and wait for you."

Boy, when God answers prayers, He really answers prayers, I thought. *Talk about a beautiful woman. You really answer prayers, don't You, Lord!* I got up, dressed, and headed for the door. Jennifer was so beautiful I was distracted by her as I asked her what changed her mind.

She said, "Kay told me I should go. She said I needed to just have some fun and get away from the daily responsibilities. I put on this coat, pulled up the collar, and put on a hat and sunglasses so the paparazzi don't recognize me. Pretty good camouflage, don't you think?" She even put gloves on her hands. "Let's go."

After hearing all the ways paparazzi can ruin your life if you are Ms. America, we arrived in Milan, Italy, where we were to change trains to go to Pompeii. Instead, she decided we should spend the day walking and talking in Milan. As the evening arrived, I asked her if she wanted to stay in a hostel. She said no. She wanted to stay in a hotel.

Jennifer and I got adjoining rooms, and before we went to bed, she knocked on the adjoining door and gave me a sweet kiss. She closed the door. A little while later, I decided to be romantic, so I knocked on the door. It took awhile, but Jennifer finally opened the door.

Jennifer asked, "May I help you . . . ?" Before she finished speaking, I stepped in her room, grabbed her around the waist, and kissed her firmly on the lips.

"Finally, Lord, thank You for Jennifer and this kiss," I thought, as I got more and more passionate.

After a few minutes of passionate kissing, Jennifer pushed me away. "Chris, stop! I can't . . . please stop," she said.

Her words didn't match her passion as she held my body against her and kissed me. There was a real disconnect between her words and her behavior.

I stopped. I was a little out of control . . . Okay, I was a lot out of control. I admit it. But I couldn't understand why Jennifer was so upset.

She summarily dismissed me, saying, "Get out!" And I returned to my room, and the door slammed behind me.

The next day, wow, she lectured me. Not that I didn't deserve it. But she really let into me for getting so fresh.

"Okay, I deserve it," I said. "I was clearly out of line. But all I did was kiss you, Jennifer. We didn't do anything else."

She continued to let me have it for my romantic behavior the night before and kept saying she was Ms. America and couldn't get involved. The scathing was pretty rough! Even the waiter told me he felt sorry for me when I paid the bill.

After we finished coffee, Jennifer demanded I take her to the train station and put her on the train so she could go home, which I was glad to do by now.

*****

In hindsight, God answered my prayer to have someone beautiful travel with me that day. Despite the grief I received, there was a happy ending to this story. I could not afford to stay in the high-priced European hotel with Jennifer. Two or three more nights at high-end hotels might have broken the bank. As it was, when I left Europe, I had less than $10 in my pocket. My credit cards didn't work in Europe, and my family would not help. I was literally on my own.

God also gave me a replacement for Jennifer. Later that day I accidentally ran into these two beautiful girls . . . the daughter of a famous movie star and her best friend. Both traveled with me throughout Italy.

*****

There is another miracle hidden in this story. At LaGuardia airport, the day I flew to Europe, I decided to buy $3,000 in traveler's checks before I left.

The banker asked me, "Would you like your traveler's checks denominated in dollars or pounds?"

"Pounds?" I asked.

"Of course, Barclays is a British bank, so our currency is pounds, not dollars."

"And you can denominate the traveler's checks in dollars or pounds?"

"Or any other European currency," he added.

"What about Swiss francs?"

"Would you like your traveler's checks denominated in Swiss Francs?"

I thought for a minute. Swiss francs were probably the best currency to hold in the world according to Professor Williams. He said the Swiss currency consistently outperformed the dollar and other European currencies.

This is almost humorous because that is not always true . . . Although in general the Swiss franc has been a strong currency, it could also drop like a rock against other currencies. So let's call it a happy accident that I chose Swiss francs as the currency for my traveler's checks. Happy accident or an accident guided by God? Who knows for sure.

I arrived home with less than $10 in my pocket. I believe the Swiss franc went up more than 15 percent against the dollar during that fateful trip. Fifteen percent of $3,000 divided by 2 is hundreds of dollars. I would have certainly run out of money if I hadn't happened to walk into that Barclay's Bank just outside of LaGuardia before I left for Europe. And a few more nights with Princess America probably would have broken the bank. So Jennifer did me another favor I didn't appreciate at the time.

By the way, one of the reasons I was late to my flight was I bought the traveler's checks before I got to the airport. Had I been on time, I never would have been able to fly to England. Another happy accident to some, but an answer to prayer to me!

*****

Before my mother was married, her dad we called Dee took her to Europe to visit family. I believe Dee took her to Europe to enjoy his last trip with his only daughter, whom he loved and whom he wanted to spoil one last time before she was married. They took a cruise ship to Europe, and they spent a full month traveling throughout Europe. My mother's favorite experience was her visit to Copenhagen. She talked about Tivoli dozens of times in my life, and she would always say she saw the aurora borealis, or northern lights, there. Knowing this, before I left for Europe, I prayed to God and asked Him if I could ride on the Ferris wheel in Tivoli and if I could please see the northern lights while I was there.

Here I was in Copenhagen. I was by myself, yes, but I was in the city. First thing I did when I arrived at the hostel was ask where Tivoli was. After getting directions, I headed there at dusk. Amazingly, I was not only able to ride the one Ferris wheel, but as I got off the ride, I looked up into the sky and I saw the northern lights. This was unusual. It was late April, and I had been told it was too late to see the aurora borealis.

I stopped cold when I saw the lights and marveled at the depth of the layers of colors hanging in the sky above me that were moving to and fro through the night sky, changing colors as they moved. People were trying to pass me on the trail, and there I stood, eyes fixated on the sky. Then I realized I had ridden the same Ferris wheel my mother and grandfather had ridden so many years before, and I got to see the aurora borealis just as my mother had described it.

I put my right hand on my face to wipe away the tears. I missed my mother and for the first time since her death realized how much I loved her and how much I missed her and my dad.

I Start Work at Arthur Andersen Consulting

I t was 1980, and I was starting my first full-time career since graduate school. At Arthur Andersen, I was to be a staff consultant. Working out of the Atlanta office, they would send me all over the United States to do different jobs. My first assignment was in Atlanta in the very hospital where the psychologist tried to push me out of the window. Worse, our offices were across from the morgue in the basement. That bothered me for a day or two, but then I got over it and got down to business. We were designing an accounts receivable system to help with medical billings and collections for Grady Hospital. I was an analyst that would help in designing and writing the computer routines.

To get to and from work, I would take the newly built Marta rail system from a station near my home to downtown Atlanta and walk to the hospital. One day I got off Marta and was walking to the hospital when someone called my name.

"Chris . . . hey, Chris."

I turned. I was a lowly staff person, and here was the manager in charge of the job calling me. I turned around and waited for Steve to join me.

He laughed and said, "Hi, Chris, I didn't know you took the train to work each day."

"Parking is a nightmare down here, Steve. I found it was easier to ride than drive."

"Me too," Steve said.

Steve was sort of an introvert and often didn't talk much, and we had to walk about five blocks to work.

My thoughts turned to a problem I had been trying to solve. I had been trying to unlock some prophetic verses in the Bible that I believed applied to us, living in the twentieth century, and I wanted Steve's opinion on my interpretation of prophecy.

I said, "Steve, I was thinking about computers and their connectivity."

Steve didn't say anything.

"I thought it would be neat if computers could be connected so that we could use that connectivity to buy things and sell things. If every person had a computer or access to a computer, imagine the power they would have and imagine how much money businesses would make if the businesses and maybe even individuals could buy things directly through computers that were somehow hooked together."

Steve didn't say anything. We continued walking, and I figured he thought it was a stupid idea.

Then he said abruptly, "But everyone doesn't have a computer."

This was 1980, and Steven Jobs had just invented the Apple computer a few years ago. The IBM PC was not yet released. Most of the large corporations had computers or were in the process of buying computers, but PCs and networking had not even been thought of at the time.

"No, people don't have computers," I said, "but I figure they will in the future. Technology just keeps improving. Simply put, I think computers could be linked together into some type of connected system like phones are connected through wires and that they could talk to each other, allowing us to buy things without going to a store."

"Chris," Steve said with a chuckle, "I think that is a good idea. I think that is a great idea. I might even mention it to William, our partner on the job."

By this time, we entered the hospital front door and went our separate ways to work.

A couple of months passed, and Steve stopped by my cubicle and said, "Hey, Chris, William liked your idea of connecting computers together and brought it up at the annual partnership meeting.

They liked your idea and assigned a couple of our best technical guys to spend a year studying your idea. What do you think of that?"

"Excuse me, did you say something?" I was working on a problem and not paying close attention to Steve. I pushed back from my desk and focused my eyes on Steve's face.

"You know . . . your idea for computer networking . . . to have computers connect together so different people can talk to each other through their computers and even buy things from businesses through a computer system?"

"Oh yeah, they liked that crazy idea?"

"Yeah, they are going to see if it is feasible. The partnership has ordered a study to see if this is possible. I'll keep you posted."

Just as quickly as Steve appeared, he disappeared. I didn't hear anything more about that for another year.

Shashi Calls

When Shashi left Atlanta, he asked me, our friends Deleep and Sunder, to be his best men at the wedding, which we were glad to do. Jennifer was a sweet young woman and was a good match for Shashi's personality. I was happy for him. Immediately after marrying her, he moved to Allentown, Pennsylvania, where he took a job with Air Products and Chemicals. This company was truly fortunate to hire such a brilliant man.

Shashi moved out of our apartment, and we said our goodbyes. We stayed in touch. Everything seemed to be going well for him. Then one day, when I was working, I received a phone call from Shashi. He tracked me down and said simply, "Chris, Jennifer is dead." It was 1984. They had not been married five years, and she was gone. I was shocked. Shashi was devastated.

I was so thankful that Shashi called me to tell me, but I was perplexed as he stayed on the line and asked me a lot of questions. Then the underlying reason for his phone call emerged. Shashi felt I talked with God. He knew about Jesus and feared Jesus, because he thought Jesus was my God. Depressed, he wanted to know if he should continue working where he was or if he should do something different. He felt that he had made a strategic error in his life by not asking me and having me intercede in prayer for him before he moved to Allentown.

"Chris, what should I do with my life?" There were tears on the other end of the line. "I hate living here without Jennifer. I am lost."

"I don't know what you should do, Shashi . . . Could you hold on a minute?"

I stepped away from the phone. I closed my eyes and prayed to God for direction. After a few moments, I took a deep breath and picked up the phone again.

"Shashi, you should move home to be with your mother. Take your children, and raise them up the way you were raised. Trust Jesus, Shashi . . . After a few years, when you feel better, you can return and work in America if you like, or you can stay in India. God will lead you if you ask Him and trust Him."

"Thank you, Chris. I really appreciate your help."

"Shashi, don't thank me. You know me too well. I believe Jesus led me to say that, and I feel that is from Him because He loves you. If you get to Atlanta, please come visit me."

"And you visit me in India anytime, Chris."

The phone call ended as we politely said our goodbyes, and I went back to work.

Two Years Later Working as a Consultant

By this time, I was working on three different job sites and would return to Atlanta to fix a problem with the computer system we designed for a large corporation. While working on-site with another client, I met a woman named Beth. She worked for the VP of Operations. Everyone was afraid of her. I had only seen her from a distance, and I learned to steer clear of this woman. One day I heard a woman's voice. She was behind me, trying to get my attention. I turned and saw the feet of a woman in high heels and straps.

I recognized her feet immediately and thought to myself, "I'm going to marry this woman, and I haven't even seen her face."

I looked up. She was incredibly beautiful. She seemed to like me, and she flirted with me. After the first day we met, she often came by to see me and chat with me. She did a lot of small talk while I tried to work. Something told me not to deal with this beautiful woman. If we continued talking, I would wind up married to her, and I wasn't ready to get married yet. In truth I was scared to death of her. But before I knew it, I found myself out with a group of women and men from the office, and they suddenly all left, and there I was alone with Beth. I had been set up by Beth. I tried to control my passions. I tried to shake her. But we continued to see each other. Arthur Andersen had a strict policy. We weren't supposed to date clients. But this was nothing I planned. It just happened. And I continually told Beth that those were not dates; we were just being friends.

Then out of the blue, I received a strange job offer. Someone called me at my hotel and tried to hire me. I did not leave a résumé with anyone; he simply got my name. Fred asked me to interview for a job. Why not, it was a free world, and he was offering to take me to lunch. I tried to blow the interview, but he offered me a job anyway. I had difficulty turning him down. He called back a week later and offered the job again. He said he really felt I was perfect for the job. I said no.

A week later, I went to dinner with the Arthur Andersen partner William. I had been promoted to senior consultant, and I worked directly for William now. We were working with a utility company in Pensacola, Florida.

"Hey, Chris," William said, "they completed the study on computer connectivity that you recommended."

"Really, I heard you had two geniuses studying my idea . . . I heard they were super-duper tech guys, am I right?"

"That's right. And they concluded that computers are not powerful enough to connect into this network thing you recommended. One company I work for just bought 1K of memory for over $1 million last month. Memory is everything, and the cost of memory is just too expensive for computers to be used in that manner."

I nodded. In hindsight 1K of memory is 1,000 bytes. One meg of memory is 1,000,000 bytes. Today my phone has far more memory than the largest IBM mainframe had at the time. My laptop has more memory than the NASA space command center had when they landed on the moon.

William added, as he took a drink from his glass, "Chris, these guys concluded that computers were not and will probably never be powerful enough to hook up together, although your idea was impressive. Actually, I thought it was brilliant, and so did the other partners, they really liked your idea and wanted to know how you came up with it."

I hesitated. I wondered how William would take my response. I decided I had good rapport with him, so I said, "I know this sounds a bit odd, but I have been studying Bible prophecy, and in the Bible, it says 'an image, some translate image to be a statue, will speak and control whether people can buy or sell.' The way I figure it is these prophets must have been talking about a computer. What else could they mean by a 'statue or image that speaks.' I figure it must be some type of futuristic computer. Then they say this computer can control whether you buy or sell. So that's where my idea originated."

William's reaction was not what I expected. "That's the stupidest thing I ever heard in my life." He was really upset with me. "Had I known you got that idea out of the Bible, I never would have recommended it to the partnership. And I'm sure the partners would never have authorized the study."

"Consider this, though," I replied. "I dated a girl whose dad was the senior VP for Univac Sperry Rand. He was asked to go to Belgium to help come up with the bar code. He told Terry, his daughter, that they decided to create a code that would have the same bar code image two times side by side so the scanner could read the bar code twice, and if it read the same thing, it would know it had scanned the code correctly."

"You know this guy?"

"No, I don't know him, I just dated his daughter. He had divorced her mother and remarried since then." I paused, and William nodded as he had been married twice. "Anyway, they needed a delimiter that would tell the scanner to begin reading, to end reading, and reread the code a second time and to end the code a second time . . . Call it a comma or period to divide the two codes. See here," I said, holding up a ketchup bottle on the table. "That bar code starts with two thin lines, has two thin lines in the middle, and two thin lines at the end. The two thin lines are also the number 6."

"That is exactly how the bar code works, Chris."

William is an expert on computers, so I was not surprised that he understood this concept.

"Well, anyway, Marvine, Terry's mom, was a very devout Christian. She talked to her husband about the Bible and said the computer was the beast and its code number was 666, as stated in the Bible. As a spoof on his wife, he got the team in Belgium to use the number 6 as the delimiter in the bar code. Three 6s are in every bar code, one at the beginning, one in the middle, and one at the end, and I felt that was confirmation that a computer could be that speaking image or statue."

William was clearly uncomfortable talking about the Bible, so I dropped the subject. My thoughts continued about the subject for a while. At the time, 666 only referred to the bar code that everyone in the world adopted, thanks in part to Terry's dad.

*****

He causes all, both small and great, rich and poor, free and slave, to receive a mark on their right hand or on their foreheads, and that no one may buy or sell except one who has the mark or the name of the beast, or the number of his name.

Here is wisdom. Let him who has under-standing calculate the number of the beast, for it is the number of a man: His number *is* 666. (Revelation 13:16–18)

As the Lord has taken me on my life's journey, I have become a Messianic Jew and spent a good part of my time studying Judaism and Hebrew. During the process I learned that the ancients did not have numbers as the Jews do today. They simply used their alphabet and the order of their alphabet for numbers. In English *A* would be 1; *B* would be 2; *C*, 3; *D*, 4; and so on and so forth. The number 666 would represent the Hebrew letter "vav, vav, vav" the sixth letter of the Hebrew alphabet. There is no letter *w* in Hebrew, but the letter *v* and *w* are considered interchangeable. So when one surfs the World Wide Web in Israel, they type in www.address.com. If I am right, the biblical reference to the number 666 may also refer to www, or World Wide Web.

*****

As the night progressed, William kept drinking. He was quite upset and getting to be quite looped. He then said it was his son's birthday that day, and he couldn't make it home because of work. He added he had missed his anniversary a month earlier because of hard work. Yes, he was a millionaire, but he would do anything to leave the partnership. He was just too highly paid to get a job anywhere else.

The remainder of that evening was quite awkward. We ate dinner, and I went back to my hotel room and planned to go to bed and never bring up the Bible to any Arthur Andersen employee again. I also concluded my interpretation of prophecy might be wrong and could just be a silly idea. If our top computer experts say computers can't be connected, I guess I had to accept their expert opinion. Perhaps I had to reevaluate my interpretation of this prophetic scripture after all.

I felt depressed. I had also found out the average partner dies in their fifties. This man lived the ideal partner life and was miserable. Then I had turned Fred down twice when he offered me a job this past week. What were the chances he would call back?

Lord, I thought. *I now believe I was to take the job with Fred, if he ever calls back.*

In fifteen minutes the phone rang. It was Fred. And this time I accepted his job offer.

This freed me up to date Beth, without fear of retribution from the partnership. I no longer had to pretend we weren't dating when we were dating. But I was still frightened by her, and falling hopelessly in love with her, though I fought the feelings with all my might. I thought I could still resist her, even though I knew the game was over.

"Checkmate!" I thought.

Funny how things work out. Beth was a woman who lived in Macon and had moved to Atlanta. When I was thirteen, the Lord told me I would marry a girl in Atlanta named Beth. I now wondered if He was referring to this beautiful blond whom I was now thinking about marrying.

I Leave the Consulting World and Work for Fred

Fred was born in Italy. He had been raised a Catholic. I liked Fred. His wife was a wonderful Christian, except she was a bit competitive in worldly terms. Fred taught me everything I needed to know to survive in big corporations. Remember, Shashi came along at the right time to teach me how to be an excellent student. And Fred came along at the right time to teach me how to be successful in the business world.

One day Fred came to the office and was gravely depressed. I knew that something was wrong. So being an employee and a friend, I went into Fred's office, closed the door, and asked him if I could help. Fred looked like he was holding back tears.

"My wife, Janie," he said, "just had a miscarriage. We so much want another child! I don't know what to do."

"Fred, I am so sorry." All I could do was be a friend. But I added, "I'll pray for you."

Fred said, "I don't believe in God."

"Fred, I assure you there is a God, and if you want a child, God will give you one if you ask Him." Fred was incredulous, and it was the wrong thing to say at that time.

After Fred had time to recover from the loss, he came to me and asked me about God.

Fred was critical of the Catholic religion. He said, "You confess to a priest and can do anything you want. Pay enough money to the church and you were guaranteed a place in heaven. This was not a God I want to worship," he said.

There it was! This was my cue to help Fred.

"Fred," I began. "Jesus is God. Read what Jesus says, not what people say about Him. He is not the Catholic church, He is not the Baptist church, He is not the Methodist or Presbyterian church, He is God! I want you to understand, if Jesus is not God, what are we doing wasting our time worshipping Him? But if He is God, is not everything He tells us the truth? I think you will be shocked to find out what Jesus really says. We are to love God with all our heart and mind and soul. And we are to love our neighbor as ourselves.

"And I believe it goes something like this. The church, the believers are not the heads or leaders of organized religion. The church are those who hear God's will and obey Him! We are all hypocrites. But the true church tries with all their heart, mind, and strength to obey Christ and do His bidding. If they fall short, they repent, pick themselves up, and don't make the same mistake twice. They are on a quest to totally serve Christ in all things. But Jesus then says the most fantastic thing when He essentially says, 'If you believe in Me and keep My law, I will do whatever you ask of Me.' So if you believe and are obedient, then all that is left to do is to ask Him for help. I promise, He will do whatever you want Him to do, provided it is consistent with His law and His will."

I knew this would be perceived as unbelievable to an intellectual, which Fred was. Fred was brilliant and sophisticated. I could not logic him into believing in God. So I simply turned him over to God.

But to my surprise, something I said might have resonated with him. He made fun of me; another man in the office chimed in; and a second man, who was a Baptist, took my side. We lost every intellectual argument that we had with the nonbelievers. I could not overcome Fred's logic. But there was someone working Fred from the other side . . . his dear wife, Janie. Janie loved the Lord very much. And she prayed daily for Fred. Finally, and to my surprise, Fred confided in me one more time. He called me into his office.

"Chris," Fred began. "The doctor says Janie has so much damage that she can't possibly have children. There is no way possible. But all I want is one more child. We have two sons, and we want a daughter. Do you really believe Jesus can help us?"

"Yes, I do, Fred. All things are possible through God. Jesus said that again and again. I will pray for you. And I know if you believe Jesus will help you, and if you commit your life to Him, you will have the daughter you want."

Was I losing my mind? I knew I read Jesus's words and believed this is what He said, but I also knew I believed in Jesus no matter what happened to Fred and Janie and their "hoped-for" baby. If I was wrong, this would be a disaster. Fred and Janie both had to believe, and they had to repent, and they had to do His will. What were the odds?

Fred said he began to pray to God for help. He took me up on my challenge, and he and Janie began to trust Christ for a child. And to the doctor's amazement, Janie got pregnant. And Fred was a near basket case for the next few months. He was horrified. He tried to hide it, but the doctors told Janie that while it was impossible for her to get pregnant, it was even more impossible for her to deliver a healthy baby. I told Fred to trust Christ. Hang in there. God could do anything. And I ran in the corner and prayed, wondering who was inserting these words in my mouth, because it was as if someone else was speaking through me.

Remember, my father was a doctor, my mother a nurse, and there was no one I held in higher esteem than physicians and nurses. And here I was saying these experts didn't know what they were talking about. Clearly an alien of some sort was possessing me, because that just didn't sound like me.

Within a year, Janie gave birth to a beautiful baby girl named Sandy. I was at the hospital with Fred that wonderful day. Fred couldn't open the double doors without my help. I wondered what was going on inside his head as his wife gave birth. It was like Fred's logical brain shut down.

So what happens to men when their wives give birth? Husbands are spiritually connected to their wives. One could understand this happening to the woman who is giving birth, but the man, it just doesn't make sense. Unless we understand the man's spirit and the wife's spirit are so intimately connected that as she is, so is he. He somehow feels her pain and stress, and he doesn't have to be in the same room with her. You see, he loves her, and he is spiritually connected to her, and he really feels her pain in a spiritual way. That's why doctors tell the men to go boil water. Personally, I think they shouldn't be allowed near sharp or hot objects, but while they stand over the water and wait for it to boil, they become preoccupied.

God had given this man named Fred and his wife, Janie, a beautiful baby girl that day named Sandy! Now I know why the seraphim continually sings "Kadosh, kadosh, kadosh [holy, holy, holy] is the Lord our God, King of the Universe." I couldn't have been happier, and once again, the Lord stretched my faith. Blessed be His holy name!

Who is this God, Jesus? Was He just a man Who was crucified on a cross? This man was a loser by any worldly definition. He was hated and killed by His government. He was hated by the religious leaders of His time. Yet others proclaimed He was the risen Messiah and God with us! But here is the most incredible piece of this puzzle. The events that transpired in Fred and Janie's life proved to me Jesus is still alive.

My Wife

I knew I was in love with Beth. Fred thought she was especially beautiful at a Halloween party where she painted her face green, her lips were bright red, and she wore a sheer black witch's gown over black leotards. But the woman I loved was no witch; she was a saint to me, and she loved me.

Beth and I were married at an uneventful wedding. Fewer than twenty people were there. Beth's family—which consisted of her parents, three brothers, two sisters, and their spouses and children—were there. My best friend Carlton was my best man. And that was it. No one else from my family showed up at our wedding.

We bought a nice house in the suburbs. I worked, and Beth worked long hours. We were active in our church. I became a deacon and treasurer of my church.

Almost miraculously, I was promoted up the ladder in the business world. Fred and I left the insurance company we worked for and moved to the very company where Beth worked. The president of this multinational business told me he planned on making me the next president of that company. He had me attend meetings with him, but I was not allowed to say anything in the meetings. I could only observe.

I worked with Fred to write two S-1 registration statements so the company could be split into three different businesses and all three would be separately traded on the NYSE.

I had been involved in writing a capital expenditure request to build a multimillion-dollar cable plant in five states in the northeastern United States. I was told by Bill, the president of our company—which was one of the fastest-growing companies on Wall Street—that I was to go up there, visit the different facilities, join the news broadcasts team on the set, visit, and view the cable plant maintenance operations and hobnob with executives that lived in the north. The last and the most important thing I was instructed to do was meet with a mysterious man at an Italian restaurant on the Rhode Island coast.

Having completed all the other assignments, I showed up at this small Italian restaurant and sat there alone and waited. A man showed up after about fifteen minutes and asked if I was Chris Morris. I said I was. He sat down at the table across from me. He asked me a lot of personal questions about my life and my background.

I answered them by saying "Yes, sir."

Obviously, this was an extremely important man, and I was quite nervous as we spoke. After a while, he got up and hugged me. Then he said, "Chris, you're a good boy." I was twenty-nine at the time. "You remind me of my son. I think we can work together. You tell those boys in Atlanta that they will get the votes they need to supply cable television in all five states."

I was confused. Before this trip I was nervous about whether we could carry three or more states votes and win their authorization to put cable television in their homes. If we had three or fewer states approve our bid, we would lose money . . . four or five, and we would make money. I wondered what the odds were that we could carry the votes in four or five states. God forbid we only won one state as that could bankrupt us.

"Did I hear you correctly, sir? Did you say you could somehow get all five states to accept our bid?"

"Yes, you did, Chris."

"Excuse me, sir, but how can you do that?"

"That is my problem and not yours to worry about. Now let's talk about you."

This blew my mind. Who was this Italian man that he had the power to get a bid approved in all five states, even if it was not the low bid?

Then he added, "I like you, Chris. I think you're a bright young man. I want you to be the chief financial officer of our company. Don't you think you should be made an officer?"

"Well, of course."

"Good, because you will be my CFO, Chris!"

And with that, this nice gentleman shook my hand and left me standing there, wondering what just happened.

When I got back to Atlanta, I talked to Fred about him. Fred had been a manager at a big 8 accounting firm and previously was a major in the Army. He had a great deal of experience in business matters that I lacked.

He said, "Chris, he must be the head of one of the families."

"Families?"

"Yes, Italian Mafia. Apparently, they have the power to get the needed votes."

Within a month, I had received word that we had won the bid in all five states. I was called into Bill's . . . our president's office.

Bill said, "Chris, I wanted to congratulate you. I am making you chief financial officer of our media company, congratulations."

I paused to take in what I just had been told. Then I said, "Bill, who was that Italian man I met with who said he could get all five states to vote in favor of our bid?"

Bill remained silent.

"Was he Mafia?"

"You can't do business in the Northeast without their approval."

"Bill, I don't feel comfortable working for the Mob. My Lord is Jesus Christ, and I don't think He would approve. I'm sorry, but I must respectfully turn down this promotion."

"Chris, I'm sorry to hear that, but I understand. I will give you some time to look for another job."

And in a minute, my joy turned into concern. Bill looked very concerned. But Bill was a good man and a Christian, so I felt . . . I mean, I hoped I wouldn't be murdered by refusing to work with the Mob.

It is funny how God operates. I am sure Bill was correct when he said we couldn't win the bids without their help. There is the power we see, and then there is the real power behind the scenes. I learned that from my dad when he worked in Washington. I also learned the CIA did some terrible things to defend American freedom, and I had concluded I couldn't work for our CIA even though their goal was for the greater good. I suppose Bill and our company had to do what they had to do to survive.

I was certainly not their judge. I understood completely what was going on. I had just made a commitment to my Lord that required me to be righteous in all things, and I could not reconcile these two worlds. Not that I was their judge, not that I thought I was better than them, and not that I felt they couldn't go to heaven.

I had simply chosen a different course for my life. I had chosen to completely dedicate my life to following Christ. And to do that, I felt I couldn't be beholden to another god or leader who might have me act against my Lord's teachings.

Then reality set in. How was I going to break this news to my wife?

It wasn't easy. Beth was upset. I had walked away from a path that could have easily led to my becoming president of a multibillion-dollar company. My wife was a Christian, but I believe she didn't see the problem I saw.

I prayed about this at length and fasted. I needed another job and fast. I told the Lord I didn't want to send out a résumé. Then out of the blue, Fred, who knew I needed a job, referred me to a man who was looking for a corporate controller. Within two weeks Ken, the Senior VP of the insurance holding company, hired me. Once again God found the perfect job for me given my skill level. I believe the Lord uses His children to help others. My help came from my friend Fred who had recently experienced a miracle when his wife Janie gave birth to a baby girl. Isn't God amazing?

Giving a Gift to Disney

When I first met Beth, we took several nice trips to places like the Cayman Islands on my frequent flyer miles I had accumulated. But the one place she loved to visit above all others was Disneyworld. If Beth married me, it was probably her love for Epcot that sealed the deal. Then when we had children, we took several amazing trips to Disney. My wife was so happy when we went there I wanted to repay them in some way, such as a recommendation to make an improvement here or there.

When I worked for Fred at an insurance company, I was often asked to eat lunch with the same group of people. Typically, four or five of us would walk to a nearby restaurant. The conversation centered around sports typically. We never talked about business. To my amazement, these executives of our insurance company knew the ERAs of the pitchers of the Braves. They knew who the best choices in the drafts for football were each year and what the odds were that Atlanta would get a good or great college player. I was amazed at their depth of knowledge of sports and players. It was like they spent all their time thinking about sports and little time thinking about work. Even our attorney, a brilliant woman who graduated from Georgetown in Washington, knew all the sports stats cold.

Then I had an idea. I had recommended Ted Turner create CNN. I wondered if he would be interested in creating a sports channel that discussed behind the scenes stats on a separate cable channel. Since I was interested in sports other than baseball, football, golf and basketball, I thought they could broadcast shows on other sports. I enjoyed tennis, my friend Carlton was a great whitewater canoeist, and most everyone in Georgia hunted everything from deer to quail to pheasants. Perhaps the world could use a cable television channel that delved into all types of sports and sports statistics. I believed there could be a huge market for this.

But I had already given Ted Turner the idea to create CNN, and I wanted to give something special to Disney. So, I decided to write Michael Eisner and recommend a sports channel that delved into all aspects of professional and amateur sports. Perhaps this was God's answer to my prayer to give something nice to Disney. I wondered what the odds were that Mr. Eisner would even see or read the letter. So, I went to the President of our company and asked him how many letters of recommendations he had received from customers. He laughed and said, "All we ever receive are complaints. I can't even get our employees to make recommendations." He paused and then added, "Except for you Chris. You're always making recommendations to help our business," and he smiled and motioned for me to go back to work, which I promptly did.

I wrote a letter the following weekend recommending this in-depth sports channel to Michael Eisner. In hopes to get Mr. Eisner to read the letter, I mentioned that I had the idea to create CNN. I then showed the letter to my wife and sent it in the mail. I never expected to hear anything else about it. But within a year another channel appeared on cable TV. It was ESPN. It took me a little research to find out that this channel was indeed a Disney channel. And once again I was pleased, as I believed that God heard my prayer and had allowed me to give a gift to Disney after all.

Over the years I made other recommendations to Michael Eisner. Some of them appeared within a year or two, others did not. I never was thanked for the recommendations. But on one occasion, Mr. Eisner's secretary called me at my office and asked me to visit Disney when they opened the Animal Kingdom Lodge. He wanted me to stay in the lodge. I had recommended he create a safari, and that he back a hotel up to the animals of the safari so that the animals could wander around the hotel. We paid the minimum price for a small room but were upgraded to one of the best suites in the hotel with a balcony overlooking several African animals, including giraffe. We watched the animals all morning and drank coffee off our balcony the day after we arrived. We thought it was the best hotel we had ever stayed at in our lives.

One evening, while we stayed there I asked a clerk in the Disney store in our hotel if I could buy a couple of masks that hung above those that had price tags on them. The woman said, "These masks are part of the hotel and are not for sale."

At which point a woman who had been following me stepped forward and said, "Excuse me, but Mr. Morris can do anything he wants." She then turned to me and said, "Mr. Morris, I will contact Mr. Eisner and see what he will charge you for those masks."

A little while later, she found me in my room, told me the price and I bought both masks. The masks hang in our den in our home to this day.

Recommendations I have made to Mr. Eisner include building parks around the world, building a parking deck and a second park in California and creating a Disney Cruise line that stopped at a Disney Island in the Bahamas. I also recommended several movies, including the Chronicles of Narnia, the Pirates of the Caribbean and the Haunted Mansion. All mysteriously appeared within a year after my recommendations. I have never been paid for these recommendations but have received upgrades into wonderful hotel rooms, like Roy Disney's favorite suite, offers to put my daughter Jessica into the Mickey Mouse club, which I declined and other special gifts that my wife and I have thoroughly enjoyed.

I never wanted to be paid for these recommendations. I just wanted to give back, at first to Disney, but then to help a troubled and lost world. God so wants to bless people around the world, and what better way for Him to bless us than through Disneyworld. It truly has been an honor to serve our Lord. And I believe improving the "happiest place on earth" was my best way to bless the most people on earth. You see God really loves us and wants to bless us and make us happy. I only wish everyone could visit Disneyworld once in their lives and see the world I believe our Lord wants to create for us when He returns.

I have struggled with whether to include this story, because I do not want to appear to be proud. That is why it is important to understand, Jesus has been the author of my life, He has created these things and done these works through me and I deserve no credit for anything, much less credit for helping Disneyworld. The truth is, God, our Lord and Savior, deserves all the credit honor and glory, and it is through Him that I have been able to make these recommendations and even more importantly that these recommendations have come into fruition. So, do not give any credit to me, but give all the credit to Jesus and to the thousands of hard working employees at Disneyworld, for all I have done has been because of Him and through Him, blessed be His Holy Name!

Jessica's Birth

During this time, my love affair with my wife grew. I was passionately in love with this beautiful girl. I don't think I have ever seen a woman who was as beautiful as my wife. We had some trouble getting her pregnant, but after prayer and fasting, God blessed us, and she became pregnant.

I was so excited about becoming a father I couldn't stand it. I remembered praying about having children. On the other hand, I knew the end-times were at hand. And given this dire prediction, the question was, Should I even have children? If the end came, would it not be a disaster to raise children during the tribulation? We did not have direct or indirect confirmation as to whether we should have children even though we both prayed for guidance.

Then an amazing thing happened. I remember having the Lord come to me in a dream one night. It was Jesus. He told me I was to go to Beth the next night and she would become pregnant with a little girl. Under the direction of Jesus, we tried the next night. A few weeks later, Beth was ill, very ill. She couldn't keep anything down. I went out and purchased her a pregnancy test and coaxed her into using it. Sure enough, Beth was pregnant, praise God.

Then one night in October, Beth started having contractions. They were about two minutes apart. I thought this was false labor, since they started out so close together, and I recommended Beth wait before she called the doctor. After about fifteen minutes, the contractions continued, so we called the doctor. The doctor said to meet him at the hospital.

I had an important meeting with Craig, the president of our insurance company, the next morning. It was a cold, rainy night, and I was concerned that after visiting with the doctor, we would have to go home and due to lack of sleep, I might make a bad presentation.

As it turned out, Beth was, indeed, in labor, and we were preparing for delivery. During the night, it became apparent that the baby, Jessica, was under stress. Her heart was racing.

It was October 24, 1984. Beth's OBGYN was late that morning. He was really late. You could tell the nurse was agitated. Finally he showed up several hours late.

He came into the hospital room where Beth was and said, "Beth, I just wanted to apologize. I got in the car and was heading out of the subdivision. It was dark, windy, there was freezing rain and lightning everywhere. I didn't see it, but there was a low hanging power line across the road. By the time I saw it and hit the brakes, it was too late. It took the roof off my car. I had to walk back to the house and get another car and call a towing service. I'm here now and glad to be here. Had I not ducked in the last second, I would be dead."

He called the nurse, got up to date on where Beth was, checked her to see how dilated she was, and had her moved into the OR immediately.

I was told to follow a nurse into a little room for instructions. This nurse sat me down to explain where I was going to sit and what I could do. I believe she said something like this: "Dr. Miller, the OBGYN and his scrub nurse will stand at Beth's feet. The anesthesiologist will be on Beth's right. In the back of the room, away from the operating table, there will be a separate table for the pediatrician and his scrub nurse. They will not show up until after the baby is delivered. I am the nurse who is not sterile, and I run the errands for the doctors as needed. If you need help with the cameras or anything else, ask me and don't touch the doctors or the nurses. You are not allowed to take pictures of the delivery, and there will be a little curtain across her stomach. You can't go past that or take pictures of the delivery. Do you understand me?" she said with a threatening look.

"Yes, ma'am," I said.

"You will be sitting down next to Beth's face on the left. You are not to roam around, but you can talk to her during the delivery and comfort her. Again, you are not allowed to take pictures below the waist, below the curtain. Have you got that?"

"No problem," I responded.

But then something unusual happened. I don't know why I said this . . . You see, it was totally out of character.

"You forgot someone," I said timidly. "Jesus will be in that room to make sure everything goes all right."

If one look is worth a thousand words, the response I received told it all.

The nurse then said, "Oh, you're one of them," and added a look of rejection that said "I don't like your type."

I did not respond. What could I say?

We went into the OR. First, they tried to give Beth an epidural that did not work. Then after the OBGYN poked Beth's toe with a needle, Beth said, "That hurt!"

The OBGYN said, "She wasn't supposed to feel that."

They did another epidural. Again he poked her toe with a needle, and Beth said, "Stop that, it hurts."

At this point they decided to do a spinal.

The OBGYN poked Beth's big toe and Beth said, "If you do that again, I'm going to deck you."

I was then asked to leave the operating room, since I was of no use when she was under general anesthesia. I stood outside the door and looked through a window to see what was going on as they tried to put Beth to sleep. In about five minutes, the nurse who hated Christians came out holding a syringe in one hand. With the other hand, she slammed cabinets and cursed loudly as she looked frantically for a bottle.

"Not good," I thought.

She found the bottle she was looking for and began to pull the liquid into the hypodermic needle. She cursed at the bottle.

Then she said loudly, "We have an emergency, call doctor 99. And get him out of here," she said, pointing at me. I realized at this point there was a nurse behind me and she was talking to that nurse.

The nurse stepped forward, grabbed my arm, and pulled me toward an open door. She shoved me into a broom closet, slammed the door behind me, and the lights went out automatically. The door was locked, and it was black. I couldn't open the door.

I thought, "This is really not good."

So I knelt to pray in the dark. I must have sounded pathetic.

"Dear Lord, once before I lost my family. One day my parents were alive, the next day they were gone and I lost my entire family. We had to sell the house and move. It was terrible. I suffered for years. For five years I went through a quiet hell. I can't take this a second time. I can't lose my family again. Not at this point in life. If my wife dies, I ask You to please save the baby. If my wife and baby die, I want to die. I know You are a wonderful God Who can do miracles, and I just want You to know I am desperate. Please don't let me go through this again. Please save my wife and child. I will raise the child as Your child. I just ask—no, I am begging You, please save my family and me."

After what seemed to be an interminable period, say two hours of continual prayer, someone turned on a light in the room. I opened my eyes and looked up. It was a doctor I did not recognize. He had opened the door widely. I walked out, and he shook my hand.

"Congratulations, Chris, you are the proud father of a baby girl."

Just like that, I felt relief all over my body. I looked back into the closet to see that I had my camera, and before I could say anything, this mysterious doctor, whom I had never seen before, disappeared. I had no idea where he went.

"Fastest getaway in town," I thought. "He must have been going to a fire."

I feared I had lost my wife and daughter during that terrifying morning. Both my wife and unborn child died in my mind a thousand times, as I played out what I was to do. And now they were alive and well. In that state of mind, I walked out of the room toward the recovery room in search of my wife. On the way I saw the nurse, the cursing nurse who hated Christians. She was crying. She walked up to me and put her right arm around my neck and locked onto my neck until it hurt.

"Chris," she whispered into my ear between sobs. "Chris," she sobbed, "you are not," she sobbed again uncontrollably, "you're not going to believe this." She was still sobbing.

There were two empty chairs to my left. I led her over where we sat down side by side. She was regaining her composure.

"You were right." She wiped her eyes with a hanky and blew her nose. "God was in that room." She was looking down at her hands and the tissue she held. "Beth died. I swear it. I don't believe it, but she was dead." At this point she cried uncontrollably as she buried her face in her hanky.

I was confused. "This doctor told me I was the proud father of a baby girl. Did Beth die and you saved the baby?" I asked.

"They never take the baby until they stabilize the mother. The baby died thirty minutes before her mother. We were not able to deliver the baby."

Now I was freaking out. "They're both dead?"

She continued her story. "Both doctors looked at the grains of Beth's eyes and pronounced her dead," she said.

"I'm confused. What happened to the baby?" I asked.

"The baby had been dead by the time the mother died, and we will not take the baby until we stabilize the mother."

Oh my god, both Beth and the baby had died. That doctor must have thought I was someone else. But he used my name and called me Chris. I had never met that doctor before, so who knows, maybe there was another Chris in the delivery room.

"I called the morgue," the nurse continued. "I put a tag on the mother's toe and told the morgue to come pick up the body. About an hour later I realized my watch was missing, so I went looking for it. I couldn't find it anywhere, so I went into the OR, and there was the dead mother. I was furious, so I called the morgue and chewed them out for not picking up the body. After I hung up the phone, I walked back into the OR around the mother and found my watch. But I heard beeping. I looked up and saw both mother and baby had a pulse. They had not disconnected mother and baby from their monitors. Seeing that they were alive, I ran out of the OR and called an emergency, and the doctors and nurses came back in and delivered the baby. The baby is being cleaned up and checked!"

That was the longest five minutes of my life. Both were alive, both were dead, and now at least the baby was alive, but what about Beth?

"Is Beth okay? Where is she?" I asked.

"Beth is being x-rayed. They are checking to see what damage was done to her lungs."

"She had damage to her lungs, how is that possible?"

"They aspirated her incorrectly."

"What does that mean?"

"It means they put a tube down her nose so she could breathe while she was under the anesthesia. They accidentally got the tube in her stomach. When the anesthesiologist pulled the tube out of her stomach, it dumped stomach acid down her lungs. That is always fatal. Beth died after this procedure. I swear, two doctors pronounced her dead." The nurse paused and looked at me as if she was freaking out. "It had to be a miracle. She was dead and now she's alive."

I stood up from the chair and started searching for Beth. Finally I found her being pushed in a bed. I followed her to an X-ray room. They brought in a radiologist who took several X-rays. They were looking for damage to her lungs. In the end, all they could find was a tiny black spot on one of her lungs.

At this point they brought in a beautiful baby girl with a bit of a pointed head into Beth's hospital room and handed the baby to Beth.

After holding the baby, Beth looked at me and said, "Would you like to hold your daughter?"

That was the proudest day of my life . . . lying in bed next to Beth holding our little baby girl, Jessica, on my chest. As she moved around in my arms, I couldn't help but reflect on what just happened. God had saved this little baby girl and her mother in answer to my pathetic prayers. I was holding a miracle in my arms and lying next to the woman I loved who had recently died and whom Jesus brought back to life.

*****

A couple of days later, Beth and I were talking about these strange events. It was apparent from Beth's reaction that she was wondering if I was telling her the truth or if I had lost my mind. I think the "lost my mind" version was winning at this point.

Then I noticed the anesthesiologist was standing at the door listening to me as I tried to explain to Beth that she had died and come back to life.

At this point she stepped into our room and said, "I am a Christian. I know you both are Christians. Ordinarily I couldn't tell you this, because of fear of being sued. But I believe you aren't like that. So let me explain what really happened. Beth, your husband is telling you the truth. As fantastic as his story sounds, I have listened to everything he said, and it is all completely true!

"This is what happened from my perspective . . . After we put you to sleep to do the C-section, things headed downhill. Something went wrong . . . I couldn't stabilize you. At this point I realized I had aspirated you incorrectly . . . which means I had inadvertently allowed stomach acid into your lungs. We watched your baby die. We then focused all our concerted efforts to save you. But then you died," she said with a tragic sick look on her face. It was apparent she was horrified that Beth and the baby had both passed away.

She regained her composure. "Both Dr. Miller and I pronounced you dead after we examined the grains of your eyes. At this point we made a note of the time of death, and a nurse called the morgue and asked them to pick up your body. We left the OR.

"A couple of hours later, we got a call to come back to the OR. We were all dumbfounded and shocked to see that you and the baby had pulses on the monitors. After some discussion, we decided to go ahead with the delivery. Everything went fine the second time.

"It is usually fatal when you drop stomach acid into someone's lungs. We tested the pH of the liquid in your stomach, and it was perfectly neutral. I can't explain it. It was perfectly neutral. Your stomach acid had a pH of 7, which is impossible. We then had your lungs checked to see how much damage was done to them, and there was only a small black spot on your left lung that probably means nothing." She paused again and looked at Beth and me for a reaction. "We will keep checking the spot to make sure it disappears.

"Beth, what your husband told you is true. I believe this was a miracle of God . . . You were dead, and you came back to life. And I am so glad, Beth, you and your baby are both okay. God is with you and your family, Beth, and everything your husband has told you is completely true."

*****

I can't say what really happened that day. I was not in the operating room. But the gist of the story was consistent between the nurse and the anesthesiologist. Both said mom and baby died. Both said they were miraculously healed. And the nurse didn't even believe in God before this event happened. Something happened to change the nurse's opinion about God, and it had to be dramatic.

Beth Signs Me Up for Flying Lessons

I had always wanted to be a pilot and talked about this often with Beth, but I had never been in a small plane. Beth and I had no children, so even though we worked long hours, we had a lot of free time. We spent a lot of time at a church, where I became a deacon and later treasurer. We wanted something fun to do with our free time, so I decided I should take up flying. But the more I looked at it, the more I realized I couldn't afford to purchase an airplane. Then out of the blue, Beth heard about a place in Chattanooga, Tennessee, where they taught hang gliding. We would drive up to Raccoon Mountain early Saturday mornings and spend the day taking hang gliding lessons. This was scarier than I thought. And after crashing the hang glider and breaking my nose . . . I barely got off the ground so it wasn't much of a crash . . . I decided this was too dangerous a sport.

At work I spoke to a friend of mine who was the company pilot. He explained to me the risks of hang gliding and did his best to dissuade me from ever doing that again. I told him about the crash, and he pointed out to me that had I been going faster, it would have killed me.

He had been a captain in the Air Force and flew jets, so I trusted him. But I believed the cost of flying airplanes was too high for me.

"Chris," he said, "you don't have to own the airplane. You can take lessons and rent airplanes for a fraction of the price. You are a very methodical person, you are careful, and you aren't a risk-taker. I think you will be an excellent pilot."

Despite these recommendations, I concluded the cost was just too high, and I needed to save as much money as I could for retirement.

But then one day I came home from work and Beth said, "Honey, you need to take me to South Gwinnett High School. I am taking a lesson in art, and I signed you up for a course in flying."

I had no idea I was going to take a piloting course. I didn't even know there was such a thing as ground school. At any rate, we went to the high school that evening, and within a month I had completed a ground school private pilot course. I really enjoyed this course as I had been a physics major in college and most of the course focused on forces and lift on a plane. They also went into how to read weather charts, which I found fascinating.

At the last class, our instructor said we had two years to get our private pilot licenses and added we should start taking lessons as soon as possible at Peachtree DeKalb Airport.

On my drive home, I prayed on whether I should take my life down this path, as I saw no real benefit beyond just having fun. It was pouring down rain outside. And it was pouring inside my mind as this tug of war went on between me and what I believed God wanted me to do. I felt God wanted me to become a pilot. But I kept arguing with Him as I told Him it wasn't a prudent use of money. I reminded God that my parents were dead and Beth's parents had no money. We had no one to turn to if Beth or I lost our job and became unemployed.

But the thought kept entering my mind: "You need to do this, Chris."

Finally, before I reached home, I decided to at least check out the costs of taking flying lessons. The following Saturday my wife and I went to Peachtree DeKalb Airport, and we scouted out all the places that taught private pilots to fly. In the end I settled on a place called Wings and Things and selected an instructor who I thought was brilliant named Rod. Rod was an amazing pilot. He had flown for Delta Airlines, retired, and taught flying for fun.

A few weeks later, I sat for the first private pilot test and passed it. Immediately after that, I began flight training with Rod. I guess I must have done quite well as Rod wanted me to apply for a job at Delta Airlines and become a pilot. In less than forty flight hours, I received my private pilot license.

Proud of myself, I went to my friend, the pilot who flew the executives around at our company. He listened to me describe how well I had done and then said, "Now, Chris, you must get an instrument rating."

"How hard is that?" I asked.

"It is more difficult than becoming a private pilot. You must pass a more comprehensive written test and then learn to fly in instrument conditions."

"Why do this?" I asked.

"You can't take cross-country trips. Truthfully, you shouldn't travel outside the Atlanta area, unless you have an instrument rating. This rating allows you to fly in bad weather and fly in the clouds without visual references. Trust me, Chris, the sooner you start on this rating, the better."

How was I going to explain this to my wife? This training was even more expensive than the private license. To my surprise, Beth liked the idea, and I started learning how to fly without seeing outside the airplane.

For fun, Beth and I would pack Jessica up, rent an airplane, and fly to the beach. We found we could leave work on Friday afternoon, take off one day, and be at Destin within a couple hours. We almost bought a condo in Sandestin Beach Resort but decided last minute that it was more fun to rent. I found a Cessna 172 I liked to rent.

One day after work, the owner of this Cessna called me on the phone. He was very abrupt. His name was Bob Loewenthal.

He said, "Chris, when you rent the airplane, you always take excellent care. You buckle the seat belts, you put everything back in perfect order, and Rod says you are an excellent pilot."

"Well, I want to continue to rent your airplane, Bob, and I would like to take care of it as if it is my own."

"That's why I am calling. I'm going to sell that plane and purchase a Cessna 182, and I would like you to be a co-owner in the new plane with me."

"Really, and how much will that cost me, Bob?"

"Let me find a plane, we'll ride in it together, and I will let you know all of the details."

Bob was a retired TV and radio announcer who loved astronomy and science. He convinced me to invest in a Cessna 182 with him and two other people. We flew the plane everywhere. We joined a club called the Flying Rebels at Peachtree DeKalb Airport, and we became good friends. Bob was an incredibly brilliant Jewish man. He reminded me of my dad, who was also a bit of a genius.

One day Bob invited Beth and me over to his house. He said simply, "Chris, I would like you to invest in an office building with me. Will you do that?"

I felt a strong urging from God, once again, to say yes. I asked him how much, he told me, and I wrote him a check on the spot. I had learned to trust Bob and thought he had excellent judgment and was a straight shooter, so I was now the proud co-owner of an office building in Tucker, Georgia.

I had no idea why God wanted me to take up flying, nor did I have any idea as to why He wanted me to become friends with Bob and to purchase this office building, but I was confident this was part of His plan.

I Am Promoted to Assistant
Secretary and Treasurer
of an Insurance Holding Company

I was responsible for all the accounting, including writing the annual reports, the 10-Ks, the 10-Qs, and monthly financial statements. I reviewed the insurance reserves usually handled only by actuaries; I handled the auditor's questions; I wrote the press releases; and I sat on the board of directors as assistant secretary of the company and took the minutes. I managed all the accountants in the company and issued the State-regulated accounting reports for the two life insurance and one property-and-casualty insurance companies. I did all this, and I was just thirty years old.

The president liked me and said I did excellent work. Our president was our investment manager. I loved investing too as I had taken every investment course that was available in graduate school. Even better, I managed my own money and made more money on my investments than I did from my salary.

I wanted to show the president my investment expertise. So I told Craig, our president, that he should purchase stock in one of my favorite companies in 1985. I had owned this stock since 1981 and made a tremendous amount of money holding it. It was a woman's clothing store called The Limited Inc. Craig was impressed with my investment recommendation, so he asked me to list three companies on a piece of paper that I thought he should consider buying. I did as he requested. A week later, he called me into his office.

"Chris," Craig said, "I asked the senior VP of Shearson to recommend three stocks to me. Here is his letter. Look at it."

I did. He recommended The Limited, Walmart, and Phillip Morris.

After reading the list, I said, "Those are the same companies I recommended, Craig."

"I know, Chris. I have asked Stan to train you to take over our investments. Stan has agreed. He will be contacting you. Congratulations."

Over the next few years, Craig and Stan trained me to manage money.

I ultimately handled the investments, with Craig's approval. I also handled cash flow management and money transfers between accounts. Excess money I either invested in stocks, bonds, or money markets. I called Jamie every day at the bank and asked him what money markets were available. The minimum cost of a CD or commercial paper was $100,000, and on my word, he would wire the money and purchase the investments. I then made sure they matured so that I always had enough cash to pay our corporate bills.

It was July of 1987. The markets had started a correction.

One day I had to go down to the Omni in Atlanta to make a press release. While down there, I decided to get my shoes shined. These two black boys talked to me the entire time about the stocks they were buying. I was in a state of shock as I listened to them. I gave them a good tip and hustled back to the office.

I then called my friend, Chuck, the history guru, and asked him, "Chuck, why did Joseph Kennedy get out of the stock market in 1929?"

"Don't you remember, Chris, he went to get his shoes shined, and the shoeshine men were talking about the stocks they owned. He figured that if the shoeshine men were buying stocks, the market couldn't go any higher, as everyone who could buy had already bought into the market. So he started shorting the market to make money on stocks as the market fell."

"Thanks, Chuck, I thought that was what happened. I wonder if this works with young black boys too."

"Say what?"

"I'll explain later, Chuck. I have to go now, talk to you later." I hung up the phone and immediately walked in to Craig's office.

"What are you doing here, Chris? Can't you see, I'm busy."

"I know, Craig, but I wanted you to know I want to sell all of our stocks today, and I thought I should get permission before I did that."

"Excuse me, Rodney, could you hold on please." Craig was on the phone. He then scratched his head. Craig said, "Rodney, I will have to call you back."

He got out of his chair and pulled out charts he used to track the markets. We looked at the charts, and he said, "Chris, it is almost impossible to get the top 10 percent or bottom 10 percent in any market. I have been worried about this market for a few months. Do you really think we are in for a bear market?"

"I do, Craig . . . I really do."

"Then go ahead and get us out of the market . . . today."

I sold all the stocks we held, except for companies we had controlling interests in. History records the markets collapsed several months later on "Black Monday." It was October 19, 1987.

On that fateful Monday morning, I got to work early. I had been studying the markets. I thought I was going to have a heart attack as the market dropped from a high of 2,396 to 1,678 on Monday. The truth is, during that Black Monday morning, my ticker tape showed the Dow drop all the way down to 500. I prayed for an hour. After an hour, the ticker tape was showing the Dow was at about 1,000. I started buying stocks as fast as I could.

Craig showed up around noon that day. I assumed he was at the brokerage firm watching the markets and talking to Stan.

"What are you doing, Chris?"

"I'm buying stocks as fast as I can. I just bought Phillip Morris for $45 this morning. It was trading at $120 earlier this summer. I also bought a few shares of Home Depot for $11, and it had been trading at $25 earlier this summer. And I bought Quaker Oats for less than half where it was."

"You're supposed to get my approval," Craig said red in the face.

"You weren't here, Craig, and I felt I had to act on the bottom basement pricing."

"What if this is the end of the world, Chris? Did you ever think about that?" Craig was visibly shaking as he excoriated me.

"I thought about that, Craig. I figure one of two things will happen. It could be the end of the world as you say. If that happens, we're all going home anyway. If it doesn't happen, these cheap stocks are too low to pass up. I only invested 10 percent of our available assets," I said helplessly.

"Are you willing to bet your job on this?"

I paused. Then said, "I am."

I could tell Craig was biting his tongue. He so wanted to fire me. In hindsight, I probably would have fired him on the spot if our roles were reversed.

Craig continued, "I'll let you know a year from now whether you can keep your job. Go ahead and invest the rest of the money in the markets today."

I understood Craig was upset. In hindsight I was crazy to buy without his permission, on such a volatile day. Craig was ultimately responsible for all our investment decisions. Happily, Craig had such a great year, due to my luck, as it really was blind luck that made us so much money, that he beat the S&P 500 handily over the last ten years when comparing our company's returns to the S&P 500. And that was largely due to my willingness to jump back into the markets that fateful day.

A year later, Craig poked his head in my office and yelled, "You can keep your job."

I didn't know what he was talking about, so I went back to his office and asked, "What was that about?"

"Don't you remember, Chris, I told you I would let you know in a year whether you could keep your job? You can keep it. Now get out of here." I did as he instructed.

I don't think we will ever know how much help we have received in this life from God. Since the mid-1980s, I have had a gift for determining when major stock market tops and bottoms have occurred, and I have been able to identify tops and bottoms within a few weeks of major tops and bottoms. All gifts come from God!

Giving Back

By now I had used almost every course I had taken in graduate school in various jobs I had held, and I knew that had my education been less thorough, I would not have done nearly as well in my career. Naturally, I wanted to give something back. The problem was I was quite young and while I was well paid, I didn't have that much money at the time, at least I didn't make enough money to really make a difference with a contribution to my university. So, I decided to pray to give something special to my alma mater.

A few days later, the Dean of Georgia State's business school called me and asked me for a donation. At first, I didn't know what to say.

Dean Black, who was my Dad's cousin, explained to me that I was perhaps the most successful student to graduate from that MBA program at that point in time. While flattered, I knew that their MBA program probably had people who had been far more successful than me. Then I thought of J. Mack Robinson, our Chairman. He was a billionaire and a nice man.

I said, "Why don't you ask Mack, our Chairman for a donation?"

"Chris, he didn't go to Georgia State, did he?"

"No, but he is a generous man who might like to have a business school named after him."

"If you can get him to talk to me, I'll see what I can do…do you think you can get him on the phone with me?"

"I'll try." I put him on hold and went up to see Mack. I had spoken to Mack on several occasions in the past regarding investment decisions and taking our company public. His secretary knew me and when I ran upstairs to his office she greeted me and without hesitation let me in to see Mr. Robinson.

"Hey Mack, the Dean of Georgia State University is asking me for a donation and I really don't have any money to give more than a small donation. I asked him if he could name the business school after you if you gave him a donation and he said he could. Would you talk to him please?"

Mack not only took the call but about a week later the Dean of Georgia State called me again to report that Mr. Robinson had made a substantial donation to them and they were going to call the business school the J. Mack Robinson School of Business.

Of course, I was truly indebted to Mack not only for the opportunity to work for him but for this generous donation. More importantly, Dean Black and Mack, unbeknownst to them, answered the prayer request I had made just a few short days before. Was this a miracle? I am confident it was as I have never been in a position to ask someone to make such a donation like that before or since. Blessed be the name of the Lord!

Jessica's Forehead Is Injured

When Jessica was about eight months old, she was learning to walk. I remember sitting on the bed watching Jessica as she played in our bedroom. She was standing up, holding on to the bed, and would let go and take a few steps, and she would walk to her mother. She turned from her mother to walk back. Suddenly she lost her balance. She adjusted by running faster to keep from falling on the ground; the further she fell forward, the faster she ran. I had never seen a young child do this before. She was running fast across the room, trying to catch her balance . . . and she slammed her head into the edge of the chest of drawers.

I dove to catch her and keep her from hitting her head but was too late. Instead I simply caught her after she hit her head. Immediately her forehead puffed out black-and-blue, and a small stream of blood was dripping down from the center.

I didn't know what to do. In a panic, I lifted her up on the edge of the bed, knelt in front of her, and prayed. Jessica was listless; her head hung down and swung loosely, with blood dripping. While her eyes were open, she was unconscious and didn't know what was happening.

Beth said, "We should call the doctor." But seeing that I was already on my knees and praying, she knelt next to me.

"Dear Lord," I said, "please help Jessica, she is too young to have such an injury. I tried to stop her from being hurt. I don't know what to do, Lord. This is Your baby girl You entrusted with us. I don't think doctors can help her now, only You can heal her." I paused, not knowing what to say. "Please, Lord, please . . . please help Jessica."

At that moment, Beth tapped me on my shoulder. I opened my eyes, looked up, and saw this black bruise with blood dripping down her forehead. The bruise was the size of a silver dollar. It puffed out about an eighth of an inch and was jet-black with blue patches. Then suddenly, magically, this wound and blood simply disappeared. The healing only took a few seconds. Once the wound disappeared, I looked at Jessica's forehead to see what marks were left. All I could see was a barely visible white vertical line that was left in the middle of the spot where the injury occurred.

At the same time, the bleeding stopped, and the blood that had been on her face simply disappeared. Then Jessica raised her head up, looked directly into my eyes, focusing her eyes as if she just woke up from a deep slumber. Her eyes expressed momentary confusion. Why were we on our knees, and why was I holding her sides? She then smiled, leaned forward, and hugged my neck. Jessica was too young to talk at the time. She was eight months old. But her actions spoke volumes. It was as if she suddenly woke up and was surprised to see us on our knees in front of her. I was so happy that she instinctively leaned forward and hugged me tight around my neck. Realizing she was okay, I lifted her off the bed and placed her gently beside me.

I was stunned. I had never witnessed anything like this. I fell backward off my knees onto my back, still in shock, and said, "I have underestimated God. If God can heal that wound and make her alert, as if she had never been injured, He can heal anything . . . heart attacks, cancer, anything! I would never have believed it if I hadn't seen it with my own eyes."

Beth started babbling something I didn't understand. She too lay back and turned her face to me.

"Chris, wasn't she injured just a moment ago? Did we or did we not see her injured?"

I didn't know what to say. I had seen something that challenged my senses.

"Yes, Beth," I said, "I am certain she was injured. Don't you remember the black-and-blue wound and the blood dripping down her forehead? Don't you remember her falling and injuring her forehead? Don't you remember I dove across the room to try to prevent her from being injured and instead caught her after she hit her head? Why else would we be kneeling and praying for her?"

I paused to try to understand what I had just witnessed. "Why, this is incredible, Beth! We have seen a miracle, a true miracle, right before our eyes. This is unbelievable! And it is something I prayed to see . . . and now we have, indeed, witnessed a miracle."

I was reminded of a CPA and his wife who were twenty years my senior who told me about a miracle they had witnessed. They had seen a crippled man's arm grow back right before their eyes. I heard them and smiled politely but privately disregarded their story as unbelievable, even crazy. I was impressed with their faith, but while describing this miracle to me, I disregarded their story as some type of hallucination or clever magic trick.

I See Jesus in a Dream

When in college, I was poisoned with an illegal drug that was put in a bottle in my dorm room by the suspicious psychologist. I nearly died at the time. Even though I had recovered, I felt my heart had been forever weakened from that experience. Odd things, symptoms, little ones here and there, reminded me of my weakened heart.

Twelve years had passed. It was a lazy Sunday afternoon. Beth and I were sleep-deprived as we started the day at 5:30 AM to take Jessica to her sitter, and the day never ended before 11:00 PM. The stress from work was challenging. I lay in bed next to my wife and went over my "to-do" list in my mind.

Thoughts flew through my mind. Remember to do this first thing Monday. Contact So-and-So tomorrow. I had to meet a tax deadline soon.

I enjoyed listening to my beautiful and sweet wife snore gently in my right ear as I lay quietly on my back next to her. My right hand wasn't but two or three inches from her, but I dare not touch her as I might wake her.

Suddenly, out of nowhere, I heard a large pop. It sounded like a branch snapped in my chest. It was a large and loud pop.

"What could that be?" I thought.

At that moment, I suddenly felt extremely weak. A violent decrease in pressure inside my body occurred. I could easily go to sleep now if I wanted to, but this wasn't that type of tiredness; this was extreme weakness that overwhelmed me and even frightened me. I had never experienced anything like this before.

"Maybe my aorta ruptured. Maybe my spleen popped. If it did, I am going to die," I thought. "But if it is my spleen, they may be able to save me. I had better wake up Beth and get to the hospital fast."

I tried to reach over to Beth to tap her and wake her. But to my amazement, my hand didn't move. I tried again. And once again I couldn't move a muscle. Strange, what a strange occurrence. I couldn't move anything. I was frozen in place, staring at the ceiling.

"I will call out to Beth and tell her to call an ambulance, and I will tell her that I love her." So I tried. But I heard nothing. I couldn't move my mouth. I was completely paralyzed. At this point I realized I might be dying. "Wait. Am I really dying? But I couldn't die now," I thought. "I had too much to do. I had to raise our daughter, Jessica. It was my job, Lord. What would happen to my wife and daughter? I had an obligation to them both. If I die now . . . I must be dying. I can't move, I can't talk . . . I must have had an aneurism."

"They say if you are going to die, you lose your peripheral vision. But I can see the entire ceiling from left to right, even the window top with my right eye."

"The artery from my heart to my body must have ruptured. Had I known I had this problem, I would never have married, Lord, I can't leave my wife in this mess. Beth needs help raising our child, Jesus save me! I can't die now. This is not fair to Jessica. I lost my parents, and it destroyed me. It's not right for me to die now and destroy Jessica, Lord. I love you, Jesus . . . but . . ."

At this point I noticed my vision was becoming restricted. I couldn't see the edges of the ceiling, and I could no longer see the top of the window with my right eye. I could only see part of the ceiling, and my vision was less sharp.

"Chris," I thought to myself, "you're going to die. There is no point in arguing with God. He is a good and righteous God. He is truly wonderful . . . and now you are going to meet Him in person."

"Jesus, why take me now?" I pleaded. "Is there no hope for me? Did I not pray to You before I chose to have children? Don't You remember, I told You my parents died before my sister, brother, and I grew up, and I felt it would be a terrible sin if I were to die before my children grew up? If You don't love me and don't want me to live, can't You remember the basis upon which I chose to have children, which was that I would never do to them what my parents did to me? I begged you that I would not have children unless I could be here to help them grow up. Please don't abandon my wife and daughter now. I don't mind dying. I know how wonderful and peaceful it is on the other side. In fact, it would be a relief to go there. But, Lord, I fear it would be wrong for me to leave my family now." I paused, knowing I was going to die, and I said in my mind, "But not my will, Thy will be done, Lord."

I momentarily thought about my sins. I was not worthy to see Him. I was inadequate and was terrified to be before Him. But I wasn't going to think about that now. I sang a prayer in my mind:

> Glory be to the Father,
> and to the Son
> and to the Holy Ghost.
> As it was in the beginning,
> is now and ever shall be,
> world without end,
> A . . . a . . . men. A . . . a . . . men.

My vision was almost gone. I was fading away. My mind was becoming unfocused.

"Well, I guess it is time to let go of this life and sing praises to God," I thought.

Hymns started popping into my mind. I wasn't afraid to die; I was just afraid to see Jesus as I was a horrible person. I just began singing praises in my mind, as I could not sing them out loud.

> Bless the Lord,
> all my soul,
> and all that is within me
> Bless His Holy Name.
> Bless the Lord,
> all my soul,
> and all that is within me
> Bless His Holy name.

He hath done great things.
He hath done great things.
He hath done great things,
Bless His Holy name.

Then I remembered that crazy psychologist who had poisoned me when I was in college. I tasted the drink . . . Just a drop touched my tongue, and my heart went crazy and raced. I fell to the floor. I couldn't stand up. Oh my, perhaps it did so much damage that it finally ruptured.

By now my vision was clearly like looking through a tunnel. I knew I was going to die. I resigned myself to certain death.

"Not my will, but Thy will be done, Lord. Thy will be done," I thought, resigning myself to certain death. This was not a bad way to die. And with that I fell into a deep slumber.

After that, nothing . . . I was asleep. Then there was a strange light in the distance.

I clearly saw the light coming closer. I ascended into the sky and entered the black void of space. There were no stairs, and someone seemed to be guiding me. Yes, I had been here before; it seemed strangely familiar. The climb seemed to take hours, but hours were as minutes.

I had arrived. There I was, before Jesus again, in heaven. He looked like a bright light surrounding a human form that moved. My eyes saw this incredibly bright light, with an outline of a man inside the light. I couldn't focus my eyes on Him . . . He was simply the source of all light in the sky. Then I heard His thoughts.

"Chris, you can stay here, or you can go back to your body."

"Lord, I have a young daughter. I have to go back and help my wife raise Jessica." I was pleading, even crying with no tears, for I felt so inadequate to be before Him.

Then Jesus said, "Then go back to your body."

All I know was after this somewhat dramatic end to this dream, I simply woke up the next morning with a terrible nagging headache, a headache that lasted for weeks.

I realized it was morning. It was just after 5:30 AM. Beth was still asleep. We had to wake up and go to work. I stumbled out of bed. What a strange dream. But the event in my chest . . . that was no dream; that was real . . . or so it seemed. God must have heard my prayer and let me come back to my body. And I can move again, I can move. Blessed be His Holy name! Holy, holy, holy is the Lord our God Almighty!

My thoughts turned to the day Jessica's head was injured. I remembered Jessica running across the room and hitting her head on the corner of the chest of drawers. Her forehead was bleeding, and she was knocked unconscious. I put her on the edge of the bed and prayed for her and the wound . . . That bruise and cut simply disappeared right before Beth's and my eyes. I had witnessed a miracle of healing. At that point I knew God could do anything. So once again, without hard scientific proof, I gave our Lord praise, for praise is always good, even if it is from a lack of understanding.

Things Head South at Work

The insurance company I worked for was growing at a rapid pace. We had the best Medicare Supplement product in the United States at that time. But I was growing concerned about our reserves, which is money that we need to pay insurance claims in the future. The reserves or savings you need to put aside for future insurance claims are calculated by actuaries. We used an outside actuary for this calculation. I took it upon myself to check the reserves calculation even though I was not an actuary. This is where my math and physics background proved beneficial. I was not certain, but based on my calculations, I concluded we were underreserved by $30 to $40 million. That was a lot of money for our small company at that point in time.

Concerned about our financial position, I told Jeff, the audit manager from Arthur Andersen, about my conclusions. He decided to check my numbers. Together we recalculated our reserve requirements. This different method of estimating reserves showed we were $32 million underreserved. I feared that if I went to Craig with this bad news, I would be fired. I also knew that if we didn't raise more than $32 million dollars, we would be bankrupt within ten years. My only hope was to get assistance from Jeff and his boss, Michael, the partner on the job.

I explained my dilemma to Jeff. He understood my predicament completely. As a result, he and I came up with a strategy. The partner would meet with Craig and force him to bring in one of the largest actuarial firms in the world to check our reserves. He hired Milliman to do this calculation. A few months later, they gave us their verdict. We were under reserved by $35 million. This meant I had to restate our publicly issued financial statements and disclose this "accounting error." Our stock tanked.

Within a month, Craig tragically died of a massive heart attack. I continued to manage our investments, but the new temporary president tied my hands and made me work closely with his brokerage firm. The person who really understood how good I was at investing had died, and this temporary president even fired our outside adviser Stan, who had spent a great deal of time training me to manage money. The investment returns since Craig's untimely death attest to my observation: that the outside adviser they hired wasn't particularly good.

My boss, Bob, was beside himself. He knew we were going bankrupt.

Then I said, "I believe we can go public. I think we should either offer more stock or do a bond offering. With our stock price so depressed, I think we should offer bonds. I will talk to my brokerage contacts and see what we can do . . . okay?"

At first Bob said that going public in our condition was impossible.

I explained to Bob that there was a money manager named Michael Milliken who was helping companies like us go public every day of the week.

I said, "At least let me try."

Bob finally agreed and said, "See what you can do."

Within a month, I started work on writing an S-2 registration statement to raise $30 million via a bond offering on the NASD. We needed more money than that, so I went to Mack, our chairman, and recommended we take our publicly traded subsidiary Rhodes Furniture public via a secondary stock offering to raise an additional $10 million in stock. We did that as well. Within six months, we had raised $40 million, which was more than enough to save the business. The public offering reduced our stake in Rhodes Furniture, so we spun it off. In the end we saved the company, and I felt I had secured a position for life.

With Craig's death, things changed for the worse. During this time, Ken—the man who had hired me and who was now president of the Property and Casualty Insurance Company we owned—

wound up in a tug of war with my boss, Bob, as both struggled to be named president of our holding company.

Bob, my boss, came in to see me one day and told me, "Chris . . . Jim, who was a president of one of the life insurance companies we owned, and I want to make some changes in this firm. We are working together to get Ken fired so I can be made president of the company . . . and we need your help. We want you to go to Mack, the chairman of the board, as you have good relations with Mack."

"I do?"

"Yes, you do. You saved the business, Chris, and Mack knows that. You also asked Mack to give money to Georgia State University, and he did that, and they named the business school after him, again thanks to you! He trusts you, Chris, as Craig trusted you!"

I said, "Mack is a good guy, but I doubt he will listen to me more than you."

"Listen to my plan. You go see Mack and tell him a story that I will give you. You are to tell him that Ken, the president of the P&C business, is a crook. After that, Jim will go in and tell him the same story in a slightly different way. Mack will not know whether to believe you two, but I am confident he will call upon me to resolve this issue. When I tell him the same story, Ken will be fired, and I will be confirmed as president of the holding company. Will you do this for me?"

"Stop there," I said. "Just stop there. I don't like dirty politics. Ken needs a job, and you need a job. I really don't think we should do this as there is room enough for both of you here."

"If you want to keep your job, you will do this, Chris."

I paused and looked directly at Bob as I thought about what I would say. "Bob, I follow Jesus Christ. He would not approve of me hurting an innocent man. Do what you want, but I will not be part of it."

"You must do this, Chris. If you don't help us, we will also tell Mack a story about you. I will make sure Mack blackballs you, and I will make sure you never get another job. Without a job, your beautiful wife will leave you and your life as you know it will end."

"I will not change my mind, Bob. Do what you must, but I will not help you do that as I will not violate God's laws. Have you not heard, 'Thou shalt not bear false witness against thy neighbor?'"

With that Bob left the room, furious. Within a few weeks, Ken was fired, Bob was made president, and I was made CFO of the holding company.

When Bob said I was CFO, he also added, "I told you to play ball or suffer. Jim and I will provide Mack with enough information to ruin your career. You will never get another job, Chris."

"I have faced worse, Bob. Do what you must."

"I will destroy you!"

I then said, "I will trust that Jesus Christ will save me, as my faith is in Him and Him alone."

*****

Within a couple of weeks, after a lot of prayer, I was offered a job out of the blue to be vice president and controller of a billion-dollar convenience store company that was built on the very place I had visited with my friend Chuck ten years before.

I remember driving Chuck to this empty piece of land, parking the car, and getting out of the car and saying to him, "One day I will be made a financial officer of a large corporation here, and I will work at this location." That prediction was now fulfilled.

Helping Chuck Colson's Ministry

After changing jobs to the convenience store industry, we discovered Beth was once again pregnant, and this time we were hoping for a baby boy. We chose not to know whether it was a boy or a girl or whether the baby had Down syndrome in advance as it would have no impact on whether we would have the baby. We would be happy with any child God provided, although we were both secretly hoping it was a healthy boy.

Just about that time, I met a minister who worked for Chuck Colson. We started working with this minister, and I felt the Holy Spirit led me to humbly help Chuck Colson's prison ministry.

Okay, I knew Chuck Colson was the strong arm that worked for Richard Nixon. I knew Chuck Colson might have been involved in the murder of my parents indirectly and might have been involved in attempts to murder me. I also knew that working with him was tantamount to insanity. Nevertheless, I believed God wanted me to help His ministry part-time, and so we did.

It was a Saturday morning. I had been instructed by Chuck Colson's prison ministries to pick up a prisoner at a church in downtown Atlanta at 9:00 AM. This prisoner was to live with us over a couple of months. The church was walking distance from my old home at Fourth and South in Midtown, so I knew exactly where it was. I pulled into their parking lot, just off Peachtree Street and Ponce de Leon Avenue, about five minutes late.

I chose to pick this prisoner up by myself without my wife, Beth, since I was unsure if this man was safe. I had to hurry because I barely had time to pick him up, take him to our home in Lilburn, and head back to Peachtree-DeKalb Airport for a flying lesson I had scheduled at ten thirty that morning. I was working on my instrument rating in the Cessna 182 I co-owned.

All I knew was the prisoner who was going to live with us for a month was supposed to be dropped off at this church at 9:00 AM. The entrance to the church was locked, so I stood outside in front of the church until 10:10 AM.

"Finally," I thought. A car pulled up, and a man hopped out. He was about forty years old, white, with brown hair and brown eyes.

He walked up to me and asked me, "Are you with Chuck Colson's ministry?"

I said, "Yes. Is your name Mike?"

"Yes, it is."

"Then follow me."

We didn't speak as we walked to my car, which was parked in the back of the church.

After getting in the car, I said, "Look, Mike, you are over an hour late."

"I'm a prisoner, and we have to wait on the guards. I'm sorry," he said mechanically, sensing I was upset.

"Well, that's not the problem, Mike. The problem is I have an appointment at 10:30 AM to fly my Cessna 182 with an instructor. I was planning on taking you home first and then going to the airport, but since you are so late, I will have to go directly to the airport."

"I know this is not exactly according to my instructions, but you seem like a reasonable guy," I continued. "I am going to give you a choice. You can either ride with me in the airplane in the back seat, or you can stay on the ground at Wings and Things. I know the owner and his girlfriend, Jenny. I'm sure Jenny will be glad to have you help her while you wait for me."

Mike started crying. He tried to stay silent, but he completely lost it and sobbed in the seat next to me. It was darn peculiar. He didn't say a word.

When we arrived at the airport, I said, "You don't have to ride in the plane if you are afraid of flying." I was trying to reassure him.

"No, I want to ride in the airplane. Can I sit in the back?"

"If you want to, of course. It's a Cessna 182 and will comfortably fit all three of us. Are you sure you want to go with us?"

"Yes, I really want to go," Mike said.

"No problem. Be cool. Some people get scared. We're going to do a few instrument approaches. I'll be wearing a hood, so I can't see out of the airplane, and so I can fly by the instruments. The instructor is a good instructor, and he can fly the plane if I have a problem. Is that okay?"

Mike said, "It's okay."

He didn't say another word. We flew three instrument approaches, and I nailed each approach.

After we were done, Mike said, "You did a good job, Chris, on all three approaches!"

He sounded like he knew something about flying. The whole incident seemed odd.

Mike would sleep in our home, get up early, and I would drop him off at a specified location on my way to work where someone from Chuck Colson's ministry would pick him up and take him to work on a Habitat for Humanity home in Atlanta.

Since Mike had never threatened to harm anyone, he was in a part of the prison where they drew a line on the ground surrounding the prison that he was told not to cross. If he did, the length of his sentence would be increased. If he behaved well, he could do special work projects and stay in a guest home like ours, while working on those projects.

Being a CPA, I knew the tax business and understood how the IRS worked. When I learned why Mike was in jail, I was shocked. You see, Mike was in prison for tax fraud. I knew they put people in jail for that, but it was rare, so I asked Mike what he had done to deserve incarceration.

Mike said, "I was a commercial pilot for a man who built malls. I flew him in his MU-2 all over the United States as he bought land and oversaw the construction of malls. When I took him to different locations, I would wait at the airports. I didn't have much to do, so I would pick up airplanes for cheap and sell them in Trade-A-Plane. I made about $100K a year doing this on the side. I didn't report all the income and got unlucky. They audited me and put me in jail for underreporting profits!"

"Wow, that's too bad," I said.

Several things about his case were peculiar. First, he should have hired a CPA to prepare his taxes. Second, any competent CPA should have been able to keep Mike out of jail. He must have represented himself and really done a poor job. And third, now I knew why Mike was so comfortable in the back seat of my Cessna 182.

"So, Mike, you're a pilot?"

"Yes, sir. That MU-2 is a great airplane. It is a turbo-charged twin airplane that seats about twelve people."

"I've never been in an MU-2, but I have seen them. How would you like to fly my plane from the left seat while you are out of prison?"

Mike got choked up again and said, "Yes, I would love to."

"You can also ride in the right seat while I practice instrument approaches, how about that?"

He was still crying.

Strange guy, I thought. Every time I talk about getting him in an airplane, he starts crying like a baby.

Mike was a model prisoner and became our friend. He worked with me on instrument approaches. I let him fly from the left seat a couple of times as pilot in command. He seemed to have a ball.

He worked hard helping build homes for Habitat for Humanity, and he always helped around the house. He even helped do the dishes. This man should never have been put in prison. It really was one of those unfortunate tragedies that could have been averted with the right advice.

After a few weeks, when we were eating dinner at home, I asked Mike why he got emotional when I picked him up at the airport. Mike was embarrassed, but he answered my question.

"Well, while I was in prison, I decided to accept Jesus into my heart. But I told Jesus that I wanted some confirmation that He was real. So I said this when I prayed, 'If you are real, I want to ride in an airplane while I am out of prison.' Then I changed my request and said, 'I would like to fly the plane as pilot in command just one time when I got out.' I told Jesus if He did that, then I would know He was God.

"And before you took me home, I was in the back seat of a small plane you owned. Then you took me up on several flights, and you let me be pilot in command on a couple of occasions. I couldn't believe it. At this point I knew, beyond a shadow of doubt, that Jesus is God."

While Mike was with us, I decided we had to buy a new car. It turns out Mike had sold cars in his past before he became a pilot. He asked me how I bought cars. I told him I looked at the sticker price and wrote a check. I thought he was going to get ill. He was trying to be polite, but it was apparent I paid way too much for cars.

He said, "Chris, do you know what salesmen call you?"

"No!" I said.

"You're a full-boat deal."

"What does that mean?" I asked Mike.

"It means the salesmen really stick it to you, buddy."

He then explained to me that I paid about $4,000 too much on my last car purchase. That was 20 percent more than I had to pay.

"So, Mike, would you be willing to help me buy a new car?"

"Sure, Chris."

Not only did he help me, but he taught me how to purchase a car at a discount. We ultimately saved thousands of dollars.

After they completed the habitat homes, Mike had to go back to prison. He was such a close friend of the family at this point that we decided to attend church at the Atlanta Federal Penitentiary. Over time, we got to know all the prisoners, and they loved us. These were our friends.

It was really a treat to go down to the Atlanta Federal Penitentiary on Sunday, as odd as that sounds. Beth looked like a million-dollar model when she dressed up in a white dress on Sunday. Our three-year-old little girl, Jessica, was a beautiful little girl, like her mother, wearing a white lace dress with pink sash, white shoes, and a pink bow in her hair.

The chaplain would look at Beth and Jessica and say, "I wish I could have married a beautiful woman like Beth and had a beautiful child just like Jessica. You're such a lucky man, Chris." He would then leave the room with tears running down his face.

When this man preached, I knew he was 100 percent sold out for God. He had given Jesus everything. And he knew he had done something very wrong in his past as he had been a prisoner himself and had even spent time in solitary confinement. Whatever he had done must have been pretty bad.

Our Chaplain

Years later I heard an interview with James Dobson and an ex-Mafia leader who co-owned a restaurant chain in Atlanta. This ex-Mafia leader, we will call Bill. He had been the "number two" man in the Gambino Mafia family.

Bill, the ex-Mafia guy, said to Dobson, "I went to the restaurant chain I co-owned early one morning. I was having a nice conversation with my partner when I realized he was high on drugs. I was furious. I told him that Paul Castillano, my boss, would kill us both if he caught either one of us using drugs. I was so angry I hit him . . . then again and again in the face until he was on the floor with blood squirting out of his face."

As he described the incident, it reminded me of a morning when I was at Steak and Ale and a big black-haired Italian-looking guy showed up. He started yelling at Terry, the owner, and he beat him with his fist, breaking his nose and causing him to bleed. Seeing what happened, I ran from my station across the restaurant to help Terry. By the time I got there, the Italian guy had stormed out of the restaurant, leaving my boss wallowing around on the floor with blood dripping down his face.

I asked Terry, "Do you want me to call the police?"

"No, no, no! Do not call the police!" Terry said as he stumbled to his feet. "This is a personal problem between me and my investor, Bill. Stay out of this please."

Then it hit me. I thought I recognized the chaplain of the Atlanta Federal Penitentiary. I just couldn't place him because he was so out of place. Could this ex-Mafia guy be our chaplain?

The restaurant chain had been sold to Pillsbury, a publicly traded food company, just as Bill, the ex-Mafia leader, described. The coincidences were mounting. If the man talking to Dobson and the man in Steak and Ale were the same person, then I understood the respect and even fear Terry had for the man who beat him up. Bill admitted that he was second-in-command of the Gambino family, and when Paul Castillano died, he was expected to become the god-father. Wow, this was quite scary.

Around the time of this beating, I felt an outpouring of the Holy Spirit on this restaurant that was unprecedented. I felt the Lord reach and touch everyone at work. God was really doing something inside this Steak and Ale that year. A black woman who set up the trays kept talking about feeling the presence of the Holy Spirit, and she would call out to Jesus over and over again during the working hours, asking Jesus to save everyone at work.

Oddly enough, Bill then described being convicted by the Holy Spirit just after he beat up his partner. He said he began to attend a small church. Then, with the help of the minister, Bill accepted Christ as his savior and became a Christian.

He then made a shocking decision. He decided to resign from the Mafia, which should have resulted in his death. You don't just quit the Mob.

In fact, Paul Castillano said, "If you follow Christ, I will be forced to put a hit on you, Bill." Translation—I will kill you, Bill.

Just after Paul Castillano told Bill he was going to have him killed, Bill was put back into prison at the Atlanta Federal Penitentiary. Turns out, Bill previously murdered a man for the Mafia. The police caught up with him for a crime he didn't commit and put Bill in prison for manslaughter. Who would think that being accused of a murder could save a person's life? But that is exactly what happened. While Bill was in solitary confinement, the Mob couldn't kill him.

One day while in solitary, Bill listened to his neighbors in the prison talk, as he so often did to pass time. But as he listened, he heard something very disturbing. The two guys described one of his soldiers whom Paul Castillano had put a hit on . . . a guy named Bill who lived in Buckhead. This guy Bill was way up in the Mafia and reported directly to Castillano. They then said they had made multiple attempts to kill him. By now Bill knew they were talking about him.

Bill listened intently as they described their numerous attempts to put a bomb under his window in his Atlanta home just after he went to bed. They would lay the bomb under Bill's bedroom window at night, they would press the detonation button, and the bomb would not detonate. They tried detonating several bombs, again and again, but the bombs failed to explode. They would then take the bombs out to an empty field, and with one press of the button, the bombs would explode.

One of the guys said, "That was the strangest thing that I had ever seen. What do you think was happening? This lucky son of a bitch was impossible to murder."

By now Bill hated these two men and wanted to kill them.

After praying and asking God for permission to murder these two men, Bill felt God tell him in his mind, "You must slay these men in the Holy Spirit as you have been slain. You are not allowed to harm them."

Around this time, Bill was released from solitary confinement. Although miffed that he couldn't exact revenge, Bill managed to testify to these lost men about Jesus. Bill explained to them why their bombs didn't explode.

Bill said, "God was protecting me, and God wants to save and protect you two men as well, so you can spend eternity with Him in heaven."

These hit men knew something was amiss when the bombs didn't explode. And with the love exhibited by Bill, love placed in Bill by Jesus, these men turned their lives over to God and quit the Mafia.

Paul Castillano happened to be gunned down in the streets of Chicago while Bill was in prison. Since no one else had a hit on Bill's life, Bill was now safe from any further attempts on his life. I might add, the other two men who accepted Christ were also free to follow Christ without fear of retribution. Isn't God amazing?

Upon exiting the prison, Bill prayed to God and asked Him what he was to do with his life. Bill felt God wanted him to become a chaplain at the Atlanta Federal Penitentiary. And it was there that

Beth, Jessica, and I met Bill while attending his services. I knew I recognized him when I first met him in prison, but I could not place his face at the time.

It was this amazing connection that all pointed back to the outpouring of the Holy Spirit at Steak and Ale. The outpouring initiating by my favorite black waitress. That outpouring led to the salvation of the number two man in the Gambino family, the man next in line to run the family after Paul Castillano died. And that outpouring also led to the salvation of two men that had repeatedly tried to kill Bill.

Our Son is Born

Since Beth had one C-section in the past, the physician recommended Beth have another section for the second child. We wanted a boy, but we were so delighted with Jessica we really didn't care. We went to the hospital, this time with an appointment. And this time everything went well. There were no problems from what I could tell as the baby was perfectly fine. They handed the boy to me, and I carried him around as a proud father and went to Beth's hospital room. While I talked to Beth, a nurse in Beth's room did not like the way the baby boy looked.

She said, "He looks gray. Something is wrong. Please let me have the baby."

"No," I retorted. "He looks fine to me."

The nurse was agitated. "Give me that baby now!" she yelled. She grabbed him out of my arms and ran out of the room down the hall.

The next time I saw our baby, he was in a clear plastic bassinet with about five hoses sticking out of him, including one taped down his throat that helped him breathe. I thought I was going to be sick when I saw our poor baby son tied down and immobilized with tubes out of his body and ties on his wrists.

I found the neonatologist, an Indian woman with a red dot in the middle of her forehead, and I asked her what was wrong with our baby.

She said, "He is critical."

"How can he be critical?" I asked.

"Apparently his lungs aren't developed. He was premature when he was born."

I said, "But he weighed nine pounds two ounces, how could he be premature?"

She said nothing. She simply walked away from me.

I left in a state of shock.

The next day after discussing our son's condition with my wife, I went looking for our son's neonatologist again. I found her alone, sitting at a desk in her office.

After reintroducing myself and reminding her which baby was ours, I asked her simply, "What are his odds?"

"I hate to give odds," she responded.

"Surely, his odds are good. Say, better than 90 percent?"

"I hate to give odds," she said.

"Would you say better than 80 percent?" There was no response. "Seventy percent," again no response . . . "Sixty percent?"

"I hate to give odds," she said again, looking perturbed.

"Are they better than 50 percent?"

Once again, "I really don't want to give odds. But it is not good."

"Are they better than 20 percent?" I asked.

Finally, she told me the truth. "Chris, your son is going to die. And if he somehow survives, he will probably have brain damage, and he will never function as a normal human being."

It was like a blow to my chest. I thought I had entered the theater of the bizarre. This couldn't be happening to me. I was sure our son's odds were better than 70 percent. It didn't make sense that God would allow our son to be this sick or die.

I asked, "Is there anything I can do?"

"You can give blood to the Red Cross for him."

I was shaken. I left her office with tears in my eyes and wandered back to my wife's hospital room as if in a daze. I told her everything.

I knelt at the side of her bed, and we prayed for our unnamed baby boy. We were both in a state of shock. I spent the night in the hospital, sleeping on a bench. I really didn't sleep that night. The next morning, I went home and changed and went directly to my office. I don't remember anything about work that day. I went through the motions. But I couldn't have been of much use. Fortunately, being the corporate controller, I was free to come and go as I pleased.

During the day I managed to call family and friends and ask for their prayers.

Then out of the blue, my friend Mike called me at home later that evening and asked, "Has Beth had the baby yet?"

"Yes, she has Mike."

"How is he?"

"Well, apparently, there are complications."

"What kind of complications?" Mike asked.

"The doctor doesn't think the baby will live. If he lives, she says he will never function as a normal baby."

There was silence on the phone. Mike sounded stunned. Then he said, "We'll pray for him. That's it, Chris. We'll pray for him! Don't worry I'll talk to the chaplain. I'll call you tomorrow at the same time Chris, okay? Don't lose faith. Remember, I'll call you tomorrow at 7:00 PM on your home phone. You'll be there, right?"

"Yes, Mike, I'll be here."

"Don't forget, Chris, I'll call you tomorrow at seven." With that, Mike hung up the phone.

The next day Mike called me at exactly seven, just as he said he would.

He said, "The chaplain has started a prayer chain. We are going to pray twenty-four hours a day around the clock until your son is healed. I'll call you the same time tomorrow to see if he is healed yet."

These prisoners did just that, and they prayed night and day for our son. Mike called me every day at seven to check on our baby's status.

The next day Mike called again. "Chris, is there any news?"

"No, there's nothing to report, Mike. The baby has tubes out of his side. He has tubes out of his mouth and a machine that is breathing for him. He's in the preemie ward. It's not good, Mike," I said, trying to hide my tears.

"The chaplain has asked us to pray for him, and, we are praying around the clock twenty-four hours a day for your son. Chris, these men are fasting and praying for him. I'm up at 3:00 AM, and it's hard to stay awake until four . . . believe me. But we are praying an hour each and rotating through to pray for your boy. I'll call you tomorrow the same time to see how he's doing."

I realized I was fighting a spiritual battle, and now I realized I was not fighting that battle alone. This ex-Mafia leader named Bill and his congregation were praying for our son, and somehow, I knew their prayers went up to heaven and would help save our son from certain death. Isn't it wonderful how God brings friends to our aid when we are in our hour of greatest need? These are friends we may have feared in the past. Friends who might have been evil. Friends recreated from the inside out by the heart and mind of Christ Jesus, our Lord. Friends who have become one with Christ.

And here, in Beth's and my greatest hour of need, it was this ex-Mafia leader and Chaplain named Bill and his "sinful men" who called upon the Lord to save our son. It doesn't take a great deal of imagination to realize that I, too, am a sinner and in God's eyes am no more special to Him than they are. That is what makes their prayer so special.

I left work early a few days later and headed home. Changing quickly, I headed back to the hospital. I think I prayed the whole time I drove without stopping. I lost it on the way to the hospital that day and wept like a child as I drove the last stretch to the hospital.

Just outside the hospital, on a country road, I came to a stop sign and paused to wipe tears from my eyes and to recompose myself.

Then the strangest thing happened. This was the second time in my life I heard a voice.

The voice said, "Chris, don't you know I love you and your family? Your son is going to be fine, and you are to name him Joshua."

Once again, I put the car in park. I hopped out of the car and said out loud, "Who said that?"

No one was there! No one was walking around the car or in the back seat. There was a cow on top of the hill on the other side of the car. He couldn't have said that, I thought. After looking all around, even under the car, I got back into the car, turned the car back on, and began to drive slowly up the road. The closer I got to the hospital, the more I realized what had happened.

"Was this an angel?" I thought.

But he said, "I love you and your family."

"Was this God? Was I losing my mind?" I didn't know what to make of this strong voice.

The closer I got to the hospital, the more I realized this had to be a message from God. After that moment, I became excited as I drove down this final stretch of road to the hospital. When I got there, I parked in visitor parking and dashed into Beth's room.

Arriving out of breath, I called to her just as I slid into her hospital room. I had on slippery moccasins that morning, so I literally slid into her room.

"Beth, Beth" I said, "you aren't going to believe what just happened. Our son is going to be fine, and we are to name him Joshua."

Beth looked at me like she was searching for something. She said quietly, looking at her hands, "Joshua."

I was delighted she liked the name, as God gave me that name, so I felt we had no choice but to name him Joshua.

Then I said, "Listen, Beth, I know he is going to be fine. Don't worry. Everything is going to be all right."

Beth still examined her hands front and back. Then she said, "Nurse!"

"Nurse?" I thought.

I looked to my left and noticed there was someone else in the room. A young nurse stood at the foot of Beth's bed. I did not see this nurse as I slid into Beth's room.

In response to Beth's call, the nurse walked up beside Beth on the other side of the hospital bed.

Beth said, "Nurse, do you have a psychiatric hospital here?"

Beth paused for a minute, waiting for the nurse to respond.

"Why, yes, Mrs. Morris, we do, it is on the third floor, why?"

"Well, I guess the stress has affected my husband." Beth paused, searching for words. "I think my husband has gone crazy."

"No, you don't understand," I interjected. "When I was at this stop sign on the country road there," I pointed out the window, "God said He loved me and my family and that our son was going to be fine. Then He said we were to name him Joshua."

I looked at the nurse, feeling completely helpless. I realized how crazy this sounded and feared what might happen to me.

Standing by Beth's side, this Jewish-looking nurse who was less than five feet tall—she had a long face, long black hair, and freckles—said with authority, "Mrs. Morris, I am a Christian, and I believe your husband is telling the truth. And instead of questioning his mental health, I think you should be praising God for the miracle that is about to occur." She turned to me and smiled as she walked briskly out of the room.

I was perplexed when she said she was a Christian, as my mother was Jewish, and this woman looked more Jewish than my mother. But my mother's family converted to Christianity, so perhaps she was a convert. It was amazing how similar her long face was to the pictures of Jesus.

"Thank God," I thought. I was relieved when this sweet nurse walked by me and didn't call the paddy wagon.

The Nurse

They started to wean Joshua off the breathing apparatus the next day. It was supposed to take four to five months to get him off the respirator and that awful hose that was taped to his mouth and that ran down his throat into his lungs.

Beth still doubted that our son would be fine, while I was confident Joshua would be completely healed . . . or at least I thought . . . or hoped . . . okay, I practically knew he was probably going to be fine. You can see clearly how much faith I almost . . . almost have!

In a few hours, Joshua was weaned completely off the breathing apparatus. The doctor said it was amazing how quickly he recovered and how strongly he fought to get off the machine.

"Wow," I thought, "that is a good sign. At least I hope this is a good sign."

The neonatologist then asked that we have Joshua tested over the next few months, including one test a year later, to see what brain damage had been done. To everyone's amazement, except for mine, our son's first tests showed no evidence of brain damage.

You see, I heard His voice. It must have been a voice commanded by God that told me not to worry, so I knew our son would be fine!

Before we left the hospital, I tracked down our neonatologist. This doctor was obviously a brilliant woman. She was still sporting a red dot on her forehead. I could only assume she was a Buddhist.

In her office, I said, "I thought our son was going to die?"

She said, "I did too. It is remarkable, Mr. Morris, how strong your son was when I weaned him off the oxygen . . . how he fought and how quickly I was able to take him off the breathing apparatus."

"Do you think he has brain damage?"

"It's too early to answer that," she said as she shook her head from side to side, "but the tests are clear so far." She then added, "I feared that if he lived, it would be terrible for you and your wife because of the severity of brain damage." Shaking her head again, she said, "We will not know for a year how much damage was done, but I am encouraged by the tests so far."

I expected her to add that it was a miracle. She never said that . . . not even once. Just as in the birth of our daughter, it was the doctor and nurses who convinced me that this was an extraordinary event. Over the next twelve months, tests were done, and they all showed that our son Joshua had no detectable brain damage.

At this point I felt the evidence indicated this was a miracle! I wanted to thank the nurses who worked so hard to take care of Joshua. My wife and daughter, Jessica, never left Joshua's side while he was in the hospital. While in the hospital, Beth held Joshua's hand until she fell asleep in the chair by his bassinet. When she woke up, she held our baby's hand. She was there for him around the clock.

I would come to the hospital and take Jessica to dinner every night and bring Jessica back with dinner for my loving wife who never left Joshua's side during those stressful days.

A few days later, Beth called me at work and said, "He's okay, Chris. Our baby is fine. And we can go home now. Will you come by the hospital on your way home and pick me up? I need to take a shower, brush my teeth, and go to bed."

Immediately I left work and went to a florist up the street. I purchased the largest vase they had and asked them to fill it with beautiful flowers. It looked like a hotel flower arrangement. It cost a lot, but I didn't care. I then headed immediately to the hospital. When I arrived, I carried the flowers into the hospital, all six feet of them, and put them on the counter in front of the nurse's station. Martha was the only nurse at the station when I arrived.

I said, "Hi, Martha."

"Hi, Chris, you brought me flowers . . . How sweet."

"Actually, these flowers are for all of you, including the Jewish-looking nurse who works here."

"Jewish nurse?" Martha paused. "Describe her."

"Well, she is roughly four feet ten inches tall, she has a long face, jet-black hair, freckles . . . oh yeah, and she says she is a Christian even though she looks very Jewish."

"Really, Chris?" Martha said as she turned her chair around facing me. "You know Sandy, Jane, and I work the day shift."

"Yes, I know each of you."

"In the evening there is Peggy, Jenny, and Carrie."

"I know each of them as well."

"And on the weekends, we have Michelle, Erica, Rosy, and Paula, right?"

"Yes, of course, I know each of them."

"Chris, there is no one who works here who fits that description. Those are all of the nurses on this wing."

"I wonder if she works in another ward and was just helping out?" I asked.

"Chris, I know all of the nurses in this hospital. No one here fits that description."

I choked and forced a smile. "Actually, these flowers are for all of the nurses who work here. We love each of you and want you to enjoy the flowers. Thank you for all of your help, Martha, and God bless," I said as I beat a hasty retreat to my wife's hospital room.

Jessica and I walked to the car, pushing Beth in a wheelchair as she held our newest family member Joshua in her arms. Martha accompanied us to the car and helped Beth and the baby out of the wheelchair into the car.

I was so happy I felt tears in my eyes. The tears were becoming a frequent problem of late.

As I drove down the road, where I heard the voice, I looked for the cow to see if she was still on top of the hill by the fence. She wasn't there.

After stopping at the stop sign, I turned to my wife and said, "Do you remember the woman who stood by your bed the day I told you our son was going to be fine and we were to name him Joshua?"

"The short nurse with long black hair?" Beth asked.

"Yes, didn't she have freckles on her face?"

"No, I don't remember freckles. But I remember her, the Jewish-looking woman who said she was a Christian. Why?"

"Because according to Martha, no one in the hospital fits that description."

I glanced to see if there was any reaction from Beth. Nothing . . . there was no reaction at all. Beth didn't move.

"I wonder, Beth . . . could that have been Mary, Jesus's mother? She did look like the pictures of Jesus."

"Bite your tongue. That is a Catholic tradition. We don't believe you pray to Mary for miracles."

"I know," I said as I accelerated down the road. Then I remembered this was a baby whom God healed and whom God named Joshua. How many people are named by God?

"I know that is a Catholic tradition, Beth, but who's to say the Catholics aren't right?" I said as we came to a stoplight at the end of the road.

*****

So why did our Lord name our son Joshua? As I studied Messianic Judaism, I studied Hebrew and discovered Jesus' name in Hebrew was Yeshua, which in the Old Testament was translated to be Joshua. Because the New Testament was written in Greek, His name was translated to be Jesus. Obviously, God was not naming our son Jesus, or Son of God, yet there must have been a hidden reason for our Lord naming our newborn Joshua. One translation periodically used for Joshua is warrior, but that is not an accurate Hebrew to English translation but is a recognition of the great acts performed by Joshua the leader of Israel after Moses.

So the mystery of our son's name must be wrapped up in the name Yeshua. What does Yeshua mean? Yasha in Hebrew means to rescue, to help, to make free, to preserve or to attain victory. A derivative of the word *Yasha* is *Yeshua*, which has been translated to mean "to seek salvation or to save." God named Joshua when he was on the brink of certain death just after he was born. On the way to the hospital a few days after his birth, I heard a voice in the back of the car say, "Chris, don't you know I love you and your family? Your son will be fine, and you are to name him Joshua." I think my Lord named our son Joshua to remind us of the miracle that was performed that fateful day, for Joshua's name can be translated into all those things: he was rescued, helped, made free, preserved, he was saved, and he attained victory that awesome day. Above all else, he received spiritual salvation because of his parents' faith in the true Yeshua Hamashiach, which is Hebrew for Jesus the Messiah. His name so beautifully fits the miracle that we witnessed that wonderful day.

Our son has since received an undergraduate degree in structural engineering at Georgia Tech. He then received a master's degree from Georgia Tech and was working on a PhD when he was hired away by a nuclear power engineering firm.

Another side note that is of interest, Joshua became a Freemason. As he went through the training, he had to memorize the first three degrees just like everyone else who becomes a Freemason. This typically takes most men three to six months, practicing six days a week. Joshua memorized each word perfectly from the first degree the second time his instructor went through the catechism. The next two degrees, he only had to hear once, and he had every word perfect. That's many pages of written words he had to memorize after one or two hearings.

Not bad for a person with permanent brain damage that will never function as a normal human being, I thought.

Later a friend of mine said, "When God heals us, He often puts in a little extra oomph in his healing. He must have done that for your son that day."

"He must have," I said as I smiled at my now-grown miracle named Joshua.

Aliens

When I was a five-year-old boy, I believed creatures with big eyes came into our home after I went to bed. They would go into my dad's and mom's room. One of these creatures would guard my door to keep me from going out. He could appear to be three feet tall, my height, he could disappear, and he could control my body so I couldn't move. My memories of these creatures were the most horrifying nightmares I ever had.

According to a psychiatrist friend, even though I insisted I saw these creatures when I was awake, I always saw them after I went to bed. He said it was not uncommon for children to confuse dreams with reality. He added, what happened to me was common.

In Texas, when I lived with my aunt and uncle, the summer after our parents disappeared, my uncle kept complaining that a blue guy about two feet tall would be in the kitchen sitting on a wide windowsill. My uncle saw him usually late at night when he heard strange noises downstairs. We all told Uncle LB he had flipped. To this day, he insisted this blue alien guy visited his home only when our family lived with him.

A physician friend of mine asked if I believed in aliens. I laughed at him and said, "Absolutely not." I was convinced such experiences were from the minds of delusional people.

When Joshua was not even a year old and Jessica was four, I had a nightmare. In my dream, I awakened from sleep because I heard a noise outside the home. It was a high-frequency, eerie sound. In the dream I got out of bed when I heard a racket at the front door . . . It sounded like someone was entering our home. When I got out of bed, I glanced at the clock. It was 2:34 AM. I ran to investigate, and I saw these little gray guys coming in the front door. They were about three feet tall; they had big black eyes; and they could project lights, like spotlights, out of their eyes that illuminated the floor in front of their feet.

In the dream I ran into Jessica's and Joshua's bedroom that was at the other end of the house on the second floor across from the master bedroom. I picked up Joshua, grabbed Jessica's hand, and headed to my bedroom. As I passed the stairs, I looked down the stairs, and these creatures, about seven of them, were more than halfway up the staircase. I tossed Joshua in bed and lifted Jessica up and put her in bed. I then went back to the door and put my left hand on the top of the door to hold it closed.

Jessica was awake but was tired and simply lay down to go to sleep. Joshua never woke up. As I leaned on the door, I heard these creatures' conversations, but I realized I was hearing their thoughts and could not understand their foreign language, which sounded like clicking, knocking, and squeaking sounds. I had turned off all the lights but then noticed a bright light illuminating the edges of the door I held closed. It wasn't too long until they walked right through the door, they walked by my legs, and came directly into our bedroom. One of them somehow coaxed Jessica out of bed, and the others surrounded her, and they led her out of the room right by me and through the door as I stood there in shock.

I was horrified. I looked in bed, and Joshua and Beth were sleeping. I woke Beth up and asked her how she could sleep at a time like this.

She said, "Chris, you know they will bring her back. They always do. Go back to sleep."

"How do you know that?" I asked.

I had no recollection of these creatures ever coming into our home before. This was my four-year-old daughter, and I was terrified for her. I paced the room and thought about what I could do to help her. I thought about calling the police. But who would believe me? I continued pacing.

After about fifteen minutes, another little guy entered our room. He walked right through the door as if it didn't exist. I thought for a minute as a physicist.

"The only way they can do that is they are going through other dimensions. Our universe must have more than three dimensions and these creatures live outside of our physical universe. That is how they disappear and reappear. They simply step into a dimension that we can't see."

This new creature stood right in front of me and froze me. I couldn't move. Looking right at him, I realized the others, several of which had entered our room after him, referred to him as their leader. Apparently, they traveled in groups. By now others had entered the room, and we now had six or seven little guys standing there that all walked together. They sounded like insects when they communicated to each other. But you couldn't hear them with ears. You could only hear their thoughts. Their insect sound was because it involved an elaborate clicking and beeping that was very fast. When they wanted us to understand their thoughts, we simply understood what one communicator put into our mind. It sounded like speech, but it wasn't audible.

Okay, before you call the paddy wagon, recognize everything I am telling you happened while I was asleep. This was all part of a complex dream I had. The communication methods these guys used was almost identical to the way Jesus put thoughts into my mind and read my thoughts.

Angels aren't ever upset or irritated. Instead they radiate love. The greatest, most wonderful love and peace I have ever felt was when I dreamed I was in the presence of my Lord and His angels. These creatures, on the other hand, were terrifying.

The leader was the same height, acted the same, but commanded all the other creatures to obey him. The only external difference I noticed was that the leader had large, granular red eyes and all the other creatures had black eyes.

The leader locked on my brain, not unlike how a computer grabs a network connection. And he immediately began to test me. Puzzles began to fly through my mind. Three-dimensional puzzles. Problems that I had to solve. I felt compelled to solve these problems. The tests got harder and harder, and the speed at which they were put into my brain increased. Finally, I missed a question. I was given the same three-dimensional problem again. About the third or fourth time, I solved a variation of the original problem. But I could not solve many more problems. They were just too difficult.

I somehow knew these creatures could not hurt me. They were prohibited from touching or injuring me. They could look, but they could not touch. They could mentally quiz me, but God would not allow them to permanently damage me. I suppose if they did touch me or harm me, they would have to repair the damage.

After the difficult test from the leader, I realized Jessica was back in our bedroom and the other creatures were in the room. Apparently Jessica was returned, and I didn't realize it. I also was surprised because they seemed to enter the house and rooms without opening doors, as if they moved through other dimensions.

Then the leader relayed a thought to me. "You did far better than I expected. I have clearly underestimated you. You will be a problem for me."

I remember thinking, "And who might you be?"

He said, "I am what you would call the devil, or Lucifer."

At this point, he began to hit the back of my head with the mental equivalent of a sledge hammer, again and again until I passed out. It hurt, and I felt I was going to die from the last impact. Clearly this guy hated me. He seemed to enjoy killing me. But of course, as with all dreams, instead of killing me, I simply woke up in the morning from this bizarre nightmare.

Because the dream was logical, introduced new information, and seemed to make sense, unlike most dreams, I wondered if this might be a spiritual experience. That morning I decided to tell my wife, Beth.

"Wow, I had a strange dream last night."

Beth said, "Yeah, I had a strange dream too." She paused and then said, "These creatures were coming into the room and you were holding the door closed, and I could see light coming into our room around the edge of the door. Then they entered the room and took Jessica.

"I remember, you were really upset about it, so I told you not to worry. I told you they would bring her back, and then I told you to go to bed. And then you wanted to call the police. I insisted you go back to bed."

"What did the creatures look like?" I asked.

"Big eyes, gray, and they could read my mind. I just wanted them to leave us alone so I could sleep."

I then explained my dream in detail to Beth. I added, "Isn't it amazing that we both had the same dream last night?"

"It was a dream, Chris."

"Yes, it was a dream . . . I wonder. I wonder if Jessica had a similar dream," I said.

I got out of bed and went down the hall and woke Jessica up.

"Hi, Jessica."

"Hi, Daddy."

"How are you this morning?"

"Daddy, these little guys with big black eyes came and took me with them last night. I don't like those little guys."

"Where did they take you, Jessica?"

"They took me to their ship. They couldn't touch me or hurt me. God wouldn't let them. But they could read my mind. They circled around me to protect me, and I knew God wouldn't let them hurt me. When we got to their spaceship, they took me inside and showed me stars. They then showed me where they were from in the stars.

"They seemed glad to see me. Then they took me back home. Daddy, they had lights that flashed out of their eyes on the ground. I knew they couldn't touch me or hurt me. God wouldn't let them touch me or hurt me, but I was scared, Daddy."

"What did they look like, Jessica?" I asked.

"They were my height and had big eyes, real big eyes. And they were smart. And they could read my mind and control me with their minds," Jessica said again, "They were my size." At the time, Jessica was under four feet tall. "They were gray and had long fingers. They were the little guys. I don't like them, Daddy. I hate it when they take me with them."

It was more than ten years later when I first heard of string theory. But that night I was introduced to the idea that we lived in a universe that had many more dimensions than the three we see in our world. String theory introduces the idea that there are ten dimensions. That means there are the three we know about, time is an irrational dimension that travels in one direction, and then there are six others. This may explain my ability to leave my body and travel to another world we can't see from earth. It also explains how the demons could walk through the walls and the doors of our home effortlessly. Of course, I am assuming that this was more than a dream, and I have no evidence or reason to believe that other than the fact that all three of us had variations of the same dream that night. I leave you with no further explanation as to what happened.

Joshua Is Choking

One evening when Joshua was about two years old, I came home from work, and Beth relayed an interesting story to me. After our normal cordial greeting, Beth asked me to sit down to tell me a story.

Beth said anxiously, "Chris, something very scary happened today. I was upstairs in the bedroom putting clothes up. Joshua was downstairs by himself in the den resting. Suddenly I had this awful feeling. I felt frightened and knew I had to check on Joshua.

"I ran down the steps and found Joshua in the kitchen. He was red and looked frightened. It took me a moment to realize he wasn't breathing. So I took him and held him on my shoulder and slapped him between the shoulder blades a few times. After a few harsh slaps, a hard candy popped out of his mouth and hit the floor. I heard a big inhale and sigh from Joshua."

"I don't know why I went looking for him. But I suddenly knew he was too quiet." Beth was shaking and crying when she said, "Oh my god, Joshua might have suffocated. I don't know why I went downstairs in such a hurry. But thank God I did."

"What does this mean?" Beth asked puzzled.

I didn't answer her. But over time I concluded this . . . I don't believe it was an accident that Beth knew Joshua was in trouble. Some would call it a mother's intuition, but I believe it has to do with the spiritual connection between a mother and her child.

Obviously, this is not a healing miracle, but I believe it was a miracle that saved our son's life.

Thank You, Lord, for saving Joshua, whom we love so very much and who truly has been a gift from You!

How many people have told me similar stories? I can't remember, but this type of story has been relatively common. Mothers are amazing. There is nothing more beautiful than a young mother with her child. That mother has an intuition, a sense about her child that can only be described as a deep spiritual connection. If I were to pick one spiritual experience that is consistent and beautiful among all peoples, I would pick a mother's spiritual connection to her children. It is as if mothers feel what their children are experiencing.

I Leave Racetrac

God had led me to the company at the very place I had taken my friend Chuck to several years before when I was in graduate school, and where I proudly announced to an unbelieving friend that I would one day be a financial officer of a large company right there where we stood. Now, in fulfillment of that prediction, I was the VP and controller for a billion-dollar convenience store business.

While in that position, I cut my staff in half, I improved the accounting department by leaps and bounds, and when the auditors from KPMG Peat Marwick were done with the audit of our firm, I was told all the numbers were 100 percent correct.

They had no adjustments, and the partner from the audit firm said to me, "Chris, I have never had an audit where we didn't change one number on the financial statements. Your numbers are perfect. But even more amazing than that, I didn't change a word in the annual report. This audit used to be a nightmare before you arrived. Thank you so much for helping my staff. You may be the best Financial VP I have ever met."

After all the improvements I made, after hiring truly wonderful staff, there was little for me to do. Having been a consultant with what was now Accenture, I was used to going into messes and turning companies around and then leaving them. Having turned this accounting department around, I was now totally bored.

My controller was a woman named Andrea. She was a brilliant accountant; she had a great attitude and was a large part of our success. Her dad had been an adviser to the president of the USA. Having this in common, we hit it off. We understood each other better than most, probably because we both knew that most of what we heard from the press was fiction. We also understood it consisted mostly of lies fed to pacify the masses and to get the desired results at the polls.

One day, Andrea asked to meet with me. It was unusual for her to schedule a meeting, but I had my secretary put her on my calendar.

When Andrea came into my office, she sat down and said, "Chris, I came here because I wanted to get your job one day. After working for you, I realize that you are the most brilliant accountant and financial officer I had ever worked for, and I have no opportunity for advancement with you here. I have decided to take a job working for Ted Turner at TBS."

"Really?" I said. "I'm sorry to see you go, Andrea. What will you do there?"

"I will be their controller."

"I'm sure you will do a great job, Andrea. I am truly sorry to see you go, but that is a great promotion for you, and I already know what a great job you will do. By the way, the Peat Marwick partner just told me the financials were perfect, and I wanted you to know, I owe our success in large part to you. You will be a great accountant at TBS, and you will be missed."

"Thank you, Chris, and I will miss you."

"By the way, have you got a minute for a brief story?"

"Sure."

"Well, it just so happens, when I was in graduate school, I met a man on a bus who knew Ted Turner years ago, I don't remember his name. Anyway, he said they were looking for a cable television business and asked me what I would recommend. I told him a news network. I recommended two channels: one that did a thirty-minute program that could run twenty-four hours a day instead of specific times, because I missed the news due to my hectic schedule when I was in graduate school. I then recommended a second channel that would delve into national and world news in detail in hopes to keep some of our government leaders in line."

"Good idea," Andrea said.

"I told him they could run the thirty-minute news and alter the news by pulling one story and replacing it with another as the news changed. But if there were no changes, they could just keep rerunning the same news over and over again. A year later CNN Headline News appeared on cable television.

"I told him I specifically wanted to keep the president of the US and others in government in check, because they were too powerful. I felt they needed to be held accountable. He was impressed with my recommendations. Another year or two passed, and Ted Turner created a second news channel that delved into national and world news in more detail."

Andrea smiled then said, "So you think CNN was your idea?"

"Truthfully, I don't know for sure whether or not they took my recommendation, but there are a lot of coincidences that point to that possibility," I said. "The strangest thing was this, Andrea. I prayed to Jesus to give me the opportunity to make this idea to create a news channel that would keep eyes on the White House, because I simply didn't trust the people in Washington. I then saw Jesus in a dream the morning I got on the bus, and He told me to hurry up or I might miss the bus. So if Ted Turner listened to my recommendation, I really have to credit Jesus for the creation of CNN."

Andrea looked puzzled and had a curious look of disbelief and concern on her face.

She finally responded, "I don't trust those government leaders either, Chris."

I wished Andrea the best with her future career, we shook hands, and she left.

*****

About a year later, I went down to the Omni in downtown Atlanta when a woman called my name. I turned. It was Andrea.

"Hi, Andrea, how the heck are you?" I asked.

"Fine, Chris, how are you?"

"I'm doing well! And how are you doing with your new impressive job?"

"I'm doing great, Chris. I love my job. By the way, you're the guy!" she said emphatically.

"Pardon me, I don't understand."

"You're the guy . . . you know, you're the guy who had the idea to create CNN."

"Really," I said. "I thought I might have been . . . I just didn't know for sure . . . How did you find out?" I asked.

"Well, Ted and the guy on the bus"—she used the name of the guy on the bus—"knew it was a graduate student at Georgia State University named Chris who came up with the idea to create CNN. So you must be the guy."

"That's amazing. I didn't expect to ever know this for sure. And now I know the truth, thanks to you."

After some more small talk, Andrea disappeared as she was late for a meeting.

As I drove back to work, it hit me how majestic and wonderful our Lord Jesus Christ truly is. I was awestruck. I prayed to create CNN to prevent a president from murdering innocent people such as my parents, and God heard me, and even better He did something about it. I didn't know what to say or think. My prayer, my faith, and God's actions changed the world. Wow! All I could do now was to hope it would change the world for the better. While Ted Turner owned CNN I believe he did an excellent job reporting the facts. I have been disappointed by the extreme bias of CNN and the inability of the news media to report the truth since he sold CNN.

Another Business Opportunity Appears

Having fixed all the problems at work, my department ran itself. I was bored. I didn't know what to do, so I prayed to God for a more challenging job. A few days later, I received a call from the top financial officer at Life of Georgia.

"Chris," Regis said on the phone. "A position just opened up, and I need someone to fill that position and oversee the accounting for our company. Are you interested?"

"Sure, let's talk."

Within a week I had put in my notice and a couple of weeks after that started work at Life of Georgia. My job was more narrowly defined, but Life of Georgia was a much larger company. We were owned by International Netherlenden Group, or ING. And I was not only responsible for our accounting, but I was to also oversee the merger of the accounting departments between Life of Georgia and Southland Life Insurance Company. Southland Life was in a little country town north of Dallas, Texas, called Plano. Now this was the type of challenge I looked forward to undertaking.

When I started, the accounting at Life of Georgia was at best a disaster. They did all their accounting using Lotus 123. Formula errors were everywhere in the calculations; the reports and the input were a disaster. It took these silly guys three months to close one month's books. It took them six months to convert the US accounting to Dutch accounting. And the statutory books were atrocious and full of errors.

Perhaps I had bit off more than I could chew, I thought. I had to not only handle the merger, but I had to clean up an accounting nightmare. I felt overwhelmed. Over the next year, I worked twelve to fourteen hours a day and all day Saturday. I refused to work Sunday as that was a day of rest. But the stress was getting to me. I had to find a way to convert this Lotus 123 accounting data into a mainframe accounting system. I went to my boss and asked to purchase insurance accounting software.

Regis said simply, "We bought the best accounting software that exists for insurance companies . . . We bought it three years ago and spent two years trying to get it running. I worked on it, and the guy you replaced worked on it. After two years we gave up. We will never get that software working. And we spent almost $1 million to purchase that crappy system."

This was the premier accounting system for insurance companies in America at the time. I decided to go with it.

"I can handle the conversion, Regis. I did this for a living at Arthur Andersen and have upgraded the accounting systems at every company I have worked for since then."

Regis laughed. Then he said, "Chris, I think it is a waste of your time. But if you think you can pull it off, go for it."

"I will need two people."

"You have your staff. You get no more people. You're going to have to make it work with their help."

I was overstaffed, anyway, I thought. I will use my two best accountants, and we will get the system converted in six months, I thought. At least I hope we will!

With my supervision, we had the system running in four months flat. It did not produce the reports exactly as Lotus 123 did, but I could get all the information that was on the existing financial statements in a slightly different format if the president and the chairman were willing to accept these new formats. I met with the president and chairman, and they gave me approval to go ahead.

After that, instead of it taking us ninety days to close one month's set of books, I was able to close the books in five workdays. That gave me two days to review and make final corrections, and I could issue the books to the president in seven workdays. Errors were eliminated; the reports were perfect. Now I was able to focus my time and energy on the merger. I kissed my wife goodbye and moved to Plano, Texas, in an apartment where I oversaw the conversion. We were done in six months, and it would have taken a year or more if I hadn't been able to get the new accounting system up and running. I then had to focus on the conversion of the US accounting to Dutch accounting.

This was the most complicated mess I had ever dealt with in my life. This was a three-dimensional accounting game. I had to go from US statutory statements (which are regulatory statements that we issued to the US states), to Dutch accounting for about half the accounts, and from US GAAP accounting (the type of accounting used in annual reports), to Dutch accounting for the rest of the accounts. Then I had to reconcile the differences that always occurred in the two different conversions. This was a nightmare. And it was all manual. I remember the day I reviewed the previous reconciliations. I was extremely upset as I believed it would take me six months to replicate what they had done the previous year if I was lucky.

I told my wife, "My job depends on me getting this darn conversion complete. The system that they used in the past is 100 percent manual and depends on the accuracy of all of the different GAAP statements and US statutory statements, or it will not balance."

"What are 'stisory' statements?" my wife asked.

"Statutory statements are regulatory statements that the States in America require us to issue each year if we sell business in those respective states. They calculate revenue, expenses, assets and liabilities differently than US GAAP.

"Oh," my wife said.

"Honey, if there is even a ten-dollar error in any of these underlying accounting reports, I will not be able to balance the US statements to the way the Dutch do their accounting without plugging one or more accounts randomly . . . and that is something I refuse to do."

"That's nice, dear," my wife said as she left the room to check on Jessica and Joshua.

It must sound like I speak a different language to her sometimes, I thought.

That night I finally knelt down and prayed, asking God for help. One wonders why we take so long to ask God for help! I suppose that is one of my failing weaknesses. My other failing weakness is not listening to God.

During the night I had a dream, and I saw Jesus. In the dream I could hear His thoughts and He could hear my thoughts. His thoughts in this case consisted mostly of pictures or images, and I had to translate them into English. This was difficult because He went way too fast for me and I had to ask Him to slow down. Finally, I realized what He was telling me to do, and I woke up.

The next day I went to work, hoping and praying that this visual model I dreamed about would work. At the office, I tried to figure out how to convert these images into a mathematical model that I could use. Then it dawned on me that I could convert the concepts I learned into a spreadsheet, and by using this multidimensional spreadsheet, I could reconcile the US GAAP to the US statutory financial statements and to the Dutch financial statements simultaneously. But what of the complicated reserve schedules that were calculated in entirely different ways in each of the three accounting formats? How would the spreadsheet do when I tried to reconcile these complicated accounts? The only way to determine if these spreadsheets would work was to complete the entire reconciliation and then balance all three financial statements. Only after I had completed each reconciliation and then built each set of financial statements and compared them, only then would I know for sure that the model Jesus gave me would work. Using these spreadsheets was where I had to step out on faith as I could not know for sure that the models would work until everything was finalized. Worse, I didn't know how long it would take to do this work.

Confident that this came from Jesus, I ignored the previous ways of doing the reconciliation, and over the next two weeks, I completely reconciled each account in all three different types of accounting models using my newly devised spreadsheet. I then built the income statements and balance sheets for all three systems and compared them. When I was done, I was amazed. I had just reconciled all three accounting methods to the dollar in two weeks, and everything balanced perfectly. This was amazing. It had never been done before in less than six months with two people working full time on it, and I had just completed the job in two weeks by myself without assistance from anyone else. Clearly the dream came from Jesus, and He gave me the solution. I was amazed and awe-inspired! Thank You, Lord, I thought. Thank You!

During this project, I identified several errors in a couple of the source documents my staff prepared for me. I found one error in the GAAP financials. I found a number of errors in the statutory statements. I was able to correct the statutory statements and annual reports before they were issued. I was also able to issue the Dutch accounting reports to Holland for the first time in February, five months sooner than ever before. It amazed me how God can help me out when I face simple worldly problems.

When done, I prayed, "You really know what You are doing, Lord." Then the thought "Is He not the Lord God Almighty, creator of the universe? Of course, He knows what He is doing."

It was then that I realized what little faith I truly have, and I felt ashamed.

The day I sent the report off to Holland, I was truly elated. When I went home, I was so excited I ran into the kitchen and said, "Beth, Beth, you're not going to believe this. I have solved the US GAAP to Dutch accounting problem with a spreadsheet Jesus gave to me in a dream. It was a miracle. I am done. And no one has ever been able to do this in less than six months. It took me less than two weeks from beginning to end. The merger is done, the accounting system is fully automated, and I have done the Dutch accounting, now all I have to do is issue the annual report."

"That's nice, Chris. Can you hand me the stewed tomatoes from the top shelf over there," my wife said, not missing a beat!

Okay, it was a big deal for me, maybe not for her, I thought.

But it was a big deal. About a week later, the chairman of the board came to see me in my office. I stood up as he entered the room, and he shook my hand.

Then Mr. Johnston said to me, "Chris, I wanted to personally congratulate you for the excellent job you did on the merger this year. Also, you are getting us financial statements, without errors, every month by the seventh workday. Yesterday the Price Waterhouse partner called David, who was the president of Life of Georgia, and told us that the audit was perfect, he didn't have to make any changes to the financials this year. I think you're the best person to occupy that job since I had your job. You're a young man . . . How old are you, Chris?"

"I'm thirty-four."

"I plan on making you the next president after David. Thank you for your excellent work," he said as he left the office.

He hadn't taken ten steps out of my office, and he turned around and walked back into my office. This time he got real close to me, leaned forward, and whispered in my ear.

"Chris, I need to correct myself. I believe you are a better accountant than me . . ." he said smiling. "But let's just keep that between the two of us." And with that, Lynn smiled and walked out of my office.

Promises, promises, I thought. This was the third chairman or president to tell me I would be the next president of a company. I then realized I had been made president of Georgia Medical a Company we owned and was put on the South Carolina Guarantee Association, both unusual honors for an accountant to receive within a year of taking a new job. So I guess I was getting recognition. I was also only thirty-four years old at the time and was in no rush to get promoted. I just wanted to do the best job I could for my company.

Each day I worked until noon. Then I would go downstairs at lunchtime to our company's workout facility, which was as extensive as an LA Fitness Center. I would change in the locker room and either play racket ball or run two or three miles around the neighborhood. I would then shower and change, rush back to the executive lunchroom, grab something to eat, and go back to work for the afternoon.

One day while I waited for the elevator, I wondered if I would do this for the rest of my life. Don't get me wrong—I was well cared for, I had a challenging job, I interacted with brilliant people, I suppose I was living the good life. But this day was unique. After a nice lunch, I remember standing by the elevator, and I asked God if this was going to be what I did for the rest of my life.

As is typical, there was no answer. I simply mused that this type of job could get boring once I mastered everything. But then my thoughts turned toward God.

"Lord, You see how successful I am in the business world. I am a thirty-four-year-old man. I have taken four companies public. I have been CFO or controller for three of the ten largest corporations in Georgia. I am currently president of a division of ING and top accountant for Life of Georgia, and I just oversaw the merger of the accounting and financial areas between Life of Georgia and Southland Life Insurance Company. And I have offered to serve You repeatedly with my skills. Yes, I talk to my fellow employees and bosses about You, but there are only a dozen people reporting to me directly that I interact with on a regular basis. And the opportunity to witness to many people is quite limited. Life of Georgia never fires anyone. So I will most likely work with these people and a few others for the rest of my life. Is this really what You want me to do?"

A few weeks later, I was wrapping up work and was about to head home. I was probably the only person left in the building that evening. I was looking out of the window at the mansions that surrounded the Life of Georgia building when this strange thought entered my mind.

"Chris, you're going to be fired."

I remember wondering where that stupid thought came from. But I had learned that when a strange thought enters my mind, that doesn't seem to belong to me. I need to consider the possibility that it came from God or the Holy Spirit.

"If that is You, Lord, clearly . . . You're mistaken," I thought. "The chairman of the company met with me a few weeks ago and said I would be the next president." I paused to consider all the contributions I made to our company. "Look at the improvements I have made here. I have implemented a new accounting system, I can close the books in seven days instead of ninety days, I eliminated almost all accounting errors, I pulled off a merger without a hitch in record time, and I found a way to produce the Dutch financials in a couple of weeks when it took my predecessor six months. You must be mistaken, Lord."

The thought occurred to me a second time. "Chris, you're going to be offered another job, but you will be happiest if you start your own business."

I had to sit down. I couldn't believe it. This must be from God because these thoughts seemed to come out of the blue as random thoughts. They were my thoughts and from inside me, but because they were something I never would expect myself to think, I questioned their origin. Then it hit me.

"Oh my god, I'm going to lose my job. And after all the improvements I made here. What am I to do?" I was in shock.

I decided not to tell my wife about my crazy thoughts when I got home that evening. I did make a point of leaving work early the next day. When I got home, I asked Beth to bring Jessica and Joshua to the car. I did not offer her any explanation as to where we were going or what I was doing.

That evening I drove Beth and the kids to a local furniture store where I promptly looked for, found, and bought a desk, credenza, and an executive chair for several thousand dollars. I paid for them with a credit card and asked the sales clerk to ship my order directly to our residence without a word of explanation to my poor wife who by now was pleading with me . . .

"What are you doing, Chris?"

You can imagine how she felt as we always discussed what we did and why we did things days or even weeks before spending thousands of dollars. Only this time I did not give her one word of explanation.

A few days later the desk, credenza, and chair arrived, and I had them moved into the basement. I then told my wife I planned on using the back room upstairs for my home office, in case I had to work at home. Beth argued with me, saying this was her sewing room and she didn't want to put my furniture in that room. Again I offered no explanation on what I was up to.

Shortly after arriving at work that Friday, I was asked to go directly to the Personnel director's office. The director of Personnel immediately invited me into his office and sat down with a grave look on his face.

I thought, "Here we go, that thought must have come from God, after all."

Michael said with gravity, "Chris, I wanted to tell you what an outstanding job you have done since you started here. But I am sorry to tell you, we are eliminating your position."

"How do you eliminate a financial officer's position?" I asked. "Did you plan this when you first hired me?"

There was no answer. I felt weak and ill. Now I had to tell my wife I had been fired for the first time in my life.

"Can you tell me why?" I asked helplessly.

"Actually, Chris, I can't tell you why. However, the good news is, while you are helping with the investment department, we now want you to take over all our investments and become our broker dealer. You will be responsible for all of our US investments as well as for all of our investment advisers."

"But I am already helping with the management of the investment department," I said confused.

"Believe me, Chris, this is not a demotion. We know you managed money for another insurance company and wanted to slot you into this position as Joel left our employment last week."

Joel had managed stocks and bonds for ING US.

"What did you say?"

Now was the moment of truth, I thought. If I say yes, I will have a comfy job with a steady paycheck. If I say no, I will be happier, according to the Lord. Should I quit and start my own business or accept the transfer?

What if that was not God and it was my own strange thoughts? I rarely have a strange thought that is from the Lord . . . Was this from the Lord?

Now I was angry with myself. "Get thee behind me, Satan," I thought. That had to be from the Lord. He has given me the option, and I want to please Him.

It must have seemed like an eternity to Michael.

Finally I said, "Michael, I appreciate the offer, but I have decided to go to work for my Lord and start my own business."

And with that I stood up, shook his hand, and left his office. I walked out of the building, sat in my car feeling completely weak and defeated, and prayed. My heart was pounding.

"Now for the real challenge," I thought, "what will I tell my wife when I get home?"

Knowing what is going to happen before it happens doesn't really help with the emotions when truth hits home. I felt a pit in my stomach. I didn't know what God was up to at this point in my life, but I knew I had to move forward and do His bidding, no matter what the challenges.

When I got home and told my wife, she took it far worse than I imagined. She sat down and cried.

"How did you know? You knew you were going to be fired. You must have done something wrong. And all that talk about the improvements you made at the company. What if we go broke? What if we can't feed our children?"

"I didn't do anything wrong," I insisted. I didn't dare tell her they offered me the job as investment officer. She would have killed me if she had known I turned that down. "It doesn't matter, Beth, God told me to start a business, and I must do what He has told me to do."

Beth cried silently and simply went to bed without me that night. When I climbed in bed with her and tried to cuddle, she pushed me away. I knew this was going to be a difficult transition, and I prayed, asking God if He really knew what He was doing, because I had no clue what He was up to.

****

That Friday evening, out of the blue one of my best friends, Chuck, called me. Chuck is the guy who went to graduate school with me, was friends with Shashi and me, and who went to the spot where Racetrac Petroleum would build their corporate offices one day.

He invited our family to meet with him and his dad up at Lake Lanier. Chuck and his dad lived in South Carolina but were visiting good friends who lived at Lake Lanier on Saturday morning. I remember telling Chuck that I was not in a good mood and really didn't feel I should go, that I had lost my job that day and was starting a CPA practice on Monday.

Chuck listened politely and said simply, "Chris, now I feel you absolutely must come. Bring your family. You will love the Millers, and . . ." He paused then said, "Their son owns a CPA practice. Perhaps he can help you out."

Finally I agreed. The next morning we all got in the car and drove up to the address at Lake Lanier. We did really enjoy the Millers, and Chuck was also correct . . . It was best that I got out of the house. Our children loved it, and Beth seemed happy to get out of the dreary house and depressed environment. In hindsight, I don't understand why I was depressed doing God's will. Even to this day, there are times when I feel I am doing God's will but have a bit of dread or concern that His will could have bad consequences on me and my family.

Mr. Miller asked me what I did, and I told him the truth that I had left Life of Georgia and was planning on starting a business as a CPA. Unfortunately, I had never run a CPA practice before and didn't know what I was doing or how to do that, but I believed I could figure it out. I didn't even have any clients yet.

Mr. Miller left the room, looking concerned, and we continued to chat with his wife. Then Chuck got up and left the room too. When they reentered the room, Mr. Miller said I was to go meet with his son, who ran a CPA practice down the road. He gave me directions and said my wife and children could stay with them while their son advised me on how to start a CPA practice.

I had no idea how valuable that couple of hours would be. I might even go so far as to say that without the help I received from Bill Miller, CPA, over the next few hours, I never would have been successful running my little practice.

I went back to the house at Lake Lanier, with ten pages of notes from Bill. After thanking the Millers for having us visit, we rounded up the kids, said goodbye to Chuck and his dad and the Millers, and headed home. I was excited when I got in the car and started driving.

"You are not going to believe this Beth. God really answers prayers. I now know what software to buy to start our CPA practice. I know what research material I should use. And I have all kinds of information on how to run the practice. Apparently, the AICPA society has manuals on setting up a CPA practice, how to manage a practice, how to hire employees, how to market your business, and how to prepare and check tax returns. I told you, honey, God was in this, and He will make sure we are successful. Imagine, the day I quit my job, I get a random call from Chuck, and he introduces me to a man who spends hours teaching me how to run a CPA practice. I don't think you have to worry, dear, it will all work out. I know it."

An Old Friend to the Rescue

A couple of years earlier, I had bought an airplane, a Cessna 182, with a friend of mine and a brilliant man named Bob. He had been a news broadcaster in his day under a different name. He retired to teach tennis and then came out of retirement to start a law practice. I really enjoyed Bob and his wife, Joan. He was Jewish and reminded me of my mother's family. He had a keen intellect and was one of the smartest men I had ever met. I trusted his judgment implicitly. If anyone could help me, I reasoned, he could.

So the first thing I did Monday morning was to call Bob and announce my intent to start a CPA practice.

"Hi, Bob, Chris. How are you doing?"

"Hi, Chris, fine . . . How are you?"

"I'm okay! Look, Bob, I just quit my job to start a CPA practice and was hoping you could give me some advice on how to run it. I am working out of my home, and I'm new at this, so I was hoping you could maybe let me buy you lunch so you could give me some advice."

There was a long pause. Bob then said, "Of course, Chris, I'll be glad to help you out. So why do you want to work out of your home?"

"I don't want to spend a lot of money, Bob, as I don't have any clients yet. I thought it would be wise if I started at home since I don't know if I will be successful."

"Chris, I want you to go to the office building we own together. You are to move into the building immediately. Let's go there this evening. I want you to pick an office and work out of that office. Is that okay?"

"I don't know if I can afford an office yet, Bob."

"Not a problem. Tell you what. We own the building together. I will give you six months free rent. You can pick the office you want. In six months I'll gradually increase your rent until twelve months, and you will pay full rent then. Is that fair?"

"I don't want to take advantage of our friendship . . ."

"Chris, I am not giving you the option. We have several open offices there. I want you to pick the office you want, but I will suggest you take the executive offices upstairs."

Thanks to Bob, I moved into the offices two days later and picked the perfect office for my new CPA practice.

That evening, Beth and I had an interesting conversation.

"Beth, honey, do you remember when you signed me up for that flying course . . . you know the one at the local high school where that guy—what was his name?—prepared me for the written pilot test?"

"Of course, Chris, I signed you up because I was taking a community school course at the high school. Yes, I remember."

"After I completed the course, I took the flight test and passed it. Having passed the test, I had two years to get my private license, so I started taking lessons, remember?"

"Yes, dear, I remember."

"I kept telling you, it was expensive to get a pilot license, but I believed God wanted me to take up flying. Remember that?"

"Yes, I do. Then you got your private license and instrument rating, and you bought that expensive airplane with Bob."

"I know. But I was convinced that God wanted me to buy that expensive airplane."

"I did like the trips to the beach," Beth added. "And we had fun traveling with Bob and Joan. Remember when we went to Virginia with them?"

"It was fun, wasn't it? Anyway, Beth, now I know why God wanted me to take up flying."

"Why?"

"Well, after I bought the airplane with Bob, he talked me into purchasing this office building in Tucker."

"Yes."

"Bob says the business would fail if I worked out of my home. He says I absolutely must move into an office building and he is going to let me have an office in our office building for free for six months. By then we should know if this business is going to succeed or not.

"I trust Bob, Beth. He is a brilliant lawyer, and he is going to help me get this business started and off the ground. So don't you see?"

I paused for a reaction. There was none.

"That's why God had me take up flying! So I would have Bob's help in starting this business. And so we would own an office building . . . That way I wouldn't work out of our home. Get it? You see, God is in control and planned this all along."

"That's nice," Beth said quietly.

Jessica Stretches Our Faith

Jessica and Joshua slept in a trundle bed that we positioned at a right angle from one another.

Every night before bed, I joined them and knelt by their beds to pray. We would pray:

> Now I lay me down to sleep, I pray the Lord my soul to keep, if I should die before I wake, I pray the Lord my soul to take.

Then we would say the Lord's Prayer:

> Our Father who art in Heaven, Hallowed be Thy Name. Thy kingdom come, Thy will be done on earth as it is in Heaven. Give us this day our daily bread and forgive us for our trespasses as we forgive those who trespass against us. Lead us not into temptation, but deliver us from all evil. For Thine is the kingdom, the power and the glory for ever and ever. Amen

After these two prayers, we would then pray for whatever we wanted or needed. I remember this cold Friday night. It was March 2, 1990, exactly one week after I quit my job. Thoughts were racing through my mind about starting the business, feeding my children, taking care of my wife, and keeping her from leaving me.

While my mind was racing, Jessica was praying, "And, Jesus, I would like to have a bicycle."

I was stunned because she had never asked for anything quite that specific before. While we each prayed for this, I remember thinking, "Maybe I should purchase a bicycle for Jessica, so she learns that God answers prayers."

I then wondered if that was fair as we were asking God to provide her with a bicycle. But I didn't want to hurt her faith if God didn't provide her with a bicycle.

Underneath I knew if the business failed, we risked being homeless. I was afraid to purchase a bicycle for her. I then prayed silently to myself and asked God if I should take my savings, which we might need for food in the future, and spend part of it on a bicycle. I went to bed praying and asking for clarity on what I should do.

The next morning was a cold Saturday morning. Around 7:00 AM, the doorbell rang. I rolled over and tried to ignore it, but it rang again and then again. Finally I climbed out of bed, put blue jeans on, and pulled a T-shirt over my head and bounded down the steps to the front door. I was ready to attack as I opened the door, and right there before me stood Kara, a sweet seven-year-old girl who played with Jessica periodically. I bit my tongue.

"Hi, Mr. Chris, is Jessica home?"

"She's asleep. How can I help you, honey?"

As most children do, she sensed I was upset and said, "I am so sorry, Mr. Chris, I came by so early, but I was so excited this morning. You see, I got a new bicycle for my birthday yesterday. It's a beautiful Schwinn 10 Speed."

"That's wonderful," I responded, feeling guilty, knowing I couldn't afford to buy Jessica a bicycle.

"But, Mr. Chris, you don't understand. I want to give Jessica my old bicycle, since I got a new bicycle for my birthday. Anyway, I wanted you to know . . . and I will bring the bicycle over later, will you tell Jessica for me and I'll come by, so we can ride bicycles together."

*****

When Jessica awakened, we all got dressed to leave the house. As we began to walk out of the house, leaning against the wall by the front door was a used green bicycle with a note taped to the seat from Kara's parents. It was a little worn and rusted but was the most beautiful bicycle I had ever seen, and it was the perfect size for Jessica. It even had training wheels.

"Jessica, look at the bicycle that Kara left for you today," I said.

Jessica walked over to the bicycle and put her right hand on the seat and turned to Beth and me and said, "I've been expecting this."

"Such is the faith of children," I said to Beth.

It was as if God was saying, "I love Jessica. Chris, you can't afford to buy a bicycle, but I can't help but give her the bicycle she wants."

We Start Our CPA Practice

The road to starting our CPA practice was rocky and far more difficult than I ever imagined. Not knowing how to get clients, I would simply drive from one group of office buildings to another and ask to talk to the owner. I would then pitch my business. This was incredibly time-consuming and, based on my calculations, would never garner enough business for me to pay our bills.

I remember one day about a month after I started the business. I had been going door-to-door to get clients and that week I had no success. I finally knelt down and prayed.

"Lord, if You really want me to do this CPA practice thing, I need Your help. Could You please send me a client through the door today?"

A few hours later, a man entered my office, sat down at my desk, and said, "Hi, I'm Jack Bishop. I drive by here every day, and I noticed your sign out front. I own a plumbing business and have been doing my own tax work, and I have decided this corporate tax return is just too complicated and I need some help. Can you help me out?"

Talk about an answer to prayer. Over the next ten years, he was the first of two walk-ins that hired us.

Jack not only became a valued client; he became a good friend. I remember more than once taking Jessica by the hand, pushing Joshua in his baby stroller, and walking up the street two blocks to Jack's home. His business was behind his home. The kids loved to go with me because they loved to play with Jack's dogs that also lived behind his home. Jack had several bird dogs and loved hunting quail, and it wasn't long before Jack got me to buy a shotgun and go quail hunting with him in the winter. I couldn't afford a vacation back then, so this was my vacation. My wife enjoyed it too. Martha, Jack's wife, would go with us, and we would hunt quail in the morning until noon, when it really got too hot to run the dogs. During that time, the women would set up a picnic lunch and talk. When lunchtime arrived, both families would sit down together at a picnic table and eat sandwiches and Kentucky Fried Chicken with potatoes. All of this came to us because of prayer.

God really met our needs in the early days after we started the CPA practice. Bob, our lawyer friend, a partner in the plane and building, was instrumental in referring several key clients to us that were needed over the coming years to pay our bills. About 25 years later, when Bob passed away, I prayed and thanked God for Bob. As I silently prayed, I felt the Holy Spirit come upon me.

"I sent Bob to help you, Chris."

Tears came to my eyes as I knew just having Bob's help was a miracle and we never would have been successful without his help. Who says God doesn't love the Jews?

During the early years of starting a business, we had been attending a small prayer group. This group was closely knit Christians that behaved much like the early church. If anyone needed money or food or clothes, they helped each other out. I believe if we had gone bankrupt, they would have been glad to help us, but fortunately that never happened. In the interim, I helped them build a church building, using skills I learned from my grandfather. We often got together and ran three or four miles in the early morning, and we enjoyed family "get-togethers" that usually centered around eating lunch or dinner.

A member of our prayer group, Jerry, was frequently trying to promote our CPA practice. He referred me to a furniture business that became a valuable and helpful client over the next couple of years. One day Jerry referred me to a young woman who did telemarketing for CPA firms. For the last few months, I had been in my car driving to different office buildings and selling my services door-to-door. Fewer than 2 percent were interested in hiring our CPA firm, and I could only meet with four or five prospects a day.

So I gladly took up Jerry's offer and met with Alyson to learn how she telemarketed CPA practices. Alyson came by our office and gave me a script. We paid her for a few hours while she demonstrated the process. The next day, full of hope, I began telemarketing. Wow, this was exactly what I needed. It took eight hours of calls to get one appointment, but that was a lot better than driving door-to-door. The problem was this: while I could schedule five appointments a week, I could not do the telemarketing and meet with the prospects at the same time.

I had a brilliant idea. I called my wife Beth and asked her to come to the office and work with me full time. Her job was to telemarket while I drove to each appointment she scheduled for me to sell our services. Beth also did her part-time work for a missionary organization.

We set up an office for Beth and a separate office for our kids. We gave Jessica and Joshua a TV, a computer, and video games, and we often stopped and played with them during the day. They could always leave their office and come and visit with us anytime, and their needs took precedence over anything else we were doing. Even if we were in meetings with clients, the kids were free to come into our offices and talk to us.

At any rate, Beth was far more successful as a telemarketer than I was and could book an appointment for me every four hours of phone calls. By doing that, she could schedule me for ten appointments a week. I would then have a full-time job going from appointment to appointment, signing up new clients. I converted about 40 percent of her referrals to new clients. That meant we were picking up a new client each day.

Because of help from friends, as guided by God, within a year, our business revenue matched the salary I previously made. Don't think I made as much money, because our revenue before expenses only matched my salary, and I still had a lot of expenses to pay. But we were able to make ends meet. There was another problem we encountered. Within six months, I realized I had to start doing some accounting and tax returns to keep up with the workload, and it wasn't too long until we had to completely abandon telemarketing and focus all of our time on doing the work we had sold.

By year two, once we got busy, we never had time to market our business again. Jerry, hearing of our plight, introduced us to Emily, one of the women in the prayer group who was looking for work, and she telemarketed for us for another year. Jerry's business sold furniture they manufactured. So Emily would call businesses and offer our CPA services. If they were happy with their CPA, she would talk to them about custom-made furniture, and if they weren't interested in the furniture, she would ask them, "Do you know Jesus?" I would shake my head when I listened to her, because she really connected with people. Emily was in her forties and had received two marriage proposals that year over the phone.

By now it was apparent that God had provided several miracles to get our business started. These things may sound small, but they were huge to us, and they occurred exactly when we most needed help. Without any one of these events occurring our business would have failed. It was by the grace of God that our business prospered.

I learned over the years that had God made us rich; we would have learned to worship money instead of Him. Money is an idol, and the Jews teach us that the worship of money is something that the Gentiles do. God doesn't want us to worship money. He wants us to learn to rely on Him. He is sufficient for all our needs, and He is ready and willing to step in and help us whenever we need His help, provided we first trust Him and have the courage to step out on faith.

Animals

The faith of children is simple and amazing. For the first time I was beginning to understand why Jesus said we needed to have the faith of children. In Matthew 18:2–5, Jesus says the following:

> Truly I tell you, unless you change and become like little children, you will never enter the kingdom of heaven. Therefore, whoever takes the lowly position of this child is the greatest in the kingdom of heaven. And whoever welcomes one such child in my name welcomes me.

But our children . . . well, everything they prayed for, they seemed to receive. We did not have riches or fame or fortune. What we had was faith. Jessica prayed for a dog, and the next day a client brought a dog into our offices, asked to see Jessica, and then gave her the dog. Jessica and Joshua prayed for several kitty cats, and in short order were given two cats. Everything Jessica and Joshua prayed for, they seemed to get given to them, and Beth and I never participated in answering their prayers. They were simply given to them, or in some cases, wild cats that professionals had been trying to catch for years, simply allowed themselves to be caught by Jessica and Joshua. At first this was freaky. But before long, it was expected. We were no longer surprised when prayers were answered. We were only surprised when it took a few days for the prayers to be answered.

> Jesus said to him, "If you can believe, all things *are* possible to him who believes." (Mark 9:23)

The only thing I could figure was happening was that our children were not burdened with the world and were not yet tainted by the lusts and desires of the things of this world, so they had an easy time connecting their spirit to the Lord's Holy Spirit.

We Need Help

We had been in business for two years. By now Beth and I had stopped marketing and simply relied on referrals to grow our business. Beth was an excellent accountant, so I bought another computer for her and set her up to do the monthly bookkeeping. I would do the complicated books and tax returns, and she would do the normal books and 1040 tax returns.

While she had done accounting at Rollins Inc., she did not have much tax experience. One of my best friends, Phil, had been a tax manager at Arthur Andersen. We asked Phil to be a partner in our business, and he trained Beth to do taxes and assisted me with immensely complicated returns. Phil was a devout Christian, and he and his wife, Donna, became great friends of ours. They even attended the small church I played the piano for, and we shared season tickets to the Braves baseball games and would sit together and catch up during the games.

How many CPAs have access to a "big 8" accounting firm manager for help when complex problems arise. On several occasions Arthur Andersen partners saved our clients. Phil and the partners were always happy to help us out with simple, clear advice at no charge, provided the answers only took a few minutes over the phone. Having Phil's help was clearly another miracle provided by our Lord.

*****

One day a local karate school called. They wanted to hire us to do their accounting. Tucker was a small town, and they knew we had two very young children. They wanted to trade karate training for Jessica and Joshua for accounting services. I realized Beth and I needed to exercise more, so I signed the whole family up for lessons. We habitually went to the karate studio at lunchtime for training. There were typically twenty-plus people in the room. The students lined up from front to back with our best karate student, Kora, at the front right of the class. Since Beth and I were new, we stood at the back of the room, which was the lowest position. We learned quickly that when you enter the studio you bowed, when you left the studio you bowed, and you never spoke during lessons. Only the instructors spoke.

One warm summer Friday, Beth and I were about to go to karate class and then lunch. We had worked long hours and were exhausted.

Beth said to me, "Chris, I am completely worn out."

"I know how you feel, honey, I'm exhausted too."

"At what point do you think we should hire someone?"

"I'm not sure we can afford to, but I believe we need to hire someone or we will die from exhaustion," I said.

"You agree with me?" Beth asked, surprised that her slave driver husband might consider hiring help.

I grabbed Beth by the hand and pulled her to her knees next to me. "I think it is time that we go to God in prayer and ask Him for His help."

On our knees by my desk, I closed my eyes and prayed, "Lord, we are at our wits' end. I don't think Beth and I can continue to work this hard, and I believe we really need help. Could You please send us someone who can work for us and help us out? I believe we could do the work, but we need to spend time with our children. Plus, our children need to get out of the office and spend time with other children their age. Lord, You know what we need better than me, I only ask that You provide the best help You consider appropriate, and not my will but Thy will be done."

Immediately after we prayed, we stood up and rushed out of our offices, locked the doors, hopped into our car with the children, and drove over to the American Karate Studio . . . And once again, we were late. Beth and I changed into our karate gees in a NY minute. We bowed quickly and rushed to the back of the room without saying a word and joined in the exercises.

Mr. Cape, our instructor, said, "We're glad you could make it, Chris and Beth," which was a nice way of scolding us for being tardy.

We joined our class by doing karate punches. When we paused after the punches, Kora, our best student, who was about to test and become a brown belt said, "Chris . . ."

"Yes, Kora?" I said. Speaking during class is not something you do, but Mr. Cape said nothing.

"Chris, God told me that I'm supposed to work for you. When do you want me to start?"

"Begin front kicks," Mr. Cape commanded.

The entire class kicked and chimed in unison, "Hiya, hiya, hiya, hiya, hiya."

Out of breath, I said, "Kora, we would love to hire you. You can start anytime, even this afternoon if you want."

"No, I can't start this afternoon!"

"Begin left side kicks."

"Hiya, hiya, hiya, hiya."

"What if I start on Monday?" Kora said between kicks. "Can I show up at your office at 9:00 AM on Monday?"

"Sure," I said, "anytime you want, Kora."

"Begin right side kicks."

"Hiya, hiya, hiya, hiya."

"We look forward to working with you," I said, out of breath.

"How should I dress?"

"Begin back kicks."

"Hiya, hiya, hiya, hiya, hiya!"

"Casual," I said as we finished our back kicks.

My thoughts were simply that of disbelief.

After the lesson, Beth said with excitement, "Can you believe that we prayed and within an hour God provided someone to work for us? He must really be a part of our business after all."

I answered, "I know you are stressed, as I am, but if you want proof that we are doing what God wants us to do, you don't have to look any further than this miracle to see that He is with us and our business."

Kora Is a Blessing

Kora was not interested in doing accounting. But she was interested in helping raise our children. We paid Kora, and she did secretarial work in our offices. But she did so much more. It was not uncommon for us to need office supplies or to deliver or pick up tax work or accounting work. Without missing a beat, Kora would take our children with her and her two children and run errands for her and for us. She was like a nanny to our two children.

We often prayed in the office and talked about God and His blessings and miracles. Kora was a devout Christian and would listen, but often not talk.

One day I took the whole office to lunch. Kora sat next to me.

As we waited to be served, Kora said, "Chris, I was raised in an orphanage by missionary parents in Korea. I was the youngest child and the only person my missionary parents took into their home. They were white, not Korean, and they raised me as their daughter, probably because I was so young at the time. When I was seven, I was the first Korean orphan to be adopted by an American family and raised in America."

"Clearly the Holy Spirit is with you, Kora. Your parents did a great job teaching you about the Lord."

"That's true, Chris. A few years ago, after I was married to Ted, I thought of these wonderful missionary parents who raised me. I prayed to the Lord and asked Him if I could meet my missionary dad again . . . you know, the man who raised me in Korea. A few weeks later, I was attending church, and a guest minister was speaking. The man stopped the service when he saw me. He left the pulpit and walked down the middle aisle into the congregation. He stopped at my aisle, looked directly at me, and asked if my name was Kora. I said yes. He cried, and I cried, and we had a wonderful reunion right there in church.

"I got to spend time with my missionary dad who raised me and loved me so much. He had prayed to see me one last time too.

"A few short weeks later, my missionary mom called me to tell me he had died of a heart attack the day before. You see, Chris, God answers my prayers too, and I got to see my missionary dad one last time."

Kora's husband at the time was doing his residency in nuclear medicine at Emory. She worked for us for a few years. Ted, her husband, decided to do another residency in Tennessee, to become a radiologist. It was with tears that we said goodbye to this family that God brought into our lives, and we will always love them and are forever thankful for the blessings they were to our children and to us.

I Pray for a Vacation

I had worked with a stockbroker at Robinson Humphrey—a CPA named Peggy—since I became a corporate controller of Atlantic American. We became good friends over the years, and she was the person I went to for stock advice and the person I went to when we needed to take Atlantic American public. Due to her introductions to senior management at her company, Robinson Humphrey underwrote our bond offering and helped save our insurance company from bankruptcy.

Peggy was gay and knew I was a devout Christian. I think she was surprised that I never said a negative word about her sexual preferences and that I treated her with the love and respect she so rightly deserved. I knew that I, too, was a sinner and was not her judge. That said, the time it took you to read this was the time it took me to consider Peggy's shortcomings, and the thoughts of her private life were forgotten just as quickly. I really did care for Peggy. I was not worthy to be her judge, and I wanted the best for her.

After I started our CPA practice, Peggy left Robinson Humphrey and started her own CPA practice. Out of the blue, I decided to talk to her and learn what she was doing as she had built a very successful practice. We met at her office that warm summer, and I picked her brain, and she took me on a tour of her office. Turns out when Peggy was a stockbroker, a client of hers, a dentist by trade, had set up an accounting and tax practice. He couldn't handle the accounting business and his dental practice too, so he asked Peggy to quit her brokerage job and run his accounting practice. He had over a hundred dentists he did accounting for at the time, and he gave Peggy the practice.

I had recently started working with ACCPAC accounting software, and Peggy said she knew the head of ACCPAC's marketing program. Turns out this ACCPAC person, Lisa, was also gay, but kind words were sent from Peggy to Lisa, and before I knew it, I was given many quality referrals to do ACCPAC computer consulting.

In hindsight, I suppose God tests us. Do we really love one another, despite each other's shortcomings, or do we elevate ourselves to the position of judge? I had already learned I was not the judge and was not worthy to criticize others, and I think that led to an important set of connections that I could have just as easily ruined had I believed differently.

We had been running the CPA practice for several years by now. Beth and I were working twelve-hour days six days a week, and Beth and I were on the verge of collapse. So I decided we needed a vacation, but knowing our financial situation, as our debts were continuing to mount, I felt I needed work that could double as a vacation and pay for the vacation. So that night I prayed to God for a consulting or audit or accounting client that was by the ocean, so our children could go on vacation with us to the beach.

I remember thinking, "I would like them to go to the beach at least once in their lives."

A few days after my prayer, I received a call to meet with Kevin, a sales manager at ACCPAC. Larry, my computer consulting buddy, and I went over to meet with Kevin, and he simply handed us several leads in Atlanta.

Then he held one in his hand and said, "Chris, I don't know if you are interested in traveling to South Carolina, but I have a lead here for a fire station in Beaufort, South Carolina."

I did not know where Beaufort, South Carolina, was, but Larry immediately became excited.

Larry said to Kevin, "I'll take that referral, thank you," as he reached over my shoulder to grab the referral sheet. "My wife and I love to go to Beaufort," Larry said. "There is a little restaurant there where the water ebbs that we love to eat at."

Kevin looked at me and said, "Okay, Larry, I will give it to you, but remember, Chris is our certified ACCPAC adviser, not you, and he has to be there while you do the work."

"I taught Chris everything he knows about computers," Larry said. "And don't worry, I will not do any work without Chris' help."

Larry was instrumental in helping me with computer hardware and networks, while I taught people how to do the accounting and answered their ACCPAC questions. Together we made a good team. The following Monday, Larry and I took a trip to Beaufort where we were hired as the ACCPAC consultants to fix this fire department's ACCPAC system.

Most of the issues they had required accounting training. But they did have some outdated computers and networks that Larry was able to fix.

Best of all, their fire chief Al and his staff loved Larry. Larry took a vacation every year for a couple of weeks in Hilton Head, which turns out was just down the road from the fire district, and Larry loved to go down there and talk to the fire chief Al. A few months later, Al told Larry he needed a new auditor as they were paying way too much and not getting decent service. Larry recommended me, and before I knew it, I was back down in Beaufort, applying for an auditing job.

I was so nervous when they considered me for the audit that my voice shook when they asked me to tell them about my qualifications. I did, and despite my nervousness, we were hired.

I will never forget that summer after we won the audits. My wife and our children spent seven days in Hilton Head in a condo on the beach . . . which was an answer to my prayer I uttered a few short months before.

I would get up at 6:00 AM and either walk on the beach or swim in the ocean. By 9:00 AM, I left for work, I would work until 4:00 or 5:00 PM, drive back to Hilton Head, and then spend the evening with my wife and children playing on the beach and then eating a nice seafood dinner—all paid for by the audit work I did during the day. This was a real blessing that God provided to us and was an answer to a prayer I uttered one night months before.

The following year, we went to the beach to do the audit, and this time we brought Kora. While Beth and I worked on the audit in Beaufort, Kora would take care of all four children . . . hers and ours. Kora would take the kids crabbing, fishing; she would feed them at lunchtime and play with them at the beach; and we would join back up with them after work and have a wonderful time playing at the beach and cooking seafood or eating out.

All thanks to a merciful God Who answers prayers.

Jessica Wants a Menagerie

Beth and I concluded Jessica didn't want a dog or a cat; she wanted an entire farm. Jessica got smart, and she asked Joshua to agree to pray with her . . . and oh my god, the faith of innocent children . . . And each time the kids prayed, the Lord gave them exactly what they wanted.

I remember one night, we were on our knees, praying, and Jessica asked the Lord for two bunny rabbits. There I was, trying to figure out why she wanted two bunny rabbits instead of one; but before I could ask her, she finished the prayer and pulled the cover over her shoulders and closed her eyes.

I went to bed perplexed and said to my wife, "You're not going to believe what Jessica asked for tonight!"

Beth said, "I heard . . . two bunny rabbits."

"Why two?"

"Who knows?" Beth said looking at me as we crawled into bed together.

"I understand her praying for a bunny rabbit, but really? She's asking Almighty God for two."

Beth closed her eyes and said, "I think one's for Joshua."

I laid down my head and drifted off to sleep, wondering who the alien was that possessed my daughter.

The next day the whole family left work in the car to visit a client who made cabinets. We were going to pick up our client's check stubs so we could prepare their financial statements. Jessica had never met this client or been to their offices before.

We entered the front door, and there was the owner's daughter, Marjorie, sitting at the entranceway. I held the door open for Beth, who held Joshua's hand, and finally Jessica entered.

Marjorie looked straight at Jessica as she entered the office and said, "You must be Jessica, Beth and Chris's daughter."

Jessica stopped and looked at her directly and said, "Yes, I am."

Marjorie then said, "Wouldn't you like to have two bunny rabbits, Jessica? I happen to have two I would love to give you."

Initially I was upset because Marjorie didn't ask "the parents" first, but knowing the source and power of Jessica's prayer, we graciously accepted the gift.

"Come with me, Jessica, the bunny rabbits are in the warehouse where my dad is watching the guys build cabinets."

The rabbits were in a cage underneath a work bench. Marjorie pointed at the cage, the rabbits, and the feeder, and she looked at me and said smiling, "They're yours."

I said, "We will have to go buy a cage and food for the rabbits."

"It's a package deal. Take the cage with the rabbits. Oh, and the food is over here," Marjorie said, pointing at a bag of rabbit food under a different work bench.

Who knew you could buy rabbit food in a bag.

*****

A few months later during our prayer time, Jessica said, "And, dear Jesus, I would like to have a horse!"

My thoughts ran a bit amuck. Praying for a bicycle, a dog, or a cat and having those prayers answered is one thing . . . but a horse? Really? I then realized that when these kids prayed, God answered their prayers, so my mind flipped from a lack of faith to where were we going to put a horse.

At that moment, Beth came into the room and was visibly upset.

"You get out of bed, and you get back on your knees, little girl. We are praying against that horse right now. How can we feed it and care for it?"

Beth began to cry and shake; she was so upset. She knew if Jessica and Joshua prayed for a horse, we would get it, while I knelt there wondering how God would pull off this miracle. Beth already knew it was a done deal and wanted to undo it, because we could not afford to stable a horse.

I stood up and took my weeping wife in my arms and whispered in her ear, "Beth, maybe we should pray that if we get a horse, God would provide someone who would take care of it for us. Don't you think God could also answer that prayer too?"

Beth said in my arms as she regained her composure, "I agree to this prayer, only if we don't have to take care of the horse."

We all knelt down together, including Beth and I, and we prayed together.

I said, "Dear Lord, we would like to get a horse, but we simply can't afford to stable a horse at this point in our lives. So if You are so inclined to answer Jessica's and Joshua's prayer, would You please provide a way to have it stabled for free?"

The next day was a Wednesday, and no horses were offered to us. The following day was a Thursday. That night Beth and I congratulated each other as we made it through another day without being offered a horse. The only thing unusual was that Mary called us and asked us to come to her house and pick up her tax work. She was a new client, and it was common for clients to have us come meet with them before we started work.

Mary said on the phone, "Chris, I would like you to come to our home this Saturday to pick up my work and to meet with my partner, my dad. He has some questions for you before you start work. Is that okay?"

"Where are you located?"

"Just down the road from Chateau Elan."

"Beth and I love to visit Chateau Elan," I said. "We will be happy to come by on Saturday. Yes," I said.

"Oh, and one more thing, Chris, please bring your whole family, please bring Beth, Jessica, and Joshua, as I want my dad to meet your whole family."

"Actually," I said, "I would love to take them to see Chateau Elan on Saturday. When?"

"How about noon?"

So on cue, that Saturday morning we all got dressed and piled into the car and headed for Mary's home in the country.

Mary greeted us when we arrived and invited our family into her living room. Her dad was sitting there, and she introduced us to him. He had specific questions on corporate taxation and how to handle the growth of her new business. We spent an hour answering tax questions she had and did our best to help her and her dad understand what tax and accounting issues they would face when they incorporated this new business.

When we were done with the meeting, Mary asked Jessica, our seven-year-old, if she wanted to ride one of her horses. Jessica politely nodded and said yes, she would love to. Up to this point, we didn't even know Mary had horses.

We went out the back of the house to the stables, and Mary pointed to the saddle, which I retrieved off the wall hanger, and I helped her put the saddle on the back of the horse. I lifted Jessica up so she could put her foot in the left stirrup and helped Jessica onto the horse. Mary and I adjusted the stirrups to the proper length, and Mary started teaching Jessica how to ride a horse. At this point I backed off and let Mary take control of the training.

Holding the reins, Mary led Jessica around the ring several times and explained to Jessica how to ride the horse. When Mary was done with Jessica's first riding lesson, Mary walked the horse and Jessica to where we were standing.

Tying the rein of Lulu, the horse on the wooden rail, between us, Mary walked back over to Jessica and said, "Jessica, I know your dad and mom can't afford to take care of the horse, and they have no place to put her." That sounded pretty offensive to me even though it was true. "So I will give Lulu to you on one condition. You must leave the horse here on my farm, and I will feed her and take care of her. As you get older, if you want the horse, you can take her with you. I am giving you Lulu, do you understand me? That means you are responsible for riding the horse at least a couple of times a month. You must brush her and bring her apples and carrots to eat. Anytime you want the horse, she is yours, you just let me know. All you have to do is ask. In the meantime, you can ride her here as often as you want."

I then offered to at least pay for the feed, but Mary would not accept any money from us. Surprised but not shocked, Beth and I recognized the majesty and beauty of our Lord and His willingness to answer the prayers of innocent children with faith.

A year passed, and one day Mary called me and told me she had lost her business and the lenders were foreclosing on her farm and she was filing bankruptcy. Mary was having to dispose of the horse and wanted to know if we wanted to move the horse to another stable. Of course, we were brokenhearted for Mary's loss. We had no idea that her business was in that much trouble, as Mary had not said a word about having financial difficulties and the tax return we prepared was based on her old business, not the newly created company.

I said, "I so thank you, Mary, that you offered your horse to Jessica. But you need what you can get from selling Lulu now more than we need a horse. God bless you, and please sell the horse and keep the proceeds. We freely give her back to you."

A New Used Car

S ince our children went to a private Christian school that was underfunded, the parents were asked to kick in and help out. The women were involved in the curriculum and school lessons and did a better job than most of us men ever could do. Most of the women in this school were stay-at-home moms, so they had time to get heavily involved. But the men were expected to help as well, and since I owned a business, I had more flexibility to take off from work than most of the dads. So I often volunteered to do things that required a half day or more off work, which included driving the kids to special events. Every year we went to a puppet show in Atlanta that I thoroughly enjoyed. We also went to hear the Atlanta Symphony Orchestra when they had a morning for children. But my favorite trip was to NASA at Huntsville, Alabama where dads and children spent two days doing astronaut things and learning about space flight.

After helping in this way for several years, I was called into the principal's office and told I could no longer drive the children to events unless I had a van. Initially I was hurt as I was the only driver who did not have a van, and at the time I felt I could not afford to buy a van.

That night, before the children went to bed, we knelt down together. I asked Jessica and Joshua to pray for a van.

Jessica then said to me, "What type of van do you want, Dad?"

"Jessica, should I dare tell God what I want? Will God not think we are being pushy and stepping out of line by asking Him for material things?"

"So, Dad," Jessica said, "how is God going to know what to get for you if you don't tell Him exactly what you want?"

I was flabbergasted. I had to think about this. On the one hand, I could see her point. But did I dare tell God what I wanted? Was I that brazen? Who did I think I was? I was a lowly unimportant Christian that God helped in times of emergency. Who was I to step over the line and ask Him for material things?

"Daddy, if you're not going to tell God, tell me what type of van you want."

I could do that, for sure, I thought. "Well, let's see. Uncle Speedy has a Caravan that he likes. So maybe we ought to ask for a Dodge Caravan," I responded.

Jessica asked, "Anything else?"

"Well, how about a Grand Caravan. I would prefer to have a big van over a small van, so I could better haul paperwork back and forth to Hilton Head to do audits."

"Anything else?" Jessica pressed.

"If it's a big van, we probably need a big engine, because I can't afford to pull out of our neighborhood with traffic bearing down and not be able to accelerate. Let's say a six-cylinder engine."

"Anything else?"

"It would be nice if it had low mileage. Say below 25,000 miles. And by the way, while we are at it, I would like to pay wholesale for the car . . . and I can't afford to pay over ten thousand dollars . . ." I paused as I thought about what we could afford. "No, I can't afford $10,000. Let's change that to $8,000. It must be less than $8,000."

"Good, Daddy, what color do you want?"

"My used-car dealer friends tell me to only buy red, black, or white cars. We have a black and a red car . . . How about a white van?"

"Good, Daddy, so let's pray," Jessica said. Then she began praying, "Dear Lord, you know what we want, please Lord, please . . . provide Daddy with the car we need."

"Amen," Joshua said, after which I chimed in and added a quiet "Amen."

The next morning, I arrived at the office first, as I had to prepare for a meeting with the IRS. Beth was going to bring the children in later. It was 8:00 AM exactly, and as I was unlocking the door, the phone was ringing. I finally got the key in the lock and opened the door.

I rushed into the office and picked up the front office phone and said, "Hello."

"Hi, Chris, is Beth there? This is David."

David was a car wholesaler who had just hired us a year ago to do his taxes.

"Hi, David . . . No, Beth, has not arrived yet, she will be in by ten. Do you want me to have her call you?" David was from Australia originally and had a thick Aussie accent.

"Look, Chris, I'm really busy, so I will tell you. Beth said she wanted a van about six months ago. Well, I ran across a van yesterday that I am not interested in purchasing, but I thought she might want."

"Really, what type of van is it?" I asked.

"It's a Caravan."

"Is it a Grand Caravan or regular Caravan?"

"Regular."

"Okay, does it have a big engine?"

"Yes, it does have the V-6 engine."

"How many miles does it have?"

"Twenty-four thousand."

"That's good, David, what color is it?"

"It's white."

"Wow, sounds like an answer to prayer, I'm really interested. Do you think I can get it for wholesale?"

"No. There is no way in hell he will sell it to you for that low a price. You'll have to negotiate the price. Are you still interested?"

"Yes, I am, David. Thank you so much. Where is it?"

"Go over to Kelly Toyota off Beaufort Highway. Tell Bill McIntyre, the used-car manager, that I sent you."

"Thanks, David. I will give you a deal on your tax return if I buy the car."

"I expect at least that," David said as he hung up the phone.

I carried paperwork into my office, brought up my computer, and saw my day was packed solid. There was no way I could get over to look at the car until after work. I decided I needed to have my mechanic check it out and see if it was clean. I had a mechanic client at the time, so I picked up the phone and called him.

"Hey, Bobby, this is Chris. I was thinking about buying a car at Kelly Toyota and was wondering if you could check it out for me before I bought it. Could you do that today?"

Dead silence. "Yeah, I think I can get over there for you, but it will have to be at lunch."

"Tell Bill McIntyre, the used-car sales manager, that David Murphy sent you to check it out for me. He'll let you look at it."

"Be glad to. Let me write those names down . . ."

"Bill McIntyre is the used-car sales manager, and David Murphy is the wholesaler who referred me to him. By the way, Bobby, how much will you charge me for checking it out?"

"Don't worry about it, Chris. Just take good care of my taxes for me, will you?"

"Of course, Bobby, I'll be glad to do that," I said.

About three that afternoon, I got a call from Bobby. He said he checked the car out, and it was clean. It needed about $150 worth of work, and I could pay him to do that after I picked up the car. I then called up Bill at the dealership and asked him if he would sell me the car for wholesale.

Bill cursed me out on the phone then added, "No, you can't get it for blankety-blank wholesale. Who do you think you are? Your price is $7,800! Take it or leave it."

"Don't get mad at me for asking, Bill. I'll take it. Can I pick it up this evening after work?"

"Yes, I'll have it ready for you. I leave at 7:00 PM. Be here before six if you want the car."

That evening our whole family showed up at the dealership to purchase the car sight unseen. As I talked to Bill, I asked him how much over wholesale was I paying.

"Wholesale is $7,300, but you're not getting it for that. Your price is $7,800."

"Okay, Bill, I'll pay $7,800. Can you at least detail the car for me?"

"Not for the price you're paying!" Bill was a crusty old guy. "If you want the car, go upstairs and pay for it."

As I walked upstairs, a black gentleman saw me and said, "I heard you talking to Bill. He's just that way. I like you, and I'll be glad to detail that car for you. You go up and pay for it, and I'll have it ready for you when you come back down."

What a kind gentleman, I thought. I really didn't expect that type of service.

"Thank you so much, Mr. Wilson." He had his name tag on. I always went out of my way to treat older black men as equals as they so often acted inferior, and there was no call for that especially with me. God loves the humble ever so much more than the proud.

After paying for the car, which seemed to take forever, we came downstairs, and Mr. Wilson found me and led me to where he just finished washing the car. But as I was looking at the car, I realized Bill, the used-car manager, had made a mistake. This was a Grand Caravan, not a regular Caravan.

I said to Mr. Wilson as he handed me the key, "Isn't this a Grand Caravan?"

"Why, yes, it is. I think you'll be happy with this car," he added.

"Are you sure this is the right car?"

"You are Mr. Morris, aren't you?"

"Why, yes, I am. Mr. Wilson?"

"Call me Smitty."

"Smitty, is this my car?"

"Yes, sir, these are your papers, and this is your car."

I couldn't believe it. Our family piled into the car, and I drove it to the used-car office. I parked the car and found Bill inside.

"Bill, it appears you made a mistake. I believe you sold me a Grand Caravan. I will be happy to pay you for the difference. I don't want to take advantage of you."

Bill followed me as I walked to show him the car. Bill looked upset. "Have you paid for the car yet?"

"Why, yes, we have." We just went through the door, and I motioned to the car. "See?"

"Let me see the paperwork."

I handed it to him.

"It's your car. And who the hell detailed your car?" The car was still dripping with water.

I refused to answer as I didn't want to get Smitty in trouble.

"By the way, Bill, how much did I pay above wholesale?"

Bill pulled the black book out of his pocket. "You paid whole-sale to the dollar," he responded as he threw the book at me.

The book bounced under the car. I climbed in the car as quickly as possible, and I waved to Bill as we drove off.

"Jessica what did we pray for last night?"

"A van Daddy... and we're driving home in it now," Jessica said with enthusiasm.

"Let's see, I told you I wanted a Caravan,"

"A Grand Caravan," Jessica corrected me.

"With a V-6 engine, with under 25,000 miles. I wanted to pay under $8,000, and I wanted to pay wholesale."

"And you wanted a white van," Jessica added.

"It looks like God answered our prayer right down to the letter," I said.

"Don't you have to fix the car Chris?" Beth asked.

"Yes, that's true, but the way I figure it, we paid $7,800 and Bobby said he would fix it for $150. All told that is less than $8,000 isn't it?"

Jessica said, "That's $7,950 Daddy."

"You're pretty good at math aren't you sweetheart?" I complimented Jessica.

"Yes, I am Daddy."

"That doesn't count the taxes," Beth added.

"Now we're splitting hairs," I said. "You're also not considering that we will probably tax deduct about half the use of the car this year, because I drive a lot for business. 15,000 miles times 27.5 cents a mile is a little over $4,000 in tax deductions. I think we safely paid under $8,000."

I shook my head and considered my faith, or sadly, my lack of faith. Once again, I realized I had underestimated God.

Trip to Lake Tahoe

When Jessica was eight and Joshua was five, I decided I wanted to take them out West to ski.

One day I received a copy of *National Geographic*, and it had a story that described Lake Tahoe with beautiful pictures of the lake.

Recognizing that our kids had a talent for prayer, I carried the magazine with pretty pictures of Lake Tahoe into their office. I sat on the floor and had them sit on the floor next to me, one on each side. I then showed them the pictures of Lake Tahoe in the magazine.

I said, "Jessica and Joshua, wouldn't you like to see that beautiful lake?"

"Yes, Daddy, yes, that is a bea-u-ti-ful lake, Daddy," Jessica said with enthusiasm.

Joshua nodded as well.

"Can we go there?" Jessica asked.

"I would like to," I replied. "Why don't we pray tonight that God would allow us to visit Lake Tahoe sometime . . . perhaps this Christmas? Do you think God would answer that prayer?"

"Yes, Daddy, let's pray to Jesus to go there," Jessica said.

I looked over at Joshua, and he nodded in agreement.

"I would like to take you skiing out West this winter. Maybe God can help us take a skiing trip there," I added.

We had stayed at a friend's house on Beach Mountain in North Carolina and had gone skiing once before. The conditions were terrible; we all fell dozens of times on the man-made snow that had turned to ice. I promised our children that I would take them skiing on real snow out West sometime in the future.

That night Jessica, Joshua, and I knelt down together by Jessica's and Joshua's bed, and we prayed to go to Lake Tahoe. Beth said nothing while we prayed.

When I entered our bedroom, she said simply, "And how are we going to pay for this little trip?"

"Beth, if you recall, I specifically told God I could not afford to pay for the trip and I asked Him to help us find a way to pay for this. Let's see what He does. We will know if He wants us to go or not."

The next morning, as we drove Jessica and Joshua to their Christian school, our radio show travel expert Clark Howard said simply, "A family of four can fly round trip to Lake Tahoe for $600."

Never had I heard Clark Howard say a family of four could fly anywhere, but he did that morning. Bingo, I thought, that is God telling me to make reservations.

So when I got to work, I called a travel agent to book a week vacation over the Christmas Holidays to Lake Tahoe. I didn't have the money to pay for the trip, but I did have a credit card, and I simply charged it. My wife had some choice words to chastise me with after I told her I had paid for the trip.

I said simply, "Honey, don't worry, God will help us pay for this trip, I promise."

"Chris, you just don't understand how difficult it is for me to make ends meet, and I am going into debt, and I can't pay all of our bills. I am worried night and day that we will go bankrupt. I just don't know what to do," Beth said.

Beth was our company's accountant, and she did our books. But she could not seem to let me see the books. I threatened before to hire an outside CPA to do our books, but she resisted as she felt what she gave me was adequate. What's the saying? "A cobbler's kids have no shoes." So a CPA has no books. The tragedy was, I did not know how much debt had accumulated, largely due to my blind steering of the ship without financial statements.

I stopped all work and started reviewing our bills with Beth. I spent the next few days catching up our financials so I could see exactly where we stood. When I was done, it was clear she was correct. Our business was bleeding cash, and we were not yet able to pay all our bills. The business had run up $30,000 in credit card debt I didn't know about, and the debt was expanding every month. Then when you factor in the 18 percent interest rates, we were on a collision course with bankruptcy in two years if I didn't do something and fast.

Fortunately, I had investments that I had been building for a while, so I wrote a check out of my retirement account to pay off our credit card debt. But that was all I had left in savings at the time.

The problem was more severe because we weren't making money; we were losing about $1,000 a month after expenses. It turns out Beth was right. We really didn't have the money to take this trip to Lake Tahoe. But it was too late to undo the booking, and I felt we were committed, especially when it was apparent, at least to me, that God answered our prayer about sending our family of four there.

The following day I visited our travel agent and told her we needed to go to Lake Tahoe on a shoestring and a prayer. I added that I still wanted to teach the children to ski and wanted to know about any package deals they had.

She informed me that if we stayed at South Lake Tahoe, there were casinos that helped fund the hotel bills, and she found a hotel room that would sleep all of us for $45 a night. It was a Best Western, and I was okay with that choice. She then found us an economy car for something like $10 a day. And she said she could get me lift tickets at a discount if I bought them in advance. She added that they would have discounts for the two children if I enrolled them in ski school, but I would have to do that at the school. This was going to cost us fifteen hundred dollars, I thought, but I was determined to go, even if I had to put this on a credit card.

As the days approached to go to Lake Tahoe, we checked on the snow conditions. I had worked at a ski resort as a boy with a friend who owned a small resort in Pennsylvania. We then went to Sports Authority in Atlanta to purchase ski gear for the whole family. I bought helmets for everyone, thermals, ski coats, ski pants, ski gloves, and pull-on hats—all of that for a little over $300.

My wife asked, "And how are you going to pay for this pray tell?"

I pulled out my Mastercard, smiled as I showed it to her, and handed the card to the cashier. I tried to keep a positive attitude and keep my wife happy, even though I was really concerned about our financial situation.

As the days to go skiing approached that fall, I watched the snow reports on the Weather Channel. Unfortunately, there was no—and I repeat, no snow—in Lake Tahoe. I had bought the tickets, bought all the snow gear, except skis. We were ready to go, and there was no snow.

In desperation, when I knelt down to pray by the children's bed one evening, after our normal prayers, I said, "Jessica and Joshua, we have a problem. I was planning on skiing in Lake Tahoe this Christmas, but there is no snow. Will you all join me and help me pray for snow?"

"Yes, Daddy. And I will ask them to put this on our prayer list at school," Jessica said, "and we can get the whole school to pray for snow in Lake Tahoe."

I had heard that Jessica's teacher had a prayer journal at school and would ask the children each morning if they had any prayer requests. They even wrote down when each prayer was fulfilled by God, as they all were.

So I added, "Good idea, Jessica, please ask your entire class to pray for snow in Lake Tahoe, let's make this a school and home prayer request."

"I will do that," Jessica said.

After our standard prayers, I said, "Dear Lord, perhaps I should not have booked this trip to Lake Tahoe. I know we really can't afford it. But it has been several years since we started our business, and we have not taken one true vacation other than to go to Hilton Head on business each year . . . and the one trip two years ago to California for money management training. I am truly thankful for that answered prayer, but I have perhaps unwittingly bought airfare and ski gear for the trip, and it would be really nice if we had enough snow to ski on while we were there. We may never go back, and I thought this would be a special vacation and an opportunity for Jessica and Joshua to learn how to ski."

The next morning Jessica asked the school to pray for snow in Lake Tahoe. I checked with the teacher, and she said the entire class was praying for snow.

It was the week before Christmas of 1994 when we went to the airport to go to Lake Tahoe, with ski gear in the bags and no snow on the ground.

As we walked to our gate early that morning, I heard CNN announce on the air, "Lake Tahoe has received seven feet of snow in one twenty-four-hour period."

I stopped and went over to the TV to watch the report about all the snow Lake Tahoe had received that night. When they confirmed that they had seven feet of snow, I was so excited that I started jumping up and down, and Jessica, Joshua, even Beth joined in with me as we cheered, and everyone in the gate heard me say, "God has answered our prayer. God has answered our prayer. We're going to ski in Lake Tahoe!"

We flew to Reno, Nevada, that morning and rented a car to drive to Lake Tahoe. The drive was beautiful. There was this long valley with mountains in the distance. The road I took led straight to those mountains. As we climbed the road into the mountains, the temperature dropped, and snow flurries appeared. People were pulling over and putting chains on their cars. I had bought chains for the tires, so I, too, pulled over and put the plastic chains on the front wheels. But when I read the manual, it said, "Do not put chains on those wheels." The car rental place assured me I could use chains, and I ignored the warning. Once we reached the top, the snow was blowing. It wasn't long until we essentially came to a complete stop.

We had been on the road for four hours and were now surrounded by snow. The snow was coming down heavily. It was beautiful. But by now I realized I needed a restroom. So I decided to get out of the car, hide behind a tree, and relieve myself. I put the car in park, got out of the car, and headed for the tree; and as I stepped off the side of the road into the snow, I fell straight down into the snow with the snow over my head. I was completely buried. I lifted my head back and looked up to see a tunnel of snow over me with light from the sky at the end of the tunnel. I must have walked off a bit of a cliff, and the snow was so deep it looked like there was ground when I stepped off the road, and there was no ground there. Seven feet of snow, I thought, and now I'm buried in it.

Not knowing what to do, I tried the backstroke until I felt ground with my right hand. I spun around and took hold of the ground behind me and pulled my way back up onto the road. I said a brief prayer, thanking God that I didn't freeze to death.

But I still had a need to find a bathroom. Realizing we had passed a gas station about a half mile back, I got the entire family out of the car, and we started to walk on the road back toward the gas station. As we walked, windows were rolling down, and people were asking me, "What the heck are you doing? You're just going to leave your car in the road like that?"

"We're all going to the bathroom and buying supplies at the store back there. We've only moved three car lengths in the last half hour."

When I told them this, they, too, put their cars in park and followed us to the gas station. Almost every family and driver abandoned their car for a quarter of a mile and followed us to the gas station where we all lined up and relieved ourselves and bought supplies for the long commute to our hotel.

When I returned to the car, I advanced the car one car length. It took us many more hours to drive several miles due to terrible snow conditions. But we got there late that evening and collapsed in bed. The next morning, we went to Heavenly Ski Resort and signed Jessica and Joshua up for ski lessons for three days. I prayed this time that both children would be able to ski the beginner "green" slopes with me before we left. I recognized that Beth would probably not get off the "bunny" slopes, because she didn't like this skiing business. I prayed doubly hard that the kids would be able to keep me company on the slopes.

After three days of lessons, on the fourth day, Jessica informed us that she had lost one of her gloves. So we went to buy another pair of gloves at Heavenly's ski shop.

Standing in line to buy the gloves, a gentleman wearing a ski patrol outfit walked toward me and, in a demanding voice, said, almost punitively, "Excuse me, is this your daughter?"

I didn't know what to say.

"Is this your daughter?" he repeated, staring at me.

"Why, what did she do?" I responded sheepishly.

"So she is your daughter," he continued.

"Yes, this is my daughter, what did she do?"

The stranger stuck his hand out to shake mine and said, "My name is Robert, and I'm in charge of the ski team here. Your daughter is a gifted skier, and I need her on my ski team. I think she has Olympic potential."

His voice changed to be more sincere and personable. "Look, ah… I have trained five people who became US Olympic team skiers. I'm not as young as I used to be. I believe Jessica can be my sixth Olympic contribution, and then I will retire. Would you consider bringing her here every weekend so she can be on my ski team?"

"If you can pay the commute costs," I responded, laughing out loud.

"I think I can help reimburse you. Where are you from, San Francisco or Los Angeles?"

At this point I realized he was serious. "We're from Atlanta," I responded.

"Oh no, oh no," he grumbled. "She has such talent." He walked away from me, turned in a circle a couple of times, and then returned to me. "What do you do?"

"I'm a CPA, and I have a small practice in Atlanta."

"Can you move to San Francisco or Los Angeles?"

"I don't think so."

"Wait, maybe I can get you a job here at Heavenly. I bet I can get you a job working here as an accountant," Robert said. "Look, we need her here on my team. We're talking about making your daughter an Olympic skier, Mr. Errrr."

"Morris . . ." I helped.

"Mr. Morris."

I reached in my pocket, knowing this was a futile idea, and pulled out a business card. "Here's my card, let's talk when I get back to Atlanta," I said.

I was tempted for about three seconds to send Jessica there, but what of my business, and what of our lives and homes we had built? Plus, he thought he could get me a job working at Heavenly. But to be safe, I later reviewed the size of Heavenly Corporation, and I had been president of a company that was ten times larger than this company. There was no way they could afford to pay my salary, and it would ruin my résumé if I were to take an accounting job at such a small company. It just didn't seem like God was in this decision. Just the same, I asked God for confirmation that Jessica could be an Olympic skier.

The next day when I took Jessica and Joshua to the ski slopes, I was amazed at both of their skiing skills. That day we stayed mostly on the greens and tried a few easy blues, which are intermediate slopes. Neither Jessica nor Joshua had any problems skiing blues. Within three days, both kids were tearing me up on the blacks and double blacks, and I fought to keep up with them. I was amazed that Jessica maintained perfect form throughout her skiing. It was as if she had spent her entire childhood living on skis. Joshua was also an excellent skier, but he did not have perfect form like Jessica had.

After three days of skiing, I decided to go to another ski resort other than Heavenly. The drive wound up the side of the mountain and crossed a two-lane pass with thousand-foot drops on both sides of the bridge. As I began to cross the bridge, my car spun out and did a 360-degree turn before bouncing off the curb and back into the lane facing forward. We were a few yards from plummeting to our death. The road looked clear, but it had a fine sheet of black ice all the way across the bridge. I went into the trunk, pulled out the plastic chains, and put them on the car. While I did that, three more cars passed my car and spun out. Amazingly, none of the cars hit any of the other cars, but they too bounced off the curb and slid into random places on the road. None of us were driving more than ten miles an hour when we spun out. Having put the plastic chains on the car, I skipped skiing that day and headed down the mountain to the Reno airport where I traded the car in for a four-wheel drive SUV. It was a good thing I did that. Over the next few days, the snow continued, and the banks mounted. Several feet a day of snow built on top of the seven feet we started with. By the end of the week, I believe we had received over ten feet of snow.

Before we left Atlanta, I had called Alex and Jodi, friends who lived in Lodi, California, to tell them we were skiing in Lake Tahoe and asked them if they wanted to ski with us. They said no, but they wanted to know if we were staying in South Lake Tahoe, and I said yes. Excited, they said they would take off from work on Friday, come up Thursday night, and they wanted me to join them in Harrah's, a casino in Lake Tahoe. We were going to check in and stay through Sunday, and they had enough points to comp us a room for free from Thursday night through Sunday.

That Thursday evening, after skiing, as we walked to Harrah's, I held Jessica's hand, and Beth held Joshua's hand.

When the casino lights were clearly visible, and we began to cross the street toward the casino, Jessica yanked her hand out of mine and said, "Daddy, Daddy, we can't go there." She pointed her hand directly at the entrance to the casino. "The devil lives there."

I had never told her what a casino was, nor had I told her anything about gambling; she simply looked at the casino and knew beyond a shadow of a doubt that the devil lived in that building. Jessica was crying.

I paused to assess the situation. I concluded that Jessica and Joshua had to learn about the world, that there was evil in the world, and that they had to live among the evil.

I decided to convince Jessica and Joshua . . . now Joshua was crying . . . that it was okay to enter the casino and that I would not let anything happen to them. I quoted scripture to them.

"Jessica, Jesus tells us in Romans: 'For I am convinced that neither death, nor life, nor angels, nor principalities, nor things present, nor things to come, nor powers, nor height, nor depth, nor any other created thing . . . will be able to separate us from the love of God, which is in Christ Jesus our Lord.' If I am right, there is nothing in there you need to worry about." I knelt down to see her face. "Jessica, is it okay if we go there now?"

Jessica didn't say anything, but she stopped crying, nodded her head suspiciously, and held her hand out so I could hold it. We all walked quietly across the street toward Harrah's. We happened to walk through the casino to get to the hotel lobby, and Jessica squirmed the entire way there.

Alex and Jodi arrived at Harrah's promptly at 8:30 PM, just as planned. We waited as they checked into the hotel at Harrah's and gave us room keys.

I said, "Alex, there is a family restaurant up the street we like. They have a nice diner."

Jodi gave me a strange look.

Alex then said, "Chris, let's eat at Harrah's, they have a huge buffet upstairs, it's all you can eat, and it's very inexpensive. You'll love it, I promise . . . they even have steak and lobster . . . and did I say it's inexpensive?"

Beth looked concerned but said, "Fine."

Dinner was excellent, and while it was reasonable, it was still more expensive than I had hoped it would be. After dinner, we dropped the kids back at our hotel room with Beth. Then Alex, Jodi, and I headed for the casino.

Jodi and I followed Alex to the Pai Gow poker table, and he grabbed a seat and began to gamble. I sat down too and played a couple of hands. But this wasn't my cup of tea.

I turned to Jodi, and she said, "If you don't like this, Chris, why don't you join me at the craps table?"

In college we had a gambling day with fake money, and I managed the craps table, so I knew how to play that and thought it would be fun.

I followed Jodi to the craps table. She carefully picked the first table. She reminded me how to play and what the best bets were. I placed a $3 bet on the Pass line and started to play. I then paused, stepped away from the table, and prayed silently. Jodi matched my bet, and we won. We did this again and again, and more times than not, we won.

I came to the casino with only $20 in my pocket. By now I had won over $100. But then the table turned on us, and we began to lose.

After several losses, Jodi looked at me and said, "Chris, this table is cold, let's move to another table."

She closed her eyes to help pick the next table. I said, "Jodi, let's pray to God for guidance on where to bet next."

Jodi looked at me suspiciously and said, "Chris, I don't think it's wise to pray . . . you know, in a casino?"

"Of course, it's wise, Jodi. He's with us wherever we go, and we need to win . . . not lose."

"If you say so," Jodi said, forcing a smile.

I prayed, and Jodi looked around nervously. When I was done, she said, "Now where too?"

"I will let you pick the table."

Jodi led me to the last table on the right.

When it was my turn, Jodi said, "Throw a 7, Chris."

I threw not one but five 7s in a row. Then she said, "Throw a 6," and I threw a 6. I had to throw a 6 again to win after throwing the 6 the first time. Sure enough, I threw a 6. This continued until the manager of the casino showed up.

Everywhere we went, the manager followed me and Jodi from table to table. Every time I rolled the die, he would break the die with a little hammer. He only broke the die when I rolled them, not when anyone else rolled them.

I finally asked him, "Excuse me, but what are you doing?"

"You're cheating, and I'm going to prove it," he said smugly.

"But I swear, I am not cheating," I said helplessly, as I quietly continued to pray before I rolled the die.

Jodi would say under her breath, "Chris, don't let them see you pray!"

He never said a word about my praying. Finally, somewhat exhausted, Jodi and I returned to our hotel room to check on Beth and the children. They were all asleep.

I woke Beth up to check on her, and she started to cry, then said, "We don't have that much money, and here you are gambling away what little we have . . ."

I reached in my pocket and pulled out five $100 bills and handed them to her. That didn't seem to calm her down, so I handed her two more bills.

"I made all of that on $20, dear," I said.

Even better, I had another $700 in my other pocket to gamble with. I then looked at Jodi and she said, "Are you ready to go back, Chris?"

"Sure," I said with confidence.

We stayed out until after 4:00 AM gambling. That night I won enough money to pay for the entire trip, including lift tickets, ski lessons, airfare, and the hotel.

I never showed Beth all the cash I had made, but I had won in excess of $2,500 that night. The next few nights, I went briefly with Jodi and Alex to the casinos with $20 each night and lost it all in less than fifteen minutes, except for one night when I won a couple hundred dollars. I left the casinos, returned to the room with my wife, and left Alex and Jodi to their gambling ways.

Sunday finally came, and after a short-day skiing, we said goodbye to Alex and family and thanked them for joining us. They said they had a great time, and we hugged each one of them and told them we had a great time, and this was something we would never forget. That evening we packed the car up and went to bed early.

We left the following morning at 4:00 AM their time. I checked out of the hotel. We carried the sleeping children to the car and latched them into their seats. Beth and I loaded the rest of the luggage into the car, and we climbed into our four-wheel drive SUV and headed down the mountains toward Reno, Nevada.

It was still snowing. It was pitch-black, and I was so tired I was having trouble staying awake.

Then I remembered a dream I had the night before. It was in the dark, and it was snowing. I was driving the car. Then I fell asleep, and with a bang, I woke up as our car careened over the edge of the mountainside and we began to fall. I woke up terrified.

I was having trouble keeping my eyes open when I thought of that dream. It looked like I was reliving that exact experience when Beth yelled at me, "Wake up, Chris. Wake up, you're falling asleep."

I was so frightened when she said that; adrenaline pumped into my body. Thank God, I didn't fall asleep. I was wide awake for the rest of the trip.

The sun came up as we departed the mountain range and lit up the highway on the plain toward Reno. The lakes on both sides of the road seemed to stretch from the base of the mountains right up to the edge of the highway. They were beautiful as they reflected the mountains in the distance.

Beth said, "These are the most beautiful lakes."

I said, "They remind me of a lake in Vevey, Switzerland where I walked along the shore and the snow-covered mountains loomed in the background and reflected in the lake.

"Beth," I said, thinking about the lakes, "I don't recall seeing lakes as big as these when we drove in from Reno. There were a couple of lakes, but they were on one side of the road, and they were way in the distance."

Beth didn't respond.

"Wait a minute," I said concerned. "Beth, I am sure there weren't but a couple of lakes way in the distance and nothing that extended up to the road like this when we drove to Tahoe."

At this point, I realized something was wrong.

Looking out into the distance, I noticed clumps of grass growing out of the lakes. Then I noticed a cow and then another cow walking on the water.

"Look, Beth, there are cows walking on the water," I said. "These aren't lakes; these are floodwaters."

I remember looking in the rearview mirror. I hadn't seen a car for at least an hour. I hit the brakes and slowed the car down. I stopped in the middle of the highway, put the car in park, and jumped out of the car. I went to the right side of the highway and looked over the edge. Water was within a few inches of coming over the top of the road. I then looked for oncoming traffic, there was none, and I went to the other side of the highway. Water was just reaching the road, but I could see it rising as I looked at it. Oh my, I thought. These were floodwaters, and they were rising on both sides of the road. We were in real danger of being stranded in the middle of nowhere. If the water crossed the road, I would not be able to see where the road was as it would look like it was part of the lake. That meant that if the water got on top of the road, we would have to stop the car and wait and could possibly drown before help arrived.

My heart was pounding; my hands were even shaking as I climbed back into the car, snapped my seat belt, and asked Beth, "Honey, could you please wake our children up."

"They're asleep, Chris, let's leave them be."

"Beth, this is not a joke," I said with a raised voice. "Wake them up now."

"How?" Beth asked.

"Take off your seat belt and turn around. Shake them if you must, but wake them up." Beth was a bit perturbed but did as I asked. She undid her seat belt, turned around, and grabbed Jessica's legs. She told Jessica to wake up as I began to drive down the road.

Then I said, "Listen, Jessica and Joshua, do you see the lakes around us?"

"Yes, Daddy, but can I go back to sleep?" Jessica asked.

"In just a minute, sweetie . . . Could you pray with me that the water will not cross the road until we arrive at the airport?"

"Yes, Daddy, but I'm tired," Jessica said.

"Please, Jessica, we need God's help."

Jessica said, "Okay!"

"Would you make sure Joshua is awake, Jessica?" I asked.

She shook Joshua. "Wake up, Josh, we have to pray, we have an emergency." After a few moments, Jessica said, "Okay, he's awake now, Dad." Jessica whispered to Josh, "Joshua, Joshua, we have to pray, wake up, it's okay, wake up."

"Okay, everyone, listen up. Dear Lord, Heavenly Father, creator of the universe, we may be in danger. The snow we prayed for is now melting, and it has formed these huge lakes on both sides of the road. I haven't seen a car in over an hour. We are the only people left on this highway. We need to get to the airport. If this water crosses the road, I don't know how we will get home safely as I will not be able to see where the road is. Please, Lord, please, protect us and give us speed as we drive across the plain to Reno. Let us not have any water on the highway. It is only a couple of inches from cresting over the road top, Lord. Please protect us."

With that prayer, I sped the car up to over ninety miles an hour and headed for Reno. My hands were still trembling, and we were flying down the road. Fortunately, the road was straight as an arrow. There was no risk that I would fall asleep now. The trip seemed to last for an eternity. But we eventually arrived at Reno without incident. A little hill here and a second hill there, and I finally felt we had reached safety in Reno.

To my amazement, we never once saw any water on the highway. We arrived at the airport in Reno and turned in the car. As I handed in the car keys, I told the clerk at the desk that we had just arrived from Lake Tahoe and water was rising and almost cresting above the road.

I then said, "Don't let anyone go down the highway to Tahoe because I am sure it will flood shortly."

The young man at the desk said, "That's amazing. I don't know how you made it. They closed the highway from Tahoe to Reno early this morning, and no cars were supposed to be on that road."

"We left before 4:30 AM," I said.

"That must be it. You must have left before they closed the road. You're lucky you got here safely."

They shuttled us to the airport. I was anxious until the wheels of our airplane rotated and lifted off the runway later that morning.

After we arrived back in Atlanta, we watched CNN, and they reported the runway in Reno was underwater. Also, the roads from Tahoe to Reno were flooded out. Even some casinos were closed due to flooding, and it was the first time in history that they had closed a casino. CNN showed pictures of houses sliding down the side of the Tahoe Mountain Range. Our prayers had saved us from what could have been a calamity when we left Lake Tahoe.

But a nagging question bothered me. Had our prayers brought calamity on others? I didn't know how to interpret what had happened and prayed for the people who were hurt by the snow and flooding in the Lake Tahoe area.

I then called our good friends, Alex and Jodi, to see if they got home safely. Before they left, I told Jodi I would have the kids pray for nice weather and a safe trip home for them. Jodi told me on the phone that among all the disasters and bad weather that had occurred in the Lake Tahoe area, their trip home to Lodi was uneventful. As they descended the mountains and got on the road to Sacramento, the weather cleared, and they drove the rest of the way with sunny skies and clear roads. I thanked them for an unforgettable trip and said goodbye.

After the call, I took Beth by the hands, we sat down, and I said, "Alex and Jodi got home safely."

Beth said, "Good."

I then said, "Beth, let's pray. Dear Lord, thank You, Father, for a safe trip home. Thank You for keeping me awake and not allowing me to fall asleep on the road down the mountains. Thank You for keeping the water at bay as we drove to Reno. Thank You that we caught the plane and got out of there before the runway flooded. And thank You for providing us with money we needed to pay for the trip. Thank You, thank You, Lord Jesus . . . We praise Your Holy Name."

And with that, Beth said simply, "Amen."

I then leaned over and kissed her and said, "I love you, Beth. And didn't I tell you that if God wanted us to go to Lake Tahoe, He would provide a way for us to pay for the trip?"

Our Business Grows

Around four years after I started my business, my church friends called me on the phone and recommended I contact a guy who owned a tire store near Georgia Tech. I called him up on the phone, and he scheduled me for an interview. As I drove there, I was very nervous as I was still in the early stages of starting our business. When I arrived at his offices, I realized I had frequently driven by his business each day when I drove to graduate school. I then remembered the strange feeling I had whenever I drove by this building. This specific place gave me an impression of familiarity and spiritual peace in an area of Atlanta that was spiritually dark.

As I sat in the lobby to wait to meet the owner for the first time, I considered this peaceful spirit. I reasoned that the familiarity I felt meant he would hire me. My early nervous jitters were replaced with a calm demeanor when Wallace came out of his office, greeted me in the lobby, and shook my hand for the first time. I was not surprised when he hired me later that day and was happy because this was the largest client to hire our firm to date.

Wallace was at least twenty years my senior, he was a multimillionaire, and he became one of my best friends. He took an interest in me and tried again and again to persuade me to become a Seventh-Day Adventist.

I have learned in the business world almost all businessmen say they act in their clients' best interests and they say you can trust them. Then there are the few rare people whose word means something. They tell you what they will do, and then they do it. Their word is golden. I describe these people as righteous men. One doesn't even need a written contract with them. Every one of these men and women that I had met had strong faith in God.

Wallace and I were kindred spirits here, and we strengthened each other's faith.

It was common for Wallace to recommend I join the Seventh-Day Adventist church. He was disappointed that I never actually did. Yet he had a more profound impact on my thoughts than he knew. During our friendship, my thoughts returned to my mother and her Jewish background. Wallace had convinced me that the Sabbath was on Saturday, not Sunday, the very day Jews keep the Sabbath. I understood why the pope changed the Sabbath to Sunday in honor of Christ's resurrection. But I couldn't help but think that Jesus kept the Sabbath on Saturday, not Sunday, and this bothered me, as I wanted to do exactly what He would have me do.

These thoughts led to my mother, and I was particularly saddened that my children never knew who my mother was, as I was certain she would have been delighted with them and spoiled them rotten. My thoughts returned to the kippah my mother gave me as a young lad, the Jewish harp, the dreidels and chocolate money I received as a boy. I find it fascinating that when we have thoughts about things, opportunities present themselves to us, and in short order, I was invited to attend a Passover service by the organization Jews for Jesus. I took our whole family. Tears came to my eyes during the service as these Messianic Jews were really on fire, and being Jews, they reminded me of my mother's family. Our family started regularly attending their services on Saturday, and we continued to attend church on Sundays as well.

The services were fascinating. Christians sat on the right side of the room, while Jews sat on the left. The Christian rabbi would link the two religions together beautifully. He would ask a question that all the Jews and none of the Christians could answer. A little while later, he would ask a question that all the Christians and none of the Jews could answer. Then it hit me. Jesus was a Jew, and He never converted to Christianity. It was at this point that I realized there were large gaps in my understanding of Jesus since I did not understand Judaism completely. I then took it upon myself to learn everything I could about Judaism and teach my children, initially as an academic exercise, but over time our family would adopt these traditions as our own.

Wallace, indeed, had an impact on me. I was never meant to be in a traditional church. I was meant to be a Messianic Jew.

Wallace also helped our business become profitable. Shortly after Wallace became a client, I helped set up a consulting business. That business also added to our income. Around this time, I recommended a bridge around Hilton Head to the Beaufort County controller. He liked my idea but told me it was the wrong bridge. He wanted to build a bridge across Hilton Head in another direction but could not afford to do that given their tight budget. I said he should make it a toll bridge. After some discussion, he checked into my idea and started construction. He said he couldn't pay me a referral fee but decided to build a little park at the far end of the bridge for my two young children as a gift to them. I laughed and thanked him. He then referred me to Daufuskie Island's fire district and asked me to start auditing their books as well. As a result, our time in the low country increased, and our children were having a blast at the beaches there.

Because of this recent growth, we were finally able to pay our bills and stop the negative cash flow.

Joshua's Fight with Other Boys

When Joshua was nine years old, he was playing softball in our front yard with our three other boys in our neighborhood. I was planting flowers in the front and listening to them. The two brothers who lived next door were cheating. One of the four boys lived across the street. He was a son of the minister, and after consistent cheating, he finally called the two brothers cheaters and went home.

I expected Joshua to quit as well, but instead he said, "I know you boys cheated, and I think what you did was wrong. But Jesus would want me to forgive you, so I forgive you."

Joshua continued playing with the boys. The boys stopped cheating and began treating Joshua with respect. Their respect carried forward after that date, and they became good friends until they moved out of the neighborhood.

Trip to Hawaii

After our trip to Lake Tahoe, my wife mentioned that she would like to go to Hawaii. If we didn't have the money to go to Lake Tahoe and needed casino winnings to pay for the trip, how could we afford to go to Hawaii? I thought.

When I had powerful spiritual experiences, I either had a dream where I was instructed by Jesus to do something, or I felt thoughts in my mind that were inconsistent with my thoughts, like they came out of the blue. These events were rare. I could count these spiritual experiences on my right hand. But I had learned something about my wife. When she had a feeling that we should do something, we probably needed to do it. She never described having a dream where she saw Jesus. Not once did she say, "God has told me to do this." She would simply say, "I think we should do . . ."

The day before she mentioned that she wanted to go to Hawaii, I had a thought—a very strange thought that I would be in Hawaii within a year—and I wondered if that was one of those spiritual thoughts planted by God. So when Beth brought this up, I naturally didn't mention that I also had a feeling that we should go to Hawaii. Instead I told her the truth . . . It would be too expensive, and we couldn't afford to go.

Twice before, Beth and I had planned trips to Hawaii. Each time something came up that stopped us. The first trip we made a deposit. Then my boss told me I had to pass the CPA exam the first time or he would fire me. With such a weight on my shoulder, how could I expect to go to Hawaii before the exam? We forfeited our deposit, and I passed the CPA exam the first time.

The second time my sister decided to get married the same week our CPA Society was going to Hawaii. I asked her to move the wedding to another date, and she said, "No can do." We got back half of our prepaid deposit from the CPA Society. So Beth had a right to ask to go to Hawaii. Twice I had promised her we would go, and each time we backed out. I felt guilty and decided I should search for a way to take my lovely wife to Hawaii.

If God wanted us to go, I thought, He would provide a way. Then the thought occurred to me that I might be able to pay for this trip by putting on a seminar there. What if I were to invite all my clients to Hawaii and put on a seminar that would be extensive enough to make the trip tax deductible? Who doesn't like Hawaii? Most of my clients were rich and could easily afford to go. I felt almost all of them could learn how to legally take deductions and stay within the rules, and that would be a great topic for the trip.

We prayed that night to go to Hawaii. To my surprise, Joshua had heard of the volcanos in Hawaii and asked the Lord that night if we could see a volcano erupt. Apparently, he had been studying volcanos in school that year. I remember praying that God would keep us safe if the volcano erupted and we saw it. Joshua then informed me that the Hawaiian volcanos were shield volcanoes, and that made them safe to observe from a distance. Over the next few weeks, we continued to pray every night to go to Hawaii, and Joshua followed every prayer with a prayer to see the volcano erupt. Unfortunately, there was no apparent answer to prayer even though I expected to hear something from someone about how to go to Hawaii on a five-dollar-a-day budget.

About six months before the planned excursion, I sent out an invitation to all my clients to see who would like to go to Hawaii. Over the coming weeks, I systematically called all my clients and invited them to go to Hawaii. I called hundreds of clients. Sadly, only two women said they wanted to go. During that time, I had done research on airfare and hotels. I was shocked to find out one doesn't save money by traveling as a group. In fact, airlines and hotels charge more to groups. Who knew?

I then called the Hawaiian Volcano National Park and talked to a park ranger.

I asked her, "What are the odds that we might see the volcano erupt?"

She responded flatly, "Sir, I am sorry, but it's practically impossible. Whenever the volcano erupts, the flights fill up, the hotels fill up, people camp in tents to see the eruption. By the time you hear the volcano is erupting, it's typically too late to book the trip. The other problem is, you have only a day or two to witness the lava flow, and then the eruption stops. That's how sporadic the lava flow is."

This led me to the conclusion, we had six months until we would go to Hawaii, if we could even pull it off, and the only hope we had to see the volcano erupt was prayer. So every night we prayed to go to Hawaii and see the volcano erupt.

Another month passed. We sent out two more rounds of letters inviting everyone we knew to attend tax deductible seminars in Hawaii. Again, there was no answer. Finally, after several months of trying, I gave up. I remember the night I told Beth that we couldn't afford to go and that God must not want us to go as no one was signing up for the trip. Beth was a trooper as she smiled and said she still loved me and understood.

The next day I went in to work, and I called Mary Clayborn and Lanida Solera to tell them the bad news. Neither person accepted my change of heart. In fact, they both lectured me and told me that I was taking them to Hawaii, and if I didn't, it would be over my dead body. To my surprise, I was relieved. I guess we would just have to use credit cards.

Two days after this interesting conversation, Lanida called me on the phone and said, "Chris, I just heard Clark Howard on the radio. He says Hawaii is on sale. We can go round-trip from Atlanta for $199 a person. But we have to buy the tickets now."

That price was a third the normal airfare. I told Lanida I had to talk to my wife and I would call our travel agent and I would go ahead and book reservations within thirty minutes. I immediately told my wife. She agreed to buy the tickets. I then called Mary, and she wanted me to get tickets for her, and then I called our travel agent and had her find the discounted airfare over a two-week period that worked for everyone; and before we knew it, we all had tickets to go to Hawaii from Atlanta.

The total cost per ticket with taxes was under $250 per person round-trip. Thank you, Clark Howard, thank you, Clark Howard! The next problem was how to see the Hawaiian Islands on a shoestring. So I headed for my travel agent's offices. Unfortunately, she couldn't find any real values. Hawaii was far more expensive than I realized, especially if you stayed at their touristy hotels. It was not uncommon for the hotels to charge $1,000 a night and more, something we could not possibly afford.

Wondering how on earth we could pay for the trip, once again Clark Howard came to the rescue.

We heard Clark on the radio a few days later say, "So many people are going to Hawaii from Atlanta that I will tell you how to get the best specials over the next few months."

We followed his recommendations, and by the time we were done, we were staying in great hotels that were $1,000 or more a night for less than $100. Suddenly the impossible had come true. This was a nail-biting experience, but it all worked out in the end. Our whole family was elated. We were going to Hawaii!

We finally headed for the airport to travel to Hawaii. Our family sat in tourist class, but our wealthy clients upgraded to first class. On the jet to Hawaii, Delta Airlines played the movie *Dante's Peak*, which was about a volcano exploding. After the movie, Joshua looked white as a ghost. He was horrified.

I asked him, "What's wrong, Joshua?"

Joshua was sitting on my right and whispered, "Dad, we prayed to see the volcano erupt. What have we done?"

Joshua's faith was so great that he knew God would answer our prayers.

What did Jesus say in Matthew 17?

> He [Jesus] replied, "Because you have so little faith. Truly I tell you, if you have faith as small as a mustard seed, you can say to this mountain, 'Move from here to there,' and it will move. Nothing will be impossible for you." (Matthew 17:20)

Joshua didn't hope God would answer our prayer; he knew Jesus would answer our prayer. Feeling sorry for Joshua, I leaned over to him and whispered in his ear, "Remember, Joshua, every time you prayed to see the volcano erupt, I prayed that we would be safe and that no one would be hurt. Why would God answer the first part of our prayer and not the rest?"

Joshua sighed and said, "I guess you're right."

Then I said, "Joshua, I called Volcano National Park and spoke with a park ranger last year. She said that it would be a miracle if we saw the volcano erupt. Apparently, it only erupts once a year at most, and when it does, it only lasts for a couple of days and stops. We are only going to be on the Big Island for a few days. When I told the park ranger this, she politely told me not to plan on seeing the volcano erupt.

"Dad, God always answers our prayers," Joshua said, looking at me in disbelief. His point was well taken.

"I'm sorry, Joshua, you are correct, God does answer our prayers," I said as I thought how cool it would be to see an erupting volcano.

We had been awake since 4:00 AM EST, and by now it was around 10:00 AM EST, and boy, I was tired. So I put a pillow behind my head and dozed off. While I slept, I suddenly found myself being led back to heaven. When I arrived there, I stood in front of Jesus. By now I was more comfortable talking with Him through my thoughts, and I now saw Jesus as my friend. I knew He was God, but I talked to Him more like He was my dad, out of love.

His first thought was "Chris, I want you to go to the Island Molokai."

I thought, "Mola-what?"

I thought for a moment about our trip. "We are flying to O'ahu. We are then flying over to the big island known as Hawaii. After that we are flying to Maui. The only other habitable island that I know exists is Kauai. There are many uninhabited smaller islands, but I doubt I can get to those islands.

"I wonder if the Lord is mistaken," I thought, "because I have been planning for this trip for several months now, and I do not remember an island called Molokai." It is difficult to adjust to a place where every thought you have is immediately heard. "Why are those angels staring at me? Oh my, everyone heard me. I have sinned, I called the Lord a liar . . . Look at the way they are staring at me . . . I feel so ashamed. Please understand, my thought wasn't out of disrespect, Lord, I just don't remember an island called Molokai. Please forgive me, Lord."

Then the Lord thought again, "Chris, I want you to go to Molokai."

An image appeared in my mind of Jack Paar on the tonight show when I was a young child. Mr. Parr was visiting an island in Hawaii where lepers lived.

I directed my thoughts to the Lord, "Is that the island where the lepers live?"

He said, "Yes."

"Of course, Lord, I will do whatever You want." It was as if there was a sigh of relief from all the angels around our Lord.

There was no response from Jesus.

I was now overcome with grief as my mind went in several directions at once. This is the Lord God Almighty, not my daddy. I lowered my head in shame.

"Yes, Lord, of course I will go to Molokai, I will do whatever You want. I'm just trying to figure out where this island is and how to work this into our hectic schedule. The only free time we have is when we are on the island of Maui. Can I work it in then? Can You help me do this and . . . ah, can You help me with my wife? She gets upset when I make last-minute changes to plans, could You perhaps keep her calm when I tell her that I must go to Molokai? And what do You want me to do in Molokai anyway?"

Jesus then changed the subject and thought, "What size volcano do my children want to see?"

It confused me when He referred to my children as His children. But I had to realize, they were truly His children and I was merely their temporary sitter.

I was reminded of our nightly prayers where I told the Lord Jessica and Joshua were His children.

I thought, "Lord, a very small volcano, we don't want to hurt anyone. Remember, when we prayed for snow in Tahoe, we saw homes flowing down the mountain, and many people were hurt from flooding."

With that the Lord turned toward an angel. I remember seeing the angel move toward the earth faster than any rocket ship I had ever seen. I was amazed.

Watching the angel fly toward the earth at incredible speed was the last thing I remembered before awakening. Still groggy, I thought about the dream's unconscious revelation. What could this dream possibly mean, and what is my unconscious trying to tell me? But as I gained consciousness, I realized this dream had provided me with information I did not know previously. Plus, it was too coherent, too factual and too conversational to have been just a dream. My only possible conclusion was that it must have been a message from Jesus . . . at least I thought it was Jesus . . . although I wasn't 100 percent sure.

The Bible says in Joel 2:28:

> And afterward, I will pour out my Spirit on all
> people. Your sons and daughters will prophesy,
> your old men will dream dreams, your young
> men will see visions.

I suppose I was just dreaming one of those dreams.

When we arrived in Hawaii hours later, we deplaned on the tarmac and walked toward the terminal. I let Beth lead with the children. Strangely, someone grabbed me from behind and held my stomach area for a few seconds. As I prepared to deck him, he let go. I turned and saw a Hawaiian man running from me. At the time I did not know what to think of this man who grabbed me around my belt and held me tight. Later I wondered if he somehow cursed me or knew I would get extremely ill right where he grabbed me, on my liver.

After a few days on Oahu, we flew to the Big Island. I rented a car and drove to our hotel, arriving at dusk. We were put in their best suite and charged $150 a night. I don't know why they did that, but they gave us a spectacular view of the rocky ground disappearing into the ocean. It was the most beautiful hotel view I had ever seen. The next morning, I went down to talk to the concierge about scuba diving. In front of his desk was a sign that said, "Ask me about the volcano." So I did.

The concierge said, "The volcano is erupting. We have helicopter tours where you can see the eruption if you like."

"How much is the helicopter tour?"

"$300 per person," he said.

He may as well have said one million dollars because there was no way I could pay $1,200 for our family to see the volcano erupt, and Mary would kill me if I told her she had to pay $1,200 too.

"When did it start erupting?" I asked.

"We have had a series of earthquakes lately," he said. "There were thirty or more small earthquakes and a larger one that began the eruption, when one side of the crater fell into the caldera," he said.

"Exactly when . . . what day and time did the volcano start erupting?"

He had a computer in front of him. He typed into the computer, and then he said, "It started erupting on Saturday . . . shortly after 5:00 AM."

There was a six-hour time difference between EST and Hawaiian time. That meant it started erupting when I fell asleep on the fight to Hawaii, plus or minus an hour.

I then booked the scuba diving trip for that day. I believed if God started the eruption when I was asleep, it would still be erupting when we planned to go to Volcano National Park a few days later. I also realized that Jesus would provide a way for us to see the volcano erupt other than taking the expensive helicopter tour. We had a lovely time scuba diving in Kona. But after a couple of days seeing the sights, we decided to head for the eastern most part of the island to visit the rainforest in Hilo.

When we arrived in Hilo, I noticed a sign for an airport in town. After checking into the hotel at Hilo, I took a trip to investigate this little airport. It had many small airplanes that were for rent. Since I had a pilot's license, I asked a flight instructor at the FBO if

I could rent an airplane and fly up to see the volcano. I was told I could if I took a flight instructor with me. Lanida did not join us on this part of the trip, so I had to fly Mary, her two children, my wife Beth, and our two children and decided I could easily handle this in a larger single-engine airplane with the instructor in two flights. The cost per hour was $125. That meant we could all see the volcano for under $500. I signed the paperwork and we took off within the hour.

I flew the Cessna 182 over the volcano twice with the passengers and had a picture-perfect view of the lava. The first lava we saw was Aa lava, and it was jet-black. There were lines of it that didn't seem to move much, but occasionally it would pile up and tumble over itself. Then when we approached the crater we saw the Pahoehoe lava, which looked effervescent and flowed like a river. The view was incredible. At the crater we saw the lava shooting into the sky, and I flew above and around the column of orange-red lava several times for a spectacular view. I was amazed at the size of the volcanic lava flow, which had to be over a thousand feet high.

On the second flight, the sun was setting, and the Aa lava looked like red-hot charcoal that occasionally tumbled over each other. On the previous flight this Aa lava was black. But the amazing thing was, I felt like I could see through the Pahoehoe lava as if it was opaque and luminescent. The view was surreal, and no photos could do this vision justice. I turned the plane to the coast and followed the lava to the sea, where it flowed into the ocean, and I saw steam vents and heard the steam exploding as the lava hit the ocean.

When we arrived home from Hawaii, we learned that the eruption had continued nonstop since I saw the angel fly toward the earth. I might add, last time I checked, it was still erupting decades later without ceasing.

At home after the trip, Jessica found a Christian CD she liked. She listened to it again and again. It was about a boy who prayed to move a mountain. The singer was looking for that boy . . . He wanted to find him. When I heard the lyrics, I told Jessica and Joshua, I knew who that boy was . . . It was Joshua!

A few days later we were in Maui. I enjoyed the trip to Hana. I drove a jeep. We forded several rivers, and these jeeps filled up to our waist in water as we crossed some of the rivers. I was warned that we would have to do this but was unprepared for the cold water as it entered the cabin of the jeep and covered our legs.

On Saturday Beth and I awakened around 6:00 AM. Everyone else was sound asleep. I decided to take Beth on a tour of the expensive hotels in Maui. She agreed. After writing a brief note to Mary, telling her where we went and when we would be back, we snuck out of our room and headed for our car. I pulled into the parking lot of the Westin. We walked to the coast, along the beach, and then walked back to the hotel between water fountains that shot water high into the air on both sides of the sidewalk.

As we headed for the lobby, I suddenly recalled the dream on the flight to Hawaii. By now I had ample proof that I really did talk to Jesus. Yet I had not made any arrangements to go to Molokai. I didn't even know where that island was or if it existed. I shuddered internally as I realized I was disobeying God. It was Saturday morning, and I needed a travel agent. Saturday and Sunday were the only days I had to travel to this strange island. I began to panic.

I stopped and turned to my wife. "Beth, we need to talk." She stopped walking and looked at me.

"Well, you know that I had a dream where I was told I would see the volcano erupt. Well, we saw it erupt . . . the volcano Joshua prayed to see."

"Yes."

"During the dream on the flight out here, Jesus told me," my voice got faint, "that I had to go to Molokai."

"What is Molokai?" Beth asked.

"Apparently, it's an island here in Hawaii," I responded sheepishly.

"If God told you to go, then you have to go."

I couldn't believe what I heard. My knees felt weak. "But, Beth, it is Saturday, and all the travel agencies will be closed, and I have no idea where Molokai is."

Beth said, "Maybe they have a travel agency in the hotel. Let's go check."

I was anxious, and I prayed as we walked to the hotel. When we entered the hotel, I turned to the left and directly ahead of me at the end of the hall was a sign that said "Travel agent." There was a desk in front of the sign, and someone was sitting at the desk.

"Thank God," I said to Beth. "A travel agent who works on Saturday."

We walked hastily to the desk, and I asked, "Are you a travel agent?"

"Yes, my name is Anita."

"Hi, Anita, my name is Chris. Anita, I need your help. You see, God told me I have to go to an island called Molokai, and I really don't know where Molokai is or how to get there."

She didn't miss a beat. "Well, Chris, if you look out the window there, you will see an island."

I turned, and sure enough I saw an island.

"That island is Molokai."

At this point she pulled out several typed pages that were stapled together and flipped through the pages.

She found what she was looking for and said, "There are two trips today. One leaves at 9:00 AM, and the other at 10:00 AM." It was around 7:15 AM.

"Where is the airport? Can I get there from this island?"

"The airport is just down the road."

"Oh, thank God, it's here on Maui?"

"Yes."

"I need to get my children and pick them up if we are to all go to Molokai."

"Mr. Morris, children under the age of eighteen are not allowed on the island. There are lepers there."

I looked at my wife. Beth said, "That's fine, Chris, you go ahead, and I will stay with the children and take them to the beach today. You have a nice trip."

"Are you sure you don't want to go?"

"Believe me. I need a day of rest! You have fun, dear, and do what God asked you to do."

I looked helplessly at Anita.

"Chris, I recommend you leave at 10:00 AM, because the tour doesn't really start until the second group arrives. That will give you time to pack a few things. You will need to pack a bag lunch and drinks. I think Molokai is the most beautiful island in Hawaii. You will learn about Father Damien and many other things on the tour."

"What is the price?"

"It is $180 for the tour."

After paying, we drove back to the condo, I packed a backpack, and then Beth and the children rode with me to the airport. After kissing and hugging everyone goodbye, I boarded a twin airplane.

On the way over, I sat next to a beautiful woman with her mother. Turns out this woman was an actress I recognized from an *Indiana Jones* movie. We saw spectacular cliffs and waterfalls as we approached the island. When we arrived, we waited at a deserted World War II vintage airport. After about an hour, a bus arrived, and we were escorted onboard.

We went on a wonderful tour of the island that included detailed explanations about the history of the lepers of Hawaii. I was so impressed with Father Damien. He worked so closely helping the lepers that he tragically contracted leprosy and died.

The Hawaiians were a gentle, loving people, prior to the arrival of the Christians, who really messed things up. Except for the occasional execution of the king's enemies, usually by throwing them off the top of cliffs, the people were downright civilized. They really took care of each other as Jesus asked us to care for one another.

There was a dark side to some of these people. There was no mercy for the lepers and their families. They were treated like murderers. Their entire families were rounded up and sent to Molokai to die . . . even if they didn't have leprosy. Often the lepers were taken by sailboat to the island and cast overboard, hundreds of yards from shore. No attempt was made to determine whether these people could swim. If they couldn't, they simply drowned.

Father Damien gave up everything to help these lepers, eventually contracting leprosy.

"There was a great man of God," I thought. Surely God wanted me to know that wonderful things were done by the church for these lepers.

We drove from stop to stop, learning about the history of leprosy and the history of the island. It was fascinating.

But the entire time, I kept asking myself, "Why did God send me here? There must be a reason beyond the obvious lesson about great priests and nuns."

Yes, I enjoyed talking to the actress and her mom. I also enjoyed learning about Father Damien. But I believed there had to be a more important reason that I was sent here than to take a history lesson.

The highlight of the tour was when we stopped at a beautiful little church. The view around that church was heavenly. We entered the church, sat in pews, and our guide, who by now had impressed me with his intellect, sat in the pulpit and described the sacrifices of the Catholic priests and nuns who saved his ancestors.

As we boarded the bus to head for the airport, our guide stopped me and asked me a question.

"You look like an intelligent man," he said.

I didn't know what to say.

"I need your help."

"I would be glad to help any way I can," I said.

"My name is Jim, and I am the sheriff of Molokai. I am sworn to uphold the law. Well, you see, the lepers are missing eyes or have bad vision, poor coordination, and bad judgment driving sometimes. They could not get licenses to drive anywhere else in Hawaii. And the State authorities want me to take away their licenses. The problem is, I know these people, and if they lose their right to drive, they will probably give up and die. I suppose I have to do what is right, but I just don't know what to do."

This must be why God sent me to Molokai. I paused and evaluated the situation, then said, "Jim, is it?"

"Yes."

"Hi, Jim, I'm Chris. Let me ask you this. Who else lives on the island besides the lepers?"

"Only the lepers live on this island."

"I see. How many tours are there on this island?"

"This is the only tour."

"I thought you pointed out some people in the distance heading up a mountain earlier today."

"Oh yes, that is another tour, but they stay on the other side of the mountain and hike up that volcano over there. There are no roads for cars over there. Those are trails for horses."

"I see. So we are the only tour on the island?"

"Yes."

"Look, every time you stopped the bus, you pulled way off the road behind a bunch of trees and told us to stay away from the road. I wondered why you did that, but now I understand. So there is no way anyone could hit any of us on the tour."

"They would have to go fast and plow through several trees."

"That's not going to happen, is it? Tell me, what is the greatest risk to the people driving their cars?"

"Well, they might drive off one of these cliffs to their death."

"What would they choose, the possibility of driving off a cliff or not driving at all?"

By now everyone had gathered around and was listening to our conversation.

"They would take the risk of driving off the cliff."

"Why would they do that, Jim?"

"We have a commissary where all of our food is served for breakfast, lunch, and dinner. If they can't drive, they will slowly starve to death. Also, all the social activities take place there. If they can't drive, they will sit in their homes and die."

"Jim, you just spent all day telling us how Father Damian sacrificed his life to help out the lepers. What would Father Damian do?" I watched Jim's chin tighten. "Wouldn't Father Damian do what was right? You yourself have said the lepers are no threat to anyone. There isn't anyone on the island for them to run into? I recommend you tell the Hawaiian government you're not going to enforce the law."

"You don't understand, Chris. They will fire me and replace me with someone who will enforce the law."

I chuckled. "That's easy, Jim. It was my idea to create CNN. You tell those Hawaiian officials that you will not enforce the law. If they have a problem with that, you have a friend at CNN who will show up with cameras rolling, and we will show the world how the Hawaiian government is persecuting the poor lepers."

"You think that will work?"

"Here is my business card. Call me if you have a problem. I will be glad to help out."

I knew I was bluffing. I did have the idea to create CNN, but I doubt Ted Turner would take my phone call. My best bet was to call Andrea and ask for her help and introductions. Either way I believed that I could get someone from CNN who would believe the story was newsworthy. While I debated this in my mind, I also believed God's Holy Spirit had entered me and used me as a focal point to help Jim stand up to the Hawaiian officials.

I knew Jim would give it his best effort. I wrote Jim's phone number down and said I would call to follow up and make sure everything went well.

I expected to hear from Jim within a month or two but heard nothing. About six months later, I found a note on my calendar that said call Jim. I picked up the phone and called. It took about a week of calls before I finally caught Jim at home.

"Hi, this is Jim speaking."

"Hi, Jim, this is Chris Morris. I went on a tour with you about six months ago, and we talked about how the Hawaiian government wanted to take away drivers' licenses from the lepers on the island. Remember me."

"Yes, Chris, how are you?"

"Fine! How are you?"

"I'm doing well."

"Jim, I just wanted to follow up and see if you needed my help with CNN as we discussed?"

"Chris, it all happened just as you said it would."

"Really? Tell me what happened."

"Well, I went to meet with my committee in Oahu, and they asked me if I had given eye tests to the islanders and taken away drivers' licenses from those who didn't pass the test yet, I told them I would not do that, and I would not enforce that law.

"My boss got angry, and he threatened to fire me and replace me with someone who would enforce the law. I told him that I had a friend at CNN who thought it would be great news to show how the Hawaiian government persecuted its leper citizens.

"At that point, they left the room for about half an hour. When they returned, they said simply, 'We have decided we will not take the drivers' licenses away from the Hawaiian lepers on Molokai until the last leper dies. Only after the last leper dies will we enforce the State laws.'"

I felt tears come to my eyes as he explained this to me. "That's great news, Jim. Great news! Well, I wish you the best, Jim."

"Chris, if you ever come to Molokai, we would love to see you again."

"Thanks, Jim. Thank you. God bless you, my friend."

I Miss an Important Warning!

Sunday was our last full day in Hawaii. We were going to head home on Monday. So that night we went out to a nice seafood restaurant to celebrate and conclude our Hawaiian vacation. I ordered the Ahi, which is semi raw tuna. When they put the food in front of me and everyone began to eat, I had a strange thought.

"Don't eat that, Chris."

At first, I wondered if that was from God. I then wondered how I could return food at this nice restaurant without taking a bite out of it. I debated in my mind. Was that little voice in my mind God's, or was it my own? I debated back and forth. Everyone was eating. I concluded it had to be my silly thoughts run a bit amuck, so I tasted the tuna . . . and it tasted fine, so I ate dinner.

That night I got ill, extremely ill. I spent the night running to the bathroom. By morning there wasn't anything left in me. The good news was, I fasted the next day and didn't eat anything as we flew home to Atlanta. There was nothing left in my body, so while I was sick, I just hurt.

Unlike most food poisonings, I didn't get over this in a few days. I stayed sick for a week. Finally I went to my doctor. He ran blood tests and asked me to come back to his office to talk. When I got there, the nurse looked at me like she was really concerned. The doc arrived and sat at his desk.

"Chris, do you drink alcohol?"

"Really the most I drink is a half a glass of wine a year, and maybe some spiked eggnog at Christmas."

"Spoken like an alcoholic."

I had not worked with this doctor but once before. I asked him to look at my last lab results. He looked at the chart and saw that the last tests showed no liver damage.

"I apologize, Chris, I should have checked, but your liver, it is failing and looks like a standard case of cirrhosis. In fact, your blood tests look like a man in his seventies, not his forties. So what could have caused this liver damage?"

"When I was in Hawaii, I had some bad Ahi that made me sick. This was just a week ago. I have been sick ever since I ate that tuna."

He said, "The damage to your liver is so severe that you have three months to live. You might make it six months. But you need to make arrangements now because you could die any day. Your liver has completely failed. That's why you are sick. Whatever you ate poisoned and essentially killed your liver."

I was speechless. I had been warned by God when I ate the Ahi. Why didn't I recognize His voice? Yes, it would have been embarrassing to return the Ahi, but that wasn't the real reason I disobeyed God. I disobeyed because I wasn't sure that was Him. I remembered the man who put his arms around my gut, directly over my liver. How did he know?

Then I thought about my children and my wife. The business was just beginning to grow and would not survive without me. I did have a million dollars in life insurance and wondered if it was enough.

While contemplating my family's fate I noticed a picture on the Doc's desk. It was a picture of him and his family on top of a ski run.

"Where is that ski resort?" I asked.

"That is at Breckenridge. I took my whole family there two years ago."

"Is that in Colorado? I have never skied in Colorado."

"Yes, it is, Chris."

I thought about my children. I prayed silently to myself. "Dear Lord, please let me live to see Jessica and Joshua ski one more time. I would like to have a picture taken with them in a place like Breckenridge, so they would have a picture of me when I am gone."

I left the doctor's office partly in shock, partly in disbelief, and ultimately resigned that I was going to die. The problem wasn't *if*, it was *when*.

I deserved it. God warned me, and I didn't listen, and now I was going to take the medicine. I really didn't fear dying. We all die. I should have died in college from lymphoma. A few years later I died in bed after something in my chest ruptured. Jesus saved me both times, but I realized while He could save me again, I would ultimately die. I just didn't want to suffer.

"Six months, Lord, that's all I ask for, six months and one last time to watch my children ski at a ski resort." I prayed this again. "That's all I ask for." I didn't cry. I found it difficult to cry for myself.

When I arrived back at the office, I went in to see Beth and told her the doctor's diagnosis. She didn't believe it. At lunchtime she went to the health food store in Tucker and bought a book called *Nutritional Healing*, which talks about cures for different ailments. Before that day was over Beth handed me a handful of pills to help heal my liver. She handed me pills three times a day after that to take.

Each day I went to work my thoughts became foggier and foggier. My blood was polluted. I had sewage running through my body and it was killing me from the inside out. This was not going to be an easy death. I began to realize that my mind was going to go sooner than six months, and I would not be able to enjoy the ski trip.

Our children loved to roller blade. It was the summer, and I needed to exercise. I hoped that some exercise would help. The two children already had rollerblades, and I wanted to spend more time with them. So I bought a pair of rollerblades for Beth and me. That night we went rollerblading over at Tucker High School. We skated around the track behind the school. I caught a crack with my right skate, tripped, fell facedown, and slid ten feet on my hands and knees. The hand protectors and knee protectors I was wearing worked as advertised. I didn't have a scratch on my body. I got up and continued to rollerblade. We skated for half an hour. It was hot outside, and I was sweating up a storm. Oddly enough, my sweat really stunk. I stunk like a skunk. Not just under my arms. My whole body stunk. What was also odd was after that skate, I had more clarity of mind. I thought about what had happened. I decided that my sweat was helping my body eliminate some of the toxins in my blood.

I then started rollerblading with the kids at least an hour a day, and often two and three times a day. Over the next few days, my mind improved so much that my mind felt almost 100 percent clear. After that, whenever I started having clarity issues, I would put on the Rollerblades, get Jessica and Joshua, and we would skate all over the little town of Tucker. Beth continued to feed me pills.

I went back to see the doctor, but my liver was still shot. I prayed to God, asking Him to heal me, but nothing. I knew I didn't deserve to be healed as I had not listened.

As September rolled around, the routine of pills from my wife and rollerblades continued. One of my friends, Cliff, the guy who thought the government might kill me, was an avid skier. One day we were chatting about skiing, and out of the blue he asked me if Beth and I would like to go with him and his family to ski in Colorado. He had found an inexpensive hotel just outside of Breckenridge.

"Now, that must have been from God," I thought. "I had been praying to get a last picture with my children like the one the doc had in his office."

Believing this was a gift from God, I said, "Yes, count me in, let's all go there this Christmas."

Cliff agreed, and we all booked a trip to Colorado that winter.

There was no miraculous cure this time. I gradually improved. I continued to rollerblade or run that fall and into winter. I also took the pills Beth gave me.

A few weeks before the trip to Breckenridge, I went back to the doc and after a careful examination, he said simply, "It's the strangest thing. Your liver is fine. I can't explain it. You had extreme cirrhosis of the liver, and now your liver enzymes, while slightly elevated, seem to be almost normal. I just can't explain it."

I couldn't cry when I was told I was going to die. But now that I was told I was getting better, tears came to my eyes. I couldn't believe that God would be merciful enough to heal me again as I knew I didn't deserve it.

After the doctor's appointment, I went out to my car and sat there for a while thinking about God. I closed my eyes and praised the Lord with all my heart and soul.

"I knew You could heal me, Lord. But I certainly did not deserve to be healed as I did disobey You. It just confirms what a loving God You are and how much You care about us. Even when we disobey You, even when we step out of line, You are there with us. I don't deserve to call You my friend, but You are my best friend, and I truly love You with all my heart. Forgive me, Lord. Please forgive me for all my shortcomings. Thank You for being a forgiving and loving God. And blessed be Your holy name, for there is none like You. There is none like You. You deserve all the honor, all the praise, all the honor, all the praise, all the honor, all the praise, for worthy are You, the Lamb of God, and I am forever thankful for You, Jesus, and the Holy Spirit Who comforts me when I am in pain. Hear, O Israel, the Lord our God, the Lord is one, blessed be the name of the Lord. And thank You, Lord, thank You, Lord, thank You, Lord, for I truly love You!"

That Christmas we all went to Breckenridge, Colorado. The altitude was higher than we were used to, the air was thinner than we were used to, and it was cold and brisk. But it was a heavenly place. Not only did we have a lot of fun skiing, but we had a lot of fun with Cliff and his family.

One morning when we got up in the dark to go skiing, I stepped outside with Joshua. The light was beginning to come up behind the white snow-covered mountains in the distance. You could still see stars overhead. The snow was two feet deep around my legs. Joshua stood quietly next to me. I heard something to my left and turned my head. It was a hot-air balloon heading our way. It was heading directly toward us. Josh and I stood there in awe looking at this balloon floating just above us in the air. The hot-air balloon flew directly over us, and we could hear the people talking and the intermittent sound of the gas burning as it floated overhead. The wind changed, and the balloon headed for the mountains. Joshua and I watched as the balloon went up, up and away; it got caught up in the upslope wind. It crested the mountains, barely missing the peak and disappeared over the top of the mountain range. I wondered as it disappeared if they planned to cross the mountains like that when they departed and worried about the downslope wind on the other side of the mountain, which could blow them into the side of the mountain. I said a prayer to the Lord and asked Him to protect those people.

I decided to use my cell phone to call 911 and tell them about the hot-air balloon as I feared their balloon crashed. The path and speed of that balloon across the valley was too high; it had to be unexpected. The dispatcher on 911 acted like she didn't believe me.

Several years later, I watched a show on TV where they showed a hot-air balloon that left in the early morning in Breckinridge, in the dark, and was swept over the side of the mountain range. They crashed. I believe one of the members was killed. Another injured person managed to call 911 for help, and they were found on the other side of the mountain. I wondered if the balloon we saw was the same balloon and if God wasn't showing me the rest of the story, possibly because I asked God to save them. I was sad that one person died. Another partially answered prayer? I wondered as I realized God was ultimately in control and was righteous in everything He did!

The sun was now lighting up the sky. So we went in our room, gathered the two families together, and headed out for a day on the slopes. Jessica and Joshua were truly excellent skiers. After doing the normal runs, we decided to take a towline up the mountain. When I worked at a ski resort, that was how we went up the mountains. There weren't chair lifts for this run, only one towline, and I wanted the kids to experience riding a towline. Joshua and I went side by side. The bar fit behind his back and behind my thighs. It was an odd way to be pulled, but we managed to make it to the top.

When we got there, I was stopped by a ski patrol.

"Sir, you may be breaking the law, did you know that?"

"No, why?"

"Your children are too young to ski on this double black slope. I could put you in jail for this . . ."

"You don't understand . . ." I began to tell him.

While we spoke, Jessica and Joshua started to ski down the hill. Seeing them leave, he interrupted me and took off down the slopes after the children. Once again, about fifteen minutes later, after an arduous ski for me, I finally caught up with the children at the bottom of the run. I realized the ski patrol was probably correct as the slope was more difficult than I imagined.

As I arrived by the kids, the ski patrol, who was standing by them, said simply, "These kids can ski wherever they want. They are expert skiers. But I don't think you should be on this slope. I think it is too difficult for you, and you're liable to get hurt."

"That's what I was trying to tell you," I said as he turned and disappeared over the next cliff.

****

I will never forget walking down Main Street in the little town of Breckenridge that Christmas Eve. It was snowing big snowflakes all around us with no wind. The street lamps glowed in the dark. Stores and shops had Christmas lights all around them. The mountains loomed under the full moon in the distance. It was a heavenly beautiful Christmas Eve. I held Jessica's hand, and Beth held Joshua's hand as we walked down the sidewalk with snow lightly falling in the cold night air.

"God made all of this for us," I thought.

I knew He was present in and around us. I also knew I didn't deserve to be here this winter. I now wished to walk with Him and hold His hand as my children held my hand, and I wanted Jesus to enjoy the snow, the Christmas lights, and the Christmas trees that honored Him. I wanted Him to be part of the love our family enjoyed together and the love that was in all people this Christmas Eve. But wasn't the love that was there with us emanating from Him as He is the first giver of love?

My thoughts turned to the Lord. "I hope You are enjoying this moment together with my family as much as I am enjoying this time together. For You, Lord, deserve to enjoy everything we enjoy, and more. Somehow, I know You are here and You are a part of my mind and a part of each of us and You are enjoying this evening with us. I am eternally thankful for You and Your gifts, Lord. Blessed be Your holy name."

Back to Work

In Breckenridge I had a picture taken of Jessica, Joshua, and me on top of the mountain—just like the picture I saw my doctor had in his office that originally inspired me to pray to be healed and to see my children ski one more time. I proudly displayed that picture on my credenza when I got home, and it resides there to this day, as a reminder of God's mercy and miraculous healing.

BRECKENRIDGE
1998

My liver enzymes stayed elevated for many years, but other than that, I felt completely normal and was fully operational when we returned home after our vacation in Breckenridge.

My wife took over management of the tax practice. We had lost all our audits in 1998 when we tried to raise our prices, and I needed to do something to bring in new revenue.

Since I managed investments for insurance companies, I reasoned, I could manage investments and sell insurance to small-business owners. After much prayer and fasting, I decided in 1998 to pivot our business into financial services. I moved offices and added two friends to help me enter this new business venture . . . One was a seasoned insurance professional, and the other, a seasoned broker.

This change of business was the greatest challenge I ever faced, but it also led to some of the greatest blessings I ever received. I was confident the Lord gave me the necessary tools and provided me with a trail of petals that I could follow in setting up this new business, blessed be His holy name.

The Mummy

After I had left Life of Georgia to start a CPA practice, I attended an alumni meeting to hear my previous boss who was now retiring, the Chairman of Life of Georgia, Lynn Johnston speak. As he spoke I felt guilty about helping Georgia State University and not helping Emory. What little money I had at the time, I felt needed to be saved for getting the business going. But I believed Jesus could do anything, so I prayed for a small miracle that would help Emory.

After the meeting, Jessica, Joshua, Beth and I went to an Egyptian exhibit that was on display at Emory. It wasn't the best museum I had ever seen, but it was interesting. That weekend, given our new interest in Egypt, we watched a TV show about the mummies of Egypt. The woman who spoke was considered the leading authority in the world on mummies and she explained in detail the traits of a great pharaoh's mummy versus other mummies. Jessica, Joshua and I sat and watched the entire show.

A few days later we were going with a friend to Parliament in Canada to help him run an errand. We decided to fly to Buffalo and drive there, but I wanted to spend a couple of days at Niagara Falls. We stayed in a hotel on the Canadian side, that overlooked the horse-shoe bend of the falls and the view was spectacular. The price was low too as the Canadian dollar had dropped quite a bit against the US dollar. After touring the falls from top to under the falls, we decided to go on a drive to see the US side of the falls. When we arrived, we drove through the little town of Niagara Falls. It was dead. There were for sale signs on almost all the businesses in town. There was even a for sale sign on a little museum in town. But the museum was open, so being curious, we all went in to the museum. It was a tiny one room Egyptian museum. But the exhibit was quite interesting, since we were now interested in Egyptian artifacts. In the middle of the room, there was a mummy.

At first, I simply glanced at the mummy. But then I noticed a couple of things the expert said separated the pharaoh mummies from average mummies. There was no doubt, in my mind that this mummy had details that appeared to be that of a great pharaoh. I called Jessica and Joshua over.

"What do you think about this mummy?" I asked.

Jessica studied the mummy from the other side of the glass enclosure. Joshua stood next to me while he examined the mummy.

Jessica looked at me and said, "Dad, I think you know what this is," and nodded as if she believed it was an important mummy.

Joshua then said with excitement, "Dad, this mummy is..."

I put my hand over his mouth and said, "Shhhh" before he could say anything else.

I glanced at the curator of the museum who seemed to be busy doing something behind the cash register. He didn't hear us.

"Let's talk outside kids," I said as I motioned to them.

We all went outside and stood by the car that was parked in front of the museum. "What were you going to say, Joshua?"

"Dad...don't you realize that mummy is a mummy of a pharaoh?"

I looked to Jessica. "Did you see the work around the finger nails? And the nose was perfect. This was a pharaoh, Dad."

"That's what I thought too. Don't say anything inside as I'm going to ask how much he wants for this museum before we leave. Can I trust you to keep quiet Joshua?" I asked.

"Yes Dad, I promise, I won't say anything."

With that we went in and I discussed the price of the museum. At this point Beth joined us.

"Sir, I am asking $40,000 for the entire museum. You can have it lock stock and barrel for $40K."

Beth's eyes looked like a woman gone mad who was about to commit murder, and I was going to be the recipient. "And where are we going to put this museum Chris?"

"We can put it in the basement?"

"The basement? Really? You mean the crawl space. You're going to put a mummy under our house."

It was a losing battle. I thanked the curator of the museum and we left.

The weekend after we returned to Atlanta, we all returned to Emory's Egyptian museum. I asked the cashier, if she could summon the curator of the museum for me.

"I'm the curator," she said.

"Great. My name is Chris Morris. I'm an Emory alumnus and want to give you a gift."

"What kind of gift?"

"I want to give you a great mummy, a mummy of a pharaoh. But to get the gift, you must travel to the American side of Niagara Falls. There is a little museum in town and it is for sale. The purchase price the owner is asking is $40,000. I assure you that if you purchase that museum, you will purchase a priceless mummy."

This young woman looked at me as if to say, "I don't believe you." Instead she simply stared at me and said, "I have no reason to go to Niagara Falls."

I tried to argue with her but to no avail. Then my daughter said, "He's not kidding. You can get a great pharaoh. We examined the mummy and we can all assure you this is truly the mummy of a great pharaoh. We listened to the leading expert on Egyptian mummies on a TV show a couple of weeks ago and this mummy has all of the characteristics of a great pharaoh."

She was not convinced.

Joshua then in tears defended me. "My Dad never lies. He is telling you the truth. You need to go there and buy that mummy." I could tell his plead shook her but I was not sure she would take us up on our offer.

I forgot about that conversation for months. Then one Saturday evening I caught the Egyptian mummy expert again on the History Channel. She was examining a mummy that Emory University had acquired. As she studied the mummy she announced on television, "At last we have found the mummy of Ramesses the Great. This is the greatest find ever...we have been looking for this mummy for over one hundred years."

I was surprised to find out Emory received the gift and then simply gave the mummy to the Egyptian authorities. Not what I would have done but it was their mummy and they could do with it as they pleased. And that is how God answered my prayer to give Emory a gift.

A few years later, Jessica and Joshua joined me in California at Disneyland. As we entered the Indiana Jones ride I explained to them that Indiana Jones found a rock, but my two children found the mummy of the greatest pharaoh ever to live. And that's why I thought they were greater archaeologists than Indiana Jones! At which point Jessica said, "God found that mummy Dad, in answer to your prayer." Of course, as usual, she was right.

Trip to Costa Rica

In Hawaii I went scuba diving, and an instructor on the boat convinced my wife, Beth, to allow Jessica to go with us. Jessica was thirteen at the time. I was quite upset because I felt Jessica was too young and scuba diving was too dangerous. But after talking to the instructor, I decided to let Jessica dive with the instructor and me. The instructor and I spent the dive holding Jessica's hands, and the instructor stayed two feet from Jessica's face, looking at her the entire time to make sure she was okay. We only descended about ten feet. As usual, Jessica's performance was exemplary. After a fifteen-minute dive, we took Jessica to the surface, and then I joined the other divers for a spectacular reef dive.

Since I complained that Jessica had to be certified to dive, Beth signed Jessica up for scuba lessons when we returned home to Atlanta . . . I think she did this to make me happy. It was 1998, and Jessica was fourteen years old and Joshua, eleven. Oh my god . . . I thought Jessica would be in college before she was certified. But her mother signed her up with a friend of ours, Tom, the same person who had spent the night in Castro's closet during the Bay of Pigs invasion talking to President Kennedy on whether to kill Castro.

Tom was a great Navy scuba diver, and was a client of ours. Beth had me drive Jessica to the classes five nights a week, and I attended every class with her as a refresher course, as it had been years since I had been scuba diving. To my surprise, Jessica did better than the adults did on the written test. And when we got in the water, Jessica was practically perfect.

But then came the challenge. Having completed the written test and training in the pool, Jessica now had to complete an "open-water checkout" dive. Initially I thought we would drive to the Florida

Keys to do her "open-water checkout" dive. But after checking the costs, it was less expensive to fly to Costa Rica and dive there than it was to drive to the Keys and dive there, so I booked a trip to Costa Rica to complete Jessica's scuba training.

Two nights before our trip to Costa Rica, I had a nightmare. First, I saw my Lord Jesus. He showed me an incredible vision of the future. I saw a little road at the base of a volcano. I was floating in the air above me, my family, and Tom, the scuba instructor. I watched all of us standing on the shoulder of the road, side by side. Everyone was looking up at something, so I looked up to see what they were staring at. In front of us was a volcano. We were at the base of the mountain slope, and above us were lava flows coming down the flank of the volcano. It was a different type of eruption than what we saw in Hawaii. Boulders the size of cars were hitting the side of the mountain, breaking apart and rolling toward us.

Jesus said, "You will see this volcano erupt, and you will be safe."

Suddenly the scene shifted. I was hovering behind myself and watching me, Tom, and my family walking on a sandy beach. We were at a narrow cove. There were palm trees on the beach, and people were selling jewelry. The people who sold jewelry had nailed wooden planks between palm trees and laid black felt on top of the wooden planks and displayed their jewelry there. There were several different people selling jewelry in this manner. The five of us were on the beach donning snorkeling gear, and one by one we jumped into the water. It was an odd cove in that there were no waves. Tom went into the water first, Jessica and Joshua next, then I walked in, and finally, after putting on her scuba boots, Beth slipped into the water. We then took off in different directions and were looking at the underwater reefs.

The scenery changed. It was now evening. Tom, the dive instructor, was pointing at a small sailboat leaning against two trees to the left of the cove. We were soaking wet and were holding our fins and masks in our hands. Tom went to get the little sailboat. Beth and Jessica joined Tom and were hauling the dingy into the water. I was running around on the beach, frantically searching for the owner to rent the boat. We found the renter, and I took him to the boat and asked Beth to pay him. Tom and I dropped our snorkeling gear, and we pushed the little sailboat into the ocean. Beth and Jessica were to stay ashore. Tom got on the boat by the tiller, and I climbed onto the bow, and we set sail out on the water, looking for something.

I could hear our conversation, and then I heard Tom say, "He has to be around here. I am going to do a checkered pattern, and I want you to help keep me lined up with the trees or rocks so we don't miss anything."

I wondered who we were looking for. Everyone on the beach was accounted for. There was Beth, Jessica, Tom, and me. Joshua, I thought. We were searching for Joshua. Apparently, we had all been snorkeling, and when we came ashore, everyone reported in except Joshua.

The scenery changed again. The sun was going down, and we had little time to find Joshua. As we worked our way further and further out to sea searching for Joshua, even though I was outside my body, I could feel my panic growing and my heart sinking.

The scene changed again. It was a dark moonless night; you could see the stars overhead. The water was calm, as oceans go, but you could barely see the surface of the ink-black water. I was beside myself with panic and grief. Tom and I searched for what seemed to be an eternity. We searched all night long, into the early-morning hours. People helped by building a bonfire on the beach. We were getting so far out to sea that the only visible light was the orange light radiating from the bonfire.

Another scene change occurred in my dream! Sunlight at last. We were still searching and could finally see into the water. Both Tom and I were exhausted. We had been searching all night long. The panic and grief had turned to dread.

Then the Lord said, "Joshua has drowned."

"Where is he, Lord?" I asked.

"He is far out to sea now, more than a mile from where you are."

I was in shock. I couldn't believe this had happened.

"How could this have happened, Lord?" I asked. "Why has the current not pushed Joshua back to shore?"

There was no answer. In my grief, I said, "Lord, I will pray that You will reverse this night. Surely You can take us back in time and prevent this tragedy. Jesus, please." I was begging Him. "Please, Jesus, take us back in time, Lord, please, do something . . . anything to reverse this so Joshua doesn't drown. I know You can do that. I am at fault, Lord, I killed my own son. I can't live with myself. Do something, Lord, please save him."

By now I was weeping between requests. I knew Jesus could save Joshua, I knew it.

I woke up terrified. That cove . . . I would never forget that cove. The people selling jewelry and the soft sand, the bamboo back-drop, the sailboat on the left.

"Was this a future that had to occur, or was this a future that might occur?" I thought to myself.

I did not know what to tell Joshua that morning, if anything. As Joshua and I got into the car for me to drive him to school, I noticed he had lost his halo or aura overnight. I was examining Joshua's face, and there was death . . . only death. From what I could tell, his halo was so weak, he did not have long to live.

Joshua and I sat side by side in the car as I was about to crank the car. But after seeing that he was going to die, I decided to teach Joshua how riptides can pull you out to sea. I then began telling him how to swim parallel to the coast to free himself from riptides.

Then I said, "Joshua, I had a dream last night about the trip we are going to take tomorrow to Costa Rica. In my dream, we all went to a cove to go snorkeling. While we were snorkeling, we got separated, because the water was a little murky. Apparently, you drifted in one direction and got caught in some kind of riptide. You were pulled out to sea. We didn't know you had been caught in the current until we had finished snorkeling. When we realized that you were missing, Tom and I found a little sailboat, a dingy leaning up against a couple of trees. We took that dingy and searched for you . . . All night long we searched for you. In the morning, Jesus told me that you had drowned during the night."

Joshua cried, and I held back tears so I could talk.

"Joshua, we need to pray." I prayed for God's protection. "Dear Lord, You have shown me a terrible event. I know You love Joshua . . . You named him. You told me You loved me and my family. If there is any way to prevent this terrible thing from happening, please show me and Joshua what to do."

After we prayed, Joshua opened the car door. "Dad, I have to get my backpack. I left it in the house."

I sat in the car while Joshua was gone and wondered, "Was this future event I saw something that had to happen, or was it a vision of the future that was given to me of what might happen?" I then wondered, "Why would God take me into the future and show me an event that could happen if I could not reverse or change the event?"

I immediately thought about canceling the trip and not going to Costa Rica at all. I began to feel sick to my stomach and helpless.

Joshua emerged from the house, but as he emerged, I noticed his halo had returned to him. He opened the back door of the car and threw his backpack into the car. He then climbed into the front seat next to me. I took a minute to really look at him to see if his halo was really that bright. His halo was as bright as ever.

Just a few moments ago, when Joshua climbed out of the car, he had death all over his face. Now upon returning, he had life. I began to realize, this must be a sign from God that we can change the future.

I asked Josh, "What happened while you were in the house? Your halo has returned."

"Dad, I decided not to swim in the ocean. I will stay on the beach and not enter the water. I know you, Dad. You are never wrong when you say things will happen."

I was so proud of Joshua when he said that. Of course, that was the correct answer.

*****

The next day we went to the airport, got on the plane, and flew to Costa Rica. I sat with Tom, the instructor, and we talked about war stories he lived in Vietnam.

We arrived in Costa Rica. It was beautiful. The hotel room we had overlooked the ocean at Tamarindo, with a view that was amazing. I went down to the front desk, after we checked into our room and asked about the surfboards they had in the lobby and the beautiful white waves at the beach. I was told this was one of the top ten surfing areas in the world. But that if we went to the beach to be very careful, because the riptides and currents were deadly. I went back up to the room and rounded up everyone and told everyone to put on their bathing suits. I offered to rent everyone bodyboards. Jessica and I were the only ones who wanted bodyboards. We went to the lobby, picked up two bodyboards, and headed to the beach. Dozens of unusual shells lined the beach. Tom and Jessica immediately went into the ocean and swam out to the breakers.

Before I went into the water, I walked over to Joshua, and he said, "Dad, don't worry about me, I'm going to look for shells, I'm not going into the water."

Beth was standing there, looking perplexed. I looked at Beth and said, "Do you want to go in the water?"

"No," Beth said, "I will put out a beach towel, and Joshua and I will look for shells. I don't want to go into the water either."

"Josh, I think you can go up to your knees, but stay out of the deep water, okay?"

"No, Dad. I'm not going into the water at all."

Ever since we arrived at our hotel, I looked at this beach. It was straight as an arrow to the left. To the right, a couple of miles out, there was a peninsula that stuck out into the ocean. This was not like anything I had seen in my dream. But to be safe, I agreed with Joshua that he should stay out of the ocean.

Tom took off swimming while Jessica and I swam out to the waves and bodysurfed for a while. The waves were ten to fifteen feet tall. When they hit you, they had more power than any other waves I had ever encountered. Wow, we rode hundreds of yards on each wave we caught. It was so much fun. But when the waves broke on you, it hurt. After a significant pummeling by these giant waves, I headed ashore with Jessica. We rounded up Beth and Joshua, who were collecting shells. Then we returned to our hotel room and watched the sunset over the ocean.

The next morning, I went to the lobby and asked detailed questions about the beach, the rocks we had found under the waves, and safe places to bodysurf. I got wonderfully detailed instructions on where to rent scuba gear, where to swim, and what boat to rent to take Jessica out to sea for her open-water checkout dive. This guy recommended we rent a fifty-foot wooden sailboat they called the "Pirate Ship" for the scuba diving lesson, which I thought sounded like great fun. Problem was, the sailboat wasn't available until Thursday or Friday, and this was Monday, so I booked the sailboat for all day Thursday.

As we talked, I noticed a beautiful picture of an erupting volcano on the wall. I asked about the picture and was told, "This volcano is called Mt. Aranel. They have a beautiful hotel on top of a mountain that is next to Mt. Aranel called Observatory Hotel. It is the best hotel in all of Costa Rica. You should go there and see the sights."

We talked it over, and due to decompression risks of driving up into the mountains after we scuba dove, we decided it was best if we went directly to the top of Mt. Arenel the next day before we went scuba diving. We could then return the following day, and we would have plenty of time to take Jessica out on the boat and get her checked out.

The next day we drove to Mt. Aranel. We spent about five hours driving through the Costa Rican jungle. We saw monkeys, lizards, and parrots in the trees. We stopped in a little town and had a cheese-and-bread lunch on the side of the road. When we arrived at the base of a mountain range, we left the paved road and started driving up a dirt and gravel road that ascended the mountains. As we drove up this gravel and dirt road, rain began to fall. The storm worsened the higher we ascended, and the rain smelled like sulfur. Then I realized the worst of the rain and lightning seemed to hang directly over the volcano that was barely visible in the distance.

After a grueling seven-hour drive, we finally arrived at Observatory Hotel. The hotel lobby shared space with the restaurant and had a large two-story glass wall that faced the volcano. After checking in, we entered the restaurant and sat down. While we waited for our food to be served, I noticed what looked like large, black boulders flying out of the top of the volcano. At first I wondered if I was seeing things, so I asked the others if they saw the lava flying out of the volcano. Beth said no. But then after a while, Jessica and Joshua confirmed seeing streams of lava flying out of the top of the volcano. These streams of lava became more and more pronounced as the sun set, and they changed from black trails to orange strings of fire that shot across the sky and covered the mountaintop.

We were given a room in a hotel that had one side from floor to second story in glass that faced the volcano. And in the moonlight we could see the silhouette of the black volcano with white clouds billowing out of the core of the volcano. Emerging from the clouds of smoke were red streaks of fire shooting like stars out of the cone and lighting up the clouds with a brilliant red. It was beautiful and surreal.

We went to sleep, and in the morning, we awakened to the tune of a bird that called out a loud screeching and then cooing sound. I thought it was a monkey squealing instead of a bird. But as I studied the forest, I saw the culprit, a giant black bird, sitting on top of a branch.

We ate a wonderful breakfast. Tom, the Navy diver, spent much of the night and morning quietly complaining about the dangerous volcano and said he didn't sleep a wink. We discussed why they had a hotel less than a mile from the crater of an active volcano. Hawaiian park rangers would not let people go within three miles of a very safe volcano.

After breakfast I asked the concierge if there was anything fun we could do in Costa Rica. He recommended we hire a tour guide to take us through the rain forest, and everyone agreed to go. We walked through the jungle with a native and was glad he led the trip, as there are anaconda snakes that could drop out of trees onto your head if you weren't careful. We finally arrived at the base of the back side of Mt. Aranel. We were now at the edge of the forest. In front of us were giant volcanic boulders, and to the right loomed the gray-black ominous cliffs ascending to the top of the active volcano that summited at a caldera looming about five hundred feet above us. We could see clouds of fumes billowing out of the side of the volcano and rocks and boulders pounding into the top of the volcano from above. Up close the mountain looked even more menacing. Our guide said he had stood down the path and came within a hundred yards of the rock we were now standing on when it was liquid lava.

I asked if there were any laws that prohibited us from going up the volcano.

The tour guide said, "I took a man here to show him the volcano a year ago. He set out on foot to climb up the volcano. About halfway up that mountain, I saw him fall. He screamed. Then there was silence. I never heard or saw him again." The guide shook his head from side to side as he concluded this tragic story.

He continued. "This is Costa Rica. It's a free country. You can do whatever you want. There are no rules prohibiting you from going up that mountain if you want. But I will not go any further. I don't like that volcano."

After looking at me to see if I was going further, I said, "No, I have no interest in going any further either."

Our tour guide then said, "The tour ends here. Now it is time to return to the hotel."

On the return trip, Jessica found a coral snake, and Joshua confirmed it was a coral snake by the stripes. The two men, Tom and our guide, cornered the snake for me so that I could capture it on film. I filmed the snake with my movie camera. Then it reared up at me and showed it had pits and two big teeth that it aimed at the camera. I backed off instantly, and the snake dropped to the ground and quickly found its way down a hole on the side of the path. I was perplexed as I knew coral snakes were not pit vipers. Clearly this was another more menacing snake that just looked like a coral snake.

Having heard of hot springs that originated from the volcano, we all decided to drive to the other side of the mountain to see the springs. After paying admission, we entered the hot springs and walked in the water, with the water up to the calves of our legs. Being in the tropics, the hot water made us all extremely uncomfortable, and we were covered in sweat in short order. Jessica, Joshua, and I played in the hot springs for about an hour. We even found a cold stream that poured into one section of the hot springs that fish lived in. When the children and I were done playing in the hot water, we walked back to our SUV and found Tom in the front seat looking through binoculars at the summit of the volcano. He handed me the binoculars, and I clearly saw lava shooting out of the volcano and hitting the summit of the volcano and rolling down the mountain.

I got out of the car with the binoculars. Everyone else got out of the car, and we all walked across the parking lot onto the shoulder of the two-lane road that bordered the active volcano. We stood there and watched boulders hit the side of the volcano, split apart, and roll down after us. This was exactly where we stood when I had the vision with Jesus showing me the future. The only difference was I floated above us and looked down on this exact scene in my dream. At one point an eruption occurred, and the ground shook, and a gray cloud ascended into the air and rolled down two-thirds the side of the mountain and stopped just short of us.

Tom was visibly shaking at this point and said, "This is the craziest thing I have ever done in my life."

Joshua said, "Tom, you'll be okay. My dad saw Jesus in a dream, and Jesus said we would see the volcano and we would be safe."

Tom said, "Jesus may protect you, but I'm not so sure He'll protect me." Tom's voice was shaking as he spoke. "I think we need to get out of here while we can."

I looked at Joshua and Tom and said, "I agree. It's time to leave."

We all crossed the road to the parking lot, and we climbed in the SUV.

I decided to talk to Joshua before we drove back to the beach.

"Josh, I love you, but clearly this dream came from God. I saw this volcano erupt in my dream the other night, so the rest of the dream must have come directly from Jesus as well. I want you to stay out of the water for the rest of this trip. Is that clear?"

"I will, Dad. I promise! I'm not going into that ocean. And, Dad, I'm not going on that Pirate Ship with you either."

Then Beth said, "Y'all go ahead on the Pirate Ship, and Josh and I will stay at the hotel room."

My immediate reaction was that the Pirate Ship would be safe, but before I said anything, I decided Joshua and Beth were right. It was probably best if she and Joshua stayed behind. We then drove back to the hotel. This time instead of going through the jungle, we went on a highway, and it took us a couple of hours to return to the Best Western on Tamarindo Beach.

The next day we left on the Pirate Ship and went out to sea. Jessica's checkout dive was uneventful. She passed with flying colors. We had fun looking at the small fish and the reefs in Costa Rica. The boat was fun to sail. I climbed up the ratlines to the crow's nest and prayed, thanking God for the safe trip. When done, we returned to the hotel exhausted.

After a couple of more days at the beach, we decided to check out the best snorkeling area in Costa Rica. It was about three miles from where we were staying. Everyone piled into the car with bathing suits, T-shirts, and flip-flops. We each carried bags with flippers, snorkels, and masks. We also wanted to check out the high-end hotels in case we ever visited Costa Rica again.

After a nice tour of the area, we headed to the beach. Snorkeling gear in hand, we walked from the parking lot, past a huge pool and outdoor restaurant through a stand of bamboo to get to the ocean where we planned to snorkel. As I stepped through the bamboo, I looked ahead at the cove, and a cold chill ran down my spine. The cove had a peninsula with ragged rocks to the left and another peninsula to the right that was flat. It was the exact place I saw in my dream. I dropped my snorkeling gear and felt weak in my knees as I assessed the situation. Joshua was walking by me.

I grabbed his arm and said, "This is the place I saw in the dream, Josh. Stay out of the water."

There were several women selling jewelry on black felt covered boards nailed between trees. On the left was that dingy sailboat, just as in the dream. It was leaning against a couple of trees. There was a blackened circle with rocks around it, the very place they built the bonfire in my dream. The cove was exactly the same place I saw in my dream. It was as if I had been catapulted into the future and saw this place in my sleep. The only difference was that we stayed out of the water this time.

Tom didn't hesitate. He was in the water in a NY minute, checking out the reefs near the shore. I stepped off the edge of the water and was up to my waist on the second step. This was an odd place to swim. I got out of the water and stayed out of the water.

As Tom swam, I noticed lightning in the distance. It was getting closer. I did not remember the approaching storm in my dream. But the lightning in the distance and occasional rumbles of thunder seemed to say "Don't go into this water."

Beth and I decided to leave the beach by going through the bamboo stand at the edge of the beach. On the other side of the bamboo, we headed for a swimming pool, with Jessica and Joshua in tow. I sent Beth and the children to the pool and told them to play.

I found the manager who ran the restaurant and pool area. I asked him, "Have you ever had anyone drown in that cove before? I mean, has anyone ever gone swimming there and never returned?"

"Yes, sadly, it happens all too often. We had a young man disappear from here about two weeks ago."

"How does this happen?"

"You see, the current comes in from the north and wraps around the right side of the cove then exits on the southern side straight out into the ocean. People who drown swim on the left side and get carried out to sea. The current is strong, more than five knots an hour, when you get a hundred yards offshore."

"Why don't you post warning signs for the tourists?"

"It's a free country, sir, anyone can do whatever they want in Costa Rica."

"You ought to at least put a warning sign so people know the dangers," I said, disgusted by his answer.

I went to find Tom to tell him where we were and to warn him to stay to the right. After walking through the bamboo trees, I jumped into the water and swam out to him on the right side of the cove to catch his attention. By now the lightning was closer, and I felt nervous swimming in that water. After I got his attention, I told Tom we would be at the pool just past the bamboo on the left. I added he should not swim on the left side of the cove.

When I returned to the pool, Joshua, Jessica, Beth, and I had a wonderful time playing in this gigantic but shallow swimming pool. After about thirty minutes, Tom arrived and we exited the pool, dried off, and sat down at the cafeteria for an outdoor lunch.

As I sat there, patiently waiting for them to serve lunch, I mused on the fateful question I asked before we went on the trip. Now I knew the answer. Yes, we can change the future with God's help. I was not bound to any future path, even though Jesus showed that alternative future to me in a dream.

Then the thought occurred to me . . . I remembered pleading with Jesus in the dream to reverse this drowning. I knew Jesus could take me back in time. I wondered, was this dream a warning of future events, or was this dream something that really happened, and that God answered by taking us back in time, so we could change the future? After pondering this problem, I decided to let it go as it did not matter, and as I was not qualified or capable of understanding the mind of God.

Either way our son Joshua was safe and sound. By now the food had arrived. We all held hands, including Tom. I closed my eyes and gave thanks to our Lord for the food, for the day, for His blessings, for protecting us at the base of the volcano, and for protecting us from the dangerous cove. I then praised the Lord silently to myself. And we all ate lunch.

Joshua never entered the ocean that trip. The thunderstorm we encountered at the cove was a harbinger of things to come. A hurricane hit Central America over the next week with winds topping two hundred miles an hour. This was essentially a giant tornado the size of a hurricane, and it destroyed parts of Central America, including Nicaragua, killing thousands of people. This storm was heading for Costa Rica and turned north the last minute, just missing us to the north. At the time, we had no idea that our lives were in jeopardy.

When I heard about the damage the hurricane did, my thoughts turned to our flight to Costa Rica. We all knew there was a hurricane to our east as we flew south, so the crew flew over Mexico, across Nicaragua, and onto Costa Rica.

When we crossed Nicaragua, Joshua said to me, "Dad, I feel evil below us. I feel it."

"I feel it too, Joshua," I said. "It makes my skin crawl." I was relieved when we passed over that country and arrived safely in Costa Rica.

The message is clear. It is important to fear the Lord. Knowing the Lord is a complicated relationship that balances fear, reverence, friendship, respect, and love. The greatest may be love, but fear is an appropriate emotion.

Thousands of people died or lost their homes that week due to this terrible hurricane. My heart went out for those people and the tragedy they endured. We prayed for the survivors.

On this trip, I encountered a beach that I had foreseen in vivid three-dimensional color with a plot that played out quite differently in person than in the nightmare. But the greatest part of this trip was leaving Costa Rica knowing our son, a boy who undoubtedly put his faith and trust in our Lord, was fine and was coming home . . . All honor and glory be to our Lord and Savior, Yeshua Ha Ma Sheach, Who is truly God! All honor and glory to Him forever and ever! Amen.

The Great Business Challenge

Our income had improved, and I was now making as much as I did when I left industry. But the year 2000 loomed.

I knew from my money management training that the eighteen-year expansion of the economy would end in the year 2000. I expected a slowdown. I even believed we could have another depression that could last for sixteen to seventeen years. What I didn't anticipate was how bad our business would be affected by the depression we were entering. And I did not anticipate that we would lose almost all our clients either through retirement or bankruptcy over the next sixteen years.

After the year 2000, we found ourselves with a tax practice that was ever contracting. Fortunately, I had already entered the financial services business.

The early years were hell. The brokerage firms I dealt with wanted to hold us captive and make the most money they could, to hell with our clients. This was how the financial services business worked.

All I wanted to do was take care of my clients and help them be financially successful so they never would run out of money. Apparently, I was the only person in America who insisted on taking care of his clients, and I found myself moving from broker dealer to broker dealer, looking for the one firm that would back my goal, which was simply to take care of my clients. Add to this the recession / depression we were entering, and I found myself struggling to keep my head above water.

During this time, the audit partner I worked with from KPMG Peat Marwick contacted me and got me work with what would be a billion-dollar chemical company. This helped us out during the transition to the financial services business. Also, friends at Gold Kist stepped in and hired me as a consultant. These opportunities sound like good luck, but to me they were a gift from God, and I worried what was around the river bend if I needed this much help now.

By the year 2000, the chemical company offered me a full-time job to be the CFO of their company. While flattered, I did not want to take another salaried job. I had worked too hard to start a business, and I had my wife working with me and did not want to give up what we had created. Plus, I felt an obligation to take care of my clients, who would be thrown into a den of wolves if I took a salaried job and closed my practice, something I felt God would not appreciate.

Ski Utah

Cliff and Linda once again asked us to join them for another Christmas vacation ski trip, only this time they wanted us to go with them to Park City, Utah. I asked Cliff to go with us to Breckenridge. Just a couple of days before that, I had prayed to Jesus and specifically asked if we could go to Breckenridge, because I thought we were supposed to go there instead of Park City.

Cliff listened to my explanation and said I would love Park City as the snow was drier and it was not as high in altitude. I asked him again to go to Breckenridge, but he was adamant and said they were going to Park City and I could share in the cost of a condo, or he would get someone else to go with him. At which point I agreed to go, as it sounded like great fun and it would be less expensive if we shared costs.

When I told Beth we were going to Park City, she first thought it was a good idea. But a couple of weeks later, she said she didn't want to go and thought I should cancel the trip. When I asked her why, she was unable to give me a good reason; she just didn't feel we should go.

Over the coming weeks, I too began having reservations, as I was having recurring nightmares where I was involved in a skiing accident . . . then I would wake up. By then I had bought lift tickets, airline tickets, I had paid for the condo rental, and I had promised Cliff—a valuable tax client—that we would go with his family. As far as I could tell, it was essentially impossible to back out now.

I was concerned that I might not be listening clearly to the Lord, so I specifically prayed if I should cancel the trip . . . nothing, no answer was forthcoming . . . so I concluded it was okay for our family to go to Park City. Clearly these were just warnings from God. But to be safe, we needed to be careful when skiing . . . extra careful.

The vacation started out badly. The snow layer was thin. Ice, rocks, and treetops stuck up through the snow and increased the odds of injury. Prayer for additional snow hit a wall. There was no answer to our prayers. We had previously been able to rely on God to give us more snow when we prayed. Then, to make matters worse, on the flight to Park City, Cliff and his son took turns running to the bathroom to vomit. This concerned me as we were sitting next to them and they were clearly contagious. It was at this point that I really wondered if I had made a bad decision.

Cliff and his family went their own way, and we went our way, something I had not planned on either. In fact, I felt Cliff and Linda were avoiding us on this trip. Beth and I talked about it, and she reminded me that they were fighting the flu, plus I was not sensitive to their needs for family time as it was Christmas week. So we planned our skiing and meals separately.

The first day we skied at Alta, which we loved. At Alta, I could let the children pick their own routes, because Alta is a giant bowl and all routes led to the same point. I almost always managed to keep them in sight, no matter what path they took, even though I might take entirely different runs. Even when they were a mile from me, I could spot them and their helmets in the distance, and I would eventually catch up with them.

The next day we went to Snowbird. I knew we were in trouble when we sat down for breakfast at the base of the mountain and Joshua threw up on the table. Here came the flu we were trying to avoid. Jessica was feeling peevish, but she at least agreed to ski with me. Joshua stayed behind with Beth at the Ski Lodge.

Beth argued with me. "Maybe you should skip skiing today, honey, and go tomorrow when the kids feel better."

"But, Beth, we have leased the skis. I have already bought the lift tickets. I really don't want to let them go to waste."

"I think we should forget the investment and do this when the kids feel better."

"Jessica and I'll just ski for a little while, dear. I'll come back at lunchtime, okay?"

With that Jessica and I took off and headed for the lifts. The conditions were terrible. The winds were blowing. There were white-out conditions everywhere. The mountain had many exposed rocks. The snow was thin. Due to the poor weather conditions, a blue slope seemed like a black slope, and there were few blue slopes on this difficult mountain. As Jessica and I warmed up, we found some wonderful runs and began to loosen up and have some fun.

At the bottom of a lift, Jessica and I joined a young twenty-something-year-old man who looked pale. I was making small talk. We chatted in line and on the lift. After the lift picked us up, he confided in me that he was a drug addict. My heart went out for him. I had to tell him that I was impressed with his openness and that I thought he could get help from AA. I said my father was a psychiatrist and felt AA was the best way to overcome addictions.

Then I felt the Holy Spirit enter me and speak through me. "Let me tell you about Jesus," I began. "He loves each of us and wants to help us out, and I'm sure He wants to help you, Jim."

Then I began to weave together several stories about the miracles my daughter and son had seen in their short years. I told him that God had healed me more than once. And if he could heal someone like me—an old imperfect person—surely, he could help him with his addictions. We parted company at the top of the lift. I felt better, and for the first time I believed that I had turned a mostly negative vacation into a worthwhile trip.

Jessica and I came down the mountain at lunchtime to eat lunch with Beth and to check on Joshua and to see if he wanted to ski with us. To my surprise, Jessica wanted to quit for the day, and Joshua had no interest in skiing. After lunch, Beth, Jessica, and Joshua found a TV set and plopped down at the bar, and Beth ordered a drink. Beth kissed me goodbye and sent me on my way.

Having had some success in the morning, I wanted to do one more run off the gondola from the top of the mountain. Two of the skiers in the gondola said they did movies of extreme skiers and complained as we rode up the mountain, saying this was one of the most difficult days they had ever encountered on Snowbird. I wondered if I should take the gondola back down and not ski. But I ignored my feelings and jumped off the gondola and started skiing.

It was tough up there, though the wind had subsided; whiteout conditions surrounded me, and I apparently couldn't see the sign for Upper Chip's Run on my left that I had planned on taking. Instead I continued straight on "High Baldy Traverse," which was a double black run. I continued skiing along the top of this run for a while. Realizing I missed my turn, I took the next run to my left and carefully picked my way through some trees. As I approached the next turn, I stopped in front of four people sitting or lying down on their backs blocking me. I asked if they were okay. They said they were all fine. While we talked, another skier flew down behind me and crashed headlong into the snow as he tried to avoid the bodies in the snow. He was okay. Trees were on both sides of these people, making it impossible to pass them.

I took the only course available, which was to swing to the right through the denser woods. I emerged from these trees and found myself on an open powder slope in whiteout conditions. I really couldn't see anything, so I simply kept my skis facing forward and strained my eyes from side to side, looking for an opportunity to exit this run. I saw no exit opportunities. After skiing for a while, the slope dead-ended into a steep cliff. I realized I had discovered a tough run and I was the only person on this run.

In front of me was a cliff face that was a double black nightmare with rocks, ice, the tops of trees sticking out of the snow, intermixed with soft snow. I stopped and considered walking back up the slope. It was more than a mile, and the sun was going behind the mountain. It would have taken me hours. The only direction I could go was down the mountain. The soft snow alternated with invisible patches of ice and intermixed with rocks and treetops that stuck out of the snow.

I began to ski down the slope, picking my way between the tip-tops of trees and rocks, and turned carefully avoiding the tall trees. After skiing a few turns, I chose to stop and investigate the next area before continuing. It was so steep. When I was stopping, my skis hit a patch of ice, and I spun to my right facing uphill. I parted my skis in a V shape to stop sliding backward. Then in an instant, I fell backward. My left ski detached and disappeared. My body careened backward down the slope. To stop my fall, I slung my right ski tail down into the soft, deep snow, abruptly stopping my fall and jerking my right knee. I heard two loud pops as ligaments behind my knee gave way.

There I hung, on my back, on a steep slope, with nothing but my right ski dug firmly into the ground, holding me. I couldn't move. It was like being suspended by a broken leg, and the pain was so great that when I bent to release the bindings, I would fall back in agony. Finally, after a brief prayer and plead for help, I made a last-ditch effort to grab my leg above my knee, which I did successfully. Holding my calf, the pain lessened from behind my knee. I was then able to climb up my lower leg, putting one hand over the other, until I reached the bindings. I pounded on the tab behind the boots until the bindings released my boot, and I took off sliding down the slope backward. I dug my hands into the snow to slow down my descent. As I slowed, I managed to turn around on my seat, legs facing down-hill as I came to a stop on a rocky outcrop. I stopped there, assessing my predicament. I knew I had seriously injured my right knee. My skis were missing. I feared I had torn my ACL.

I decided to climb, digging my arms into the snow up to the ski that was planted firmly in the snow. It took me awhile, but I was finally able to dig the ski out of the snow. Then I slid on my back to the other ski, which was caught on a treetop that stuck inches out of the snow. It was difficult, and tears were freezing on the side of my eyes, making it hard to see.

Having recovered both skis and lying on my back, I wondered if anyone would see me so I could get help. But I was way off the normal paths on double black slopes and on an unmarked slope that should have been closed by the ski patrol. I realized that I had been there for a while and I had not seen one skier since I passed those other skiers at the turn.

I decided to do the only thing I could do, which was to slide down this run on my back. There was a catwalk hundreds of yards below me. I decided to take aim and pick the best route and let go, hoping I wouldn't be injured. I slid twenty feet or so and hit a tree-top that stopped me. I aimed again and once again hit a rocky patch that slowed me. This continued until I eventually slammed into the catwalk path on my left side, holding my right leg in the air. I dusted myself off and pulled myself up so I could sit in the snow on the side of the path.

With great pain from my right knee, I finally put enough pressure on my right foot and second ski to lift my left boot and slam it into the bindings. I held the other ski in my right hand, pushed off the hill, and headed down the run on one ski, holding my right ski against my chest. I prayed, asking God to not let me stop, as I feared I couldn't walk up a hill on one ski. There were no people on this path until I merged with another run. This catwalk was perfectly slanted and smooth, so I gently skied easily until I reached a bridge. The bridge slopped uphill. Seeing the uphill slope, I picked up the pace and skied rapidly up the hill and across the bridge. On the other side of the bridge, others joined me, and I carefully navigated around them on one ski. I then saw another bridge. I picked up the pace again, and crossed that bridge easily. From there it was a short descent directly to the lodge. Thank God, I thought. I made it just in time for the sun to disappear behind the mountain. It was after four in the afternoon, but the sun had completely disappeared behind the mountains, making it dark. Bright lights shone from the roof of the ski lodge in my face.

I paused and prayed for help. I asked the Lord to send my wife to help me.

"I need my wife now, Jesus," I prayed in a soft voice. "I need Beth."

I knew if I sat down, I would not be able to get up. So I stood there with my poles in the snow and my right ski leaning against my chest. I then used a ski pole to undo the bindings, hopped out of the left ski, leaned over, picked up the ski, and began to hop on one boot back toward an exit from the roof of the building. Each time I hopped, I thought my lower right leg was going to break free from my knee, and the pain was excruciating.

But as I headed for the door, my wife emerged from the crowd and saw me. Jessica and Joshua were behind her. I thanked God for sending them to me, just when I arrived at the lodge. This was clearly an answer to prayer. I gave the kids my skis and poles, and I put an arm around my wife.

I hugged her and kissed her and said, "Beth, I injured my knee."

She was not happy. "I can tell that, honey. I told you not to ski without the children."

"I know, you were right. I was wrong. I am sorry."

"Do they have an emergency room here?" I asked.

"Downstairs, Daddy," Jessica said.

"She is the smartest kid I ever met in my life," I whispered in my wife's ear. "She's like her grandfather."

Beth said, "She's like her dad."

With Beth and the kids' help, I hopped slowly to a staircase. Holding on the railing, I hopped down the stairs and eventually emerged at the ski lodge's emergency room. My wife then returned my skis and boots; she went to the locker to get my things and returned to put dry socks and tennis shoes on my feet.

It was Christmas Eve. The wait at the emergency room was long. The room was packed full of injured skiers and snowboarders who sat on the floor, on chairs and leaned against walls. We were told the number of injuries they had that day were the worst they had seen all season. The conditions on the mountain were described as horrible and dangerous. An aide then told me the wait might be more than five or six hours or even longer. So Beth and I agreed not to wait at Snowbird but instead to head for the main hospital in downtown Salt Lake City.

Beth went ahead to get the car, while the kids helped me hop to the front of the lodge. When we arrived at the entrance, there was Beth in the car waiting for us. I eventually climbed into the front passenger seat with assistance from the kids, and we headed for the hospital.

When I arrived at the main hospital, we found the emergency room wait was over three hours. We were told it was a full moon and the emergency room had been packed all day. I asked a nurse what he would do. He told me about an orthopedic surgeon who could help me a hundred feet to the left from the emergency room.

With one arm around my wife and another around my daughter, I hopped on one leg out of the emergency room, up the little hill, and into the doctor's office. Jessica opened the door for me, and I entered the office leaning on my wife.

"Finally, we are where I am going to get help," I said to Beth.

No one else was in the waiting room except a couple of nurses who headed our way. I became concerned as these nurses gave us the evil eye. I thought my injury would get sympathy.

Instead we were immediately ejected out of the office and told, "You do not have an appointment. It's Christmas Eve, it's after five o'clock, and we are going home."

We left the doctor's office disappointed and went down the hill back to the emergency room.

Outside my wife said, "I will see if I can find another orthopedic surgeon here," and she took off, leaving me, Jessica, and Joshua standing there. Standing twenty feet in front of the emergency room entrance, afraid to move for the pain, we huddled in a little circle, and I prayed out loud for God's help. People stared at me as they walked by, but we ignored them and continued praying. Beth found the only other orthopedist's office was closed. When she returned, she informed us of the situation.

I said, "That's it, if God wanted me to see someone, He would have provided a way. He must not want me to be treated by a doctor. Let's go home and go to bed, and we are going to pray to be healed. I believe God will heal me tonight."

Beth added, "Then we will go see a doctor tomorrow and check on your leg. I know it is Christmas tomorrow, but I will find someone who will see you then."

"I will be healed by tomorrow, Beth," I said.

Beth reluctantly agreed and drove me home.

At the condo, I climbed in bed. Beth and the children sat around me, and we prayed that Joshua would be healed from the flu and that my leg would be healed. Beth tucked the kids into their couch that made into a bed. I then lay down next to my wife and tried to sleep, but I had serious problems sleeping because my knee kept popping in and out of joint. I didn't even move, and it popped in and out of joint by just breathing. And the darn thing hurt. It was excruciating.

"How could I sleep with this excruciating pain?" I thought.

I then felt tears on my cheeks—because of the pain, because I knew I was suffering the consequences, because I didn't pay attention to God. I hated to cry. I found it humiliating, but tears wet my cheeks that night anyway.

"God, forgive me for my foolishness," I thought. "You warned me, and because I didn't want to hear Your warning, although I don't remember You saying don't go on the trip . . . I disobeyed You. Lord, I disobeyed You and was injured. I deserved to be injured. God forgive me."

Much later, in the early-morning hours, I finally drifted off to sleep. I was exhausted. But it wasn't long when I awoke from a horrifying nightmare. Once again, this was not a typical dream as it was too logical and sequential.

In my sleep, I was taken before my Lord Jesus. He glowed like the sun. But this time He was not happy to see me. He was upset and disappointed in me.

"Chris, why are you asking me to heal you? I told you not to go to Park City. I warned you that you would be injured."

"He's angry," I thought. "This is like the movie The Wizard of Oz, only Jesus is Oz, He is mad at me, and I'm the cowardly lion shaking and wanting to jump through a window."

This was undoubtedly the most difficult conversation I ever had with Jesus. Fear was more dominating than love. I knew I had been bad, and I was miserable.

"Lord," I began, "we had made large deposits that we would lose. I felt it was irresponsible to waste money that belonged to You that could be used in other ways for Your glory. Forgive me, I know You warned me, but I thought that warning was to be careful on the trip. I didn't know You wanted me to cancel the entire trip. I would have canceled the trip had I known."

"Chris, you asked if you could go to Breckenridge, and I approved of that trip. You did not ask me if you could go to Salt Lake City."

This was another reason He was angry! Who am I to do anything without first consulting my Lord? He is always there watching over us. He loves us like a father loves his children, like I love my children.

I began to realize the magnitude of the problem I had created. He deserves our respect and love. He takes care of us right down to the very details. And He loves us like a father. But disobedience, and not discussing our desires with Him, is not what He wants from us.

I dropped my head in humiliation and sadness. I had failed the Lord my God Whom I love.

"I should have asked You before going on the trip. I should have sought Your will. I thought I did ask for clarity on whether to go . . . Forgive me, Lord."

I then felt love and understanding return to His demeanor. It did not make me forget what I had done or diminish the sin I had committed, but I did feel better.

He said, "Chris, I will heal your leg. But I will not heal you or your children from the flu. Go back to your body."

I remember thinking, "Excuse me, I have the flu?" That was precisely when I woke up feeling terrible.

When I woke up, I realized I had to go to the bathroom. That was the last thing I wanted to do with my leg throbbing. But I had to go. So I climbed out of bed in great pain, hopped into the bathroom on one leg, grumbling under my breath, as my leg popped in and out of joint with every hop. Not being able to balance on one leg, I sat down on the toilet. I twisted my lower leg to better align it with my knee as it tended to move freely when I hopped, and it hurt when it wasn't aligned properly. Then I smelled the most powerful scent of roses. The smell was more like burnt roses.

I was reminded of my Egyptian missionary friend Maggi, who was put in prison in the Sudan as he waited to be beheaded. He slept in a room four by four feet tall that had no windows. He slept in his own urine and feces. He knew he would die soon. But then, when the smell became intolerable, he called out to our Lord.

"Dear Jesus," he said, "please take this horrible smell from me and fill the room with the fragrance of flowers." And sure enough, the room smelled like roses.

Then he saw an angel in the room, who was sent to help him.

The angel said, "I'm here to free you." The angel disappeared.

A little while later, one of the guards unlocked his door, took him out into the sunlight, hosed him down, gave him a towel and his clothes, and sent him on his way.

My missionary friend said, "All of this had to be a miracle. No Christian has ever left a prison in the Sudan alive. He must have been told to release someone else and released me by mistake. It had to be a miracle."

Remembering this story, when I smelled burnt roses, I started looking for an angel. I never saw him or her, but I felt some presence was there.

Then the thought occurred to me, "Chris, I'm here to heal your leg."

Shortly after this thought, my right knee began to tingle. It grew warmer until my right hand and fingers that rested on my quadriceps was burned. That burnt hand turned bright red, as if I had held it over an open fire.

After a few moments, my leg cooled enough so I could touch it again.

Believing it was better, I tried to stand up. Amazingly I stood up with ease. I then began to test my knee gingerly, carefully, to see if it was still injured. Nothing. It was fine. I finally mustered enough courage to put some minor pressure on my right toes, increasing pressure a little here and a little there. I then pushed on my toes and then straightened my leg out and pushed on my heel. I felt some pain in my calf, but my knee was fine.

"Praise the Lord, praise the Lord . . . my knee is healed," I thought.

Around this time, another thought entered my mind. "Chris, I am going to check on the children to make sure they are okay." I suspected that thought came from the angel whom I could not see.

I focused on the twinge in my calf muscles as I continued to test my right leg to see if it was completely healed.

"It's okay," I thought, "I've been healed. My calf hurts, but it will get better on its own."

I walked briskly through our bedroom to the living room to thank the angel and found Jessica and Joshua asleep on the couch now made into a bed. Apparently, the angel was gone. Feeling exhausted, and wanting to protect the kids, I climbed into the couch-bed with them and fell asleep.

During the night, Jessica, Joshua, and I took turns running to the bathroom to throw up. Yes, indeed, I got the flu and threw up repeatedly. I hate the dry heaves. But that illness was a mere inconvenience when compared to the injury in my leg that was now healed. I was so relieved I could walk to the bathroom to throw up. I never would have made it with the injured leg. I prayed all night long.

"We praise You, Lord, and give thanks to You! We love You, Jesus, and don't deserve Your love and mercy."

The next day was Christmas Day. Beth took me to the only open "Doc in a Box" in town to check on my leg. As expected, the female doctor examined my leg, moved it all around, and concluded that I had pulled my calf muscle. She showed me how to massage the muscle to help it feel better, but she said it would heal on its own. She also gave me a salve for my burnt right hand.

When she asked me how I burned my hand, I said, "Uh, I . . . ah . . . I guess I just burned it."

She looked perplexed then said, "I see. You burned it."

My wife then said, "What about his leg? He seriously injured his knee."

The doctor patiently explained to my wife that my calf injury was a minor pulled muscle and not to worry about it.

After the appointment, we went to eat lunch out. I was delighted to be able to drive the car again and hopped out of the car into the only open restaurant where we all ordered cereal, except for Beth. After eating lunch that day, we returned to the condo and stayed there for the rest of the vacation.

The next day Beth called our minister, Ron Crews. She was frantic to talk to someone.

Everyone here is throwing up," Beth said. "I'm the only healthy person. If I get ill, there will be no one to take care of all these sick people. Please, Ron, please pray for me, my family, and please pray we will get well. By the way, Chris hurt himself, and I guess Jesus healed him. Tell the congregation that Chris was healed but have them pray for everyone because everyone has the flu. I'm the only healthy one left. And please pray that I stay healthy. Someone has to clean up after them and take care of them!"

*****

The condo was stocked with plenty of wood. I fed logs into the fireplace, we watched television, and Beth cooked broth for those who wanted to eat. As the evening progressed, we all got sicker, except for Beth, who remained completely healthy the entire time. It was the worst vacation we ever had as a family.

When we arrived at home in Atlanta, I talked to Beth about our trip. Sitting in our den, I asked her, "I wonder what Jesus wanted us to do in Breckenridge?"

"Breckenridge is such a beautiful town, isn't it?"

"Yes, it is, dear," I said. "But I've been wondering . . . Jesus wanted us to go there instead of Salt Lake City. I've been wondering . . . what person or family needed our help or prayers?"

"Maybe no one needed our help."

"What harm did we do to those people by not going to Breckenridge?" I thought quietly. I was glad I talked to Jim in Salt Lake City. But clearly our Lord had a plan for us that we did not fulfill. "I hope the Lord was able to get someone else to help in our absence."

"Of course, He did, dear."

"Beth, I wonder what blessings we will miss out on because we went to Salt Lake City instead of Breckenridge."

"I hate Salt Lake City, and I hope we never go there again."

*****

Over the years, we returned to Salt Lake City several times, and Beth learned to love Park City, especially when we went with Cliff and Linda. They even had an indoor swimming pool in Park City that she could use when we went skiing.

I never returned to Snowbird and really don't ever want to ski there again. That painful experience is something I would rather forget.

I Meet Several Extraordinary People

Around this time, I attended a computer consulting event where I met a young woman named Sofia. We struck up a conversation and hit it off, as I tended to connect quickly with intelligent people. Sofia hired me as her CPA. But over time, I learned she was from Afghanistan. Not only was she from Afghanistan but her dad had worked for the prime minister of Afghanistan before he moved to America. Over the years, Sofia and I had many conversations about Christianity and Islam. Sofia was well informed about Christianity and seemed to be in touch with the Spirit of God. In our conversations, she allowed me to call Jesus God, and she even called God "Jesus," which was not a part of Islam. She confided in me one day that the Koran essentially defined Jesus as the greatest of prophets and the one who would bring God's Holy Spirit into the world. She believed Jesus had introduced us to God's Holy Spirit yet continued to see herself as a Muslim. She explained to me that the challenge we all have is to get in touch with what the Spirit of God is telling us and to be obedient to Him.

Sofia's computer consulting business expanded when she brought on a partner named Bob. Their consulting business became a real force in the Southeast, and they brokered hundreds of computer consultants around the southeast. Sofia even used my company's letterhead when she started her business and simply added "Consulting" to our company name.

Ultimately her partner Bob, who had become quite wealthy running this consulting business, sold his shares to another foreigner named Shahid. As I worked with Sofia and Shahid, I learned that he had been a finance minister for Benazir Bhutto, a previous prime minister of Pakistan. Shahid was a brilliant man. He brought his uncle in from Pakistan to interview me and to make sure I was competent to advise them before they bought the consulting business.

Without Bob's connections in the computer world, the consulting business slowly unwound and became less and less profitable. I was really saddened by this turn of events as it hurt Shahid and Sofia—two wonderful, intelligent, and kind people.

To try to grow his business further, Shahid called upon his friend Benazir Bhutto to help him. She came to America and was willing to invest in a new business opportunity in America and to find partners for such an investment. Shahid invited me and my wife to meet her at a party one evening.

We went to the party with bells on as I really wanted to see them build a successful business in the future and was happy to do anything I could to help them. Mrs. Bhutto sat quietly by herself, so I brazenly sat down across from her and struck up a conversation. I was amazed at her intellect.

"Chris, all I want to do is to help out the people of Pakistan. I so love the people. I want to be their mother and help them."

"Did you not have the power to do this in the past?"

"No, the military controls the government. I wasn't allowed to rule the government, I was only allowed to be the social caretaker of the people."

As we spoke, I felt the Holy Spirit take control of me and speak through me. "This is not about you and your power, is it?"

"No, Chris, it is about helping out our people, who are in such need."

"Do you want peace between the Muslims and the Christians?"

"Yes, of course, I do. I too believe in Jesus, and I believe in His message."

"I believe Jesus can help you, if you trust Him."

Our conversation went for quite a while. What a beautiful and brilliant woman.

"She may be the smartest person I ever met. She may be smarter than Shashi Kapoor," I thought. But what impressed me the most was her desire to help others and do good for the people of Pakistan.

The conversation was almost surreal. I was talking to a woman who had been the head of a Muslim nation, and she was lecturing me on the teachings of Christ and how she wanted to exhibit that love to her people. She was opposed to the terrorists. She was opposed to radical Islam. And she wanted to reach out to Christians and reconcile the differences between Christians and Muslims. And the whole time I felt the Holy Spirit's presence during the conversation.

I then added something odd, which was uncharacteristic of me.

"Jesus said, if you believe in Him, you will do His bidding." It was odd, because Jesus never actually said that; this was an interpretation of what I believed He meant. Then I added, "Talking about wanting to help the people in Pakistan does not help the people. Talk is cheap. The actions you take demonstrate your willingness to help." This was so out of character for me to talk to her in this way. Fortunately, she didn't take it negatively but liked my comment and repeated it back to me in her own words.

I had talked to her for quite some time and wanted to give others an opportunity to meet with her, but then she said, "I want to go back into Pakistan, Chris. I want to once again lead our government."

"I have a friend," I thought of my Rambo friend, "I would like you to meet. He worked for President Kennedy and was often used by our government in difficult operations. I think he may be able to help you."

We spoke about her return to Pakistan, and I felt dread the more she talked about her intentions. Musharraf ran the Pakistani government at the time. I had seen him on television several times and recognized the dark evil aura around his eyes. His aura was rare, as I had only seen this type of aura on Mafia leaders and mass murderers before then. Clearly this man could not be trusted. During our conversation, she began to talk about the CIA. It was obvious that she thought I was CIA.

As our conversation concluded, I said, "I will do my best to find Tom, and I will put some calls in to a few other people I know who are high up in our government to see if they can help you, Mrs. Bhutto. I think the people of Pakistan would be truly blessed to have you return and lead your people again."

With that, I stood up, shook her hand, and bowed my head in respect to one of the most influential women ever to live, whom I had learned to respect and love as a God-fearing person who exuded the love of Christ in all she said.

Over the coming weeks, I tried to track down Tom, my Rambo friend, but was unable to reach him. Tom was one of those people that you could reach out to, with no guarantee that he would get back with you. I could only leave word and wait for him to contact me, which he did not do for months.

I then called my Aunt Hank and spoke to her about Mrs. Bhutto's desire to return to Pakistan. At the time George W. Bush was president, and I hoped she would reach out to President Bush and ask for his assistance. Aunt Hank listened but explained that she had retired and felt she couldn't help. Clearly it was in our nation's best interests, at least that was what I thought at the time, to get this woman back in power. But instead of supporting my recommendation, I ran into outright opposition. I contacted several other people, but it became apparent, over time, that our government felt they could control Musharraf and wanted him in charge. They didn't want to stir the pot.

It wasn't long before Mrs. Bhutto started on her journey back into Pakistan. A bomb was detonated, and several people who were traveling with her were killed. It was later reported to me by Shahid that Musharraf had approved of her reentry into Pakistan. But I was not so trusting of him, nor did I believe America wanted her restored as prime minister.

A couple of weeks later, I was in Colorado on a ski vacation with my family. I woke up early in the morning, turned on the TV, and all over the news was the report "Benazir Bhutto is dead."

They spoke about her brave return to Pakistan. The tragic assassination of her father. And now her assassination. They played a recording of her in an interview where the interviewer said, "returning to Pakistan was too dangerous."

In response she said, "Saying you want to make a difference doesn't help. It's the actions you take that matter." I was ill. I didn't know what to do. I knelt and prayed for what seemed like an eternity.

While I prayed, I either fell asleep or fell into some sort of trance. I saw Jesus.

"What is wrong, Chris?"

"Benazir Bhutto is dead, and I encouraged her to go back to Pakistan."

"It is not your fault, Chris," Jesus said.

Then He took me back in time, to the evening when I sat at the table across from Mrs. Bhutto. I was floating behind my shoulder, watching the conversation we had a couple of months ago. Then it hit me. I realized that Jesus was controlling everything I said and that the words that I spoke came from Him. Not one word that I spoke came from me. I can't explain how I knew that; I just recognized He was speaking to me and I was repeating His words.

Then the conversation changed from talking about her faith in Jesus and God, and it became a conversation about her reentering Pakistan. At that point, God was not speaking through me any longer, and we left the conversation.

"But, Jesus, Mrs. Bhutto is a Muslim, and I did not have time to witness to her, and now she is dead and may be in hell because of my failure to convert her to Christianity."

This is a case of my thinking, and Jesus hearing my thoughts and my inability to filter what I am saying to Him before I speak. It was clear to Him I was devastated by her death.

"Last time I checked," Jesus said as He leaned toward me, "you are not the judge."

This comment made me feel as small as a mite. Who was I to judge another person, and who was I to question my Lord's authority?

He continued, "She is in paradise with Me forever. She did everything I asked her to do."

With that I woke up. I was perplexed. I had been trained my whole life that you had to "believe in Jesus" and you had to be "baptized" to be saved.

But then the thought occurred to me: "What does it mean to believe in Jesus?" Muslims believe in Jesus; they just don't believe He is God. For that matter, even demons believe in Jesus. So clearly that's not correct. Since Jesus is God, clearly the only way to Heaven is through Him as He is God. The more I thought about this, the less I understood what my dream meant.

But then I remembered this statement by Mrs. Bhutto. She told me she believed in Jesus, and she never complained once when I said He was God. Instead she nodded in approval to what I said. She also wanted to reconcile the Christians with the Muslims in Pakistan. Clearly this is not the behavior of anyone who is against Jesus. I then remembered that Jesus said, "for whoever is not against you is for you" (Luke 9:50).

"Perhaps I didn't have to witness to her after all," I thought. "Was that not the Holy Spirit witnessing to her through me, and was she not accepting what she was told, exactly as Jesus had said?"

After a confusing self-interrogation, I realized that I was not the judge and that I should simply drop the things I don't understand and trust God. I had no right to question another person's walk in faith, and who was I to question who went to heaven and who didn't, anyway? Clearly that paradigm wasn't as simple as it appeared to be on the surface. Once again, I had underestimated God and His love and His compassion for all mankind. Then my thoughts turned to Paul's words in Romans 2:12–29:

> For as many as have sinned without law will also perish without law, and as many as have sinned in the law will be judged by the law (for not the hearers of the law *are* just in the sight of God, but the doers of the law will be justified; for when Gentiles, who do not have the law, by nature do the things in the law, these, although not having the law, are a law to themselves, who show the work of the law written in their hearts, their conscience also bearing witness, and between themselves *their* thoughts accusing or else excusing *them*) in the day when God will judge the secrets of men by Jesus Christ, according to my gospel.
>
> Indeed you are called a Jew, and rest on the law, and make your boast in God, and know *His*

will, and approve the things that are excellent, being instructed out of the law, and are confident that you yourself are a guide to the blind, a light to those who are in darkness, an instructor of the foolish, a teacher of babes, having the form of knowledge and truth in the law. You, therefore, who teach another, do you not teach yourself? You who preach that a man should not steal, do you steal? You who say, "Do not commit adultery," do you commit adultery? You who abhor idols, do you rob temples? You who make your boast in the law, do you dishonor God through breaking the law? For "the name of God is blasphemed among the Gentiles because of you," as it is written.

For circumcision is indeed profitable if you keep the law; but if you are a breaker of the law, your circumcision has become uncircumcision. Therefore, if an uncircumcised man keeps the righteous requirements of the law, will not his uncircumcision be counted as circumcision? And will not the physically uncircumcised, if he fulfills the law, judge you who, *even* with *your* written *code* and circumcision, *are* a transgressor of the law? For he is not a Jew who *is one* outwardly, nor *is* circumcision that which *is* outward in the flesh; but *he is* a Jew who *is one* inwardly; and circumcision *is that* of the heart, in the Spirit, not in the letter; whose praise *is* not from men but from God.

A few weeks later, a partner of my dad's, the man who replaced my dad as head of the Army's psychiatrists, called me on the phone.

"Chris, I understand you supported Benazir Bhutto's return to Pakistan."

"That is true. She was a wonderful God-fearing woman who wanted to reconcile Christians to Muslims and end terrorism in Pakistan."

"It is a tragedy that she died, Chris. Before she died, she came to Washington and asked for assistance from our government in her quest to return to Pakistan and to become their prime minister. While there, she referred to you by name and mentioned that you were in the CIA."

I laughed. "I got the impression she thought I was CIA, but I adamantly denied it."

"Chris, you must have said some things that convinced her you were. My question is this. How is it that you know so much about our government operations that you were able to convince Mrs. Bhutto that you are CIA?"

"My dad was training me to work for him in the government, Dr. Pierce."

"I see." There was a long pause. "Do you remember when I invited you over to our home for the day and we spent time together late into the evening talking about your dad?"

"Of course I do. We had a wonderful time."

"I asked you then what you knew, and you seemed to act like you knew nothing."

"My dad and mom had been murdered. Aunt Hank told me I would be killed if I talked to anyone about their disappearance and death, so I did the only thing I could do, which was to pretend to know nothing."

Another long pause. "I thought you trusted me."

"What about the comment, if I talk to anyone I will be killed, do you not understand?"

"I see," Dr. Pierce said. "I wish you had said something. Clearly we botched handling you, and things would have been quite different for you if I had known what Gary intended for you to do, Chris."

"I did what God told me to do, Dr. Pierce, to survive. That was all I could do."

"Chris, I have been asked by this administration to warn you to stay out of politics in the future. We know who you are. We know how influential you have been in the business world. But you need to stay out of politics. Do you understand me?"

"I was just trying to help. And yes, I will do my best to stay out of politics in the future."

We then chatted about his wife, his health, his children, and our families and had a delightful conversation on the phone. I do think the world of Dr. Pierce. But Aunt Hank had warned me, and I believe the Holy Spirit had helped me bite my tongue when I remained silent at Dr. Pierce's home many years ago.

Conclusion

If I had read this book when I was young, I wouldn't have believed it. This book is a progression of miracles that were done because of my initial faith and the additional faith of my wife and children. Many times I watched in disbelief as God answered our prayers. This made me bolder in faith. You don't have to believe all or even most of the miracles of this book to step out on faith.

When we learn to walk, we crawl first. Then we pull ourselves up. Then we take our first steps and fall. Over and over we fall before we walk. But we keep trying even if we are hurt. And our parents encourage us and cheer us on. I believe Yeshua or Jesus is cheering you on, so listen to God's praise and believe you can walk. My hope is you will learn to pray with faith and believe with your heart that God can do anything and wants to do those things for you because He loves you.

Jesus did not lie to you and did not exaggerate when He said: "And whatever you ask in My name, that I will do, that the Father may be glorified in the Son. If you ask anything in My name, I will do it." John 14:13-14 And Paul did not lie when he said: "I can do all things through Christ who strengthens me." Philippians 4:13

Consider the miracles the Jews experienced. The sea was parted for Moses' faith. The walls of Jericho fell for Joshua. Gideon took 300 men and went to war against 120,000 Midianites and prevailed. And a young lad named David challenged a giant warrior and defeated him with a slingshot. These stories really happened for those who had faith. So, if God will do that for them, what will He do for you? I believe that's why God gave us His Bible, to strengthen our faith.

I send you into the world as a teacher sends his students on life's journey. Yeshua or Jesus in English, is cheering you on and like a parent, wants to help you learn to step out on faith. He is pulling you up off your knees as he pulled my family up again and again to teach us to have more faith.

I hope you have a great journey as you follow Jesus with your newfound faith and step out on the most exciting journey imaginable, with the help of Yeshua, also known as our Lord and Savior Jesus Christ. Maranatha.

Paul in His Letter to the Romans Chapter 8:

For I am persuaded that neither death nor life, nor angels nor principalities nor powers, nor things present nor things to come, nor height nor depth, nor any other created thing, shall be able to separate us from the love of God which is in Christ Jesus our Lord. (Romans 8:38–39)

Post Analysis

I remember Jim Rohn, author and motivational speaker, saying something like this:

Jesus did the Sermon on the Mount. When He was done, some of the people were confused. They didn't understand Him, while others made fun of Him and ridiculed Him. A little while later, Jesus did another sermon. Once again there were many who were confused, and they called them "the perplexed." Others who ridiculed Jesus they called "the scoffers."

Jim Rohn goes on to say, "The people who were confused in later sermons were probably the same people who were confused in the first sermon. That's why they called them 'the perplexed.' And the same people that ridiculed Jesus and made fun of Him at the Sermon on the Mount, were probably the same people who ridiculed him at other sermons. That's why they called them 'the scoffers.' I'll bet you Jesus wasn't talking to either 'the perplexed' or 'the scoffers.' No, he was talking to those who got it."

Jesus left His kingdom in heaven, came into this world, and spoke His sermons to reach those who would get it. There will always be the perplexed and the scoffers. Jesus knew that before coming into this world. So why did He go to the trouble to come into this world if it was not to share His message with those who would get it?

Jesus's kingdom is here. It is all around us, it is in us, and it is through us. It is invisible and can't be seen or touched. Nevertheless, it is as real as you and I are.

A blind man knows there is light even though he can't see. But not seeing does not invalidate the light. I bear witness to this truth. I am not the truth. I am a beneficiary of the truth. I do not cause miracles nor create miracles. Again, I am merely the beneficiary of miracles.

I am like a physicist that has turned a telescope to the center of our galaxy to search for a black hole. The telescope can't see the black hole itself. The gravity of a black hole is so great light can't escape from the black hole. Therefore, there is nothing to see. That's why they call it a "black hole." Instead physicists look for the existence of a black hole by observing the motion of the stars and matter around the black hole. A physicist recently said that the winds at the outer edge of a black hole travel hundreds of thousands of miles an hour. And physicists can see the stars moving erratically as they are caught in the gravitation pull of a black hole.

Jesus came to bear witness to the spiritual things that make up His kingdom of heaven. We know of worldly things, because we are of the world. We care for worldly things like money, power, conquests, and happiness. But the love of these things masks or hides the spiritual from us. Jesus came from the spiritual world to bear witness to it, and He gave us a pathway to enter this spiritual world.

Jesus wants us to have faith in God and to demonstrate that faith in unseen things. He says we need faith the size of a mustard seed, which—if you haven't seen a mustard seed—is very small, indeed, but adds that a mustard seed grows into a large bush, just as our faith can grow into a large spiritual awakening.

If we take little steps toward this unknown spiritual universe, Jesus will meet us halfway. He will help us comprehend this invisible world. He says we must die to self before we can see. In a sense, we must abandon the physical "here and now" if we want to touch and experience the spiritual. When we die, all things we value in this world will be gone from us . . . money, power, sex, physical well-being, health, home, cars, airplanes, jets, television sets, and other idols . . . all the things we value and worship will be lost.

We have a chance while we are here to discover this spiritual world, the spiritual part of ourselves, . . . and to commune with the Roo-ach Ha Ko-desh, or Holy Spirit. We have a chance to grow and enhance that part of who we are. We even have a chance to commune directly with God, if we will let Him into our spiritual heart.

To do that, we must turn off our physical senses, close our eyes to the world, cover our ears to blot out the noise around us, and hold our nose to eliminate the smells of existence. Only then can we hear the still, small voice, that spiritual voice, however faint, the voice that resonates all around us, in us, and through us. We need to learn to listen to the spiritual things and to connect to God. We need to store up these things, for they are all that we can take with us into the next life. That is why Jesus said we must die to self and be reborn . . . reborn into the spiritual realm.

It is at the point of death that spiritual awakening occurs or becomes self-evident to us. I died once and came back to life. But God saved me because I asked Him to save me and because He wanted to save me. I died to self and was reborn in the spirit to live for Him. It is in this agreement between my being and God's will that I was granted the power to come back to life. Similarly, it was in this agreement that my son's prayer to move a mountain moved a mountain.

Put another way, it is in reaching out to the spiritual that we can touch the very face of God. When we connect with the spiritual, we are connecting with God directly, and we can become one with Him. Then if we let Him, He will direct us and show us what He wants us to know and understand. It may be spiritual enlightenment. It may have to do with the physical world. Either way if we are obedient to Him, He will become one with us, and if we will listen to Him, we will become one with Him. At that point and under His direction, if we pray for a mountain to move, it will move. It is then that all things become possible through Him.

This is like the Jedi in *Star Wars*. When they describe the force, I understand what they are trying to communicate. They are describing the spiritual connectivity between man and God. To touch those things, they must die to the things of this world.

As Yoda says, "Death is a natural part of life. Rejoice for those around you who transform into the Force."

The Jedi feels God's Holy Spirit in *Star Wars*, and this spiritual force works through the Jedi. The difference is subtle, yet the difference is everything. I do not tell God what to do, I let God tell me

THE ACTS OF THE HOLY SPIRIT

what to do, and it is in responding to His will that I see wonderful and miraculous things. These are not things that I do but things that He does that I accept should be done.

In *Star Wars* the Jedi too often take credit for God's accomplishments and become proud and arrogant in what they witness. They don't give credit to God and at times deny God by calling His work "the force" instead of "the Lord's force." Believe me when I say, there is no force apart from God. The Jedi also use the force for worldly power. This conflicts with what Jesus teaches. Jesus showed us worldly power is irrelevant. He doesn't need it as He controls the universe and everything in it.

Jesus says He is the door or the entranceway to the spiritual. Noah's ark had one door or one entrance. People and animals could go through the door and live or stay outside and die. It is interesting that the Hebrew word for *pitch*, the mud put between the logs of Noah's ark, translates to salvation. This mud was, indeed, salvation when the floodwaters rose. Noah's ark was the only way to be saved, or to find salvation. The true door to salvation was Yeshua Ha Mash-ee-ach, or Jesus, the Messiah, a future Messiah, who would bridge the gap between God and man. If you pass through this door, God will give you the gift of the Holy Spirit, and you can become one with God. Then if you die to self and listen to that still, small voice, you will know what to do and become a manifestation of God on earth.

The pyramids are going to ruin. All our possessions will rot away and disappear. Even the gold that covered the Ark of the Covenant has been melted down and sold. Nothing in this life is permanent, except for our love of God, the love of others, and the evidence of that love.

Alas if you read this book, you too will die, and all your worldly possessions will pass through your hands like water through fingers. This book is my testimony to you of the spiritual world. God is real. Jesus is one with God, and He is King of the spiritual, yet his kingdom is not of this world.

Physicists are grappling with the idea that there may be eleven dimensions—seven of which, we can neither see, hear, smell, nor touch. Like the black hole, we can't see it, touch it, or even prove it exists except through circumstantial evidence. Physicists know that light is the only particle that never dies. The entire universe revolves around the existence of light. Light does not experience time. It travels at the maximum speed. It lives forever. It can't be harmed or injured. John tells us in his Gospel:

> In the beginning was the Word, and the Word was with God, and the Word was God. He was in the beginning with God. All things were made through Him, and without Him nothing was made that was made. In Him was life, and the life was the light of men. And the light shines in the darkness, and the darkness did not comprehend it.

In the beginning the light came together and became alive, and only light can take advantage of all the dimensions of the universe. The Bible speaks of a spiritual part of us that lives when we die. Many people have seen this spiritual light leave the body when people die. I believe this is the part of us that really matters.

I have given you evidence of this light.

Gary Morris, my Dad, was the psychiatrist for several people who died around the time of Watergate. My Dad's office was broken into during Watergate, and this break in was well documented in the press. He was also a psychiatrist for Martha Mitchell, wife of Attorney General John Mitchell. Martha was a friend of mine who called me frequently and kept in touch with me before and during the Watergate hearings. Richard Nixon said if it wasn't for Martha Mitchell Watergate never would have occurred. Gary Morris was also a psychiatrist for Dorothy Hunt, E. Howard Hunt's wife. Here is a brief newspaper article showing a connection between Dorothy Hunt and my Dad.

| VIP |

The Strange

Put 10/2/73

Case of the

Red Wallet

By Maxine Cheshire

The plane crash which killed Mrs. E. Howard Hunt in Chicago last December has now been officially ruled an accident but there is one bizarre coincidence which may never be explained.

In her red wallet at the time of her death she carried a slip of paper with the name of a suburban Washington psychiatrist, Dr. Gary Morris.

Dr. Morris had vanished under mysterious circumstances, nine months earlier, in March, 1972, while vacationing on the island of Saint Lucia in the Caribbean.

He disappeared along with his wife and an experienced hotel boatman, after setting out on a snorkeling picnic to another island only four minutes away.

No trace was ever found of the 15-foot motor boat or its three occupants, despite searches by the U.S. and British coast guards and a private investigation conducted by relatives.

At that time, three months before the Watergate break-in, no one connected with the Morrises had ever heard of Dorothy Hunt or her husband. There was

nothing then, or later, to link them to Dr. Morris except the discovery of his name in Mrs. Hunt's billfold the following December.

Dr. Morris' records and files are now in the possession of a brother-in-law, Stuart Knudsen, a builder, who lives in Ellicott City, Md.

A careful check by Knudsen has failed to turn up anything suggesting that either of the Hunts had ever consulted Dr. Morris on a professional basis under their own name. Knudsen did not know until last week about the piece of paper in Mrs. Hunt's billfold.

He has already satisfied himself that there was only one possible explanation for what happened to his sister and her husband.

It was a calm day when the Morrises set out with a local waterman, Mervin Augustin, from the Halcyon Beach Club Hotel for Pigeon Island three miles away.

He reasons that their boat, which had no life-saving

See VIP, B2, Col. 1

VIP, From B1

equipment, may have lost power en route and drifted out to sea. The party left at 11 a.m. and no rescue effort was launched until 4 p.m.

"If a storm had come up, they could have gone down quickly," says Knudsen. "The local authorities told me that had happened once before, 10 years ago."

Knudsen conducted his own search and followed one rumor which took him to the coast of Venezuela, where a couple and a boatman had put in for gas that day. It turned out to be someone else.

The Morrises, who left three children, were presumed lost at sea. His office at 4501 Connecticut Ave. was closed.

There were three other psychiatrists sharing that suite. Since learning that Mrs. Hunt was carrying around Dr. Morris' name, they have made discreet inquiries of their own. But they have failed to turn up any link.

One possible explanation is that Mrs. Hunt had been referred to Dr. Morris by someone who did not know that he was missing.

This is the theory held by another Washington physician whose name also appeared in Mrs. Hunt's wallet.

Dr. Marvin Korengold, a neurologist, says that Mrs. Hunt had never been a patient of his either. He did not know Dr. Morris, but learned from other medical sources recently that the psychiatrist had used hypnosis as one of his tools for therapy.

He says: "If Mrs. Hunt, or some member of her family had suffered migraines, for instance, it is conceivable that she could have been referred to both a neurologist and a hypnotist. If we could locate Mrs. Hunt's family doctor, he might clear up the mystery, but so far we haven't been able to do so."

© 1973, The Washington Post-Chicago Tribune—New York News Syndicate, Inc.

E. Howard Hunt, Dorothy Hunt's husband, was one of the burglars caught trying to break into the safe in the Democratic National Committee's offices that was in the Watergate Hotel. E. Howard Hunt went to prison for this. Then before he died he confessed to participating in the Kennedy assassination and provided a tape of that confession to his son, St. John Hunt. He also listed several other people who worked with him to assassinate Kennedy. Howard Hunt admitted in one of many books he wrote to being responsible for training the Cuban troops to liberate Cuba from Castro. During the Bay of Pigs invasion, a World War II vintage airplane that our CIA did not know Castro had at the time gunned down our Cuban trained invasion force. Kennedy did not provide air support and shoot down the plane resulting in the failed invasion and the death of many Cuban troops our CIA trained. Hunt and other military and CIA leaders were incensed by this. They had spent years training the Cuban invasion force and were devastated to see so many of their friends die in such a useless and tragic way. This may have inspired the military and CIA operatives to get revenge on Kennedy.

The mafia had converted Cuba into a playground for gambling, alcohol, drugs and sex. The loss of their Cuban resort to Castro resulted in huge financial losses. They wanted revenge for the failed invasion by Kennedy more than anyone and were probably the main impetus behind the assassination of President Kennedy.

Lyndon Johnson was a man focused on becoming President. His boss was a member of the Texas mafia. Read the book, *A Texan Looks at Lyndon, A Study in Illegitimate Power* by J. Evetts Haley. By participating in the assassination of Kennedy, he knew he would be the next President. The timing of the assassination was perfect to ensure Johnson would win the next election as Kennedy died one year before the election and the sympathy vote would easily propel Lyndon Johnson into the office of President.

These players, Lyndon Johnson, who redirected the path of Kennedy through Dallas that fateful day, the mafia and the CIA conspired together to kill President Kennedy. But there is one more player. There is no proof to this, but I believe Richard Nixon was instrumental in killing President Kennedy. Why else would Nixon leave a trail of dead people? These people knew a lot about Nixon, some had been with him throughout his career. Why else was it so important to President Nixon to pay off Howard Hunt to keep his silence? Why else was it so important to kill Hunt's wife Dorothy Hunt, a brilliant CIA operative, by poisoning the pilot of the plane she was on with strychnine? Why else was it so important to threaten Howard Hunt's children with execution, to ensure Hunt's silence?

Just before Hunt died he confessed to his son that he was involved in the Kennedy assassination.

There were over one hundred participants in the assassination of both Kennedy brothers. Essentially this could be described as a military coup that our Government has gone to great lengths to cover up. If Nixon's involvement in the assassination had become public knowledge, he not only would have been impeached but he probably would have been tried and possible executed.

Lee Harvey Oswald was CIA. Jack Ruby, who assassinated Oswald was also CIA and only had a few months to live when he killed Oswald, so he was willing to sacrifice himself. Ruby was dying of cancer at the time. The CIA knew Oswald was a communist sympathizer, so they could claim the assassination as politically motivated. They also knew he was weak minded and would talk if interrogated. The simple assassination and payment of funds to Jack Ruby's wife ensured the plot to kill Kennedy was kept silent.

Aunt Hank was friends with Dorothy Hunt. Howard Hunt and Dorothy Hunt were CIA operatives, according to E. Howard Hunt and their son Saint John Hunt. St. John Hunt wrote three books about his parents and he connected his mother's death to my parents, Gary Morris and his wife Jane Morris. I had met Dorothy Hunt and Howard Hunt, along with the Secretary of State, and high ranking military officers at our home during parties my parents hosted when I was in high school.

In the movie titled NIXON, Richard Nixon admitted killing three innocent American's and cried in the movie as he confessed to the executions. In one of Nixon's tapes he also confessed to these strange killings. I believe those innocent people were my parents and Dorothy Hunt, although it is probable he also ruined the life of and caused the early demise of Martha Mitchell, which would make the number four. Many others were killed as well, either by Nixon or the Democratic National Committee. We will call them collateral damage. Below is a list of some of the people who died or were murdered during the Nixon administration. It is a long list with a lot of names including Gary and Jane Morris, Dorothy Hunt and Martha Mitchell. President Lyndon Johnson, J. Edgar Hoover and several Congressmen were on the list as well.

30 Watergate Witnesses
Have Met Violent Deaths
(From *Midnight,* July 12, 1976)

What are the odds of 30 people — all involved in the same horrible scandal — dying within four years?

Because that's what happened with Watergate.

Since the break-in at the Democratic National Headquarters on June 17, 1972, there have been 30 deaths — many of them violent — all of people involved in one way or another.

The odds are at least 100,000,000,000,000,000 to one. (One hundred million billion to one.)

An actuary of the London Sunday Times worked out that figure after witnesses in the assassination of President John F. Kennedy died within four years of his death.

MAE BRUSSELL

Now Watergate has surpassed even that violence.

By MALCOLM ABRAMS
MIDNIGHT Staff Writer

The CIA is behind it all. That's the conclusion of Mae Brussell — one of America's foremost assassination experts — a researcher who has collected every pertinent newspaper story, every book, every document since the Watergate break-in four years ago on the night of June 17, 1972.

Miss Brussell is the only person in America who perceived the gruesome string of deaths that stretches from Watergate to now.

She believes that a faction within the Central Intelligence Agency is responsible not only for Watergate, but for the assassinations of John and Robert Kennedy.

She believes, as President Nixon stated on the Watergate tapes, that everything horrible that's happened in American politics is connected, starting with the Bay of Pigs.

Some of the 30 people who died, she says, knew only about CIA involvement in Watergate. Some of them knew much, much more.

A few of the dead, like Martha Mitchell, Lyndon Johnson, Congressman Hale Boggs and Mafia hoodlum Sam Giancana, are well-known. Others might have been — if they had lived and told their stories.

But 30 are dead. And there's no reason to believe that there won't be more.

1. Beverly Kaye, 42, died of a "massive stroke" in December, 1973, while riding in the White House elevator. She was Secret Service agent John Bull's secretary and her job included the actual storing and preservation of the White House tapes.

It is almost without question, says Mae Brussell, that she knew what was on those tapes, including the 18 minutes of recorded conversations which were mysteriously erased.

As reported in the West Coast news service, "Earth News," on June 5, 1974, from the stories she told her friends and neighbors, she was convinced that the president and his aides were involved in the Watergate bugging and cover-up.

2. Murray Chotiner, a long-time friend of Nixon's was killed when a government truck ran into his car on January 23, 1974. At first it was reported that Chotiner suffered only a broken leg, but he died a week later.

According to a March 31, 1973 article in the Los Angeles Times, Chotiner may have been one of the people who received the tape recordings made inside the Democratic campaign headquarters in the Watergate building.

3. William Mills, the Congressman from Maryland, was found shot to death — an apparent suicide — one day after it was disclosed that he failed to report a $25,000 campaign contribution given to him by President Nixon's re-election finance committee. Mills, 48, was discovered with a 12-gauge shotgun by his feet and an "alleged suicide note" pinned to his body. In all, seven such notes were found, apparently written by Mills, although this was never verified.

According to Miss Brussell, the $25,000 came from the $1.7 million dollar secret fund for "dirty tricks" used by the Committee to Re-Elect the President.

4. and 5. James Webster and James Glover, key men in Congressman Mills' campaign, were killed in a car accident in February of 1972. Another campaign worker stated in the Washington Post on

May 23, 1973, that the illegal $25,000 contribution was delivered to Mills' campaign manager James Webster.

6. Hale Boggs, the Congressman from Louisiana and a member of the Warren Commission, died in July of 1972, one month after the Watergate arrests. Boggs and two other men disappeared when the light aircraft in which they were flying crashed in Alaska.

The Los Angeles Star, on November 22, 1973, reported that "Boggs had startling revelations on Watergate and the assassination of President Kennedy."

Richard Nixon made some unintelligible remarks about Congressman Boggs which were recorded on the White House tapes, just seven days after the Watergate break-in.

7. <u>Dorothy Hunt,</u> the wife of convicted White House "plumber" E. Howard Hunt, was killed, along with 41 other people, when United Airlines Flight 553 crashed near Chicago's Midway Airport on Dec. 8, 1972.

Mrs. Hunt, who, like her husband, had worked for the CIA, was allegedly carrying $100,000 in "hush" money so her husband would not implicate White House officials in Watergate.

The day after the crash, White House aide Egil (Bud) Krogh was appointed Undersecretary of Transportation, supervising the National Transportation Safety Board and the Federal Aviation Association — the two agencies charged with investigating the airline crash.

A week later, Nixon's deputy assistant Alexander Butterfield was made the new head of the FAA, and five weeks later Dwight Chapin, the president's appointment secretary, was dispatched to Chicago to become a top executive with United Airlines.

The airplane crash was blamed on equipment malfunctions.

8. and 9. Ralph Blodgett and James Krueger, attorneys for Northern Natural Gas Co., were killed in the same airplane as Mrs. Hunt.

The two men, Miss Brussell contends, had documents linking Attorney General John Mitchell to Watergate, and documents of a secret transfer of El Paso Natural Gas Co. stock made to Mitchell after the Justice Department dropped a $300 million anti-trust suit against the company.

The money from these stocks may have been used for political espionage.

Blodgett told friends before boarding the plane in Washington that he would "never live to get to Chicago."

10. and 11. <u>Dr. and Mrs. Gary Morris</u> died in March of 1972 when their boat mysteriously disappeared off the Caribbean Island of St. Lucia. Their bodies were never found. But their names were on the dead body of Mrs. Dorothy Hunt, according to an article in the Oct. 3, 1975 Washington Post.

"The plane crash that killed Mrs. Hunt in Chicago has now been officially ruled an accident," the story stated. "But there's one bizarre coincidence that may never be explained.

"Her red wallet at the time of her death had a slip of paper with the name of a Washington psychiatrist, Dr. Gary Morris, on it."

Neither Howard Hunt nor his wife were patients of the doctor, who was already dead at the time of the plane crash.

It is interesting to note, Mae Brussell says, that Dr. Morris was an expert in hypnosis and that Mr. Hunt used "mind control" in his espionage work.

12. J. Edgar Hoover, head of the FBI, died on May 1, 1972, a month before Watergate. There is considerable evidence that he may have known about the White House "dirty tricks."

An article in the Harvard Crimson quotes Felipe De Diego, a Cuban exile who took part in the break-in at psychiatrist Daniel Ellsberg's office, as saying:

"Two burglaries took place at Hoover's Washington home. The first was in the winter of 1972 to retrieve documents that might be used for blackmail against the White House.

"After the first burglary," according to Diego, "a second burglary was carried out; this time, whether by design or misunderstanding, a poison, thyonphosphate genre, was placed in Hoover's personal toilet articles. Hoover died shortly after that."

Thyonphosphate genre is a drug that induces heart seizures. Its presence in a corpse is undetectable without an autopsy. No autopsy was ever performed on the body of J. Edgar Hoover.

13. Sam Giancana, the Mafia chief, was murdered on June 22, 1975, as he was about to testify before Sen. Frank Church's Senate Committee, investigating the use of underworld figures by the CIA, for the purpose of assassinating foreign leaders. Giancana had ties to E. Howard Hunt and the CIA.

His murder is unsolved, although police say "it didn't look like a Mafia hit." His former girlfriend, Judith Campbell Exner recently revealed her secret romance with JFK.

14. Lyndon Baines Johnson, the former president, died on January 20, 1973, in a helicopter ambulance en route to San Antonio, Tex.

Three months before his death, Johnson was quoted in the San Francisco Chronicle as saying, "We've been running a damn Murder Inc. in the Caribbean." This was two years before Sen. Church's committee revealed the plots to assassinate foreign leaders.

"Coincidentally," Mae Brussell says, "Johnson died in the arms of a secret service agent Mike Howard, who in 1963 had been assigned to protect Marina Oswald after her husband was killed."

15. George Bell, assistant to Charles Colson, special counsel to the White House, died of unreported causes on June 30, 1973. When questioned about President Nixon's infamous "enemies list," Colson told the House Subcommittee Investigating Watergate that the "late George Bell" was responsible for the list of 200 celebrities and politicians whom the President considered dangerous.

16. Lee Pennington, Jr., a CIA agent, died of an apparent heart attack in October of 1974. Immediately after the Watergate arrests two years earlier, he had been sent to ransack burglar James McCord's home. Richard Helms, the CIA chief at the time, did not reveal this fact to any investigators.

It was not until June 28, 1974, four months before Pennington's death, that the new CIA director, William Colby, reported to Sen. Howard Baker:

"The results of our investigation clearly show that the CIA had in its possession, as early as June, 1972, information that one of its paid operatives, Lee R. Pennington, Jr., had entered the James McCord residence shortly after the Watergate break-in and destroyed documents which might show a link between McCord and the CIA."

17. J. Clifford Dieterich, a 28-year-old secret service agent assigned to Nixon, was killed when the president's helicopter crashed off the Bahamas in May of 1973.

Dieterich was one of seven men in the helicopter, but the only one to die. Miss Brussell believes that in guarding Richard Nixon, he may have come to know too much.

18. Clay Shaw, who years earlier had been acquitted of conspiracy to kill John F. Kennedy, died of a heart attack, on August 16, 1974.

His death came just weeks after Victor Marchetti, author of "The Cult of Intelligence," revealed that Shaw had worked for the CIA. He had been on assignment in Mexico in 1963 at the same time as CIA agent E. Howard Hunt and Lee Harvey Oswald.

Shaw was cremated. There was no autopsy.

19. Merle D. Baumgart, an aide to Rep. Peter Rodino of the House Judiciary Committee on Impeachment, was killed in a traffic accident on May 20, 1975. Washington police described his death as "a routine traffic accident" — until they received an anonymous call to "look into it."

According to the Portland Oregonian of June 30, 1975, U.S. agents joined the probe but kept it secret because of the "stature of some individuals who might be involved."

Miss Brussell speculates that in his work to impeach Nixon, Baumgart may have come across some dangerous information.

20. Nikos J. Vardinoyiannis, a Greek shipowner who contributed funds to Nixon's presidential campaign, died of undisclosed causes in 1973. Watergate prosecutor Leon Jaworski was investigating Vardinoyiannis when the Justice Department declared that the Greek's contribution of $27,000 was not illegal.

The Department reached this conclusion, Mae Brussell says, even though the contribution was made after one of Vardinoyiannis' companies was contracted to supply fuel for the U.S. 6th Fleet, and even though federal law bars foreign contractors from contributing to U.S. political campaigns.

21. Joseph Tomassi, the 24-year-old head of the American Nazi Party in California was shot to death on the front steps of his Los Angeles headquarters, on August 15, 1975.

Two years earlier, the Los Angeles Times had reported that "the Committee to Re-Elect the President gave $10,000 in undisclosed funds to finance a surreptitious campaign to remove George Wallace's American Independent Party from the 1972 California ballot."

The Times went on to say that "$1,200 of the fund found its way to Joe Tomassi, head of the Nazi Party in California."

22. Mrs. Louise Boyer, Nelson Rockefeller's assistant for 30 years, fell to her death from a 10th story New York apartment on July 3, 1974.

At the time, as a consequence of Watergate, Rockefeller was being considered for the vice-presidency. Accusations had been made that he had been involved in the illegal removal of gold from Ft. Knox. It's believed that Mrs. Boyer supplied the investigators with this information.

23. Jose Joaquin Sangenis Perdimo, a Cuban exile who worked with the CIA at the Bay of Pigs, died mysteriously in 1974. Code-named "Felix," he had worked with Watergate plummers Hunt and Barker. In 1972 he was awarded a secret merit medal by the CIA.

24. Rolando Masferrer, another Cuban exile employed by the CIA, was blown to bits when his car exploded on October 5, 1975. Masferrer had worked with "plummers" Hunt, Sturgis and Barker.

According to Miss Brussell, "He would have been investigated for his activities in connection with assassination attempts on foreign leaders, had he not been killed."

25. Lou Russell, an old friend of Nixon's from the "Red Scare" days, died of natural causes on July 31, 1973.

In testimony before the Senate Select Committee on Presidential Campaign Activities, Nixon's secretary Rosemary Wood stated: "I met Lou Russell once when he came to the office. He said he worked on the old House Un-American Activity Committee and that he needed a job."

Russell found a job alright, with "McCord Associates," a CIA front run by Watergater James McCord.

26. Jack Cleveland, a partner of the president's brother Donald Nixon, died in Canada in November of 1973. At the time he was wanted for questioning in connection with a possible government pay-off to Howard Hughes.

Cleveland was suspected of being a go-between in a deal whereby Nixon's brother gained an interest in a large Nevada ranch allegedly in exchange for the president's clearing the way for the billionaire's takeover of Air West.

"When Watergate came apart," Miss Brussell says, "this deal came under investigation."

27. Richard Lavoie, chief of security for International Telegraph and Telephone, died of a heart attack on December 27, 1972.

At the time Lavoie was guarding Ditta Beard, an ITT secretary who claimed she had a memo that her company had contributed $400,000 to Nixon's campaign fund so that John Mitchell would not bust up some of ITT's holdings.

When columnist Jack Anderson broke this story, Miss Beard was moved from Washington to Denver, Colo., where she was hospitalized for an apparent heart attack. She was whisked away, Anderson claimed, so that she couldn't testify.

Miss Brussell suspects that Lovoie may have heard too much from Dita Beard.

28. Mrs. Andrew Topping, the wife of a man arrested for plotting to kill Nixon, died of gunshot wounds on April 6, 1972, two weeks after the Watergate break-in. Her death was declared a suicide.

Andrew Topping told police that "pro-rightist forces" beyond his control caused his wife's death.

29. James Morton was President Gerald Ford's campaign treasurer. According to a New York Times report of November 2, 1973, Ford was being questioned by a senate committee prior to his appointment as vice president, and was asked about a secret sum of $38,000 used in his campaign for the House of Representatives.

438

The Times story stated, "Ford confirmed under questioning that a committee organized in Washington raised $38,216 for his re-election in 1972... but Ford said he did not know the names of the donors because the committee treasurer, James G. Morton is now dead."

Like so much of the Watergate money, Miss Brussell notes, no records were kept.

30. Martha Mitchell, estranged wife of the former attorney general, died on Memorial Day, 1976. A constant "pain in the side" of the Watergate conspirators, she was the first person to point the finger at Richard Nixon and suggest he resign.

The question that I attempt to answer in the book is speculative, and that is, what was in the safe in the Democratic National Committee's (DNC's) offices that Howard Hunt and the other burglars were trying to retrieve? Everything in this story hinges on that question. If Martha Mitchell caused Watergate, she must have pressed Nixon into that burglary. In his tapes, Nixon often referred to the Bay of Pigs. H. R. Haldeman, in his book, *The Haldeman Diaries, Inside the Nixon White House* said when Nixon talked about the Bay of Pigs he was referring to the assassination of Kennedy. The reason Nixon used a code name was he knew his conversations were being taped.

I assert that the list in the DNC offices was the names of the people who conspired to assassinate President Kennedy. I heard that from two different reputable sources but have no written proof to back up that theory. Whatever was in that safe, Nixon was desperate to get it out of that safe and out of the hands of the DNC. I also believe my Dad, Gary Morris and Martha Mitchell were the principal people pushing Nixon to get that prized document and they may have threatened to expose Nixon as a co-conspirator in the Kennedy assassination, if he didn't cooperate. Why retrieve that document? If I am correct, it was to save the lives of over 100 CIA and military operatives, some of whom worked for my Dad that participated in the assassination of President Kennedy.

Nixon resigned from the office of Presidency, not because of the Watergate break in, but because of the many innocent people he had executed and for fear that his involvement in the assassination of Kennedy would be exposed.

It was repeatedly revealed to me that my Dad was a General in the Army, but his rank was classified. Remember, he was a General and reported to the Secretary of State, high rank for a "lay psychiatrist in the Washington area," as reported by the press at the time. The military also held a ceremony for our family after our Dad and Mom died. They placed a plaque with our Dad's name on it on a wall of plaques. We were told the wall of plaques was for fallen military and intelligence heroes of America's past.

If the document in the DNC safe was not a list of those who conspired to kill Kennedy, it was something that implicated Nixon with the assassination of Kennedy. At this point I guess we will never know for sure what was in that safe.

After the break in, Dorothy Hunt, whose husband was in jail, continued the push to expose the Nixon cover up. St. John Hunt believed she was extorting Nixon. Nixon in turn went to the mafia to get payoff money. It was also clear that not only was her life threatened but her children's lives were on the line as well, as documented in the book *Dorothy, The Murder of E. Howard Hunt's Wife - Watergate's Darkest Secret*, written by St. John Hunt.

> **At the very end of his life Papa [E. Howard Hunt] confessed that he thought that her [Dorothy Hunt's] death was a homicide. He confessed to being afraid that his children would be killed. He confessed to having involvement in the JFK assassination. He confessed that Dorothy had been in a losing battle with the President of the United States of America.**

I would believe the death bed confession of Howard Hunt over the words of the living who stand to lose a lot if the truth comes out. Sadly, St. John seemed to be going through much of what my sister, brother and I went through around the same time.

I know it's hard to believe that our Government works in this manner, but if you want more evidence of the things our CIA and Government do at the behest of the President, read the book, **Overthrow**: *America's Century of Regime Change from Hawaii to Iraq* Kinzer, Stephen, Brand. After you read that your eyes should be opened to understand that our Government is not innocent and passive as suggested by our media,

Our Government uses CIA operatives who work for the press and others like E. Howard Hunt to write books and articles of disinformation in the news. Martha Mitchell was portrayed as a completely insane woman by the press. E. Howard Hunt was a simple burglar with no connections to the CIA or President according to the news media at the time, yet based on his responsibility **and the fact that he worked in the Nixon White House,** I would guess he was one of the seven heads of the CIA. These are stories of fantasy promulgated by our CIA to cover up the truth. It doesn't take a lot of research to get to the truth in America. It is out there, you just need to use your head and read between the lines to determine what articles are plants or fantasy and what are factual.

For information as to the mafia's involvement in the Bay of Pigs invasion watch the Godfather series or read the books. These movies are based on fact and are historical accounts of what happened during that timeframe. For information as to Lyndon Johnson's involvement in the Assassination of Kennedy, read the book *The Man Who Killed Kennedy: The Case Against LBJ* Stone, Roger

For further information about Nixon's cover up there are many books, and several of these books reference my parents' disappearance and connect their deaths back to Watergate.

The Watergate Conspiracy Conviction and Appeal of Assistant Attorney General Robert Mardian
Rochvarg, Arnold

Hidden History: An Exposé of Modern Crimes, Conspiracies, and Cover-Ups in American Politics
Jeffries, Donald

The Essential Mae Brussell: Investigations of Fascism in America
Brussell, Mae

JFK and the Unspeakable: Why He Died and Why It Matters
Douglass, James W.

American Spy: My Secret History in the CIA, Watergate and Beyond
Hunt, E. Howard

Bond of Secrecy: My Life with CIA Spy and Watergate Conspirator E. Howard Hunt
Hunt, Saint John

Nixon's Secrets: The Rise, Fall, and Untold Truth about the President, Watergate, and the Pardon
Stone, Roger

Plausible Denial: Was the CIA Involved in the Assassination of JFK?
Lane, Mark

Coup D'Etat in America: The CIA and the Assassination of John F. Kennedy
Canfield, Michael

All the Government information I reveal in this book is readily available in print, in the movies or on the web in one form or other, except for an explanation of what was in the DNC safe. Articles that shed light on Watergate are listed below:

Mary Ferrell Foundation "Confession of Howard Hunt"

"E. Howard Hunt Dies" By John Kennedy White, January 23, 2007 in JFK Assassination Debate Recommended Posts

Fair Play Magazine "The Strange Death of Dorothy Hunt" November 1994

Online Journal Associate Editor "Hunt's Deathbed Confession Reveals JFK Killers The Last Confession of E. Howard Hunt – US government/CIA team murdered JFK" by Larry Chin

Watergate and related scandals (Main article: Watergate scandal) -- The Rockefeller Commission is owned by the Rockefellers. The Rockefellers essentially owned the Republican Party so any report by them should be considered politically motivated and not reliable.

Rolling Stone, September 1973 "Conspiracy Central & The Late Mrs. Hunt"

In *American Spy: My Secret History in the CIA, Watergate and Beyond*, E. Howard Hunt says of LBJ:

Having Kennedy liquidated, thus elevated himself to the presidency without having to work for it himself, could have been a very tempting and logical move on [Lyndon] Johnson's part.

In Roger Stone's book, *The Man Who Killed Kennedy The Case Against LBJ*, Mr. Stone says:

All of the groups involved [in the assassination of Kennedy] benefited tremendously from the assassination. Johnson avoided political exile and incarceration; the CIA had their war in Vietnam; Big Oil had a politician in office to legislate in their favor; and the Mob had someone to call off the dogs. Indeed J. Edgar Hoover had his mandatory retirement waived by Johnson and was declared director of the FBI for life.

In St. John Hunt's book *Bond of Secrecy My Life with CIA Spy and Watergate Conspirator E. Howard Hunt*, E. Howard Hunt is reported to say:

> I had always assumed, working for the CIA for so many years, that anything the White House wanted done was the law of the land. I viewed this like any other mission. It just happened to take place inside this country.

In the TV Series 24, Jack Bauer is the equivalent of a CIA goon who carries out the orders of the White House. The audience roots for Jack Bauer as he diligently carries out Presidential orders, and often breaks the law in the process. There are times when he so wants to get good results that he ignores the order of the President for the greater good. This is fiction, but one can easily understand how a spook or goon can get carried away in fulfilling Presidential order.

Having assassinated Kennedy, Nixon now had the backing of Texas Oil money, to help him become the next president.

With that in mind, consider Mae Brussell's list of those who died shortly after the assassination. This list includes LBJ and J. Edgar Hoover. Not a surprise if you consider the real reason for Kennedy's assassination.

I have written this Appendix because I myself would find the information about attempts to murder me to be difficult to believe if I hadn't been raised by a General in the Army who was training me to work in intelligence before he died. Believe me, this book is an autobiography and everything in it is absolutely true.

Many people have read parts of the book that pertained to them over the years, including my children, my wife, Aunt Hank, and friends of mine who are mentioned in the book, both inside and outside our Government. I have asked them for corrections. The only person to give me corrections of any significance was my Aunt Hank. Her corrections were minor edits with some corrections about the political facts. That is why I can say with confidence this book is authentic, true and factual and represents what really happened.

But the purpose of the book is not political. It is spiritual. God is real. This book is evidence to that fact and the miracles He has wrought in my life are truly amazing. I have provided the information above only to confirm the accuracy of this book.

About the Author

My mother's mother was from a Jewish family that lived near Salzburg and converted to Christianity. Her dad was raised in a Lutheran church in Denmark. My mother's parents moved to Baltimore and met in Germantown during World War II. My mother's family was a hybridized Christian/Jewish family that kept many of the Jewish teachings but believed Jesus was the Messiah.

My dad's dad was a Southern Baptist minister from South Carolina who retired and became a chaplain at a hospital in San Antonio, Texas. My dad's mom introduced me to Jesus and taught me that Jesus answered prayers and took care of those who were humble and had faith in Him.

Because of my faith, my mother took me to a Lutheran church where I went through catechism and where I became an altar boy. I was an Eagle Scout and was a member of an Explorer Post. My parents both died when I was a senior in high school. My faith was badly shaken, but in graduate school, I rededicated my life to Christ and was baptized at Midland, Texas First Baptist Church.

I received an undergraduate degree in physics and psychology from Emory University. I later went to Georgia State University where I received an MBA with a concentration in finance. I worked at Arthur Andersen Consulting, went into industry, and worked for several of the largest companies in Georgia where I held titles as controller, assistant secretary, treasurer, chief financial officer, and president. I helped take four companies public during my stay in industry.

At thirty-five years of age, I followed God's lead and started a CPA practice and later added a financial planning business. I became a CPA, a CFP, and hold insurance and brokerage licenses. I taught finance and accounting at several colleges and universities and coauthored a best-selling financial book. I believe God's purpose for my starting a business and leaving industry was to serve small-business owners and those who need help with securing their financial future, and I believe God had us start these small businesses to be witnesses for Him.

During that time, I played the piano for a Presbyterian church. I traveled on a variety of missions trips, and I attended several different churches and denominations. God led me to teach my children about Judaism, and our family became Messianic Jews. We studied Hebrew, Judaism, and we learned to keep the Jewish holidays and traditions.

During this time, God's spirit led our family on an amazing journey where we studied many different facets of Christianity and Judaism. Today we consider ourselves to be Messianic Jews.